Postmodern Philosophy and Christian Thought

The Indiana Series in the Philosophy of Religion
Merold Westphal, *general editor*

Postmodern Philosophy and Christian Thought

Edited by Merold Westphal

INDIANA UNIVERSITY PRESS
Bloomington and Indianapolis

This book is a publication of

Indiana University Press
601 North Morton Street
Bloomington, Indiana 47404-3797 USA

www.indiana.edu/~iupress

Telephone orders 800-842-6796
Fax orders 812-855-7931
Orders by e-mail iuporder@indiana.edu

The paper used in this publication meets the
minimum requirements of American National
Standard for Information Sciences—Permanence
of Paper for Printed Library Materials,
ANSI Z39.48-1984.

Manufactured in the United States of America

Library of Congress Cataloging-in-Publication Data

Postmodern philosophy and Christian thought / edited by Merold Westphal.
p.   cm. — (Indiana series in the philosophy of religion)
Includes index.
ISBN 0-253-33592-2 (alk. paper). — ISBN 0-253-21336-3 (pbk. : alk. paper)
1. Postmodernism—Religious aspects—Christianity Congresses.   I. Westphal, Merold.
II. Series.
BR115.P74P67   1999
261.5′1—dc21   99-28626

1 2 3 4 5   04 03 02 01 00 99

CONTENTS

Appropriating Postmodernism

MEROLD WESTPHAL

Where is Kipling when we need him? Doesn't a title like *Postmodern Philosophy and Christian Thought* cry out for someone to insist "never the twain shall meet"? Or to ask "What has Athens to do with Jerusalem?"

From the Christian side, it is all too easy to see in postmodern philosophy nothing but an implacable enemy. Isn't postmodern philosophy little more than an intellectually sophisticated form of atheism? Is it not the latest reincarnation of Nietzsche as immoralist and Antichrist, whose anything-goes relativism is a danger to everything decent? Don't postmodern philosophers insist that the truth is that there is no truth, while Christianity stands or falls with the truth of its gospel? Should not serious Christian thought be devoted to exposing this threat and to refuting the "arguments" by which it is perpetrated?

From the other side, it is all too easy for those with postmodern sympathies to see Christianity as the embodiment of everything to which it is quintessentially (however anti-essentialist it may be) opposed. Is Christianity not a prime example of the *logocentric, totalizing, onto-theological meta-narrative* that, on the basis of exaggerated knowledge claims, seeks to impose an illegitimate hegemony on human thought and practice? (Each of the four buzzwords I italicized stands for a different way in which postmodern philosophies have accused various discourses, including religious discourses, of claiming unwarranted absoluteness for themselves.) Is this hegemony not allergic to alterity, reducing all others to the same by means of violence, intellectual, cultural, and all too often, physical?

Can the "and" in our title signify anything but moral combat?

Perhaps the situation isn't quite that simple. My own assumption is that there can and should be Christian appropriations of postmodern philosophies. I do not try to define postmodernism either as a general cultural turn or in its more specifically philosophical expressions. Instead, I point to such thinkers as Nietzsche, Heidegger, Derrida, Foucault, and Rorty, who make up, for my present purposes, the Gang of Five. In many respects, Kierkegaard and Levinas belong on the list, since they share with the others a radical questioning of assumptions that to a large degree define philosophical modernity. Although these two represent major research interests of mine, I want to keep the question of Christian appropriation both more interesting and more focused by leaving them (temporarily) aside, along with their obvious Christian and Jewish sympathies, respectively, in order to probe possibilities for Christian engagement with the secular postmodernists who so often evoke nothing but fear and loathing from people of faith.

By appropriation, I mean a certain kind of recontextualization. There is a negative side to this activity, for the need to recontextualize stems from not sharing the same assumptions or the same agenda. Thus, to appropriate is to say, "No. In this respect and in that respect I do not share your vision and find it necessary to locate myself at a different site from yours." But appropriation is affirmation and acceptance as well; and it is this which distinguishes it from simple refutation. It says, "Yes. I think you are right about that, though it will come out a bit differently in the context of my assumptions and agenda."

Any Christian appropriation of postmodern philosophy will be both a yes and a no. In this way, it will become a double challenge. On the one hand, it is a challenge to the secular enthusiasts who see postmodern philosophy as both the legitimation and celebration of the death of God. Here is a new line of defense, as they would have it, to protect us from any incursions by the God of the Bible. But by showing that major themes and arguments from the Gang of Five can be appropriated by Christian thought (in spite of authorial intentions), one shows that they are not inherently secular or atheistic and that their force, which (as I think) may be considerable, does not decide the issue for or against biblical faith.

On the other hand, the kind of appropriation I have in mind is a challenge to religious traditions and institutions that see nothing but nasty nihilism in these disturbers of the peace, forgetting that Balaam's ass once spoke God's word. Perhaps the peace needs to be disturbed by interpretations and arguments that are not inherently secular but find their motivation outside and even against faith. For the link between pious intentions and genuine insight is not tight in either direction.

Much of postmodern philosophy falls under the rubric of the hermeneutics of finitude. As such, it is a sustained protest against modern (Cartesian) and pre-modern (Platonic) claims to be able to transcend the situated finitude that makes all human knowledge perennially penultimate and not, as Hegel had hoped, absolute knowledge. But Christian faith owes no allegiance to Plato or Descartes or Hegel. It can and should incorporate a hermeneutics of finitude into its own understanding of the doctrine of creation as a reminder that we do not see things from some infinite, divine point of view. In such an effort, postmodern analyses can be helpful and illuminating (without being atheistic).

At other times, postmodern philosophy is a hermeneutics of suspicion, noting the role that desires and interests unconstrained by any Golden Rule play in shaping and sustaining systems of belief. Where Nietzsche speaks of the will to power, the Christian thinker will say that we are not merely finite, epistemically speaking, but fallen. In order to take seriously the noetic effects of sin, Christians need to incorporate a hermeneutics of suspicion into their thinking, and in such an effort, postmodern analyses can be helpful and illuminating (without being atheistic).

This was the agenda I brought with me to the six-week seminar in 1996 that bore the same title as this volume. The Calvin College Faculty Summer Seminars in Christian Scholarship (whose snappy acronym is CCFSSCS) are modeled on the National Endowment for the Humanities Summer Seminars for College Teachers but funded by the Pew Charitable Trusts. Fifteen of us spent a very intensive six weeks reading and discussing the Gang of Five, concluding with Jean-Luc Marion's *God without Being* as an example of what a Christian appropriation of certain themes from postmodern philosophy might look like. The unfettered combination of intellectual passion and good humor earned us the moniker of the Raucous Caucus. I have never had a more stimulating or satisfying experience as a scholar.

The second stage of the project was a follow-up conference at Calvin College in the spring of 1997. The essays in this volume come from that conference. Nine, begun during the previous summer, are from members of the seminar. Through the generosity of the grant from the Pew Charitable Trusts, I was able to invite four distinguished contributors to the conversation about postmodernism and religion to join us—thus the papers by John D. Caputo, Walter Lowe, Jean-Luc Marion, and Edith Wyschogrod.

I have briefly described the agenda I brought and presented to the seminar. The purpose of that seminar and of this book is to explore that agenda. While the idea of a Christian appropriation of postmodern philosophy gave us a starting point for conversation, I hardly need to say that neither in the seminar nor at the conference did that model monopolize our discussions. Several essays in this volume challenge it quite directly in various ways. Taken as a whole, this volume defines a broad spectrum. At one end, one finds the sense that there is little recontextualizing to be done because one or another of the postmodern philosophers has pretty much said it as it needs to be said. At the other end, one finds the sense that the postmodern world is the problem to which the gospel is the solution. In the one case, appropriation is hardly necessary; in the other, it is distinctly unadvisable. One of the reasons the conversations in the seminar and at the conference were so stimulating is that there were many interesting and important differences among us. We didn't just talk about difference; we talked differently.

But in one respect we were all the same—and postmodernly the same at that. Nobody posed as Pure Reason, as disinterested, disengaged, de-situated Objectivity. Nobody checked her or his religious commitments at the door in order to be academically serious. Each of the seminar members and each of the invited speakers participated, honestly, passionately, and without apology, from the religious and intellectual standpoint she or he actually occupied. The resultant polyphony was sometimes harmonious, sometimes dissonant, and once in a while almost atonal. But it was and, I believe, remains, a musical feast.

The first four essays locate postmodern philosophy in conceptual/cultural space. Jay Wood's essay boldly explores the possibility of a double appropriation, one by a Christian thinker who is also an analytic philosopher. Within modernist frameworks, the normative element in epistemology has largely been deontological in character. The notion of epistemic justification is tightly linked to notions of epistemic rights and duties. Virtue epistemology is the application to the theory of knowledge of notions from the ethical theories of the likes of Aristotle and Aquinas. To Wood's surprise, he found in the hermeneutics of suspicion developed by Foucault a kind of vice epistemology that is a natural corollary to his own work in virtue epistemology. In theological terms, it is a way of making sin an epistemological category, in keeping with a tradition that stretches back from Karl Barth and Kierkegaard to Luther and Calvin and eventually to Augustine and Paul. To place Foucault in that company is to appropriate with a vengeance.

Too much vengeance? Gary Percesepe worries that the very notion of appropriation signifies a violence aimed at possession. Appropriation means to be had by the other. In effect, this essay places postmodern philosophy in the world as seen by postmodern philosophers, more specifically by Nietzsche, Foucault, Derrida, Deleuze, and Guattari. It is a world in which the possibilities for dialogue and conversation are minimal. Contests for power or market share are more common than genuine openness to the thought of the other. Gossip and demonization are so frequent that when philosophers restrict themselves to concept creation they are on their good behavior—but not in conversation. This is a good reminder that while the Cold War may be over, the culture wars are not. And if conversation among friends is displaced by competition among rivals, we may need to return to virtue epistemology for some reflection on what constitutes a fair fight.

The next two essays question the possibility of appropriation from rather different directions. Lee Hardy argues that modern philosophy is largely constituted by the confluence of a representational theory of knowledge (Locke's "Way of Ideas"), a correspondence theory of truth, and a strong foundationalist strategy for gaining knowledge; that Nietzsche's analysis of knowledge stays within this framework; that his skepticism is thus more a rigorous application of modernist assumptions than their rejection; and that postmodern philosophy can represent a break with modernity, not by being Nietzschean in epistemology but by distancing itself from him. The exegetical work is devoted to showing that this remains true, against the work of Maudemarie Clark, even for Nietzsche's final perspectivism. The critical side is devoted to problems of self-reference raised by Nietzsche's global falsification thesis, leading to the conclusion that Christian thinkers who see the virtue of epistemic humility in the anti-realism of Nietzsche's perspectivism should find a way to cultivate that virtue within a realist framework.

Brian Ingraffia comes to our question from literary theory, but he is no less skeptical than Hardy about possibilities for a Christian appropriation of postmodern thought, in this case paradigmatically postmodern novels by Thomas Pynchon and Don DeLillo. He finds the protagonists of *The Crying of Lot 49* and *White Noise* to be what Nietzsche would call incomplete nihilists, modernists seeking meaning in a postmodern world from which both God and Reason have disappeared. Against the suggestion that postmodernism is more hospitable to Christian thought than modernism, that it represents a kind of re-sacralization of the world or "something like a religious revival," Ingraffia argues that these novels represent less the recovery of spirituality than the parody of Christian faith. Postmodernism differs from modernism by being hostile to Christianity in a different way.

Postmodern philosophy is about language and discourse. Since theology is God-talk, the possibility of Christian appropriations of postmodern thought raises this question: what would a postmodern Christian theology look like, that is, a theology that knowingly or unknowingly was sympathetic to one or more postmodern themes and

incorporated them into its discourse about God? The next three essays
address this question in various ways.

Garrett Green suggests that such a theology might look a lot like
Karl Barth's. Of course, being theistic enough to affirm the reality of a
personal creator and Christian enough to affirm that God was in Christ
reconciling the world to himself fixes a great substantive gap between
Barth and, say, our Gang of Five. But Green suggests that convergence
might occur at the level of conceptual tools rather than substantive
content. Thus, if Derrida's critique of the metaphysics of presence and
of the notion of a transcendental signified, together with his positive
analysis of the economy of *différance,* did not help to generate Barth's
theology, they can help us to understand what is going on in it. The
tensions between immediacy and mediation, revealing and concealing,
presence and absence that make Barth's theology dialectical have an
astonishing resonance in Derridean thought. And Barth's distinction
between primary and secondary objectivity not only shows that theistic, Christian faith need not interpret its knowledge of God in terms
of the metaphysics of presence and the transcendental signified, but
also shows that the alternative to these is not an anything-goes subjectivism where discourse is subject to no constraints.

Walter Lowe suggests that a postmodern Christian theology would
go easy on appeals to the experience of transcendence, which may be
flights of rebellion rather than acts of genuine piety. Modernity, he reminds us, is more than the Enlightenment and the Newtonian worldview. It is also romanticism, including, in particular, Byron's *Cain,* a
text that enacts a gnostic form of the unhappy consciousness in its
striving for an Infinite it finds it cannot have. Some forms of postmodern theology, Lowe suggests, in their eagerness to break with the
Enlightenment, come too close to repeating the gestures of Byron's
character, Cain, and become totalizing in their critiques of totalizing
thought. Derridean deconstruction, by contrast, which does not equate
undecidability with indeterminacy, sticks to the task of thinking the
finite from within the finite. It might be of use in helping theology
stick to the finite determinacy of creation, incarnation, and *the* Incarnation. It would be interesting to compare the "Nietzschean" Christocentrism implicit in this account with the Barthian Christocentrism
implicit in Green's account.

Jean-Luc Marion is one of the most creative contemporary philosophers, whose work as a phenomenologist is closely linked to theological interests. In works such as *God without Being, Reduction and Givenness,* and *Étant Donneé,* he has joined a widespread ongoing discussion
and debate about the idea of the gift. Its theological importance is evident from its obvious link to such notions as revelation, salvation, for-

giveness, and grace. Drawing on the works just mentioned, this essay takes as its point of departure Derrida's recent discussion, especially in *Given Time*. In a series of arguments that Marion succinctly summarizes, Derrida points to the paradoxical or aporetic character of the gift such that the gift disappears if either the giver or the recipient is aware of the gift as such. Marion seems to read this as a critique which denies the possibilities of genuine giving, though it is also possible to read it as a typically Derridean claim that there is no *pure* gift, no gift completely eccentric to the economy of exchange. Through a detailed phenomenological analysis, Marion seeks to find an exception to Derrida's analysis in the gift that gives itself, a notion whose theological import is obvious. At the very least, the argument shows that we need concepts quite different from those involved in talking about the "exchange of gifts" at the holiday office party if we are to make sense of fundamental Christian themes.

The next three essays address familiar loci from Christian theology: the possibility of natural theology, the meaning of creation, and the meaning of the cross. George Connell asks why Heidegger encourages the religious instinct in precisely those modes that often give rise to natural theology, namely cosmological and teleological wonder, while denying theistic satisfaction to this instinct. Is he closer to the epistemological and theologically motivated suspicion of natural theology to be found in Kierkegaard and Barth or to the metaphysical and atheistically motivated suspicion of Nietzsche? When Heidegger argues against natural theology the notion that faith is the proper basis of the religious life and that the ontic/causal character of proofs for the existence of God could at best yield a false God not worthy of religious devotion, he sounds very much like Kierkegaard and Barth. But when he gives priority to the question of Being over the question of God, he seems, if not as overtly hostile to theism as Nietzsche, at least indifferent. The ambiguity leaves open possibilities of appropriation for Christian thought, and Connell notes that the larger issues involved here involve God-talk as such, and not just natural theology.

Steve Bouma-Prediger places the Christian doctrine of creation in the context of the homelessness that seems a hallmark of postmodern culture. He sees homelessness as coming to expression in three features of postmodern culture: a suspicion bordering on cynicism about the socially constructed character of our truths and meanings and their instability in the ebb and flow of economies of power; a sense of the self as nomadic; and a sense of the global ecological degradation of what otherwise might be our earthly home. In such a world, can the Christian story redemptively address "suspicious postmodern nomads living homeless on an increasingly fouled earth"? Yes, he answers, but only if it can take the form of "a non-violent meta-narrative of God's love affair with the cosmos."

Such a story will affirm that we are indeed sojourners not yet at home. In that regard, the postmodern analysis of both our finitude and our fallenness is not simply set aside. But such a story will also affirm that we have a home and that we are homeward bound. So it will set aside the cynical despair to which such analysis sometimes leads. The basis for both the eschatological hope and the ethic of present responsibility implicit in the notion of being homeward bound is the doctrine of creation, not as a piece of cosmological explanation but as the reminder that creation is the good gift of a loving God, a God who accompanies us on our journey homeward and who requires that we treat the earth given to us in creation with both love and respect.

If Bouma-Prediger is near one end of the spectrum described above, John D. Caputo is closer to the other. That makes it especially useful to read their essays back to back. Caputo compares sustained readings of Augustine's *Confessions* by Heidegger and Derrida and boldly suggests they represent two postmodern versions of what Luther called *theologia crucis*. This does not mean that they are theories of the Atonement. Rather, the suggestion is, they can be read as differing accounts of the *imitatio Christi*, what it means to bear one's own cross. Heidegger's reading occurred early in his career, while he was developing the hermeneutics of facticity that would culminate in the analysis of *Dasein* as Care. Beneath the neoplatonic philosophy of the *Confessions*, he seeks to uncover the sense in which the life of faith is one of struggle, trials, and tribulations. The difficulties of life *coram deo* lead Heidegger to find in Augustine and in the New Testament a *Kampfsreligion* that left him easy prey for the *Kampfsphilosophie* of the Nazis later on.

Less macho, but much to be preferred, in Caputo's view, is the Derridean reading which focuses on suffering, solidarity with those who suffer, and an ethic of compassion. He finds in Augustine "not the combative strength of a Christian soldier but the weakness of a suppliant begging God's help" and weeping for the sufferings of his mother. On Caputo's reading, Derrida's appropriation of Augustine reveals a whole host of questions about possible appropriations of Derrida for Christian thinking.

Since postmodernism is often portrayed as the continuation of Nietzsche's immoralism, the presumed corollary of the death of God (God is dead; everything is permitted), questions of ethics become at least as important as questions of theology. Jack Caputo and Edith Wyschogrod have argued, respectively, in *Against Ethics* and *Saints and Postmodernism*, that postmodern philosophy opens new vistas, or the recovery of old resources for the moral life, precisely by undermining not moral responsibility or moral idealism but a certain kind of ethical theory. Emmanuel Levinas plays an important role in these arguments, and in her essay here, Wyschogrod presents a famous Talmudic saying by Rabbi Hillel as a miniature, a homologue of the larger analysis of the relation of self to other in *Totality and Infinity*. Levinas makes it clear that he seeks to interrupt the ontological discourse that hails from Athens with an ethical discourse that stems from Jerusalem, and standard readings emphasize his critique of Heidegger as the latest variation of Greek thinking and his drawing on Hebrew resources from Rosenzweig to do so. But in her reading of Hillel, presented in dialogue with earlier readings, Wyschogrod seeks to show not just the tension between the Greek thinking of self and the Hebrew thinking of the other, but their need for each other and their ultimate inseparability.

Levinas is also a powerful presence in the essay by Norman Wirzba, though here he is in the background rather than the foreground. When speaking about reason's fall from innocence through the discovery of its interestedness, Wirzba adds Levinas' name to those of the usual suspects, Nietzsche, Heidegger, Derrida, and Foucault, in order to suggest that the moral life may have more to gain than to lose from the collapse of pure reason (as Caputo and Wyschogrod have also argued). Rather than turning directly to Levinas, however, he contrasts Heidegger's conception of thought embedded in care *(Bekümmerung, Sorge)* with his own notion of a Christian reason rooted in *agape, caritas, Liebe*. Heidegger's strength was to show compellingly the rootedness of thought in affect and interest, and Wirzba traces this through the early Freiburg lectures to *Being and Time*. But neither in his early studies of Christianity (Paul, Augustine, Luther, and Kierkegaard), nor in his turn to Aristotle, nor in *Being and Time*, does Heidegger interpret care as care for the other, for the neighbor. Wirzba begins the task of spelling out a Christian conception of reason as reason-for-the-other rather than reason-for-the-self. Before the Other we must learn to think otherwise.

What, then, of the Christian's relation to other religions? Andrew Dell'Olio seeks to articulate a postmodern Christian philosophy of other religions that, while posed in terms of the question of truth, does not disguise the deeply political character of the issue. After probing critiques of both the exclusivism that claims, well, exclusive possession of the truth and the pluralism which denies that there is any privileged religion, he argues for a Christian inclusivism that maintains that divine truth is revealed definitively in Jesus Christ, but that the Christian religion is too human to be in full possession of this truth. Accordingly, its teachings and practices do not enjoy absolute status vis-à-vis the other religions, which may also legitimately lay claim to revelation. What is postmodern about this position is the way it invokes the hermeneutics of suspicion against exclusivism and the hermeneutics of finitude against pluralism, charging the latter with being forgetful of its own particularity.

All of us involved in this volume are deeply indebted to The Pew Charitable Trusts for funding the seminar and the conference; to Calvin College for administering the grant and hosting our activities; and, in particular, to C. Stephen Evans, director of the Summer Seminar program, Sandra Van Kley, coordinator, Anna Mae Bush, secretary, and all the support staff at Calvin who made our visits to Grand Rapids comfortable and who made us feel so much at home.

Whatever Derrida and Marion may eventually conclude about the Gift, we know that we have encountered a rare generosity that our gratitude will not erase. To the above thank-yous from all of us, I would like to add my own personal thanks to each of the fourteen members of the seminar, including those who for various and good reasons were not able to contribute to this volume. You have given me a gift whose value I shall not attempt to calculate and whose memory I shall always treasure.

1. Placing Postmodernism

1

On the Uses and Advantages
of an Epistemology for Life

W. JAY WOOD

In his article "Overcoming Epistemology," Charles Taylor rehearses many standard postmodern indictments of traditional Cartesian epistemology as voiced by Heidegger, Rorty, Merleau-Ponty, Derrida, Nietzsche, and others.[1] These criticisms include many that are commonplace in today's anti-foundationalist philosophical scene: objections against efforts to adopt a transcendental "view from nowhere," against hyperbolic notions of certainty, individualism, and representational realism, as well as criticisms of modern epistemology's failure to acknowledge the "darker" forces motivating claims to knowledge. Taylor sees two strands to postmodernism's rejection of traditional epistemology. The radical approach, which he identifies with Nietzsche and Foucault, takes an eliminitivist posture toward epistemology, one which is ready to jettison altogether notions of truth, rationality, and anything remotely resembling the traditional projects of epistemology. The less radical approach, which Taylor identifies with Jürgen Habermas, continues to defend a version of critical reason. Taylor does not definitively settle the differences between these two voices, nor does he propose what a suitably chastened post-foundationalist epistemology should look like.

I propose that postmodern philosophy has not altogether outgrown the need for epistemology, and that an epistemology which takes seriously the notion of intellectual virtues is one alternative very much worth considering. I will argue that many elements of a virtue epistemology are congruent with dominant themes within postmodern discourse. To support these contentions, I will enlist the aid of both Nietzsche and Foucault, the two voices Taylor identifies as offering the most radical dismissal of traditional epistemology. I will claim that while neither thinker considers himself to be developing a replacement for traditional epistemology, each offers suggestive remarks that invite seeing links between aspects of their work and a virtue epistemology. For both Nietzsche and Foucault underscore the importance of thinking responsibly within a certain form of life; each, in his own way, hints of a virtue epistemology in the service of life.

I. Virtues and Vices

The notion of a virtue is, of course, not postmodern but pre-modern, as old as philosophy itself. According to Aristotle, virtues are well anchored, reliable dispositions that people acquire over time, enabling them to think and feel and act in ways that contribute to their fulfillment and, sometimes, to the fulfillment of those with whom they interact. They allow us to negotiate gracefully and successfully the tasks of life as they arise and to overcome obstacles in the path of accomplishments. Vices, by contrast, are acquired traits of character that undermine human flourishing. Compassionate persons, for example, must have powers of moral perception and judgment that reliably indicate to them persons who are in need. Moreover, their judgments will be qualified by, or perhaps prompted by, a corresponding emotion or set of emotions. Compassionate persons have enduring concerns that motivate them to ameliorate the suffering of others. Because they want to relieve the suffering of others, they will be disposed to a feel a range of emotions commensurate with their circumstances. They will typically feel pity and sadness that some person is living in deprivation, and they will feel joy if another's needs are met. Such emotions indicate abiding concerns for the welfare of others that serve as an ongoing source of moral motivation. Additionally, compassionate persons act appropriately to alleviate need, such action often requiring careful deliberation. Indulgent parents or codependent spouses may give lavishly, but they do not give appropriately and hence not virtuously. This way of analyzing the virtues shows just how closely moral virtue is intertwined with excellence in such cognitive abilities as deliberation and judgment.

Following the model of a moral virtue, we can analyze an intellectual virtue as an abiding, acquired trait that reliably allows us to orient our intellectual lives—our believings, reasoning habits, and cognitive powers—in ways that contribute to human flourishing, most notably to success in cognitive endeavors such as gaining understanding, acquiring truth and avoiding falsehood, being able to revise one's beliefs in the face of new information, and so on. Traits such as wisdom, understanding, foresight, attentiveness, and teachableness are representative intellectual virtues. An epistemic vice, by contrast, is a trait (an attitude, affection, or disposition) that bears unfavorably on some aspect of our intellectual life. Intellectual vices are such traits as gullibility, folly, superstitiousness, closed-mindedness, willful naïveté, and unteachableness. We can think of intellectual virtues as habits of mind we cultivate in the service of a way of life, and epistemology, then, as the discipline which systematically explores the nature of these traits, their causes, their various interrelationships, as well as the different conceptions of a flourishing life that such traits are meant to serve.

Intellectual virtues, like moral virtues, often come accompanied by emotions. Do we not feel "gratification" upon understanding some complicated matter or take delight at discovering the truth? Linda Zagzebski, a leading advocate of a virtues approach to epistemology, argues that a deep underlying concern to "make cognitive contact with reality" provides the motive force disposing us to a whole range of intellectual virtues and, I might add, to a range of emotions depending on how successful we are in achieving this end. Intellectual virtues also share with moral virtues the capacity of sometimes being action-guiding. I say "sometimes" because not every moral and intellectual virtue automatically issues forth in some concrete action. For instance, I might be virtuously hopeful or humble without those virtues leading automatically to some specific action. Rather, we should say that the virtues, moral and intellectual, dispose us, as appropriate, to various courses of action.

Let me distinguish between purely natural intellectual abilities, intellectual skills, and intellectual virtues. Someone born with perfect pitch or a photographic memory will obviously excel in discovering a certain range of truth. Though such abilities are admirable on some level, they are not virtues; indeed, they may be found in some idiot savants. Similarly, a person who is defective intellectually (an Alzheimer's or attention deficit disorder sufferer, for example) is in a lamentable state vis-à-vis the intellectual life but is not thereby intellectually vicious. Many cognitive defects may thwart our intellectual efforts without their being attributable to some underlying personal failing.

Consider next someone with an acquired skill in doing proofs in deductive logic: here too the agent will be adept at discovering a certain range of truth and of avoiding falsehood. He or she will know, for example, the correct procedures for constructing a *reductio ad absurdum* argument. Though such skill requires effort to acquire, and granted that such skill is better to have than to lack, it still does not constitute an intellectual virtue in a robust sense of term. For such skills can be cultivated and deployed in ways relatively disconnected from human flourishing. (This is one of the lamentable features of the Unabomber's life.) Such skills may contribute to one's being a better logician but not necessarily to one's being a better person.

A mature intellectual virtue, on the other hand, arises out of a particular vision of human flourishing. A part of practical wisdom consists in an agent's ability to survey the shape of his or her life, to monitor his or her strengths and weaknesses, and to undertake strategies of self-improvement where possible. Viewed this way, intellectual and moral virtues have an integrating function; they draw together the threads of a person's life and weave them together into a coherent and vital whole. While moral and intellectual traits can be separated on rare occasions, they are not usually separated or separated for long. For persons lacking the intellectual virtues of prudence and discretion have little prospect for long-term success in the moral life.

The root idea of a virtue epistemology, then, is rather simple: as thinking persons, we should cultivate traits such as attentiveness, understanding, prudence, and other intellectual virtues, and shun their opposing vices. For the activities we pursue in life—work, parenting, friendships, politics, the arts—are better served when they arise out of and are nourished by traits such as creativity, open-mindedness, intellectual honesty, and practical wisdom. None are better served by being rooted in prejudice, superstition, self-serving beliefs, obtuseness, dogmatism, or intellectual arrogance. Still less are any long-term goals to shape our lives in particular ways served by such vicious traits.

But how does this suggestion bear on the traditional discipline of epistemology? What becomes of long-standing concerns about knowledge, belief, justification, memory, and skepticism? Are they abandoned or recast along different lines? One might use the resources of a virtue approach to epistemology to reconsider traditional problems such as defeating evil demons, solving riddles of induction, generating reflective certainty for the foundations of knowledge, uncovering the necessary and sufficient conditions for justified belief, addressing Gettier problems, and so on. One could, for instance, devise from the resources of a virtue epistemology an account of epistemic justification that conferred positive epistemic status on any belief acquired in an intellectually virtuous fashion. One wonders, however, to what extent many of the problems traditional epistemologists have labored over weren't problems generated by a flawed understanding of the entire epistemological project. Do away with demands for self-reflective certainty and transcendence, unimpeachable foundations, unrealistic levels of autonomy, and many of the traditional epistemological worries disappear, along with the projects undertaken to allay them.

Ironically, we receive encouragement for the idea that epistemologists ought to pursue new agendas from William Alston, a premier practitioner of epistemology in the traditional vein. In a remarkable display of the virtue of intellectual honesty and humility, Alston argues that it is a mistake to search for the necessary and sufficient conditions of epistemic justification, a task to which he had been a chief contributor. He says of his thesis: "[It] is an iconoclastic and revolutionary one, a bold departure from the well trodden pathways of the discipline. It implies that a large proportion of contemporary epistemologists, including myself, have been misguided in their researches, fighting under a false banner, engaged in a quixotic tilting at windmills."[2] Neither Alston nor I wish to disparage all that goes on under the heading of traditional epistemology. Nevertheless, it failed, in a way virtue epistemology does not, to address themes and goals that are important to living a full human life.

An alternative epistemological project would be to explore the different understandings intellectual virtues receive in the larger systems in which they are embedded. Let me explain. The concept of a virtue on the above analysis is rooted in the notion of human flourishing, from which it follows that contrasting notions of human flourishing will correspondingly give rise to differing accounts of the virtues and their various interrelations. Traditionally, theories of virtue and vice and the concepts they employ are embedded if not in an account of human ends and purposes then at least in some broader notion of human flourishing or happiness. Whether a trait is virtuous or vicious hinges on our beliefs about where our lives as a whole ought to be headed. Thus, what we regard as intellectually virtuous and vicious behavior will vary as we are committed to one or another account of human flourishing. Consider how notions of human flourishing and the goals of cognition corresponding to them change as we alternatively embrace the ideals of Aristotelian eudaemonia, Stoic apatheia, the Christian beatific vision, or Buddhist annihilation. Our analyses of intellectual virtue and vice, as well as what we take to be the distinctive features that make certain traits good or bad, are situated in larger philosophical commitments that impart to them their own distinctive grammar. A new task to which epistemologists might be called, then, is that of analyzing the virtue concepts as they arise in their distinctive frameworks. Epistemologists might even do comparative analyses between frameworks.

Let me illustrate. We in philosophy prize analytical rigor; we work to cultivate this skill, which allows us to dissect concepts into their component parts and note their various logical interrelations. Sometimes, we think, the full truth about the world is revealed only after logical dissection. Zen Buddhists, by contrast, condemn such thinking as intellectually vicious, as symptomatic of an underlying spiritual defect that keeps us bound to the wheel of rebirth. The Zen master Shibayama writes: "For the attainment of incomparable satori, one has to cast away his discriminating mind. Those who have not passed the barrier and have not cast away the discriminating mind are all phantoms haunting trees and plants."[3] The variability of notions of flourishing makes the notion of a virtue highly adaptive, as seen by the starkly different philosophical settings in which the notion has functioned. This fact will become apparent as we examine below the elements of a Nietzschean virtue epistemology.

II. Points of Intersection between Pre- and Postmodern Thinking

My central claim of this section is that an epistemology rooted in the virtues is congruent with several crucial themes being sounded in our postmodern climate. Any suitably chastened epistemology for a postmodern age must reckon not just with the limitations imposed upon reason by time, place, and language, but also with those darker forces of pride, power, economic advantage, and idolatry that subvert reason and keep us from the truth and other desirable ends of intellectual activity. Of course, such concerns are not incidental to virtue epistemology, but integral to it. For the flip side of any epistemology of virtue is, obviously, an epistemology of vice. The historical companion to the study of personal traits that lead us to understanding and *phronesis* and the other intellectual virtues is the study of ways in which our thinking subserves the interests of self, rather than those of truth or understanding or practical wisdom.

It should not surprise us, first of all, to find postmodern and virtue theorists united in recognizing the prominence of passions in our thinking and theorizing. Beginning with Augustine (especially Book 10 of the *Confessions*) and throughout the period of medieval philosophy, Christian writers steeped in the philosophy of the virtues wrote of the ways in which various self-interested passions undermined the life of the mind. Even Aquinas, not as easily given as Augustine to ruminations about our darker nature, writes in the *Summa Theologiae* about the ways that passions and intentional neglect undermine virtuous thinking:

> Hence when man ceases to make use of his intellectual virtues, strange fancies, sometimes in opposition to them, arise in his imagination; so that unless those fancies be, as it were, cut off or kept back by frequent use of his intellectual habits, man becomes less fit to judge aright, and sometimes is even wholly disposed to the contrary, and thus the intellectual habit is diminished or even wholly destroyed by cessation from act. (Ia–IIae, Q 53, 3)

And Hobbes, still very much influenced by this ancient and medieval tradition, pinpoints the role of the passions in promoting intellectual vice in *Leviathan:*

> The passions that most of all cause the difference of wit are principally the more or less desire of power, of riches, of knowledge, of honor. All of which may be reduced to the first—that is, desire for power. For riches, knowledge and honor are but several sorts power. . . . For the thoughts are to the desires as scouts and spies, to range abroad and find the way to the things desired, all steadiness of the mind's motions, and all quickness of the same, proceeding from thence." (*Leviathan,* pt. 1, chap. 8)

These passages have a very contemporary ring to those whose philosophical diet includes writers such as Merold Westphal, Michel Foucault, and Jacques Derrida. The last, for instance, notes in several places the power of wayward passions to subvert philosophical reflection. In "Structure, Sign, and Play in the Discourse of the Human Sciences," for example, he comments on the ways our desires to master anxiety and achieve reassuring certitude prompt us to arrest the force of play. Not only do fears of ambiguity and uncertainty distort thinking, but so do the hubristic impulses for a kingdom: preferably one where we preside. As he writes in "Différance," "Not only is there no kingdom in différance, but différance instigates the subversion of every kingdom. Which makes it obviously threatening and infallibly dreaded by everything that desires a kingdom, the past or future presence of a kingdom."[4] At the very heart of the intellectual life, then, lurks the tendencies toward fear and self-aggrandizement.

Aquinas' reference to the relationship between passions and intellectual virtue underscores a second important theme virtue epistemology shares with some contemporary postmodern writing: a holistic account of the person. Epistemology as practiced by many in the tradition of onto-theology has taught that knowledge is sought best by the unaided intellect, when the knowing agent applies, as Plato at one point

remarks, "his pure and unadulterated thought to the pure and unadulterated object, cutting himself off as much as possible from his eyes
and virtually all the rest of his rest of his body, as an impediment . . .
to truth and clear thinking" (*Phaedo*, 66a). Descartes no less than Plato
views human cognizers as pure *res cogitans*, as disembodied minds, ignoring, by and large, the connections between the life of the mind and
the rest of our human nature. So, in the *Discourse on Method*, we read:

> I knew that I was a substance the whole essence or nature of which was to
> think, and that for its existence there is no need of any place, nor does it
> depend on any material thing; so that this "me," that is to say, the soul by
> which I am what I am, is entirely distinct from body.[5]

This precedent in turn has yielded accounts of the rational life based
on a very "thin" account of the person. Descartes' is not an epistemology of the whole person but an epistemology done from the neck up—
a docetist epistemology that fails to acknowledge our full humanity as
knowers.

The brief account of virtues given above should already have sig-
naled the incompatibility between these purveyors of "pure reason"
and the classical virtue approaches to knowledge. For a properly functioning mind is not, as Descartes put it, one that has been "liberated
from all cares" but one that has been suitably trained to care about the
right things. For virtues are closely connected to our emotional or feeling states in ways Descartes does not acknowledge. Emotions typically
serve as the motive forces directing us to various ends concerning ourselves and the world. If I love justice, I shall orient my thinking toward
ends commensurate with desires for justice. As a juror, I shall endeavor
to weigh evidence carefully and avoid the influence of rumor and in-
nuendo.[6]

Consider a case cited by Oliver Sacks concerning a judge whose cognitive functioning was damaged by a shell fragment in the frontal lobe
of the brain.[7] As a result of the injury, the judge was left incapable of
experiencing emotion, a condition one might suppose ideal for someone whose job is to render impartial determinations of guilt and innocence. Though he was able to understand the information presented
by the lawyers and to draw correct inferences from it, he nevertheless
resigned from the bench because, as Sacks puts it, "he was no longer
able to enter sympathetically into the motives of anyone concerned,
and that since justice involved feeling, and not merely thinking, he felt
that his injury totally disqualified him."[8] One part of determining guilt
is to ascertain whether persons charged with crimes had sufficient mo-

tive to commit the acts with which they are charged. But to make such determinations requires that we have insight into the motivational structure of other human beings. to get inside their hearts, as it were. This often requires a sort of sympathetic understanding, a capacity to reason by analogy from one's own case. This facet of judicial reasoning was exactly what the brain-damaged judge lacked.

A third point of intersection resembles the second; postmodern writers and virtue theorists are allied against characterizing intellectual beings as cut off from communities and social contexts which, for good or ill, exert tremendous influence over our intellectual formation. Heidegger, as is well known, writes about how the representations we form of the world arise from our manner of engagement with the world, from our having been "thrown" into concrete, particular settings at specific moments in time, and from the "facticity" of our being. "Dasein," he writes in *Being and Time*, "tends to understand its own Being in terms of that being to which it is essentially, continually, and most closely related—the world."[9] But these are claims from which no virtue theorist would demur. In the *Nichomachean Ethics*, Aristotle stresses repeatedly the important role played by socialization in cultivating the virtues. Whether we are becoming morally or intellectually virtuous depends very much on the training to which we are subject as well as to the nature and quality of the polis wherein we reside (1103a–1103b). Clearly it is not just we, strictly by our own efforts, who determine whether and to what degree the virtues take root in us; it is also the communities in which we are bound up. Does anyone doubt that virtues such as justice and honesty are better fostered in a community of morally sensitive persons than in a thieves' den?

Fourth, and finally, we see thinkers of both a virtue and postmodern persuasion rejecting methodological approaches to knowledge. If modern epistemology had one goal, it was to impart to the moral sciences the same axiomatic method Newton had employed with so much success in the natural sciences: the "Baconian Method," Descartes' *Discourse on Method*, Locke's "Historical Plain Method," "Mill's Methods," and Husserl's "Phenomenological Method" being chief examples. Aristotle, for one, would have found such methods odd. In book 1, chapter 3 of the *Nichomachean Ethics*, Aristotle remarks that "it is the mark of an educated man to look for precision in each class of things just so far as the nature of the subject admits." The *phronimos*, the person of practical wisdom, realizes that algorithmic approaches to justice, wisdom, and the other virtues don't exist. Suppose with Aristotle that virtue is a mean between extremes. How do we determine what is too much or too little reliance on authority? What is the right balance between continuing to search for more evidence and reaching closure on some matter? How shall we decide whether the resistance we display to criticism of our beliefs constitutes a suitable amount of tenacity of belief or displays a lack of honesty about their shortcomings? Clearly we have no formulas to determine such matters. Here Aristotle and John Caputo concur: "The real obstacle," writes Caputo, "to understanding human affairs lies in the tendency to believe that what we do . . . admits of formulation into hard and irrevocable rules. . . . Hermeneutics pits itself against the notion that human affairs can finally be formalized into explicit rules which can or should function as a decision procedure, whether in scientific theory or in ethics."[10]

III. An Objection Considered

At this point, we must consider an objection against the very idea that the pre-modern concepts of virtues may be so happily harmonized with a postmodern philosophical context. After all, does not the notion of a virtue imply that humans have an essential nature whose telos is achieved only along the path of virtue? Surely Richard Rorty rather than Aquinas best represents the postmodern temper on this score. Speaking approvingly of Freud's picture of a merely contingent self, Rorty urges that we not "see humanity as a natural kind with an intrinsic nature, an intrinsic set of powers to be developed or left undeveloped. . . . To abjure the notion of the 'truly human' is to abjure the attempt to divinize the self as a replacement for a divinized world. . . . it is to get rid of the last citadel of necessity, the last attempt to see us all confronting the same imperative, the same unconditional claims."[11] Does a virtue epistemology turn on philosophical assumptions which can no longer have any purchase?

Michel Foucault is right to note that "there is no value in a period which is not our period . . . it is not anything to get back to."[12] Yet I want to argue that while the notion of intellectual virtues has historically been situated amid talk of human essences and a common human telos, such a context is not conceptually necessary. Recall, first of all, that even in the ancient world, the notion of virtues flourished in divergent and incompatible philosophical contexts. Aristotelian, Stoic, Christian, and Confucian worldviews all made ready use of the notion of virtues, each with its distinctive anthropology and view of human ends and ideals. Obviously, then, the notion of virtue is not captive to any one account of human ends and purposes, religious or otherwise.

As an act of unabashed appropriation, I would like to argue that both Nietzsche and Foucault, voices Taylor associates with the radical elimination of epistemology, offer fascinating hints for the practice of a virtue epistemology, not now of an essential self, but of a purely contingent self. For each thinker, in his or her own way, not only fashions an account of a life worth living and pursuing but identifies traits of mind and character that best accompany the realization of this life, as well as traits that would detract from its realization. In short, each person specifies what intellectual traits mark the thinking of someone who embodies his or her respective ideals.

Consider, first of all, Zarathustra, a self-described inventor of a new virtue, the virtues of the overman. One of Nietzsche's purposes throughout this work is to contrast two competing visions of human excellence. Each puts forth an ideal for human life together with the traits of character that constitute it as the distinctive form of life that it is. Nietzsche derisively characterizes the Christian ideal as marked by goodness, justice, sham wisdom, false knowledge, pity, kindness, chastity: these are the virtues, he says, that "lull [us] to sleep" and "make us small"; these are the virtues of "wretched contentment":

> I walk among this people and I keep my eyes open: they have become smaller, and they are becoming smaller and smaller; but this is due to their doctrine of happiness and virtue. For they are modest in virtue, too—because they want contentment. But only a modest virtue gets along with contentment.[13]

An alternative doctrine of happiness and virtue must therefore supplant the Christian doctrine if these "objectionable" traits are to be avoided.

To this end, Zarathustra offers a different human ideal: that of the overman. The attributes of the overcomer range over both moral and intellectual qualities. The overman is proud, powerful, courageous, noble, strong-willed, and a self-conqueror. Specifically intellectual traits include honesty, creativity, a "will to the thinkability of all things," a lover of knowledge "that breaks the old tablets," and wisdom. Nietzsche is clearly recommending a way of life whereby one strives to realize a certain human ideal. "I love him who loves his virtue," "who wants to be entirely the spirit of his virtue," "who makes his virtue his addiction."[14]

While Zarathustra doesn't develop an epistemological theory per se, the structure for one may nevertheless be extracted from the totality of his advice. The epistemological task is one pursued, first of all, in the service of a vision of human life. Some remarks Nietzsche makes in another context about history are applicable to this discussion of epistemology.

> We need history, certainly, but we need it for reasons different from those for which the idler in the garden of knowledge needs it. . . . We need it, that is to say, for the sake of life and action. . . . We want to serve history only to the extent that history serves life.[15]

What constitutes the well-lived intellectual life, and thus what contours shape our epistemology, what concerns should mark our lives as thinking persons, will very much depend on what sort of life one thinks valuable and worth living. Second, a virtue epistemology, whether Nietzschean or not, will endeavor to identify and provide an in-depth analysis of the intellectual characteristics that qualify excellent lives and what would constitute its opposing vices. Third, it will specify what regimen must be undertaken to cultivate such traits: do we need a sage to guide us? A community? A certain sort of polis? Fourth, epistemology practiced in this way will explore the logical and causal interconnections between the various virtues. Are some virtues prerequisites for the formation of others? Are there connections between the intellectual and moral virtues? Are some of them capital virtues in the service of which other virtues manifest themselves? What are the causal processes that contribute to the formation of a virtue, and once formed within us, what are its causal consequences? Fifth, Nietzsche models for us a valuable sort of comparative study showing the differences between contrasting visions of the well-lived life and the system of virtues that contribute to that life. Not only does he juxtapose contrasting forms of life, but he polemicizes against those he finds inadequate—most notably the Christian way of life—and argues in support of his own virtue system.

   Michel Foucault's project of presiding over the formation of the self can also be viewed as a favorable context for the sort of epistemology I am advocating here. Consider some of Foucault's commendatory remarks in "On the Geneology of Ethics" concerning "*epimeleia heautou*," a powerful Greek notion which means taking care of one's self: "From the idea that the self is not given to us, I think there is only one practical consequence: we have to create ourselves as a work of art" (p. 351). Among the many fascinating things Foucault says about the project of self-formation, I am especially interested in his remarks about the relation between knowledge and care of the self. The project of self-formation, he says, "implies attention, knowledge, technique" (p. 360). The Greeks from whom he is drawing inspiration taught that "the one who cared for himself had to choose among all the things you can know through scientific knowledge only those things which were relative to him and important to life" (p. 360). Note again the pursuit of knowledge in the service of a way of life.

According to Foucault, knowledge contributes to the project of self-formation in the very same ways it does for Zarathustra. It requires, first of all, that we consider the kind of being we wish to become in behaving in a moral way. "For instance, shall we become pure, or immortal, or free, or masters of ourselves, and so on? So that's what I call the telos (teleologie)" (p. 355). The task, he says, commending certain ancient Stoic thinkers, is to "constitute a kind of ethics which was an aesthetics of existence." Another phase of a person's "constituting himself as a moral subject of his own actions" is to ask "what are the means by which we can change ourselves in order to become ethical subjects?" (p. 354). This requires, he says, "a kind of adequation between all possible knowledge and the care of the self" (p. 360). One needs to be a careful student of the traits one is wishing to acquire and the means by which such traits are cultivated. Thirdly, Foucault speaks approvingly of the notion of virtue which consists "in perfectly governing oneself, that is, in exercising upon oneself as exact a mastery as that of a sovereign against whom there could no longer be revolts" (p. 363). Part of the "training of oneself by oneself" of which Foucault speaks requires that we carefully monitor our own interior lives so as to determine how we stand in relation to the self we are going about the business of fashioning. To this task, Foucault mentions the importance now and in the ancient world of *hypomnemata*, various writing we do about ourselves in order better to recollect teachings, recall things heard and read, and serve as a repository for later meditation. Foucault is quick to contrast that form of writing, which, as practiced by Plato, seeks to gain ontological knowledge of the soul's being, from that writing done as an exercise of the self upon the self simply as a mode of psychological contemplation. Finally, Foucault underscores the importance of comparative analyses for techniques of the self. "Techniques of the self, I believe, can be found in all cultures in different forms. Just as it is necessary to study and compare the different techniques of the production of objects and the direction of men by men through government, one must also question techniques of the self" (p. 369).

In conclusion, we see that Taylor is right about Nietzsche and Foucault: while they certainly don't advocate anything remotely approximating the project of traditional epistemology, they are nevertheless keenly interested in the cultivating certain habits of mind and avoiding others. For in fact, each offers the rudiments of an epistemology cultivated to serve not the search for the universal structures of all knowledge, but a way of life. Knowledge, and the habits of mind associated with it, subserve the goal of realizing a certain conception of the well-lived life. But this is precisely the goal that Aristotle, Aquinas, and others have long insisted are served by virtue epistemology. At the very least, their suggestion deserves attention.

Notes

1. Charles Taylor, "Overcoming Epistemology," in *After Philosophy, End or Transformation?*, ed. Kenneth Baynes, James Bohman, and Thomas McCarthy (Cambridge, Mass.: MIT Press, 1987), pp. 464–88.

2. William Alston, "Epistemic Desiderata," *Philosophy and Phenomenological Research* 3 (September 1993): 541.

3. From Zenkei Shibayama, *Zen Comments on the Mumonkan*, in *Sourcebook in Asian Philosophy*, ed. John M. Koller and Patricia Joyce Koller (New York: Macmillan, 1991), p. 361.

4. Jacques Derrida, "Différance," in *Margins of Philosophy*, trans. Alan Bass (Chicago: University of Chicago Press, 1972), p. 22.

5. Rene Descartes, *Discourse on Method*, in *The Philosophical Works of Descartes*, trans. Elizabeth Haldane and G. R. T. Ross (Dover Publications, 1955), p. 101. One finds similar remarks in Plato; see *Phaedo* 65d–66.

6. For a more complete account of the relationship of the emotions and virtues, see W. Jay Wood's *Epistemology: Becoming Intellectually Virtuous* (Downers Grove, Ill.: Intervarsity Press, 1998).

7. The case of the judge resembles that of Phineas Gage, discussed at length by Antonio D'Amasio. An injury to the frontal lobe rendered Gage incapable of feeling the normal range of emotions, resulting in an impaired ability to reason in accordance with social conventions and ethical rules. "The unintentional message in Gage's case," writes D'Amasio, "was that observing social convention, behaving ethically, and making decisions advantageous to one's survival and progress require knowledge of rules and strategies and the integrity of specific brain systems"; D'Amasio, *Descartes' Error: Emotion, Reason, and the Human Brain* (New York: Avon, 1994), p. 17.

8. Oliver Sacks, *An Anthropologist on Mars* (New York: Vintage Books, 1995), p. 288.

9. Martin Heidegger, *Basic Writings*, ed. David Farell Krell, trans. Joan Stambaugh (San Francisco: Harper Collins, 1993), p. 58.

10. John Caputo, *Radical Hermeneutics* (Bloomington: Indiana University Press, 1987), pp. 212–13.

11. Richard Rorty, *Contingency, Irony, and Solidarity* (Cambridge: Cambridge University Press, 1989), p. 35.

12. Michel Foucault, "On the Geneology of Ethics: An Overview of a Work in Progress," *The Foucault Reader*, ed. Paul Rabinow (New York: Pantheon Books), p.

347. All subsequent quotations of Foucault are taken from this essay and are noted parenthetically in the text.

13. Friedrich Nietzsche, *Thus Spoke Zarathustra,* in *The Portable Nietzsche,* ed. and trans. Walter Kaufmann (New York: Penguin, 1982), p. 281.

14. Ibid., p. 127.

15. Friedrich Nietzsche, "On the Uses and Disadvantages of History for Life," in *Untimely Meditations,* trans. R. J. Hollingdale (Cambridge: Cambridge University Press, 1983), p. 59.

2

Postmodernism as a Kind of Modernism

Nietzsche's Critique of Knowledge

LEE HARDY

The mind, in all its thoughts and reasonings,
hath no other immediate object but its own ideas,
which it alone does or can contemplate.
—John Locke, *Essay on Human Understanding*

(nature = world as idea, that is as error)
—Nietzsche, *Human, All-Too-Human*

I

Of the several features characteristic of Western philosophy in the modern period, the representational theory of consciousness—what Locke called the "Way of Ideas"—is surely one of the most pervasive and deeply entrenched. The core of that theory, roughly stated, consists in the claim that the direct objects of our experience are not the "things themselves," but rather images or representations of things displayed, as it were, on the inner surface of our minds. Our basic cognitive situation resembles that of Plato's cave dwellers: in our naïveté, we take the shadows projected on the screen of consciousness for reality itself, not realizing, as David Hume informs us, "that nothing can be present to the mind but an image or perception, and that the senses are only inlets, through which these images are conveyed, without being able to produce any immediate intercourse between the mind and the object."[1] Although representational theory has many versions that differ in important respects, its central claim formed one of the assumptions shared by partisans of both the rationalist and empiricist camps; it served as a common conceptual platform from which sophisticated arguments both for the possibility and for the impossibility of knowledge were launched; and it was regularly combined with metaphysical positions of both dualist and idealist persuasion.

The general picture of the mind as a self-enclosed sphere of representation, in conjunction with the traditional correspondence theory of truth and the Cartesian demand for certainty, defines the deepest and most basic problem of knowledge in the modern period as one of securing, by way of rational demonstration, the agreement between our mental representations, or some privileged subset of them, and external reality. If we are to be philosophically justified in claiming to know anything beyond the familiar proceedings within the "chamber of consciousness"—to use Nietzsche's image[2]—then, it seems, we must be assured that our mental representations do indeed represent the world correctly.

But there's the rub: what do we have to go on in this crucial endeavor but our own mental representations? To convince ourselves of the veracity of our experience, we cannot momentarily excuse ourselves from our seats in consciousness and take a peek at reality as it is in itself. For any access we have to reality will involve some form of consciousness and its representations. It is as if we were born and grew up in a movie theater and were then assigned the task of determining, without leaving the theater, if the images dancing on the silver screen accurately represented the world outside. We would have to work from the inside and infer with good argument to the outside.

At any rate, this is the task we would accept if we set out to demonstrate the possibility of knowledge. The party of the skeptics, on the other hand, try to show that our representations, or a vast majority of them, do not, or cannot, correspond to the way the world is—or, more modestly, that we have no good reason to think that they do. For my purposes, it is important to note here that the skeptical denial of the possibility of our knowing the truth about a wide swath of reality does not amount to a rejection of the correspondence theory of truth. Rather, it assumes that theory and tries to show that a good deal of our beliefs fail to meet its requirements.

I argue that Nietzsche's critique of knowledge, often taken as the prototype of postmodern epistemology—or the postmodern rejection of epistemology—remains firmly within the grip of the representational theory of consciousness, the correspondence theory of truth, and the Cartesian demand for certainty. I will thereby suggest that postmodern epistemological commentary, to the degree that it is derived from Nietzsche's work, remains firmly ensconced within the conceptual space carved out by modernism in the philosophical sense. That is, the postmodern report on the current status and prospects of human knowledge is best conceived as a product of a particularly rigorous application of principles of modern epistemology, not a rejection of them.[3] An unavoidable implication of this claim is that those who wish to appropriate postmodernism's anti-realist account of human knowledge will not thereby advance one inch beyond the territory already defined by the deep commitments of modernity.

Nietzsche's epistemological reflections were something less than systematic, both in presentation and substance. Maudemarie Clark, among others, has suggested that the welter of his striking statements on human knowledge, and some of their apparent inconsistencies, can be straightened out when they are aligned in a three-part developmental scheme: first, a form of Kantianism, where Nietzsche, following Schopenhauer, posits a mysterious thing-in-itself behind the veil of representation; second, a "neo-Kantianism," where Nietzsche rejects the concept of the thing-in-itself and restricts his analysis to knowledge within the sphere of representation; and third, "perspectivism," a position of Nietzsche's own device, one that has received widespread currency in postmodern circles.[4]

Clark argues that the first two positions are deeply informed by the representational theory of consciousness and therefore lead to a global—and hence paradoxical—skepticism. In the first position, reality *in toto* recedes behind the screen of representation, unknowable in principle; in the second, reality is given in the stream of sensations but is unknowable by means of conceptual representation because it is radically individual and constantly changing. In both cases, Clark maintains, the epistemic status of Nietzsche's own claims are threatened by the very skepticism he seeks to advance. With the articulation of the third position, the perspectivist theory of knowledge, however, Nietzsche decisively broke with representationalism, gave an account of knowing that allows for a good deal of our beliefs to meet the correspondence requirement, and thus evaded the vexing paradoxes of his earlier positions.

In what follows, I contend that Clark is right about the first two positions and entirely mistaken on the third. I will attempt to show how Nietzsche's perspectivism is controlled by a broadly representationalist account of perceptual experience. In addition, I argue that Nietzsche himself drew explicitly skeptical conclusions of a global sort from his perspectivism; hence he presents us with the same kind of paradox that attended his earlier positions. In the early 1870s, Nietzsche made the following entry in his *Philosophenbuch:* "Truths are illusions which we have forgotten are illusions" (*NTP,* p. 84). This claim, I will argue, remained at the center of his philosophical convictions throughout his productive period, unmoved by the successive shifts in his conceptions of human knowledge. Thus on all three accounts—Kantian, neo-Kantian, and perspectivist—"knowledge," for Nietzsche, is a kind of error, and what passes for truth among us is but a fiction, devised for vital purposes.[5]

II

In the philosophical assessment of this deeply anti-realist position, and all like it, a key question is whether the skeptical claim advanced concerning the epistemic status of our beliefs is global, thus including within its scope the claim set forth by the position itself; or whether Nietzsche, and those with similar ambitions, have granted themselves a special exemption from the consequences of their own analysis and are therefore in a position to state the sober truth about the human cognitive situation. Is the claim that all of our "truths" are little "t" truths—good for us to believe, perhaps, but ultimately false—itself a big "T" truth, one that gets it just right, one that tells us how the world is set up such that our truths must always be spelled with a little "t"; or is the claim that all of our truths are little "t" truths itself a little "t" truth, that is, nothing more than a useful fiction?

There are problems with both options. The first option divides the extension of putative truths into those that do not correspond to reality and those that do. Those truths that do correspond to reality are the ones stating that, and why, the other "truths" do not correspond to reality. If the position on truth thus escapes the analysis it proposes and counts as the big "T" truth about "truth," then big "T" truth is possible after all, while the analysis it proposes makes its epistemic status altogether mysterious and its assertion seem like a form of special pleading. Moreover, if big "T" truth is possible on this point, why not elsewhere? It would seem just arbitrary, apart from some demarcation theory, to claim truth with a capital "T" for oneself while denying it, on the basis of a general account of knowledge, to everyone else—especially to those who disagree.

The second option is equally troubled. If, in the interest of consistency and fair play, the proposed analysis of knowledge is itself advanced as a little "t" truth—that is, one falsehood among others—it has little to recommend it but its non-epistemic quality of utility. Although it appears to be a universal claim about the status of human knowledge that should command assent by virtue of the cogency of arguments given in its favor (and such arguments are given), the real basis of its acceptance, as it is a self-confessed falsehood, must be located not in the way the world is but in the practical needs of its audience. Those needs, however, are particular and not philosophically compelling. Here, as in other cases of practical preference, people should be allowed to pick and choose as they please. Can those who advance an epistemically self-abasing theory with passionate philosophical argument, then, be disappointed if others walk away from it for reasons wholly unconnected to the grounds they adduced in its support? It would seem not. If philosophers are really just sales reps for a tool company, they have little ground for complaint when the need for their particular product is something less than universal.

Secondly, it would seem that this option does not eliminate the question of big "T" truth; it only postpones it. For if the position recommends itself on the basis of its non-epistemic merits, such as its utility, its nobility, its life-affirming power, its expression of active rather than reactive forces, and the like, then, in considering the merits of this position, one must ask if it is true that it is useful, noble, life-affirming, or expressive of the right kind of force. Believing, like Nietzsche, that truth is well lost, Sarah Kofman holds that "A system must be evaluated not according to its truth, but according to its force and beauty." She then immediately proceeds to claim that "it is a question of knowing whether what made the system possible was a superabundant or a needy form of life, whether the philosopher was affirming or denying life."[6] But this is precisely the point: if we are to accept a system on the basis of its superior force and beauty, then we need to know whether it is the case that it has a superior force and beauty, whether it is true that is has the valued properties that distinguish it from its competitors.

One way to resolve the self-reflexive paradox involved in such claims as "truths are illusions" is to divide the domain of putative truths and limit the claim to one side of that division. The statement, after all, is typically given out in unquantified form. This option fills in the suppressed quantifier with the word "some." Walter Kaufman tries to help Nietzsche in this way: he distinguishes between metaphysical truths and empirical truths and then claims that Nietzsche's negative epistemological comment holds only for the former.[7] Richard Rorty lends his assistance with a similar tactic; he distinguishes between first-order claims about reality and second-order claims about first-order claims, and then maintains that Nietzsche's skepticism holds only with respect to first-order claims.[8] The problem with these forms of assistance, as we shall see, is that they are unwanted. For Nietzsche's critique of knowledge is global in scope. The reasons he gives for rejecting the truth of beliefs on one side of the proposed division typically hold with equal force for the beliefs on the other side.

Another strategy is not to divide the extension of possible truth bearers but rather the intension of the term "truth." One might distinguish a second sense of the term, then hold that Nietzsche claimed that all putative truths are fictions in one sense but still allowed for truth in another sense. Thus, it could be true in some novel sense that all truths in the traditional sense are errors. One escapes this paradox by equivocation. Arthur Danto, in his influential study of Nietzsche, makes just his claim: Nietzsche rejected the correspondence theory of truth, and "advanced a pragmatic criterion of truth; p is true and q is false if p works and q does not."[9] Like the genial American pragmatists, Nietzsche held that beliefs are true on the basis of their utility for us, not their correspondence to reality. Thus he could claim without contradiction that all beliefs that pass as true are in fact false in the correspondence sense, but at least possibly true in the pragmatic sense.

The chief difficulty with this interpretation of Nietzsche's theory of truth is that it is false. Although there are many passages in which Nietzsche explicitly associates truth and utility, he nowhere defines truth as utility. When Nietzsche characterizes our beliefs as false, he does not mean to claim that they do not work or that they are useless. On the contrary, he explicitly and repeatedly connects falsehood with utility; he speaks often and openly of the necessity of falsehood for the preservation and enhancement of life. Beliefs work because they are false; they are false because they fail to meet the relevant correspondence requirements. To claim that our "truths" are actually illusions, then, is not to reject the correspondence theory of truth but to use it as a standard. Heidegger was entirely right on this point: "Nietzsche's saying that truth is an illusion, a kind of error, has as its innermost presupposition, one that is thus never uttered at all, the traditional and never challenged characterization of truth as the correctness of representing."[10]

In those passages where he does associate truth and utility, Nietzsche's point is that utility is the criterion *we* use—whether we admit it or not—to pick out beliefs as true. We tend to believe that what we find useful, advantageous, and life-enhancing is true. "Without granting as true the fictions of logic," Nietzsche writes in *Beyond Good and Evil*, "without measuring reality against the purely invented world of the unconditional and self-identical, without a continual falsification of the world by means of numbers, humankind could not live."[11] This is an explanation of why we take a belief to be true, not what makes it true. As Alexander Nehamas puts it, "[Nietzsche] does not claim that utility constitutes, or even that it explains, truth. He writes instead that our belief that a view is useful, a belief which may well itself be false, is what makes us consider that particular view as true whether this is or is not in fact the case."[12] But Nehamas should have stated the point in stronger terms. For, according to Nietzsche, what makes for the utility of a belief, that property which makes us take it for truth, is precisely its falsehood, its misrepresentation of reality. It's not that beliefs we find useful may well be false; rather, we find them useful because they are false. If they did not falsify reality, they would not be useful. Falsehood is a condition of life, and that's why we honor it with the attribution of truth (*BGE*, §4). But paying it the complement of truth does not make it true. On this point Nietzsche was entirely clear.

III

In her careful and comprehensive study of his published pronouncements on truth, Maudemarie Clark claims that Nietzsche's use of the "metaphor of perspective" provides an "alternative to the representational model" of our cognitive situation, and therefore extricates him from the global falsification thesis of his earlier Kantian and neo-Kantian positions (*NTP*, p. 137). With his "perspectivism," as he developed it in his last six works, Nietzsche thus "overcame his early denial of truth" and the self-reflexive paradoxes that attended it (*NTP*, p. 127).

In this portion of the study, I argue that the arm of representational theory is long indeed, and that Nietzsche's perspectivism does not exceed its reach. The influence of representationalism in this case, however, is not as easy to detect as it was in his earlier positions because it comes indirectly and by way of analogy. In his final and most influential position on knowledge, Nietzsche uses the idea of perspective to suggest important and illuminating similarities between seeing from a standpoint and knowing. What I will try to show is that Nietzsche's analysis of what it means to see from a standpoint is thoroughly informed by the representational theory of perception; representational theory thus controls by way of analogy his perspectivist account of knowledge. Furthermore, Nietzsche uses the perceptual metaphor thus analyzed and applied to human cognition in order to assert the global falsification thesis once more. Finally, I indicate how Clark's own explication of the perceptual metaphor is informed by representationalism.

The epistemological implications of the metaphor of perspective, where knowledge is modeled on seeing from a standpoint, will depend to a great degree on whether one is inclined to give a representationalist or realist account of perceptual experience. On the realist theory of perception, we see things themselves by way of their appearances. We hear the violin by way of tone sensations; we see a book by way of visual appearances. Except in extraordinary cases—where the intensity of a sensation calls attention to itself, or where we are operating as phenomenologists in the mode of reflection—a thing's appearances are not the direct objects of our perception or awareness. I see a rectangular book, even though all of its shape appearances, save the one given along a line orthogonal to its surface, are variations on the trapezoid. As a skilled and competent perceiver, I move through the multiplicity of its shape appearances to perceive its shape, the one I take it to enjoy independently of its appearances to perceivers such as me—the one, in fact, that in large part accounts for why it appears to me the way it does. The appearances by which I perceive the book are clearly relative to my perception (even if they are not *wholly* relative to it). The precise dimensions and angles of the apparent figure are strictly dependent upon the book's relation to the standpoint from which I perceive it. But the spatial properties of the book I perceive are not dependent upon its relation to my perception of them. The book itself is rectangular.

In the representationalist account of perception, on the other hand, the perceptual act terminates in the appearances. The appearances of a thing, not the thing itself, are the direct objects of our perception. To use the example of the book perception again: we here perceive, on this account, nothing more or other than a relatively coherent and unified series of shape appearances. The rectangular shape appearance in that series may be preferred for practical purposes, but it doesn't count as *the* shape of the book in any metaphysically privileged sense—since it is but one possible representation among others. What we perceive depends upon our standpoint, our perspective, since the apparent shape of an object is relative to the standpoint we assume with respect to "it," and all we perceive are apparent shapes. The thing perceived is reduced to the unified manifold of its appearances.

From his early writings to his latest, Nietzsche exhibited a deep attachment to the representationalist account of perception. In "Truth and Lies in a Nonmoral Sense" (1873), he claims that philosophers typically choose to ignore the epistemologically embarrassing fact that there are other species of sentient beings. For, according to Nietzsche, different sensory equipment do not simply yield different perceptions of the same world, but different perceived worlds: "the insect or the bird perceives an entirely different world from the one that man does" (*PT*, p. 86). For any strong foundationalist who requires a correspondence guarantee for the base of knowledge, this fact is cause for some philosophical anxiety because here we have no independent access to the world as it is in itself in order to judge which form of perception is the "right" one (*PT*, p. 86). That is, we cannot guarantee the correctness of our representations.

Nietzsche claims that members of different species do not perceive the same world differently but instead perceive different worlds. He makes this claim because, in keeping with the representational account of perception, he takes it that the direct objects of our perceptual awareness are appearances and that appearances, taken together, make up a world. Since different sensory organs yield globally different complements of appearance, different sensory organs yield perceptual awareness of different worlds. In a note composed in the fall of 1886, some thirteen years after he wrote "Truth and Lies in a Nonmoral Sense," Nietzsche repeats the same point: "It is obvious that every creature different from us senses different qualities and consequently lives in a different world from that in which we live" (*WP*, §565). Different perceptual perspectives—whether constituted by different spatial standpoints or different kinds of sensory apparatus—yield different perceived worlds, not different perceptions of the same world.

To claim that all knowing is likewise a matter of perspective is to claim that there are important and illuminating similarities between seeing and knowing. One salient point of comparison is surely this: just as seeing can only occur from some particular standpoint, so does knowing. The most plausible candidate for the cognitive correlate of perceptual "standpoint" is the particular package of concepts, assumptions, needs, passions, interests, and values that we bring to the act of knowing—all things that need not, and perhaps cannot, be shared by all knowers. If it is in fact the case that our cognitive standpoint is constituted by the will to power, as Nietzsche claims (*WP*, §507), then that standpoint will surely not be held common. For the vital needs of a species, group, or individual will vary according to unique conditions, according to the particular configuration of forces at their location; hence, the concepts, assumptions, interests, and values that serve their vital needs will vary as well. There will be an irreducible plurality of cognitive standpoints or perspectives because there is an irreducible plurality of values, of conditions for the enhancement of the power of different centers of force in the cosmic system of dynamic quanta (*WP*, §635, 636). Here the perspectival metaphor cuts against the strong foundationalist notion that we possess a common faculty of evidence that makes all particularity in the realm of knowledge methodologically eliminable. But it is thus far consistent with the realist concept of knowledge. For the relativity here suggested by the perceptual metaphor is a relativity of conceptualization and justification, not truth.[13]

The realist position must be set aside, however, when seeing from a standpoint is given an analysis controlled by representational theory. For on this theory, the appearance is the object of perception. The standpoint, then, not only determines the angle from which an object is seen; it also determines the object that is seen. "The apparent world," writes Nietzsche in *The Will to Power*, is "a world viewed according to values; ordered, selected according to values, i.e., in this case according to the viewpoint of utility in regard to the preservation and enhancement of the power of a certain species of animal. The perspective therefore decides the character of the 'appearance'!" (*WP*, §567) And appearance, according to Nietzsche, is all there is to the world. There is no true world behind the apparent world. "The world . . . does not exist as a world 'in-itself'; it is essentially a world of relationships; under certain conditions it has a differing aspect from every point; its being is essentially different form every point; it presses upon every point, every point resists it—and the sum of these is in every case quite incongruent" (*WP*, §568). The perspective, then, does not simply determine the way the world appears but constitutes a world out of appearances on the basis of a particular set of values.

The application of the perceptual metaphor to cognition is this: just as in the case of seeing, where the perspective determines the appearance of the object (and the object seen just is the sum of its appearances), so in knowing our perspective determines the characteristics of the object (and the known object just is the sum of its characteristics). In the case of cognition, concepts do not discover properties of an independently structured world; they generate a world according to their plan: "One should not understand the compulsion to construct concepts, species, forms, purposes, laws . . . as if they enabled us to fix the *real world;* but as a compulsion to arrange a world for ourselves in which our existence is made possible" (*WP*, §521).

Clark claims that Nietzsche's perspectivism signifies a radical departure from representationalism. Nevertheless, like Nietzsche, she explicates the perspectival metaphor along strict representationalist lines. Consider the following passage from her study:

> There is, of course, no way things look in themselves. A thing's visual characteristics are different aspects of the way it looks from one or more of the

possible perspectives on it. Nietzsche uses the metaphor of perspective to
make a parallel suggestion about the intelligible character of a thing, namely,
that the aspects of its intelligible character are aspects of how it would be
interpreted from one or more of the cognitive perspectives on it. . . . As there
is nothing to see of a thing except what it looks like from various visual
perspectives, there is nothing to know of it except how it is interpreted from
various cognitive perspectives. (*NTP,* p. 132)

The claim that the object we know is constituted by the way we
know it—that, as Robert Legros put it, the object "is nothing outside
of the various comprehensions that grasp at it"[14]—seems wildly implausible on the face of it. Take the weight of a thing, for example,
as determined in the judgment, "This thing weighs ten pounds." Nor-
mally, we take "weighing ten pounds" to be a property that a thing
has independently of our cognitive relation to it. Granted, it doesn't
weigh ten pounds in itself, since its weight is a function of its mass and
its distance from other mass points. But it doesn't seem that the mental act of knowing that it weighs ten pounds is what makes it weigh
ten pounds. If we take "known property" to be the analogical correlate
of "apparent look" of an object, then in what sense can this property
be dependent upon our cognitive perspective? In what sense is its
weighing ten pounds a function of our knowing that it weighs ten
pounds?

Perhaps the best way to see what is going on in this extension of the
perspectival metaphor in the case of cognition is to take it as a generalization of representational theory in the following way: just as the
thing we perceive is nothing more or other than the unified sum of its
appearances whereby we perceive "it," so the thing we know is nothing
more or other than the unified sum of the intensions of those concepts
whereby we know "it." Thus the object wouldn't "weigh 10 pounds"
unless and until we had devised the concepts of weight, integers,
pounds as a metric of weight, and the like. By having our conceptual
intensions do double duty as extensions, we could then claim that different conceptual frameworks yield knowledge of different objects, not
knowledge of the same objects under different descriptions—or, more
generally, that the world we know is determined by the cognitive perspective in which we know it. Clark puts it this way: "Nietzsche's use
of the metaphor of perspective invites us to think of a thing's intellectual appearances as informed by something about the subject, its cognitive constitution, and ultimately, whatever factors are responsible for
that" (*NTP,* p. 133). I can think of no way of making sense of this claim
apart from the notion that the "intellectual appearances" of a thing,

that is, its known properties, are just the intensions of the concepts we bring to it.

Clark holds that in rejecting the notion of the thing-in-itself, Nietzsche, at the same time and for that very reason, gives up the global falsification thesis, the notion that our "truths" are actually false-hoods. For by rejecting the thing-in-itself, Nietzsche has deprived the falsification thesis of any basis of comparison between the thing as it appears to us and the thing as it is in itself. There can be no slippage, no distortion here because the term of comparison on the far side of our experience doesn't exist. The thing is just its appearances—all surface, no depth. Therefore, our beliefs about it can be true in the correspondence sense: they correspond to the way it appears to us—and there is nothing more to the object than the way it appears to us. The object is immediately accessible. It no longer hides from us. Nietzsche thus rejects the correspondence theory in the metaphysical sense but retains it in the empirical—or "minimalist"—sense. There is nothing that exists in itself that could be taken as the measure of the true and thus expose our perceptions and perceptual beliefs as systematically false. The standard of truth is cut down to human scale and knowledge made attainable. It extends not to the thing-in-itself, behind our representations, but to the thing as constituted by our representations—both perceptual and conceptual.

This is an interesting position, and one worthy of consideration. But it is not Nietzsche's. Nietzsche does not make use of the perspectival metaphor in a vigorous defense of the possibility of human knowledge. The conclusion he draws on its basis is not that we can now see how our beliefs can meet the correspondence requirement. Rather, he is at pains to point out that because of the perspectival nature of all knowing, our cognitive grasp on any object is partial, selective, and simplifying, and therefore distorting: "This is the essence of phenomenalism and perspectivism as I understand them: . . . all becoming conscious involves a great and thorough corruption, falsification, reduction to superficialities, and generalization."[15] On Nietzsche's perspectivist account, the object is the totality of properties it acquires with respect to the infinitely many perspectives that can be taken upon it (*GM*, §12). Reality is not reduced to the appearances from our standpoint; rather, it is the totality of appearances from all possible standpoints. Clearly this reality is just as inaccessible as the Kantian thing-in-itself hidden behind appearances. And Nietzsche delights in reminding us of this. He does not retract the standard of truth but turns it sideways, so to speak, thereby making the truth about the world equally inaccessible. The lack of correspondence no longer lies between appearance and reality but between our selected appearances and the totality of possible appearances. No longer does he press the skeptical point, as he did in "Truth and Lies in a Nonmoral Sense," by claiming that we have no access to the world as it is itself and therefore have no way of knowing *which* perspective is the "right" one; he now claims that *no* perspective can be the right one: "There are many kinds of eyes. Even the sphinx has eyes—and consequently there are many kinds of 'truths,' and consequently there is no truth" (*WP*, §540).

Those, like Clark, who want restore to Nietzsche a robust sense of the possibility of knowledge under the correspondence theory of truth simply miss the point: the truth is well lost; so, rather than attempt to save it, we should reconcile ourselves to the virtues of illusion. Relieved of the impossible task of getting at the truth, we should exult in the possibility of projecting many "truths"—all equally false, but many possibly life-enhancing. For "the falseness of a judgment is to us not necessarily an objection to a judgment. . . . The question is to what extent it is life-advancing, life-preserving, species-preserving" (*BGE*, §4). Rather than slavishly trying to mimic some pre-given reality, we do and must make bold to create the realities we inhabit. For the strong, this is not cause for despair, but joy. "With new values, properly chosen, there would be no longer the humble expression, 'everything is merely subjective,' but 'this too is our work!—Let us be proud of it!" (*WP*, §1059; translation modified).

IV

With this jubilant reaffirmation of the global falsification thesis, however, the self-reflexive paradox returns. Nietzsche's perspectivism is itself either an attempt to state the sober truth about the way the world is—thoroughly relational, necessarily apprehended from particular standpoints constituted by the will to power, and the like—or it is itself one among many falsifying perspectives on reality, expressive of the particular life-requirements and values of those who propound and accept it. If perspectivism is not itself a perspective on the world afforded by a particular interest, then perspectivism—as the claim that all cognitive claims are advanced from a particular perspective—is false. On the other hand, if perspectivism is itself a perspective, then it is a falsifying consciousness of a world much richer, more varied (and contradictory) than it allows. On this option, as John Wilcox pointed out, Nietzsche's truth and the errors it was meant to counteract "are, in one sense, not related as opposites; the truth is an error, too."[16]

Because the falsification thesis—unrelieved by any partition in the domain of beliefs—remains in place, the self-referential paradox remains firmly embedded in Nietzsche's epistemology and, from there, extends to all postmodern theories of knowledge inspired by his perspectivism. At the conclusion of his recent article entitled "Nietzsche's French Moment," Vincent Descombes claims that the paradoxes into which postmodernism leads us may be instructive, if only they cause us to re-examine the premises from which they followed.[17] Heidegger was already about that business in the 1940s when he challenged Nietzsche's commitment to the correspondence theory of truth:

> This concept of truth [as the agreement of knowledge with things] is the presupposition and principal standard of measure for the interpretation of truth as semblance and error. Then does not Nietzsche's own interpretation of truth as semblance become semblance? It becomes even less than semblance: Nietzsche's interpretation of 'truth' as error, by appealing to the essence of truth as agreement with the real, leads to the reversal of his own thinking and thus to its dissolution.[18]

For Heidegger, this turn of events in Nietzsche's thought serves as a clear demonstration of the inherent weakness of the correspondence theory of truth, and he quickly seizes upon the opportunity to advertise his own version of truth as disclosure. But it is not the correspondence theory of truth alone that generates the self-reflexive paradox. In Nietzsche's case, it was the correspondence theory of truth in tandem with his version of representational theory that produces the problem. If one takes the paradox as an indication of a faulty premise rather than cause for Dionysian giddiness, one always has the option of directing the force of the *modus tollens* at representational theory rather than at the correspondence theory of truth.

I have argued that Nietzsche's perspectivism does not signify the abandonment of the representational theory of consciousness; on the contrary, in his final position truth and knowledge we find representational theory intensified with the rejection of the thing-in-itself and generalized by way of analogy. Nor do we have a departure from the correspondence theory of truth; rather, this theory is assumed and used as a standard for a negative epistemic appraisal of our "truths." Nietzsche's perspectivism is therefore not a rejection of the deep and defining principles of modern philosophy but rather a particularly rigorous application of them. If I am right on this point, then postmodernist epistemology—to the degree it draws upon Nietzsche's perspectivism—should be regarded as a kind of modernism. And from this it follows that those who wish to appropriate postmodernism for religious reasons will invariably find themselves also latching onto modernism—hook, line, and sinker.

Notes

1. David Hume, *Enquiry into Human Understanding* (Oxford: Clarendon Press), 1982, §XII.

2. Friedrich Nietzsche, "Truth and Lies in an Nonmoral Sense," in *Philosophy and Truth,* ed. and trans. Daniel Breazeale (Atlantic Highlands, N.J.: Humanities Press, 1979), p. 80. Here and hereafter, I refer to this text parenthetically as *PT.*

3. In "Nietzsche's French Moment," Vincent Descombes claims that in Nietzscheanism, "We find an interrogation about the principles of modern philosophy that itself never goes outside the limits of this philosophy"; it "does not have principles other than those of the 'modern project'"; in *Why We Are Not Nietzscheans,* ed. Luc Ferry and Alain Renaut (Chicago: University of Chicago Press, 1997), p. 90. In matters epistemological, I agree with this assessment.

4. Maudemarie Clark, *Nietzsche on Truth and Philosophy* (Cambridge: Cambridge University Press, 1990). Hereafter referred to as *NTP.*

5. See Friedrich Nietzsche, *The Will to Power,* trans. Walter Kaufmann and R. J. Hollingdale (New York: Vintage Books, 1967), §453. Hereafter referred to as *WP.*

6. Sarah Kofman, *Nietzsche and Metaphor* (Stanford, Calif.: Stanford University Press, 1993), p. 19.

7. Walter Kaufman, *Nietzsche: Philosopher, Psychologist, Antichrist* (Princeton, N.J.: Princeton University Press, 1974).

8. Richard Rorty, *The Consequences of Pragmatism* (Minneapolis: University of Minnesota Press, 1982).

9. Arthur Danto, *Nietzsche as Philosopher* (New York: Macmillan, 1965), chap. 3.

10. Martin Heidegger, *Nietzsche,* vol. 3 (New York: Harper and Row, 1987), p. 35.

11. Friedrich Nietzsche, *Beyond Good and Evil,* trans. R. J. Hollingdale (Harmondsworth, England: Penguin Books, 1973), §4, translation modified; this text is subsequently referred to in text as *BGE.* See also *BGE,* §17, and *WP,* §493, 507, 609.

12. Alexander Nehamas, *Life as Literature* (Cambridge, Mass.: Harvard University Press, 1985), p. 54.

13. Brian Leiter domesticates Nietzsche's perspectivism by limiting it to questions of justification in this fashion. See his "Perspectivism in Nietzsche's Genealogy of Morals," in *Nietzsche, Genealogy, Morality,* ed. Richard Schacht (Berkeley: University of California Press, 1994).

14. Robert Legros, "Nietzsche's Metaphysics of Life," in *Why We Are Not Nietzscheans,* p. 117.

15. Friedrich Nietzsche, *The Gay Science*, trans. Walter Kaufmann (New York: Vintage Books, 1974), §354.

16. John Wilcox, *Truth and Value in Nietzsche* (Ann Arbor: University of Michigan Press, 1974), p. 163. The paradox to which Wilson alludes prompted Jean Granier to speak of an "underlying antinomy" that "disturbs Nietzsche's whole reflection," an antinomy "between a pragmatic phenomenalism and a realist dogmatism"; in Ganier, "Perspectivism and Interpretation," *The New Nietzsche*, ed. David Allison (Cambridge, Mass.: MIT Press, 1985), p. 197. It led Alexander Nehamas, in his well-known study of Nietzsche, to ask whether "Nietzsche's self-conscious genealogical interpretation [can] be both a manifestation of his will to power, of his effort to project his own values and to introduce himself into history, and at the same time *correct?* Or is it at best, as often seems to be the case, an expression of his own personal, privately motivated, and peculiar preferences?" (Nehamas, *Life as Literature*, p. 105).

17. Descombes, "Nietzsche's French Moment," p. 90.

18. Heidegger, *Nietzsche*, vol. 4, p. 132.

3

Is the Postmodern
Post-Secular?

The Parody of Religious Quests in Thomas Pynchon's
The Crying of Lot 49 *and Don DeLillo's* White Noise

BRIAN D. INGRAFFIA

> Behind the hieroglyphic streets there would either be a transcendent
> meaning, or only the earth . . . either some fraction of the truth's
> numinous beauty . . . or only a power spectrum.
> —Thomas Pynchon, *The Crying of Lot 49*

> But don't I have to believe? Don't I have to feel in my heart that
> there is something, genuinely, beyond this life . . . ?
> —Don DeLillo, *White Noise*

In a recent article, John McClure argues that the postmodern should
be interpreted as a post-secular phenomenon. This is true, he argues, of
both postmodern American culture and postmodern American fiction.

> In order to understand what is going on in American postmodern cul-
> ture, then, we need to think in terms of something like a religious revival:
> a resurgence . . . of spiritual energies, discourses, and commitments. And in
> order to understand postmodern fiction, we need to attend to the ways in
> which it maintains and revises a modernist tradition of spiritually inflected
> resistance to conventionally secular constructions of reality.[1]

A similar argument has been made by Diogenes Allen, who, in *Christian
Belief in a Postmodern World*, asserts that "the barriers to Christian belief
erected by the modern mentality [are] collapsing" because the "foundations of the modern world are collapsing and we are entering a post-

modern world."[2] And in yet another recent example, John Caputo asserts that "deconstruction must likewise be seen as a form of 'post-secularization.' For deconstruction moves beyond all Enlightenment debunking of religion and chastises the Enlightenment—as Derrida chastises Marx—for having chased away one ghost too many."[3] If these arguments are correct, then Christian thinkers should look forward to appropriating postmodern thought.

While I agree that postmodernism is anti-modern, at least in its rejection of the Enlightenment faith in reason, and therefore contains the potential to free Western thought from the secularization performed in both modern philosophy and modernist literature, I disagree with those who regard postmodern thought and culture as more hospitable to Christian thought and spirituality. In a dialogue recently published between John Caputo and Edith Wyschogrod on "Postmodernism and the Desire for God," Caputo notes how Philip Blond and Graham Ward[4] have both "pressed the claim that 'postmodern' must be understood to mean or at least to include 'postsecular,' that the delimitation of the claims of Enlightenment rationalism must also involve the delimitation of Enlightenment secularism. A critical stance toward modernism goes hand in hand with a critical stance toward secularism." Despite his sympathy with this argument, Caputo admits that at least "certain American 'postmodernist' writers . . . remain deeply and intractably modernist in protecting the rear guard of modernist critiques of religion."[5] In contrast to Caputo, I argue in my book, *Postmodern Theory and Biblical Theology: Vanquishing God's Shadow*, that postmodern continental philosophy also relies upon the modernist critique of religion.[6] Here I will attempt to make an analogous argument based upon a reading of postmodern American fiction.

McClure points to Thomas Pynchon and Don DeLillo as two contemporary American writers who are almost universally acknowledged as postmodern and whose novels perform a "reaffirmation of premodern ontologies" and a "post-secular project of resacralization."[7] To refute his argument, I will present here a reading of DeLillo's *White Noise* as representing not a rejection of modernist secularization, but rather the use of late modernist secularization as a means to recovering a secular faith, and a reading of Pynchon's *The Crying of Lot 49* as representing not a rejection of modernist secularization on behalf of a "resacralization," but rather a more radical critique of religion through a parody of narratives of religious quest and revelation.[8]

The protagonists of both novels, Oedipa Maas in *The Crying of Lot 49* and Jack Gladney in *White Noise*, search for meaning within an apparently meaningless postmodern American landscape. Both characters lament, like Jean Baudrillard, the loss of the real in a culture permeated with simulacra (including the simulacra of religious belief).[9] I will identify both characters, therefore, as "incomplete nihilists," following Nietzsche's distinction between incomplete and completed nihilism.

Incomplete nihilism faces the terror of a world in which God has died, and it sees this death as emptying the world of meaning. According to Nietzsche, the Christian-moral interpretation of the world supplied humanity with a sense of purpose and meaning, but when the falsehood of this interpretation is revealed, then humanity loses all faith and hope in finding any meaning and purpose for life. Because Western society invested so much into this interpretation, the rebound from Christianity is great, causing the incomplete nihilist to move from complete faith to total despair: "the untenability of one interpretation of the world, upon which a tremendous amount of energy has been lavished, awakens the suspicion that *all* interpretations of the world are false."[10] Because Western culture has projected all truth and meaning onto an other world, upon God's transcendent realm, the loss of belief in this God means the loss of all truth for this culture.

But if this terrified, anguished response to nihilism is the first and necessary reaction to the murder of the Christian god, it is nevertheless an inadequate and incomplete response, according to Nietzsche. The response of the perfect nihilist, the free spirit, is in many ways the opposite of the fearful response of the incomplete nihilist:

> Indeed, we philosophers and "free spirits" feel, when we hear the news that "the old god is dead," as if a new dawn shone on us; our heart overflows with gratitude, amazement, premonitions, expectation.[11]

Completed nihilism also faces the death of God and the loss of a transcendental signified as a foundation for meaning and truth; however, in contrast to incomplete nihilism, completed nihilism, rather than lamenting this loss, instead celebrates the freedom which results from this loss.

Nietzsche's distinction between incomplete and completed nihilism can help us understand the difference between modernism and postmodernism. Both the modernist and the postmodernist acknowledge the death of God, but whereas the modernist laments this death and secularizes religious and mythological narratives as a way of bringing order to the chaos of the world, the postmodernist celebrates this death and rejects attempts to bring order to the chaotic world as inevitably leading to the violent imposition of hegemonic, totalizing narratives. Lyotard defines postmodernism as "incredulity toward metanarratives," and Christian narrative is parodied in postmodern American fiction because it is seen as the source of Western society's belief in, or at least nostalgia for, a totalizing metanarrative. And as the current critical paradigm in literary theory has shifted from deconstruction to cultural studies, the belief in a totalizing metanarrative is considered not only an ontological mistake, but also a political danger. As Linda Hutcheon describes in *A Poetics of Postmodernism,* "'to totalize' does not just mean to unify, but rather means to unify with an eye to power and control."[12] Postmodernism rejects modernist attempts to impose order upon the chaos of the world, and these attempts are criticized as ontotheological, as secularizations of mythological/religious metanarratives.

Both Oedipa Maas in *The Crying of Lot 49* and Jack Gladney in *White Noise* are modernists seeking for order and meaning in a postmodern world. Oedipa's search begins when she is named co-executor—or as she thinks to herself, "co-executrix"[13]—of the will of her former lover, Pierce Inverarity, a fantastically wealthy real estate mogul who owns most or all of "San Narciso," a thinly veiled reference to the narcissistic Southern California culture which epitomizes the shallowness and cultural decay of postmodern American culture. But Oedipa, unlike her namesake, will not suffer tragedy in order to gain in self-knowledge. Oedipa will experience "all manner of revelations," but "Hardly about Pierce Inverarity, or herself" (*Lot 49*, p. 20).

The proliferation of religious revelations, or at least intimations of religious revelations, which occur throughout the novel have caused a number of critics to follow Edward Mendelson, who argues that "The religious meaning of the book does not reduce to metaphor or myth, because religious meaning is itself the central issue of the plot."[14] James Nohrnberg follows Mendelson in developing a reading of the novel which focuses upon the imagery borrowed from the New Testament, especially from the account of Pentecost in Acts.[15] First I will summarize Mendelson and Nohrnberg's excellent close readings of the biblical imagery of the novel. Then I will summarize recent objections to the contention that the novel is a religious novel as I develop my own reading of the biblical imagery as part of a parody rather than a recovery of religious, and in particular, Christian-biblical narrative.

Nohrnberg interprets the call which Oedipa receives in the middle of the night from Pierce Inverarity, the call she remembers later, after receiving the letter notifying her that she had been named co-executor of Pierce's will, as an allusion to the annunciation in Luke's gospel:

> Although she is not in the least virginal, Oedipa's story receives a Marian configuration from the moment that Pierce Inverarity, a former lover, telephones his promise to the heroine that "the Shadow" will be paying her a visit (cf. Luke 1:35: "The Holy Spirit will overshadow thee").[16]

The more immediate reference in the narrative for "the Shadow" is to the radio drama, and many critics have pointed out that the novel, like many postmodern novels, inverts the typical detective genre, the quintessential narrative of Enlightenment empiricism.[17] The Oedipus myth can also be read as a kind of detective story, with Oedipus solving the crime by discovering that he himself is the guilty one.[18] But these narratives are inverted in postmodern fiction in order to question the teleology and desire for closure exhibited in modern narratives. Nohrnberg is right to identify the Pentecostal imagery at work in the novel, but he fails to see how Pynchon inverts and parodies this eschatological narrative.

Like his Calvinist ancestors, Pynchon divides the world into the elect and the preterite; however, he inverts the Puritan valuation by identifying the elect with the rich and powerful in our society, those who run the system and profit by it, and identifying the preterite with the poor and the outcast of society, those who are sacrificed to and abused by the system. Pierce Inverarity is one of the "elect." He is the developer and owner of San Narciso. For him to come upon Oedipa and impregnate her is a parody of the annunciation and divine conception of Christ. As the narrator tells us later in the story, after Oedipa makes an appointment with a gynecologist under the pseudonym, "Grace Bortz"—that is, "grace aborts" rather than impregnates: "Your gynecologist has no test for what she was pregnant with" (*Lot 49*, p. 175).

What Oedipa is pregnant with is an obsession with her search for the meaning of the Tristero, a mysterious organization with roots in the seventeenth century, which seems to be operating as an underground communication system for the preterite or outcasts of America's consumer society. Oedipa discovers the Tristero as a result of her work on Inverarity's will. The original title for Pynchon's story was "The World (This One), the Flesh (Mrs. Oedipa Maas), and the Testament of Pierce Inverarity." Oedipa has been obsessed with interpreting the "Testament" of Pierce Inverarity, struggling to understand and execute his "will." In a Christian quest romance, the hero has to fight against the world, the flesh, and the devil.[19] In Pynchon's narrative, Pierce Inverarity plays the role of God, as author of the will and testament which Oedipa seeks to interpret; however, this god is an evil, malign god, coming to visit us not with grace but with annihilation, with death.[20]

At the conclusion of the novel, Oedipa awaits the "crying of lot 49." An auctioneer will be "crying," or putting up for bid, a "lot," or a group of objects, here Inverarity's collection of stamps, stamps which were supposedly made by the mysterious Tristero organization. Since an agent of the Tristero is supposed to be attending the auction in person,

Oedipa regards this final scene, as do many critics, as anticipating the final revelation of the Tristero. Mendelson explains the Pentecostal imagery of the conclusion:

> But why the *forty-ninth* lot? Because Pentecost is the Sunday seven weeks after Easter—forty-nine days. But the word Pentecost derives from the Greek for "fiftieth." The crying—the auctioneer's calling—of the forty-ninth lot is the moment before a Pentecostal revelation, the end of the period in which the miracle is in a state of potential, not yet manifest. This is why the novel ends with Oedipa waiting, with the "true" nature of the Trystero never established: a manifestation of the sacred can only be believed in; it can never be proved beyond doubt. There will always be a mocking voice, internal or external, saying "they are filled with new wine"—or, as Oedipa fears, "you are hallucinating it . . . you are fantasying some plot" (*Lot 49*, pp. 170–71).[21]

Mendelson is right to assert that there will always be a mocking voice, but that voice is Pynchon's. Pynchon's narrative does not want to show us that truth is only perceived by faith. Pynchon is not merely trying to caution us to inject more humility into our epistemology.

Rather, Pynchon's narrative shows that there is no truth, that we build fantasies in order to escape hearing the "words she never wanted to hear," the words Oedipa imagines hearing when "the Tristero could be revealed in its terrible nakedness" (*Lot 49*, p. 54).

> Would its smile, then, be coy, and would it flirt away harmlessly backstage, say good night with a Bourbon Street bow and leave her in peace? Or would it instead, the dance ended, come back down the runway, its luminous stare locked to Oedipa's, smile gone malign and pitiless; bend to her alone among the desolate rows of seats and begin to speak words she never wanted to hear? (*Lot 49*, p. 54)

What Oedipa does not want to hear about is her own mortality. When Mike Fallopian asks Oedipa if she has ever wondered if her search for the Tristero is based upon "a hoax, maybe something Inverarity set up before he died" (*Lot 49*, p. 167), the narrator informs us that "It had occurred to her. But *like the thought that someday she would have to die*, Oedipa had been steadfastly refusing to look at that possibility directly" (my emphasis; *Lot 49*, p. 167). Oedipa is at least in part fascinated by Pierce Inverarity's will because she sees it as his way of beating death:

> [H]e [Inverarity] might even have tried to survive death, as a paranoia; as a pure conspiracy against someone he loved. Would that breed of perversity prove at last too keen to be stunned even by death, had a plot finally been devised too elaborate for the dark Angel to hold at once, in his humorless

vice-president's head, all the possibilities of? Had something slipped through
and Inverarity by that much beaten death?

Yet she knew, head down, stumbling along over the cinderbed and its old
sleepers, there was still that other chance. That it was all true. That Inverarity
had only died, nothing else. (*Lot 49*, p. 179)

In Pierce's last will and testament, there is no overcoming of death, no
resurrection, as there is in the Christian New Testament. "Inverarity
had only died, nothing else." Nevertheless, Oedipa seeks to avoid facing
her own death through her involvement with the Tristero. But the only
revelation coming to her at the end of the novel is the advent of her
own death. As Derrida said at Villanova: "We wait for something we
would not like to wait for. That is another name for death."[22]

Oedipa's paranoid fear that the Tristero will turn malign comes true
on the final page of the novel. Listen to the imagery of the final scene.
It begins with Oedipa deciding whether or not to enter the auction
room. "She stood in a patch of sun, among brilliant rising and falling points of dust, trying to get a little warm, wondering if she'd go
through with it" (*Lot 49*, p. 183). Here she stands among the brilliance
and warmth of the world, this one, the only one there is, according to
Pynchon. As she steps inside, she leaves this world in order to pursue
her obsession, her desire to understand the Testament:

> The men inside the auction room wore black mohair and had pale, cruel
> faces. They watched her come in. . . . Loren Passerine, on his podium, hov-
> ered like a puppet-master, his eyes bright, his smile practiced and relent-
> less. He stared at her, smiling, as if saying, I'm surprised you actually came.
> Oedipa sat alone, toward the back of the room . . . trying to guess which one
> was her target, her enemy, perhaps her proof. An assistant closed the heavy
> door on the lobby windows and the sun. She heard a lock snap shut. . . .
> Passerine spread his arms in a gesture that seemed to belong to the priest-
> hood of some remote culture; perhaps to a descending angel. (*Lot 49*, p. 183)

As with other manifestations of the Tristero in the novel, the images
invoke more dread than wonder, more fear than hope.[23] Derrida remarks that "Literature concerning the secret is almost always organized around scenes and intrigues that deal with figures of death,"[24]
and the agents of the Tristero, who resemble "figures of death" in their
black mohair and with their pale, cruel faces, are in charge of preserving the secrecy of the organization. To "pierce" In-verarity's will is to
pierce behind the veil, behind the socially constructed world, behind
our self-created, solipsistic worlds, to see the inveracity, the lack of veracity, the absence of truth. The angel descending upon Oedipa at the

conclusion of the novel is not the Holy Ghost but rather the angel of death, or rather "only death" (*Lot 49*, p. 182). The auctioneer's name, Passerine, refers to the order of birds, Passeriformes, which includes the suborder Oscines, said to give omens by their cry, and suggests a demonic parody of the dove used to symbolize the Holy Spirit in the New Testament.

Oedipa Maas faces the choice between incomplete and completed nihilism at the conclusion of Pynchon's novel as she struggles to interpret the meaning of the mysterious Tristero, the holy grail she has searched for throughout the narrative:

> Behind the hieroglyphic streets there would either be a transcendent meaning, or only the earth . . . either some fraction of the truth's numinous beauty . . . or only a power spectrum. . . . either an accommodation reached, in some kind of dignity, with the Angel of Death, or only death and the daily, tedious preparations for it. Another mode of meaning behind the obvious, or none. Either Oedipa in the orbiting ecstasy of a true paranoia, or a real Tristero. (*Lot 49*, p. 181–82)

The first line, which presents the choice of "a transcendent meaning, or only the earth," can be compared with Nietzsche's deconstruction of the opposition between an apparent and an ideal world. Nietzsche denied that there is a true, transcendent realm; he asserted that there is only the earth. Nietzsche believed that "The total character of the world . . . is in all eternity chaos—in the sense not of a lack of necessity but of a lack of order, arrangement, form, beauty, wisdom, and whatever other names there are for our aesthetic anthropomorphisms."[25] All attempts to believe in an ideal realm, such as the spiritual or heavenly realm in Christianity, are regarded as being inevitably based upon *ressentiment*, upon a hatred of this world and this life. "One has deprived reality of its value, its meaning, its truthfulness, to precisely the extent to which one has mendaciously invented an ideal world."[26] Pynchon is making the same argument in *The Crying of Lot 49*. Oedipa's search for a transcendent meaning for the Tristero has caused her to become completely isolated—"her isolation complete" (*Lot 49*, p. 177)—shut off from the natural world of becoming through her search for the being of a transcendental signified.

The next opposition in the passage from Pynchon presents the choice between "either some fraction of truth's numinous beauty . . . or only a power spectrum," which can be compared to Foucault's overcoming of the dualism between truth and power, his analysis of truth as the effect of a Nietzschean will to power. The full sentence in

Pynchon reads, "In the songs Miles, Dean, Serge and Leonard sang was either some fraction of the truth's numinous beauty (as Mucho now believed) or only a power spectrum." Miles, Dean, Serge, and Leonard are the members of The Paranoids, a parody of American commercial imitations of British rock bands, like the Monkeys, and Mucho Maas is Oedipa's husband, who through the course of the novel seeks to escape from a recurring nightmare in which he sees a sign containing the acronym for the association to which he belongs as a used-car dealer, the National Association of Dealers of Automotives, or N.A.D.A., symbolizing his incomplete nihilism, his fear of the *nihil* of nihilism. After Oedipa leaves him, he begins to take LSD and hallucinates that he can do spectrum analysis of the rock music he plays in his new job as a DJ. He has a vision of universal oneness as he imagines "a couple hundred million chorus saying 'rich, chocolaty goodness' together, and it would all be the same voice" (*Lot 49*, p. 142). Therefore, we should not put much faith in Mucho's belief in the presence of the "truth's numinous beauty" in the commercials played on a rock music station for teenagers.

Mucho is just one of a cast of characters who escape from reality through what certainly should be read as a mock version of religious belief. Even Mendelson admits that "everyone in *The Crying of Lot 49* suffers from some distortion of religious faith, and almost everyone in the book eventually drops away from Oedipa into some religious obsession."[27] But rather than interpreting Oedipa as yet another example of religious obsession in the novel, Mendelson argues that the other characters "demonstrate the wrong turnings that Oedipa must avoid."[28]

Many critics have responded to Mendelson's reading of the novel by stressing the ambiguity of the novel, especially of the conclusion. They note that the list of either/or's which presents the possibility of a transcendent meaning is preceded by the questioning of either/or thinking:

> The waiting above all; if not for another set of possibilities to replace those that had conditioned the land to accept any San Narciso among its most tender flesh without a reflex or a cry, then at least, at the very least, waiting for a symmetry of choices to break down, to go skew. She had heard all about excluded middles; they were bad shit, to be avoided; and how had it ever happened here, with the chances once so good for diversity? For it was now like walking among matrices of a great digital computer, the zeroes and ones twinned above, hanging like balanced mobiles right and left, ahead, thick, maybe endless. Behind the hieroglyphic streets . . . (*Lot 49*, p. 181)

Thomas Schaub was the first to criticize Mendelson's reading, asserting that his argument "threatens to eliminate the book's essential ambiguity."[29] Mendelson himself has since become convinced of the validity of this critique. Most critics of the novel now agree that Pynchon does not intend to choose one side of the either/or questions asked.

Pynchon's presentation of the either/or between either a transcendent meaning or only the earth is similar to Derrida's now well-known distinction between the two interpretations of interpretation at the conclusion of "Structure, Sign, and Play in the Discourse of the Human Sciences":

> There are thus two interpretations of interpretation, of structure, of sign, of play. The one seeks to decipher, dreams of deciphering a truth or an origin which escapes play and the order of the sign, and which lives the necessity of interpretation as an exile. The other, which is no longer turned toward the origin, affirms play and tries to pass beyond man and humanism, the name of man being the name of that being who, throughout the history of metaphysics or of ontotheology—in other words, throughout his entire history—has dreamed of full presence, the reassuring foundation, the origin and the end of play.[30]

Oedipa believes in the first interpretation of interpretation. She dreams of deciphering the central truth of Inverarity's will to discover "another mode of meaning behind the obvious." She wants a reassuring foundation, a transcendental signified, which will function as "the origin and end of play." Oedipa's central dilemma in the novel, her quest to discover whether or not the Tristero really exists, is caused by the fact that all knowledge is mediated by language, by the fact that "there is nothing outside the text."[31] Derrida asserts that "I do not believe that today there is any question of *choosing*"[32] between these two interpretations of interpretation,[33] but this is because he believes that the desire for a transcendental signified is inherent in human thought and human language. Derrida's thought is poststructuralist in that he seeks to expose and deconstruct the enduring dualism in Western thought between presence and absence, such as the choice between either the presence or the absence of meaning and truth in interpretation. Nevertheless, in his conclusion to "Différance," Derrida champions a Nietzschean affirmation of play against a Heideggerian nostalgia and hope; he affirms Nietzsche's postmodernism over Heidegger's modernism.[34]

While I agree that Pynchon avoids closure at the end of his novel by leaving Oedipa awaiting the crying of lot 49, I think that Pynchon, by presenting such mocking parodies of belief in a transcendent realm and by showing the destructive consequences of such belief, advocates the Nietzschean belief that there is "only the earth." What he denies is that this means our lives are without worth. This is the aspect of either/

or thinking, the either/or of incomplete nihilism, which Pynchon and Derrida reject. We should give up our fantasies about finding "the direct, epileptic Word, the cry that might abolish the night" (*Lot 49*, p. 118), our desire for "the central truth itself" (*Lot 49*, p. 95), what Derrida calls our desire for a transcendental signified. As Driblette tells Oedipa, "You can put together clues, develop a thesis, or several, about why characters reacted to the Trystero possibility the way they did, why the assassins came on, why the black costumes. You could waste your life that way and never touch the truth" (*Lot 49*, p. 80). Pynchon is showing us that Oedipa should abandon her religious quest. Instead of passively awaiting the crying of lot 49, Oedipa should sound a cry, refusing "to accept any San Narciso among its most tender flesh without a reflex or a cry" (*Lot 49*, p. 181).

In the penultimate scene in the novel, Oedipa allows herself to drift aimlessly at night through the streets of San Francisco. Her goal is to try to abandon her search for the Tristero to test the possibility that it has only been created by her own paranoia. But during her nightmarish descent into the streets, Oedipa is deluged with the sign of the Tristero, a muted post horn, as she wanders among the poor and homeless. In what most critics take as the moral center of the work, Oedipa comes across an old sailor suffering from delirium tremens. She holds him in her arms and feels overwhelmed with compassion for the man. This compassion persists until she helps him up to his room, where there are "a couple of religious tracts" and the "picture of a saint, changing well-water to oil for Jerusalem's Easter lamps" (*Lot 49*, p. 127). The saint in the picture is Saint Narcissus, part of Pynchon's play with the Greek, Christian, and Freudian referents for the name Narcissus. But what has been missed thus far in interpretations of the scene is that immediately after this reference to Christian belief, "She [Oedipa] ran through then a scene she might play. She might find the landlord of this place, and bring him to court, and buy the sailor a new suit at Roos/Atkins, and shirt, and shoes, and give him the bus fare to Fresno after all" (*Lot 49*, p. 127). As soon as Oedipa begins to construct this ideal world in her head, she loses contact with the old sailor.[35] "But with a sigh he had released her hand, while she was *so lost in the fantasy* that she hadn't felt it go away" (my emphasis; *Lot 49*, p. 127). Oedipa's obsession, her fantastic search for an ideal, transcendent meaning, causes her to evade her moral responsibility and isolates her from human love.

Oedipa has become paranoid, like so many characters in Pynchon's works, in order to avoid its opposite, anti-paranoia. Anti-paranoia is the belief possessed by the nihilist, the belief that there is no purpose, no meaning to our lives that we don't create, that we are the product of chance rather than the creation of a divine will. But few have the courage of the overman to face this completed nihilism. They therefore accept paranoia, a simulacra of religious faith.[36] Like the religious believer, the paranoid believes that there is "another mode of meaning behind the obvious." But rather than believing in a divine providence, the paranoid believes he or she is the victim of a malicious plot.

Oedipa misses the revelation that I believe Pynchon hopes the reader will see. After the deflation of the scene occurs, when the sailor calls Oedipa a "bitch" for not waiting until another poor man is gone to give him $10.00 (since now he'll have to share the bottle he'll buy with it), Oedipa imagines the death of the sailor. "He's going to die," she remarks. And Ramirez, the other man, responds, "Who isn't?" (*Lot 49*, p. 128), emphasizing the theme of mortality as well as Oedipa's unwillingness to face her own death. Oedipa then imagines the sailor being immolated on his mattress:

> So when this mattress flared up around the sailor, in his Viking's funeral: the stored, coded years of uselessness, early death, self-harrowing, the sure decay of hope, the set of all men who had slept on it, whatever their lives had been, would truly cease to be, forever, when the mattress burned. She stared at it in wonder. It was as if she had just discovered the irreversible process. (*Lot 49*, p. 128)

Only by accepting this irreversible process, by accepting one's own death as the annihilation of the self, will the responsible self be formed, according to Pynchon. Derrida makes the same point in his interpretation of Heidegger's analysis of *Dasein*'s being-toward-death.

> My irreplaceability is therefore conferred, delivered, "given," one can say, by death.
> . . . It is from the site of death as the place of my irreplaceability, that is, of my singularity, that I feel called to responsibility. In this sense only a mortal can be responsible.[37]

DeLillo, in his novel *White Noise*, follows Nietzsche, Heidegger, Derrida, and Pynchon in believing that we must accept our own death in order to develop an authentic (Heidegger) or responsible (Derrida) self.

In *White Noise*, Jack Gladney has not resolutely accepted that his own death is "*not to be outstripped.*" He is obsessed by the fear of death and with "*fleeing in the face of death*" (Heidegger's emphasis).[38] This fear causes him to cross the ultimate moral boundary by attempting to murder Willy Mink, the man who has forced Jack's wife, Babette, to have sex with him in order for her to gain access to the experimental drug, Dylar, which is designed to make "the brain produce fear-of-death inhibitors" (*WN*, p. 228)—in other words, to extinguish one's fear of death.

Jack Gladney does not try to kill the scientist, Willy Mink, because of jealousy. Rather, Jack attempts to kill this doctor because his postmodern academic colleague, Murray Jay Siskind, persuades him that killing is a way of controlling death.

> "The killer, in theory, attempts to defeat his own death by killing others. . . .
> It's a way of controlling death. A way of gaining the ultimate upper hand.
> Be the killer for a change. Let someone else be the dier. Let him replace you,
> theoretically, in that role. You can't die if he does. He dies, you live." (*WN*,
> p. 291)

When plotting and carrying out this attempted murder, Jack undergoes something akin to a religious conversion. "I saw things new," he repeats as he enacts his plot to murder Willy Mink. But this illusion is shattered when Willy Mink shoots back. Jack sees that even the killer can become a dier. Jack was more right than he knew when in his classroom lecture he asserts, to his own surprise, that "All plots tend to move deathward" (*WN*, p. 26).

If killing is not the way to overcome one's fear of death, what, then, is the way? Murray Siskind, before encouraging Jack to try murder, describes other methods for overcoming the fear of death. First, Siskind urges Jack to put his faith in technology. "It's what we invented to conceal the terrible secret of our decaying bodies. . . . It prolongs life, it provides new organs for those that wear out" (*WN*, p. 285).

But while technology promises the postponement, if not the overcoming, of death, it also threatens to accelerate our deaths. Technology also "threatens universal extinction" through advances in nuclear bombs and chemical warfare (*WN*, p. 285). This ugly side of technology is represented in the novel by the "Airborne Toxic Event," which Jack and his family flee from in the middle of the novel. Jack has been exposed to this toxic cloud and medical technology has told him that "Death has entered" (*WN*, p. 141).

If technology cannot save us from death, perhaps it can at least save us from the fear of death. This is Jack and Babette's hope. Both go to extreme measures in order to secure the experimental drug, Dylar, which is supposed to inhibit the electrochemical reactions in the brain which are responsible for our feeling the fear of death. Dylar is thus reminiscent of present-day antidepressants and anti-anxiety drugs, which some hail as a miraculous medical breakthrough and others condemn as deadening the symptoms which cause us to search for true healing. Peter Kramer, in *Listening to Prozac,* summarizes Walker Percy's objection to the kind of alleviation of fear and anxiety promised by modern medical technology:

> To Percy, guilt and self-consciousness, as well as sadness, are important signals of what is wrong with us, signposts in the quest. Shame, Percy implies, links us to awareness of original sin. Anxiety is our visceral understanding of the ways in which the world is out of joint. Symptoms signify the human condition; they are mysteries to probe and savor.[39]

Percy represents the danger of technological manipulation of brain chemistry in his novel, *Love in the Ruins,* in which another "airborne toxic event" releases heavy sodium in the air, a chemical which increases rather than diminishes one's anxiety. Percy's protagonist, Tom More, believes he can save America from these ill effects, but his lapsometer fails, just like the Dylar pill does.

In DeLillo's novel, Jack Gladney begins with Percy's position. "I was not a believer in easy solutions, something to swallow that would rid my soul of an ancient fear" (*WN*, p. 211). He even articulates the reason why avoiding an easy solution can be admired: "Is it possible that constant fear is the natural state of man and that by living close to my fear I am actually doing something heroic . . . ?" (*WN*, p. 289). But as his anxiety increases, Jack becomes obsessed with the desire to try an easy solution. However, the Dylar pill does not work. Instead it leads to a completely delusional state in which one mistakes words for the things they stand for, a delusion postmodernism deconstructs by stressing the arbitrary relationship between the signifier and the signified.

Murray Siskind offers yet another solution to the fear of death: "[Y]ou can always get around death by concentrating on the life beyond" (*WN*, p. 285). Jack quickly notices the phrase "get around." He responds, "But you make it sound like a convenient fantasy, the worst kind of self-delusion" (*WN*, p. 286). Murray responds by admitting that the after life is only "a sweet and touching idea. You can take it or leave it." Jack sees no solace in the simulacra of faith, in the simulation of religious belief: "But don't I have to believe?" he asserts. "Don't I have to feel in my heart that there is something, genuinely, beyond this life . . . ?" (*WN*, p. 286). Richard Rorty, who bears an uncanny resemblance to Murray Jay Siskind, would respond no. Rorty asserts that his "fundamental premise is that a belief can still regulate action, can still be thought worth dying for, among people who are quite aware that this belief is caused by nothing deeper than contingent historical circumstance."[40] One needn't believe in the truth of one's beliefs in order for them to have pragmatic value. Zygmunt Bauman, author of

Postmodern Ethics, asserts in an earlier essay that in postmodern ethics, "choices cannot be disputed by reference to anything more solid and binding than preference and the determination to stick to the preferred. . . . one thing you cannot say about such a choice is that it follows a rule or a command—be it an injunction of reason, a rule empirically demonstrated by truth-seeking knowledge, a command of God or a legal precept."[41]

Nevertheless, after Willy Mink shoots back at Jack, Jack seeks religious solace from the nuns running the Catholic hospital he has entered. While the nun applies physical relief, Jack begins to seek spiritual relief. But the nun astounds Jack by asserting that she only pretends to believe in the Christian heaven. Here DeLillo is showing that we have entered the final phase in Baudrillard's analysis of the "successive phases of the image." Baudrillard describes this postmodern phase as "the era of simulacra and of simulation, in which there is no longer a God to recognize his own, no longer a Last Judgment to separate the false from the true, the real from its artificial resurrection."[42] In this postmodern age, God is not dead; rather, he has become what Baudrillard calls "hyperreal," that is, a model of the real without origin or reality. The nuns demonstrate that "God himself can be simulated, that is to say can be reduced to the signs that constitute faith."[43] Thus, the faith that God has overcome the fear of death, even the power of death, through the death and resurrection of Jesus Christ, is shown to be an illusion, nothing but "a convenient fantasy, the worst kind of self-delusion." Rorty explains how this leap of unfaith results from Nietzsche's rejection of our quest for truth:

> It was Nietzsche who first explicitly suggested that we drop the whole idea of "knowing the truth." . . . He hoped that once we realized that Plato's [and Christianity's] "true world" was just a fable, we would seek consolation, at the moment of death, not in having transcended the animal condition but in being that peculiar sort of dying animal who, by describing himself in his own terms, had created himself.[44]

Our only consolation is to knowingly spin out fantasies, "seeking hopelessly to fill the void" (*Lot 49,* p. 21) left by our loss of belief in the Christian God and the biblical promise of resurrection.

Murray Siskind has offered three false solutions to Jack's fear of death. All of these solutions involve the repression of our fear of death. "We're all aware there's no escape from death. How do we deal with this crushing knowledge? We repress, we disguise, we bury, we exclude" (*WN,* p. 288). Tom LeClair argues that Murray Siskind is articulating the position of Ernest Becker in Becker's work, *The Denial of Death.*

But according to LeClair, "DeLillo differs with Becker's conclusion that repression of the death fear is necessary to live."[45] But if the pre-modern faith in religion and the modern faith in technology provide no solace for Jack, where can he find the strength to live in the face of his knowledge that he is going to die?

There are hints of a secular faith in *White Noise* which show DeLillo to be, surprisingly, more of a modernist, a romantic to be more specific, than a postmodernist in his sympathies. After the Airborne Toxic Event, Jack finds comfort in watching his children sleep.

> Watching children sleep makes me feel devout, part of a spiritual system. It is the closest I can come to God. If there is a secular equivalent of standing in a great spired cathedral with marble pillars and streams of mystical light slanting through two-tier Gothic windows, it would be watching children in their little bedrooms fast asleep. (*WN*, p. 147)
>
> In those soft warm faces was a quality of trust so absolute and pure that I did not want to think it might be misplaced. There must be something, somewhere, large and grand and redoubtable enough to justify this shining reliance and implicit belief. A feeling of desperate piety swept over me. . . . In my current state, bearing the death impression of the Nyodene cloud, I was ready to search anywhere for signs and hints, intimations of odd comfort. (*WN*, p. 154)

Death is "redoubtable" in the sense of causing fear or dread, and this dread causes Jack to seek a "redoubt," a secret, secure retreat, from his fear of death through belief in something "redoubtable" in the sense of being eminent and worthy of respect. In an interview with Anthony DeCurtis, DeLillo describes his identification with Jack's sense of the sacred as a response to our fear of death, speculating that it has its origins in his Catholic upbringing:

> I think it is something we all feel, something we almost never talk about, something that is *almost* there. I tried to relate it in *White Noise* to this other sense of transcendence that lies just beyond our touch. This extraordinary wonder of things is somehow related to the extraordinary dread, to the death fear we try to keep beneath the surface of our perceptions.[46]

Like Jack, DeLillo discovers this sense of the sacred through a kind of romantic nostalgia for childhood: "Well, I think we feel, perhaps superstitiously, that children have a direct route to, have direct contact to the kind of natural truth that eludes us as adults." DeLillo relates the language of children to glossolalia, to speaking in tongues. "And I think this is the way we feel about children in general. There is something they know but can't tell us. Or there is something they remember which we've forgotten."[47]

In a central scene in the novel, Jack kneels before his sleeping child, hearing her speak "a language not quite of this world. . . . She uttered two clearly audible words, familiar and elusive at the same time, words that seemed to have a ritual meaning, part of a verbal spell or ecstatic chant" (*WN*, p. 154–55). What she says, as Jack awaits her revelation, is "*Toyota Celica*" (*WN*, p. 155). While this insertion of commercial media into the unconscious would spoil the moment for most, Jack still believes that "Whatever its source, the utterance struck me with the impact of a moment of splendid transcendence" (*WN*, p. 155). Jack holds on to a secular version of divine revelation. But what a diminished thing this revelation has become, so diminished that it reads like a parody of religious faith, especially as we compare it with Mucho's vision of a "couple hundred million chorus saying 'rich, chocolaty goodness'" in unison.

But his daughter's unconscious chanting of an advertising name is a fragment shored up against his ruin. Like the high modernists such as T. S. Eliot, Robert Frost, and Wallace Stevens, DeLillo believes that "fiction rescues history from its confusions" as "it attempts to provide a hint of order in the midst of all the randomness." And in keeping with the romantic strain of modernism, DeLillo believes in a "redemptive quality of fiction" in that "art is one of the consolation prizes we receive for having lived in a difficult and sometimes chaotic world. We seek pattern in art that eludes us in natural experience."[48] But being a late modernist, aware of the postmodern critique of imposed order, of plots as tending toward death, DeLillo opposes those who "organize their desperation and their loneliness . . . through violent means."[49]

DeLillo shows in *White Noise* that in order to impose an order upon the chaos which does not lead to violence, we must accept our own mortality. He articulates this through the voice of Jack's colleague, Winnie Richards, whom most critics read as expressing DeLillo's own beliefs. Winnie Richards asserts,

> "I think it's a mistake to lose one's sense of death, even one's fear of death. Isn't death the boundary we need? Doesn't it give a precious texture to life, a sense of definition? You have to ask yourself whether anything you do in this life would have beauty and meaning without the knowledge you carry of a final line, a border or limit." (*WN*, p. 229)

To illustrate her point, Winnie asks Jack to imagine himself "a confirmed homebody, a sedentary fellow," lost in the woods and suddenly confronted by a grizzly bear.

> "The sight of this grizzer is so electrifyingly strange that it gives you a re-
> newed sense of yourself, a fresh awareness of the self—the self in terms of
> a unique and horrific situation. You see yourself in a new and intense way.
> You rediscover yourself. . . . The beast on hind legs has enabled you to see
> who you are as if for the first time, outside familiar surroundings, alone,
> distinct, whole." (*WN*, p. 229)

In conclusion, Winnie urges Jack not to take Dylar. I think Jack's response to this message confirms my belief that the author approves of
her view: "I'm still sad, Winnie, but you've given my sadness a richness
and depth it has never known before" (*WN*, p. 230).

Winnie Richards' concept of the value of the fear of death directly
contradicts Murray Siskind's view. She asserts that we must confront
our death directly, rather than repressing our fear of death. In her rejection of Ernest Becker's view of death, she articulates a position strikingly reminiscent of Heidegger's in *Being and Time*.

In his existential analysis of *Dasein*, Heidegger asserts that inauthentic existence is characterized by the lack of resolute acceptance of our
own death. In inauthentic existence, *Dasein* refuses to accept its finitude which causes it to fall under subjection to the power of *das Man*,
the one or "the they." DeLillo illustrates how the power of *das Man* has
increased in the postmodern age. In the words of Michael Valdez
Moses: "the media enormously reinforce and heighten the illusion that
death happens only to the others. . . . The power of technology allows
its possessor or user to cover over the nearness and inevitability of personal death."[50] Thus, when Jack and his family are first confronted
with the Airborne Toxic Event, all their viewing of disaster and death
on TV causes them to deny that such a disaster could happen to them:

> These things happen to poor people who live in exposed areas. . . . I'm a
> college professor. Did you ever see a college professor rowing a boat down
> his own street in one of those TV floods? We live in a neat and pleasant town
> near a college with a quaint name. These things don't happen in places like
> Blacksmith. (*WN*, p. 114)

But despite his denials, disasters do not occur only in far-away places
seen on television, such as California, which Alfonse, professor of
popular culture, asserts is the purpose of California in the news media: "This is where California comes in. Mud slides, brush fires, coastal
erosion, earthquakes, mass killings, et cetera. We can relax and enjoy
these disasters because in our hearts we feel that California deserves
whatever it gets. Californians invented the concept of lifestyle. This
alone warrants their doom" (*WN*, p. 66). Images of catastrophic death

in the media serve to shield Jack from facing his own death: "These things have nothing to do with my own eventual death, nonviolent, small-town, thoughtful" (*WN*, p. 76). Jack's denial is illustrated again when he asks the medical technician about the effects of being exposed to the toxic cloud: "Am I going to die?" (*WN*, p. 140). As Ramirez responds to a similar question asked by Oedipa, "Who isn't?" As his anxiety increases, Jack begins to face his own mortality, to see that "Death has entered" (*WN*, p. 141).

According to Heidegger, it is the state of mind or mood of anxiety which "brings Dasein back from its falling, and makes manifest to it that authenticity and inauthenticity are possibilities of its Being."[51] In a footnote to this passage, Heidegger admits that his analysis of the phenomenon of anxiety is based on his theological studies: "It is no accident that the phenomena of anxiety and fear . . . have come within the purview of Christian theology." Heidegger goes on to refer to Augustine, Luther, and Kierkegaard, but neither Heidegger nor DeLillo, in spite of their Catholic upbringings, accept the Christian conception of death. While the remembrance of one's own finitude and death, *memento mori,* has been used in Christian tradition to spur one to live for God rather than for one's own self, Heidegger's conception of the authentic acceptance of one's own death is radically different.

Heidegger's doctrine leaves no place for the belief in Christ's victory over the power of death. Michael E. Zimmerman writes, "Evidently, there is not much room within this existential concept of authentic Being-toward-death for an existentiell concept permitting an individual to de-fuse *Angst* by believing he will not really die after all but will be saved from death by divine intervention."[52] In his discussion of death, Heidegger writes:

> *No one can take the Other's dying away from him.* Of course someone can "go to his death for another." But that always means to sacrifice oneself for the Other "in some definite affair." Such "dying for" can never signify that the Other has thus had his death taken away even in the slightest degree. (Heidegger's emphasis)[53]

This is a direct denial of the New Testament teaching on the meaning of the death and resurrection of Jesus Christ.

In his recent work *The Gift of Death,* Derrida concurs with my assertion in his interpretation of Heidegger's analysis of *Dasein's* being-toward-death in *Being and Time*.

> Death's dative (dying *for* the other, giving one's life *to* the other) does not signify a substitution (*for* is not *pro* in the sense of "in the place of the other").

> If something radically impossible is to be conceived of . . . it is indeed dying *for the other* in the sense of dying *in place of* the other. I can give the other everything except immortality, except this *dying for her* to the extent of dying in place of her and so freeing her from her own death. I can die for the other in a situation where my death gives him a little longer to live. . . . But I cannot die in her place, I cannot give her my life in exchange for her death. Only a mortal can die . . . and that mortal can only give to what is mortal since he can give everything except immortality, everything *except salvation as immortality.* (Final emphasis mine.)[54]

Derrida hears in Heidegger's analysis the denial of the Christian doctrine regarding the substitutionary death of Christ, who dies *for* sinners in just the way denied by Heidegger.

In John's gospel, Jesus says, "I am the resurrection and the life; he who believes in Me shall live even if he dies, and everyone who lives and believes in Me shall never die" (John 11:25–26). The New Testament teaches that Christ defeated sin and death by "dying for" humanity, that he has granted those who believe "salvation as immortality." This is the gospel announced by Paul: "Death has been swallowed up in victory" (1 Cor. 15:54). The writer of Hebrews asserts that this victory over death should cause us to be liberated from our fear of death: "he too shared in their humanity [cf. Derrida, "Only a mortal can die"] so that by his death he might destroy him who holds the power of death—that is, the devil—and free those who all their lives were held in slavery by their fear of death" (Heb. 2:14–15).

In contrast, DeLillo argues that our fear of death should not be overcome: "I think it's a mistake to lose one's sense of death, even one's fear of death." For both Heidegger and Derrida, for both Pynchon and DeLillo, freedom from death promised by Christianity is a nihilistic denial of our finitude and mortality. Even though the New Testament insists upon the mortality and finitude of human beings, the fact that it offers a way of attaining eternal life makes Christianity a lie and a danger to Nietzsche, Heidegger, and Derrida, as it is for Pynchon and DeLillo. Heidegger opposes the belief in freedom from death taught by Christianity, just as DeLillo makes fun of the naive faith of his characters in what he calls the "tabloid future, with its mechanism of a hopeful twist to apocalyptic events" (*WN*, p. 146). Heidegger opposes all inauthentic belief in freedom from death with the anticipation of one's own death as not to be outstripped, or what he calls "freedom for one's own death." "Anticipation . . . unlike inauthentic Being-toward-death, does not evade the fact that death is not to be outstripped; instead, anticipation frees itself for accepting this."[55]

But Jack Gladney's acceptance of his own death as not to be outstripped does not cause him to lead an authentic existence. He still feels the need of a revelation. He remains vulnerable, therefore, to Murray Siskind's suggestion that he overcome his fear of death by killing another. The fear of death enslaves; it does not free. Even Murray Siskind recognizes this: "Helpless and fearful people are drawn to magical figures, mythic figures, epic men who intimidate and darkly loom" (*WN*, p. 287). This is true of Jack Gladney, who seeks to be sheltered from his death through a study of Hitler: "The overwhelming horror would leave no room for your own death" (*WN*, p. 287). And it is true of Heidegger, who also fell under the spell of Hitler and became a servant of Hitler's National Socialist party.

DeLillo is wrong to try to persuade us that "it's a mistake to lose . . . one's fear of death." Death is the punishment which results from our rebellion against God; death is the wages of sin. Jack asks rhetorically: "If the self is death, how can it also be stronger than death?" (*WN*, p. 268). In response to this modern question, Bonhoeffer, a victim of the Nazi regime, would respond that it can't; rather, it is "God's love for man [that] has proved stronger than death. . . . The miracle of Christ's resurrection makes nonsense of the idolization of death which is prevalent among us today."[56] According to the Bible, we are not dependent upon the gift of death for our selfhood but rather upon the grace of God. The Christian hope is that "God so loved the world he gave his only begotten Son so that everyone who believes in him will not perish but have eternal life" (John 3:16). This is the good news of the New Testament, that Jesus has "abolished death, and brought life and immortality to light through the gospel" (2 Tim. 1:10). According to the Bible, death is not the final boundary we need but rather the final enemy to be abolished (Isa. 25:8). This biblical faith is in no way recovered in postmodern thought.

Postmodern philosophy is not a propaedeutic to faith. It moves no closer toward a recovery of the central scandal of the Christian faith. Derrida writes that "If something radically impossible is to be conceived of . . . it is indeed dying *for the other*," in the way Christ died as a substitutionary atonement for the sins of the world. Paranoia may at times resemble faith, just as Derrida's philosophy of *différance* at times resembles negative theology,[57] and his concept of "the structure of messianicity" at times resembles the Judaeo-Christian hope for the *parousia* of the Messiah.[58] But postmodern narrative, like postmodern philosophy, involves a "leap of unfaith." Denied full access to the central truth itself, to the Word as beginning and end, postmodernism responds not with a humbled epistemology but rather with a prideful ontology which denies that the truth itself exists.

Notes

1. John A. McClure, "Postmodern/Post-Secular: Contemporary Fiction and Spirituality," *Modern Fiction Studies* 41, no. 1 (spring 1995): 143.

2. Diogenes Allen, *Christian Belief in a Postmodern World: The Full Wealth of Conviction* (Louisville, Ky.: Westminster/John Knox Press, 1989), 2.

3. John D. Caputo, ed. *Deconstruction in a Nutshell* (New York: Fordham University Press, 1997), p. 159. See also Caputo's monograph, *The Prayers and Tears of Jacques Derrida: Religion without Religion* (Bloomington: Indiana University Press, 1997).

4. Phillip Blond, ed., *Post-Secular Philosophy: Between Philosophy and Theology* (London: Routledge, 1998); Graham Ward, ed., *The Postmodern God* (Oxford: Blackwell, 1997).

5. Edith Wyschogrod and John D. Caputo, "Postmodernism and the Desire for God: An E-Mail Exchange," *Cross Currents* 48, no. 3 (fall 1998): 293.

6. Brian D. Ingraffia, *Postmodern Theory and Biblical Theology: Vanquishing God's Shadow* (Cambridge: Cambridge University Press, 1995).

7. McClure, "Postmodern/Post-Secular," pp. 143–44.

8. Thomas Pynchon, *The Crying of Lot 49* (New York: Harper and Row, 1966); references to this text are made parenthetically in text, with the abbreviation *Lot 49* used before the page number. Don DeLillo, *White Noise* (New York: Penguin, 1985); references are made parenthetically in text, with the abbreviation *WN* used before the page number.

9. See Jean Baudrillard's acceptance of the term "nihilist" to describe himself in "I Am a Nihilist," in *Simulacra and Simulation*, trans. Sheila Faria Glaser (Ann Arbor: University of Michigan Press, 1994), p. 160. Baudrillard writes, "If it is nihilistic to be obsessed by the mode of disappearance . . . of the real, of meaning, of the stage, of history, of the social, of the individual . . . then I am a nihilist" (p. 162).

10. Friedrich Nietzsche, *The Will to Power*, trans. Walter Kaufmann and R. J. Hollingdale, ed. Walter Kaufmann (New York: Vintage Books, 1968), p. 1.

11. Friedrich Nietzsche, *The Gay Science*, trans. Walter Kaufmann (New York: Vintage Books, 1974), p. 343.

12. Linda Hutcheon, *A Poetics of Postmodernism: History, Theory, Fiction* (New York: Routledge, 1988), xi.

13. This emphasizes that her first name is a feminization of the name of the Greek tragic hero, Oedipus. For readings of the significance of this change in gender, see note 15 below.

14. Edward Mendelson, "The Sacred, the Profane, and *The Crying of Lot 49*," in *Individual and Community*, ed. Kenneth Baldwin and David Kirby (Durham, N.C.: Duke University Press, 1975), p. 191.

15. James Nohrnberg, "Pynchon's Paraclete," in *Pynchon: A Collection of Critical Essays*, ed. Edward Mendelson (Englewood Cliffs, N.J.: Prentice-Hall, 1978), pp. 147–61.

16. Ibid., 149.

17. On the relationship between Pynchon, postmodern narrative, and the detective story, see Douglas Keesey, "The Ideology of Detection in Pynchon and DeLillo," *Pynchon Notes* 32–33 (spring–fall 1993): 44–59; Stefano Tani, "The Dismemberment of the Detective," *Diogenes* 120 (winter 1982): 22–41; and Tony Tanner, *Thomas Pynchon* (London: Metheun, 1982).

18. On the relationship between Oedipa and Oedipus, see Debra A. Moddelmog, "The Oedipus Myth and Reader Response in Pynchon's *The Crying of Lot 49*," *Papers on Language and Literature* 23, no. 2 (spring 1987): 240–49; and Adrian Emily Richwell, "*The Crying of Lot 49:* A Source Study," *Pynchon Notes* 17 (fall 1985): 78–80.

19. On the relationship between *The Crying of Lot 49* and the quest romance, see Mark Siegel, "Pynchon's Anti-Quests," *Pynchon Notes* 3 (1980): 5–9; Deborah Madsen, "The Typology of the Tristero: *The Crying of Lot 49*," in *The Postmodernist Allegories of Thomas Pynchon* (New York: St. Martin's Press, 1991), pp. 54–77; and John Farrell, "The Romance of the '60s: Self, Community and the Ethical in *The Crying of Lot 40*," *Pynchon Notes* 30–31 (spring–fall 1992): 139–56.

20. Compare Tanner, *Thomas Pynchon*, p. 57: "On the title page Pynchon included this note: 'A portion of this novel was first published in *Esquire* magazine under the title "The World (This One), the Flesh (Mrs. Oedipa Maas), and the Testament of Pierce Inverarity".' Since he did not choose to give the title of another extract that appeared in a magazine, we may infer that he wanted this title definitely to appear under the main title of the book. Of course it raises the question: is 'the Testament of Pierce Inverarity' the Devil (following the World and the Flesh)?"

21. Mendelson, "The Sacred, the Profane," pp. 208–209.

22. The "Villanova Roundtable" is reproduced in John D. Caputo, ed., *Deconstruction in a Nutshell* (New York: Fordham University Press, 1997), pp. 3–28. The quotation I cite is from page 25.

23. Compare Derrida's discussion of the Christian conception of the *mysterium tremendum*, which Derrida describes, following Patocka, as "the frightening, terrifying mystery." Jacques Derrida, *The Gift of Death*, trans. David Wills (Chicago: University of Chicago Press, 1995), p. 27.

24. Derrida, *Gift of Death*, p. 10, n. 5.

25. Friedrich Nietzsche, *The Gay Science*, trans. Walter Kaufmann (New York: Vintage Books, 1974), p. 109.

26. Friedrich Nietzsche, *Ecce Homo*, trans. Walter Kaufmann, in *"On the Genealogy of Morals" and "Ecce Homo,"* ed. Walter Kaufmann (New York: Vintage Books, 1989), p. 218.

27. Mendelson, "The Sacred, the Profane," p. 196.

28. Ibid.

29. Thomas Hill Schaub, "Open Letter in Response to Edward Mendelson's 'The Sacred, the Profane, and *The Crying of Lot 49*,'" *Boundary 2* 4 (fall 1976): 93.

30. Jacques Derrida, "Structure, Sign, and Play in the Discourse of the Human Sciences," *Writing and Difference*, trans. Alan Bass (Chicago: University of Chicago Press, 1978), p. 292.

31. Derrida writes that as a result of "the absence of the referent or the transcendental signified," "*There is nothing outside of the text* [there is no outside-text;

il n'y a pas de hors-texte]." In Jacques Derrida, *Of Grammatology*, trans. Gayatri Chakravorty Spivak (Baltimore: Johns Hopkins University Press, 1976), p. 158.

One of Bortz's postmodern graduate students from the University of San Narciso mocks Oedipa's modernist quest for an historical reality outside of the text. "'The historical Shakespeare,' growled one of the grad students. . . . 'The historical Marx. The historical Jesus.'" Bortz agrees:

> "He's right," shrugged Bortz, "they're dead. What's left?"
> "Words."
> "Pick some words," said Bortz. "Them, we can talk about." (*Lot 49*, p. 151)

32. Derrida, *Of Grammatology*, p. 293.

33. Walter Lowe—in *Theology and Difference: The Wound of Reason* (Bloomington: Indiana University Press, 1993), p. 72—objects to those who read the second interpretation of interpretation as the description of deconstruction and postmodernism. He criticizes those who pass over the later sentence: "I do not believe that today there is any question of *choosing*" between the two interpretations of interpretation. I try to take this analysis into account below.

34. Jacques Derrida, *Margins of Philosophy*, trans. Alan Bass (Chicago: University of Chicago Press, 1982), p. 27.

35. J. Kerry Grant, in his outstanding work *A Companion to "The Crying of Lot 49"* (Athens: University of Georgia Press, 1994), a work to which I am indebted for its summary of the critical debate over the religious imagery of the novel, is one of the few works to recognize Pynchon's deflation of the sentimental scene with Oedipa and the old sailor: "The connection that she forges with the old sailor . . . is ephemeral, loosening irrecoverably at precisely the time she reverts to mainline expectations, dreaming about rescuing the sailor by dressing him in a suit and giving him a bus ticket" (p. 109).

36. After composing this essay, Don DeLillo's latest novel, *Underworld* (New York: Scribner, 1997) was published; in it, "the faith of paranoia" is described as a "false faith" (p. 825).

37. Derrida, *Gift of Death*, p. 41.

38. Martin Heidegger, *Being and Time*, trans. John Macquarrie and Edward Robinson (New York: Harper and Row, 1962), pp. 303, 298.

39. Peter D. Kramer, *Listening to Prozac* (New York: Viking, 1993), p. 277.

40. Richard Rorty, *Contingency, Irony, and Solidarity* (Cambridge: Cambridge University Press, 1989), p. 189.

41. Zygmunt Bauman, "Postmodernity, or Living with Ambivalence," in *A Postmodern Reader*, ed. Joseph Natoli and Linda Hutcheon (New York: SUNY Press, 1993), pp. 13–14.

42. Baudrillard, *Simulacra and Simulation*, p. 6.

43. Ibid., 5.

44. Rorty, *Contingency, Irony, and Solidarity*, p. 27.

45. Tom LeClair, *In the Loop: Don DeLillo and the Systems Novel* (Urbana: University of Illinois Press, 1987), p. 213.

46. Anthony DeCurtis, "'An Outsider in This Society': An Interview with Don

DeLillo," in *Introducing Don DeLillo,* ed. Frank Lentricchia (Durham, N.C.: Duke University Press, 1991), p. 63.

47. Ibid., p. 64. On the romantic poets' nostalgia for childhood for its proximity to the sacred, see William Wordsworth's ode, "Intimations of Immortality from Recollections of Early Childhood."

48. DeCurtis, "Interview with Don DeLillo," p. 56.

49. Ibid., 58.

50. Michael Valdez Moses, "Lust Removed from Nature," in *New Essays on "White Noise,"* ed. Frank Lentricchia (Cambridge: Cambridge University Press, 1991), pp. 73–74.

51. Heidegger, *Being and Time,* p. 235.

52. Michael E. Zimmerman, *The Eclipse of the Self: The Development of Heidegger's Concept of Authenticity* (Athens: Ohio University Press, 1981), p. 139.

53. Heidegger, *Being and Time,* p. 284.

54. Ibid., p. 43.

55. Ibid., p. 308.

56. Dietrich Bonhoeffer, *Ethics,* trans. Neville Horton Smith (New York: Simon and Schuster, 1995), p. 80.

57. "[T]hese attempts to appropriate Derrida's thought for use in theological discourse represent a misreading of Derrida, who in his essay 'How to Avoid Speaking: Denials' makes it clear that 'If the movement of this reappropriation [of deconstruction by theology] appears in fact irrepressible, its ultimate failure is no less necessary'" (Ingraffia, *Postmodern Theory,* p. 224).

58. Derrida may have turned to the "emancipatory promise" of "a messianism without religion," but in doing so he has emptied the Christian faith in Jesus the Messiah of its content, leaving us with only "the formality of a structural messianism" (Jacques Derrida, "Villanova Roundtable," p. 23). See also Jacques Derrida, *Specters of Marx,* trans. Peggy Kamuf (New York: Routledge, 1994): "but none of them [the religions of the book (Judaism, Christianity, Islam) and Marxism] can accept, of course, this *epokhê* of the content, whereas we hold it here to be essential to the messianic in general, as thinking of the other and of the event to come" (p. 59). Christian philosophy should not try to appropriate that which Derrida himself says Christians cannot, of course, accept, i.e., the messianic stripped of "all biblical forms" (p. 168).

4

Against Appropriation

Postmodern Programs, Claimants, Contests, Conversations

GARY PERCESEPE

> When you get to the point of arguing, you're past the point
> of changing anyone's mind, even though it's supposed
> to be the other way, and maybe for some classes
> of people it is, just never mine.
> —Richard Ford, *Rock Springs*

The word *against* here means an occasion for thought to consider its others. Not the killing word, the living one. Like the narrator Earl in Richard Ford's *Rock Springs*, suspicious but open as far as he can be. A bit weary; he's seen some things. But still. Is this done, *appropriation*? In the singular? But how? What are its conditions, its limits, its practices, its possibilities, its ends? What does it mean to take, to be taken? To be had, by the Other? Can a word slip the bonds of its etymological history, become a free agent—gone the violence, gone the claims to possession, the naked taking? Or does a debt arise from the gift? Within which economy of violence, according to what ledger, does one attempt to keep track of the state of the debt or escape the specters of the gift? Does appropriation open onto philosophy's dream of the "continual conversation of life among friends"—gone the violence, gone the claims to possession—or is this dialogical dream just another monologue, the sound of one voice speaking, a series of shibboleths warmly embraced and coolly ignored? But we are getting ahead of ourselves.

I

Academics are fond of appropriation. This fondness is shared by many outside the realm of what is called postmodern philosophy (there are, after all, congressional Appropriations Committees, and it is impossible to ignore the economic origins of the term), though the postmodern is the site of this essay.

To appropriate means to make peculiarly the possession of someone, to take to oneself to the exclusion of others, to claim or use by exclusive or preeminent right (I remind you during this litany that the *Oxford English Dictionary* never proved anything; it's usage we are after); to allot or attribute as specially belonging, to make suitable—to suit, to set apart for, or assign to, a peculiar purpose or use, in exclusion of all others, e.g., to appropriate money for the navy; in ecclesiastical law, to annex to a spiritual corporation for its perpetual use. Appropriation is the act of appropriating to oneself, to a particular person or use—of money or payment to the satisfaction of one or more specific debts out of a larger number; money or assets set apart by formal action to a specific use. There are *misappropriations;* for this, one can be jailed. Appropriate is a cousin to the appropriate and to the *inappropriate*—that is, the *unsuitable,* that which is not specially fitting; and also to the *proper.*

The grammar of appropriation, philosophically speaking, minimally consists of the following six points:

(1) Proper names. But how to think of them? They resemble signatures, in the paradoxical sense that it's always the same thing, yet each time it's different; each time, it is a different history, a history of effects, a different constellation of meaning structures. Can one mean by "Plato" what was meant a thousand years ago? And does "Plato" in America mean the same as "Plato" in Greece or France or Russia, or at Victory Lanes in downtown Detroit? Philosophy cannot be thought apart from its history, and yet the history of philosophy—to give it its propers—is sometimes conceived as if it were some singular thing. The best historians of philosophy (I will shortly name one) struggle with this. How to think of proper names? Think of them as waterways. James Collins did. He dared to speak of source philosophers (e.g., Plato, Aristotle, Descartes, Kant, Hegel, Nietzsche? Foucault? Derrida? Husserl? Heidegger? Levinas? Habermas? Deleuze?) and tributaries (they merge downstream: Rivers Rorty, Sallis, Davidson, Nussbaum, Williams, Westphal, Caputo—you get the idea). You want to start a fight, change the metaphor from water to light, invoke magnitude, use the dreaded "g" word, call the former "great" and the latter "lesser

lights." Leaving aside the difficult questions of how one becomes mainstream, who plots magnitude, the relationship between naming and power, and so on, we might distinguish between the *contestants* (the former list), the *claimants* (the latter list), and the resultant *canon* (it's loaded), a process that guarantees employment (if not tenure-track slots) for those willing to endlessly plot and finely calibrate the standings at academic conferences or in the dingy offices of graduate students whose charts—who's up? who's down? who's impossible!—will shortly be scanned by faculty committees.

(2) Adjectival historical naming (e.g., Derridean, Habermasian, Foucauldian, Nietzschean, Deuleuzeoguattarian, Rortyian, Rortyish, Rortyesque), sometimes linked to place, creating peculiar and amusing philosophical species of the place name (e.g., "She is a French Heideggerian; he does American Continental; he gives good Frankfurt School"); or hinting at the process by which proper names metastasize into peculiar, deadly academic nouns, *de-Marxification*.

(3) References to specific arguments or theories or concepts purportedly held by these proper names (e.g., Habermasian communicative rationality, Derridean deconstruction, Nietzschean perspectivism, Foucauldian autocolonization, Deleuzeoguattarian lines of flight).

(4) Gestures at "dialogue" or "conversation" whereby claimants seek to engage the contestants (proper names; see 1 above) and set the terms of engagement as well as its textual site (e.g., "I would like to engage with Derrida's account of *différance*, specifically with his essay by that name, page such and such"). Sometimes, in recognition of the fact that academic conferences are perhaps not the best places to try for "communicative rationality" (since tenure may be at stake, and after all, there is a performative element to giving a paper, and besides, in ancient Greece the conversation among the friends of the forms occurred mostly in the *agora* and not in the academy), efforts are made to bridge "traditions," often with disastrous results. One thinks of "dialogue" between so-called "analytic" and "continental" philosophy: beyond the usual criticism ("Such tradition-naming is absurd, like saying that two things are done in philosophy, business and Kansas"), one looks in vain for the conversation, although many views are exchanged. A few brawls have broken out. Gossip is elevated to the plateau of argument ("Did you hear the one about how Searle was set up by some continental types who launched this *Glyph* thing to further dialogue between analytic and continental—a horrible journal, really, it folded, don't worry; so anyway, John responds to Derrida, nine pages, and Derrida locks himself in this apartment in Paris and writes over a hundred pages, and the thing is, it's unreadable! and worse, he makes fun of John's name, god-awful puns, no kidding; yeah, I

know, he's not a serious philosopher; did you hear what Foucault said about Derrida, called him '*obscurantisme terroriste*,' it was in the *NYRB*, the 'Derrida Affair'; well, anyway, Ruth wrote a letter to the French government protesting Derrida's appointment to some position, but you know the French—he got it anyway").[1] Sides are chosen, teams picked. Everyone wants Kant on their side. Habermasian calls to "communicative rationality" notwithstanding, as Husserl was said to have observed, "At philosophy conferences, the philosophers meet but the philosophies don't." But still: are things really this bad? Back to the grammar of appropriation, which, I will argue (appropriating Deleuzeoguattari for my purposes), is a grammar of possession and violence, at odds with friendship—and necessarily so, according to one conception of philosophy.

(5) A resultant *recontextualization*, often called a "reading of *x*" (e.g., "on my reading of Foucauldian genealogy" or "my reading of Derrida's notion of deconstruction"). Despite a generous spirit of inclusiveness on the part of some claimants, the logic of appropriation is a logic of exclusion: not everything concerning a proper name is to be appropriated, only that which is suitable, only those insights appropriate to the appropriator's own research program, which the appropriation, of course, is meant to advance. Thus we might speak:

(6) Of a *program of appropriation* into whose service a proper name is conscripted, often against his or her intent. Claimants lay claim to what they find serviceable in a proper name; invariably, someone will object to the claim, or, in the case of living contestants (Derrida, Habermas), seek to be dis-owned. What made Marxism so widespread in academe was its serviceability; the same is true today of deconstruction. Here we have the birth of the *contest*, reinscribed for academic purposes as a conversation (see 4 above). Someone has an idea: let us bring together Gadamer and Habermas, Gadamer and Derrida! Gentlemen, start your engines! Let the contest begin. Then: Let us make a book in our image. Publishers must be sought, notified. Nothing (as Adorno rightly observed) escapes the marketplace.

My aim is not to show that programs or acts of appropriation are inappropriate—in fact, I don't know what such a claim would mean, given the history of appropriation, which, in a certain sense, *is* the history of philosophy—nor, despite the title, is this a plea for philosophers to stop appropriating (they can't). I only wish to foreground the background assumptions and to highlight the limits of "appropriation-as-a-means-of-inducing-discussion, conversation, or what is often called 'dialogue'" (which I have elsewhere called the most wistful term of the late twentieth century),[2] as well as to suggest counterpossibilities for appropriation (I do not call these nonappropriations) that emerge from a consideration of Deleuze and Guattari, and Derrida. To do this, it will be necessary, and I hope helpful, to examine two programs of post-modern appropriation, one secular (Rorty) and one Christian (West-phal) with constant reference to Gadamer and Derrida, Deleuze and Guattari.

II

Of course, not everyone is interested in appropriating insights from postmodern philosophers. In fact, if your only source on information about the postmodern were *Time* or *Newsweek*, the *Wall Street Journal*, the *New York Times*, the *New York Review of Books*, the *Times Literary Supplement*, the *Nation*, the *Village Voice*, or the *New Yorker*—publications which oc-cupy a peculiar ethico-political space in our culture and have become the site of the most brutal kind of demonization of the postmodern by academics willing to use journalists for their own purposes—you might naturally conclude that there is nothing worth appropriating. When analytic philosophers choose to go on record against the post-modern, it is interesting that they frequently do not choose respected academic journals, nor do they engage in the kind of close textual analysis one has come to expect from them in their more "serious" writings. Instead, what we get, to cite but one example, is Alvin Plantinga, in his Stob Lectures at Calvin College, railing against anti-realists and dismissing their work in a few sweeping sentences:

> Creative anti-realism can seem faintly or more than faintly ridiculous; nev-ertheless it is widely accepted and an extremely important force in the con-temporary western intellectual world. Vast stretches of contemporary Con-tinental philosophy, for example, are anti-realist. There is Existentialism, according to which, at least in its Sartrean varieties, each of us structures or creates the world by way of our own decisions. There is also contemporary Heideggerian hermeneutical philosophy of various stripes; there is contem-porary French philosophy, much of which beggars description, but insofar as anything at all is clear about it, is clearly anti-realist.[3]

But analytic philosophers are not the only non-appropriators of the postmodern. Some of the most blistering criticism of the postmod-ern has come from contemporary continental philosophers. Jürgen Habermas, in *The Philosophical Discourse of Modernity*, devotes twenty-five pages to a scorching attack on Derrida, and manages to do this despite the fact that there is not a single reference to any of Derrida's texts, although Derrida is designated by name from one end to the other as being the author of theses supposedly being discussed by Habermas. Habermas' rationale for his ignoring of Derrida's texts runs as follows:

> Since Derrida does not belong to those philosophers who like to argue, it is expedient to take a closer look at his disciples in literary criticism within the Anglo-Saxon climate of argument to see whether this thesis [a thesis claimed to be Derrida's] really can be held.[4]

Derrida's response to this is worth quoting, for it seems to bring up short anyone still willing to think that philosophy is about "conversation among friends of the great ideas" and "communicative rationality":

> Such, then, is the effective practice of a great professor and a famous advocate of communication, one who, however, reproaches me for my "performative contradiction". . . . Is there a more serious, flagrant, significant "performative contradiction" than the one that consists in claiming to refute in the name of reason but without citing the least proof and first of all without even reading or quoting the other?[5]

If Plantinga and Habermas find nothing worthy of appropriation in postmodern thinkers, Richard Rorty finds a veritable gold mine. Rorty's program is clear: recontextualize. Take what you need. Whatever suits your program. Level all differences. Flatten out all readings. Rorty's take on his predecessors as well as his contemporaries is breathtaking:

> [I]t seems best to think of Heidegger and Derrida simply as post-Nietzschean philosophers—to assign them places in a conversational sequence which runs through Descartes and Hegel to Nietzsche and beyond, rather than to view them as initiating or manifesting a radical rupture. Though I unreservedly admire the originality and power of both men, neither can hope to avoid being fitted into contexts by readers. The most that an original figure can hope to do is to recontextualize his or her predecessors. He or she cannot aspire to produce works that are themselves uncontextualizable, any more than a commentator like myself can aspire to find the "right" context into which to fit these works.[6]

Who would wish to aspire to a work that is "uncontextualizable" (leaving aside the uncommon ugliness of the word) or even think that such a thing is possible? Far more revealing in this quotation is Rorty's idea of conversation. (One wonders: what exactly *is* a "conversational sequence?") Proper names are placed, assigned sound bites in a recontextualized "conversational sequence," which is Rorty's idea of the history of philosophy in the service of his peculiar brand of pragmatism. Does this sound like a conversation that you would wish to be a part of?

Still, there are those who are more elegant than Rorty in their call to dialogue, and more serious too. They have read Gadamer. This is a good thing. But they too, wish to appropriate.

III

Let's make the background Gadamer. It's often named that way, in the beginning, and with good reason. Gadamer has some lovely things to say about dialogue. Unsurprisingly, he owes much of his insight to Plato. A sampler of Gadamerian wisdom:

> [T]he Socratic–Platonic dialectic raises the art of questioning to a conscious art; but there is something peculiar about this art. . . . The art of questioning is not the art of resisting the pressure of opinion; it already presupposes this freedom. . . . The art of dialectic is not the art of being able to win every argument. On the contrary, it is possible that someone practicing the art of dialectic—i.e., the art of questioning and seeking truth—comes off worse in the argument in the eyes of those listening to it. As the art of asking questions, dialectic proves its value because only the person who knows how to ask questions is able to persist in his questioning, which involves being able to preserve his orientation toward openness. The art of questioning is the art of questioning ever further—i.e., the art of thinking. It is called dialectic because it is the art of conducting a real dialogue.[7]

And what are the conditions of the possibility of conducting a "real dialogue," one asks? Gadamer responds:

> To conduct a dialogue requires first of all that the partners do not talk at cross purposes. Hence it necessarily has the structure of question and answer. The first condition of the art of conversation is ensuring that the other person is with us. We know this only too well from the reiterated yesses of the interlocutors in the Platonic dialogues. *The positive side of this monotony is the inner logic with which the subject matter is developed in the conversation.* To conduct a conversation means to allow oneself to be conducted by the subject matter to which the partners in the dialogue are oriented. It requires that one does not try to argue the person down but that one really considers the weight of the other's opinion. . . . Dialectic consists not in trying to discover the weakness of what is said, but in bringing out its real strength.[8]

The other person is with us, Gadamer says. There is the other, there is me, but there is also some third thing, the truth, to which we aspire. We stand before each other as human *beings*, not *havings*; with respect to truth, we are in utter poverty. We await the emergence of truth through our conversation, correcting ourselves in that direction, trusting that what has been hidden shall come to light, that we shall work out the common meaning:

> What emerges in its truth is the logos, which is neither mine nor yours and hence so far transcends the interlocutors' subjective opinions that even the person leading the conversation knows that he does not know.[9]

Gadamer recognizes the primacy of conversation even in what he terms "derivative forms" such as letters, in which, he claims, the relation between question and answer is obscured:

> Letters . . . are an interesting intermediate phenomenon: a kind of written conversation that . . . stretches out the movement of talking at cross purposes and seeing each other's point. The art of writing letters consists in not letting what one says become a treatise on the subject but in making it acceptable to the correspondent. But on the other hand it also consists in preserving and fulfilling the standard of finality that everything in writing has. The time lapse between sending a letter and receiving an answer is not just an external factor, but gives this form of communication its special nature as a particular form of writing. So we note that speeding up the post has not improved this form of communication but, on the contrary, has led to a decline in the art of letter-writing.[10]

This decline marks an interesting moment in Gadamer's *Truth and Method*, a foreshadowing of a decline in communication in general, as we shall see in a letter of Kafka's. But it is Hegel that Gadamer has on his mind here. Gadamer foreshadows what can go wrong when, just a few lines later, reflecting on the Hegelian project of dialectic as a philosophical method, he traces the transition from dialogue to monologue: "Hegel's dialectic is a monologue of thinking that tries to carry out in advance what matures little by little in every genuine dialogue."[11]

The problem is that dialogue differs from writing, differs from written tradition. What characterizes a dialogue in spoken language—the question and answer, the give and take, the messiness and unpredictability that come from talking at cross purposes and coming to see the other's point—vanishes bit by bit as the philosopher sits to write, for writing is a solitary process. But there is a deeper problem, as we shall see with Deleuze and Guattari, and it is this: philosophers create concepts, and they care more for concepts than conversation.

Nevertheless, there are Gadamerian testimonials such as that of Richard J. Bernstein, who learned from Gadamer that the basic condition of all understanding is the willingness to test and risk one's convictions and prejudgments in and through an encounter with what is radically Other in its strongest possible version. Challenged by the "quip" of a "sympathetic critic," to wit,—when are you going to take on Heidegger and the French,—Bernstein reaches a momentous decision. He will read the postmodernists:

> Only by seeking to learn from the "other," only by fully grasping its claims upon one can it be critically encountered. Critical engaged dialogue requires opening of oneself to the full power of what the "other" is saying. Such an opening does not entail agreement but rather the to-and-fro play of dialogue. Otherwise dialogue degenerates into a self-deceptive monologue where one never risks testing one's prejudgments. So the quip about Heidegger, the "French," and "postmodern" challenges was a demand to put into practice what I had been professing—to test and risk my own philosophical convictions by exposing them to the sharpest and most penetrating questioning.[12]

There is also Merold Westphal. Perhaps no Christian philosopher (with the exception of John D. Caputo)[13] has been more sanguine about the prospects of appropriating postmodern insights in the service of a Christian interpretation and critique of culture than Westphal. Whether he is taking to task Christian demonizers of the postmodern such as Roger Lundin or making the case that Kierkegaard and Levinas are postmodernists with much to teach us, or extending Ricoeur's analysis of the hermeneutics of finitude and suspicion in order to produce charitable readings of postmodernists Foucault and Derrida as well as the modern atheistic masters of suspicion Marx, Freud, and Nietzsche, Westphal's program is unabashedly one of appropriation.[14] Reading the postmodernists as thinkers of negation who relentlessly remind us of what we cannot have (Truth with a capital "T"), what we cannot say (I pause in silence), and who we cannot become (God), Westphal's work is intended to open a window to a faith purified of all idolatry, conceptually humbled and chastened, as indebted to the postmodern placeholders of negation as the Israelites were to their Babylonian captors for a prophetic word they needed but did not wish to hear. He has done yeoman's work writing, organizing, and cajoling a generation of Christian scholars and the church itself to take seriously the work of the postmodernists. Characteristically, for one who has listened for so long to Kierkegaard, his work is a product of self-examination, and ironically, as one who has listened also to Foucault, an outgrowth of his *confession:*

I conclude with a confession. For years I thought that if I waited long enough Derrida and company would go away and I would be spared the work of reading them. I resolutely played the ostrich to this bogeyman. Eventually I concluded that the movement that includes Lyotard, Foucault, and Derrida was too important to ignore, and I began the long and often painful task of reading them. I am still a beginner, and anything but a true believer. My most postmodern friends find me hopelessly metaphysical because my affirmation of the French version is qualified in ways that make them nervous. But I believe the time has long since come for Christian scholars to get our heads out of the sand and to examine critically the bogeyman interpretation of postmodernism.[15]

But let us be clear about Westphal's project of appropriation: it is a doubly violent act, a two-step operation of *rejection* and resultant *recontextualization*. The first moment is the moment of critique, the "over against"; viewing the postmodernists as heirs of the Enlightenment, serious post-Kantian philosophers who offer arguments—some of them good, some of them not so good—Westphal rejects postmodern assumptions, non sequiturs, fatal prejudices, and that which is offered without evidence. Out with the chaff. Or, to change the metaphor, having fired the furnace and burned off the dross, what Westphal believes he is left with is pure postmodern gold. This gold, it turns out— and here we are in the second moment of recontextualization, à la Rorty—is pirated Christian gold, for the postmodernists, it turns out, are thieves and plagiarizers. Just as Marx might have learned from Amos the prophet's unmasking of religious self-interest masking economic injustice, just as Freud and Sartre are modern theologians of original sin against their will, just as Nietzsche played a prophetic role in exposing Christian virtues as nothing but glittering vices,[16] even so Westphal gives us Foucault and Derrida in the service of God, a stunning reversal which mimics, in its way, the consistent word of Scripture, where every idol is cast down and God makes all things new, as startling in its way to Christian realists as Mary's Magnificat must have sounded to the rich who were sent away empty-handed. Westphal's project of recontextualization differs from Rorty's not in form but in content—structurally, it is the same operation: take what you can use, reject the rest, and then (the third step in the process) humbly invite all to join the conversation.

Before I submit this project of appropriation and recontextualization to a degree of Deleuzian torture, I want to highlight again the necessary violence of such a project. In an interview conducted in the summer of 1996, I asked Westphal about appropriation:

GP: As you describe appropriation, it may be understood as a kind of conversation. There are two moments to appropriation: rejection (the placing of oneself as "over against" the other, the notion of critique in its traditional sense) and recontextualization, to use Rorty's term. There is a sense in which there is no news here, for many years thinkers in every discipline have been engaged in this project, and yet there is something disturbing about appropriation; it has a long and violent history. As far back as Plato and even before philosophers have found it necessary to kill off the father or mother figure, in order to advance their own project. Plato had to kill off Parmenides, and did so in the *Sophist*. Aristotle did the same to Plato in his *Metaphysics*, Aquinas to the Aristotle he didn't like in the *Summa*, etc. How do you address the issue of violence and revisionist history in the project of appropriation, and in what sense can this truly be called a "conversation?" *Prima facie*, it looks more like a wake.

MW: There is an inescapable aspect of what could be called violence in rejection and reappropriation. If I say to Marx, Nietzsche, and Freud, or if I say to Foucault and Derrida, "I reject your atheism and I want to recontextualize your insights into a Christian hermeneutics of finitude, and a Christian hermeneutics of suspicion," they are not going [to be] entirely pleased. On the other hand, it seems to me that that *can* be a way of opening a conversation in the sense that one is saying, "Look, I agree with you about these insights, in so far as they have real force. Would you agree with me that they work just as well, or even better in the Christian context in which I'm placing them? In so far as it is obvious that our deepest and most fundamental disagreement is over the reality of God, is it possible to find a way to talk about that? Or must we at least for the time being just lay that aside and talk about the best way to pursue these other insights?"

GP: So are you saying that it is a form of violence, but that it is a *necessary* form of violence?

MW: Well, it would be violence if it was cut off from its conversational possibilities. In so far as it's put in the service of conversational possibilities, I wouldn't describe it so much as violence as simply identifying differences between individuals and being honest about them. I don't think that *that* is necessarily to be construed as violence.[17]

It is to this notion of "conversational possibilities" that I now wish to attend.

IV

Higher than actuality is possibility.
—Martin Heidegger

Philosophers, as rule, are not particularly good conversationalists—at least, not in their philosophical practice. The business of philosophy is the creation of concepts, not conversations. This is the testimony of

Gilles Deleuze and Felix Guattari, postmodernists extraordinaire, in *What is Philosophy?*, the book which was their last collaborative effort before their deaths. Following the great philosophers—engaging in the adjectival historical naming I mentioned earlier—involves doing what they did, not merely repeating what they have said:

> If one can still be a Platonist, Cartesian, or Kantian today, it is because one is justified in thinking that their concepts can be reactivated in our problems and inspire those concepts that need to be created. What is the best way to follow the great philosophers? Is it to repeat what they said or *to do what they did*, that is, create concepts for problems that necessarily change?
>
> For this reason philosophers have very little time for discussion. Every philosopher runs away when he or she hears someone say, "Let's discuss this." Discussions are fine for roundtable talks, but philosophy throws its numbered dice on another table. The best one can say about discussions is that they take things no farther, since the participants never talk about the same thing. Of what concern is it to philosophy that someone has such a view, and thinks this or that, if the problems at stake are not stated? And when they are stated, it is no longer a matter of discussing but rather of creating concepts for the undiscussible problem posed. Communication always comes too early or too late, and when it comes to creating, conversation is always superfluous. Sometimes philosophy is turned into the idea of perpetual discussion, as "communicative rationality," or as "universal democratic conversation." Nothing is less exact, and when philosophers criticize one another it is on the basis of problems and on a plane that is different from theirs and that melt down the old concepts in the way a cannon can be melted down to make new weapons. It never takes place on the same plane. To criticize is only to establish that a concept vanishes when it is thrust into a new milieu, losing some of its components, or acquiring others that transform it. But those who criticize without creating, those who are content to defend the vanished concept without being able to give it the forces It needs to return to life, are the plague of philosophy. All these debaters and communicators are inspired by *ressentiment*. They speak only of themselves when they set empty generalizations against one another. Philosophy has a horror of discussions. It always has something else to do. Debate is unbearable to it, but not because it is too sure of itself. On the contrary, it is its uncertainties that take it down other, more solitary paths.[18]

Deleuze and Guattari consider the objection that has come down to us from the ancient world, a dream imparted anew by hopeful professors to every class of philosophy undergraduates when teaching the *Apology*, the *Phaedo*, or the *Republic:*

> But in Socrates was philosophy not a free discussion among friends? Is it not, as the conversation of free men, the summit of Greek sociability? In fact,

Socrates constantly made all discussion impossible, both in the short form
of the contest of questions and answers and in the long form of a rivalry
between discourses. He turned the friend into the friend of the single concept, and the concept into the pitiless monologue that eliminates the rivals
one by one.[19]

We seem to be at an impasse. At this point, one might be tempted
to throw up one's hands and say, well, yes, it is true that it often turns
out in actuality that conversational possibilities are not realized, but we
must remain hopeful. Remember Gadamer. Remember Plato. Let the
ideal guide you past the ruined hulks of abandoned conversations, keep
faith with the ideal, try, try again. Westphal himself, in the interview
cited above, seems to be saying something consistent with this and perhaps not so far removed from Deleuzoguattari:

GP: The test of this is how it works out in practice.

MW: I think there is a sense in which while people are writing, they are
primarily concerned to articulate their own insights. In that sense, there will
be something less than a fully conversational posture. I think what's crucial
is what happens after writing. Or perhaps in academic situations, what happens in the discussion after the paper is read. I think sometimes real conversation across very significant barriers opens up. Sometimes it doesn't.

Indeed, sometimes it doesn't. But I am beginning to believe there
are philosophical reasons for this that run deeper than a mere failure of
an ideal, or the way we structure "academic situations" such as these.

We are haunted by the specter of failed conversations, doomed dialogues, debates which did not take place as rumored.

We have failed, in our inheritance, to do the work of mourning.

In our zeal to appropriate, even when we acknowledge the debt, we
forget the ghosts. And the ghosts carry all away, including our lack of
consolation over what we cannot have.

On to Kafka and Derrida.

V

The easy possibility of writing letters—from a purely
theoretical view—must have brought wrack and ruin to the
souls of the world. Writing letters is actually an intercourse with
ghosts and by no means just with the ghost of the addressee but also
with one's own ghost, which secretly evolves inside the letter one is

writing. . . . How did people ever get the idea they could communicate
with one another by letter! One can think about someone far away and
one can hold on to someone nearby; everything else is beyond human
power. Writing letters, on the other hand, means exposing oneself to the
ghosts, who are greedily waiting precisely for that. Written kisses never
arrive at their destination; the ghosts drink them up along the way. . . .
  [A]fter the postal system, the ghosts invented the telegraph, the
telephone, the wireless. They will not starve, but we will perish.
                                                        —Kafka, *Letters to Milena*

Derrida is as suspicious of appropriation-in-the-singular as he is of
deconstruction-in-the-singular. He wants always to know, which deconstruction? what appropriation? His suspicion of deconstruction-in-
the-singular is well known (and I myself have written a book on this
important subject[20]) for Derrida has been vigilant in distancing himself
from what he regards as the singular usage of a word he has never
liked and whose fortune has disagreeably surprised him.

> There is no one, single, deconstruction. Were there only one, were it homo-
> geneous, it would not be inherently either conservative or revolutionary, or
> determinable within the code of such oppositions. That is precisely what gets
> on everyone's nerves. . . . Deconstruction does not exist somewhere, pure,
> proper, self-identical, outside of its inscriptions in conflictual and differenti-
> ated contexts; it "is" only what it does and what is done with it, there where
> it takes place. It is difficult today to give a univocal definition or an adequate
> description of this "taking place." This absence of univocal definitions is not
> "obscurantist," it respectfully pays homage to a new, very new Aufklärung.
> This is, in my eyes, a very good sign.[21]

I must point out that it is in precisely this context that Derrida addresses the problem of appropriation, in the very next paragraph after
the one I have just cited:

> Deconstruction in the singular cannot simply be "appropriated" by anyone
> or by anything. Deconstructions are the movements of what I have called
> "ex-appropriation." Anyone who believes they have appropriated or seen ap-
> propriated something like deconstruction in the singular is a priori mis-
> taken, and something else is going on. But since deconstruction is always
> "something else," the error is never total or pure.[22]

What is true of deconstruction is true also of appropriation. Before
Derrida is willing to entertain the possibility of appropriation, he wants
to know whether the system that seems to appropriate something is or

is not modified by that which it believes it is appropriating. Thus, he answers the friendly question of Peggy Kamuf about appropriation in this way:

> Even though I do not believe appropriation to be possible in general, I am not opposed to what *you* call "appropriation": it is inevitable that something resembling appropriation take place in the university, for example, to be affected by it. Otherwise the only hope for deconstruction's remaining happily intact and pure would be for it to be utterly ignored, radically excluded, or definitely rejected. You know that this is not my foremost concern. It is perhaps the ambiguous wish of those who make opposition to deconstruction their profession.[23]

What is decisive for Derrida in determining whether something like deconstructive practices or appropriations (in the plural) are possible is the question of whether or not said deconstructions or appropriations are themselves modified by the practice. And this is a ghostly practice. The fate of texts, even texts which we have written, haunts us. Does the text come back to you precisely as it left, intentions intact, prejudices retained? Or is its identity questionable, surprising, errant in some disturbing and beneficial way? Perhaps this latter point can be illustrated by a character in a novel you are writing, who, in the midst of your writing says things that are unpredictable and uncoerced, things about which you never might have guessed; or perhaps by children you have had. —This is the way Derrida describes it in *The Ear of the Other:*

> It would be interesting to analyze closely what happens when a text you write comes back to you in one form or another. What does it mean: "to come back"? It means that another makes use of it or cites it. I've had this happen to me. . . . All of a sudden someone puts a text in front of you again, in another context, with an intention that is both somewhat yours and not simply yours. Each time it happens, it's a very curious, very troubling experience. . . . What I can say is that it is never the same text, never an echo, that comes back to you. It can be a very pleasant or a very unpleasant experience. It can reconcile you with what you've done, make you love it or hate it. There are a thousand possibilities. Yet one thing is certain in all this diversity, and that is that it's never the same. . . . [T]he text's identity has been lost, and it's no longer the same as soon as it takes off, as soon as it has begun, as soon as it's on the page. By the end of the sentence, it's no longer the same sentence that it was at the beginning. Thus, in this sense, there is no echo, or, if there is, it's always distorted. Perhaps the desire to write is the desire to launch things that come back to you as much as possible in as many forms as possible. That is, it is the desire to perfect a program or a matrix having the greatest potential, variability, undecidability, plurivocal-

ity, et cetera, so that each time something returns it will be a different as possible. This is also what one does when one has children—talking beings who can always outtalk you. You have the illusion that it comes back to you, that it comes from you—that these unpredictable words come out of you somewhat. This is what goes on with texts. . . . It's never the same *in any case,* and it never returns. This is both a bad thing and a good thing. Obviously, if it came back, that would also be terrible. One wants it to return exactly like it is, but then one also knows very well that if it did come back exactly like it is, one would have only one wish and that is to run away.[24]

There is appropriation and then there is appropriation. There is re-appropriation. And there is what Derrida terms *exappropriation.* This term appears in *Specters of Marx,* where it retains its economic etymology:

> What we have said here or elsewhere about exappropriation (the radical contradiction of all capital, of all property or appropriation, as well as all the concepts that depend on it, beginning with that of free subjectivity, thus of emancipation as ordered by these concepts) does not justify any bondage. It is, we may say so, exactly the opposite. Servitude binds (itself) to appropriation.[25]

There are appropriations that fail to acknowledge the state of the debt. That Derrida would remind of this in the context of a book on Marx, in which he develops a new concept, *spectrality,* in a work punctuated by the great shouts and cries of alarm of the opening scenes of *Hamlet,* in so doing warning us of the dangers of appropriation and suggesting exappropriation as a counter-possibility, is not without significance. Who today—among those celebrating and participating in the great work of de-Marxification with the neo-evangelistic fervor of a Fukuyama—who has time to mourn Marx? And yet Marx is part of our inheritance. The proper work of all who inherit is to mourn. Inheritance from the "spirits of the past" consists of borrowing. A question of credit, then. We answer to the dead and to those we seek to kill. As Derrida reminds us, *inheritance is never a given, it is always a task.*[26] This, in part, is what I have against Rorty: it is the voice of a smug, comfortable, bourgeois liberalism, not the voice of wailing, of mourning. Rorty is set to divide up the inheritance, to parcel out the *estate philosophico,* and to do this in the name of recontextualization and appropriation. Westphal's project strikes me as more humble, more generous in its way, more charitable. And yet his appropriation/recontextualization is no less troubling. Derrida's advice: not so fast. The end—of philosophy, of metaphysics, of Marx, of the modern lately posted, of the great emancipatory ideals of the Enlightenment—the end is not always what it appears to be. There is this matter of the apparition appearing at the inheritance, and one never inherits, one never appropriates, one never recontextualizes, without coming to terms with some specter, and therefore with more than one specter. *"Whose grave's this, sir?"* Nothing could be worse, for the work of mourning, than confusion or doubt: *One has to know who is buried where.*

The problem with appropriation in the singular is that it aims to keep the dead dead, where they cannot lay claim on us. (Reminiscent of that old quip about the crusty book reviewer, to wit: "When I review a book, damn it, it *stays* reviewed.") We take from the dead, and even from the living, whatever we determine we need; but can we take without being taken? Someone says, "Oh, I am so taken with Kierkegaard," but what can this mean but that one has been laid claim to by a ghost? Claimants who are not laid claim to, takers who are not taken, are claimants and takers to be feared, resisted, and ultimately, haunted.

No appropriation in the singular is possible; no appropriation is simple; no appropriation escapes the burden of the debt or gets out of committee without one; no appropriation ultimately evades the work of mourning, the specters of the future. Had we been paying attention, we would have seen this in the case of Kant, who learned that he could not appropriate the presumed-dead body of Hume, killed by a clumsy and brutal Wolfian interpreter, without a haunting, which awakened him from his dogmatic slumber. Ghosts trouble our sleep, not only Kant's, not only Hamlet's.

Philosophy haunts its own places as well as inhabits them. And philosophy is always more than philosophy if it is truly philosophy.

Appropriation is like the Eucharist: you take at your own risk, but not apart from self-examination, and mind the holy ghost of the Other. Some have died after partaking at the table, Saint Paul reminds us, sounding another note that Derrida hits himself: the gift of death.[27] Before you take, consider also that you too are taken, blessed, broken, and ultimately given to the world. The best interpreters are broken, grieving, haunted, humbled, errant. We needn't call the world to a holy hunt against this specter, deconstruction, against this specter, postmodern. At twilight, before or after a night of bad dreams the specter finds us, and no academic conjuring—by forgetfulness, by foreclosure, or by murder—will release us from the price of our appropriations, which bring into the world new ghosts, untimely ones.

Midway through Derrida's *Specters of Marx,* he announces, What we are saying here will not please anyone.

Is this a conversation-starter?

Notes

1. For Derrida's account of the elevation of gossip into argument that occurs in the academic world, see "Afterword: Toward an Ethic of Discussion," in *Limited, Inc.*, ed. Gerald Graff (Evanston, Ill.: Northwestern University Press, 1988), pp. 111–60. See also John D. Caputo, ed., *Deconstruction in a Nutshell: A Conversation with Jacques Derrida* (New York: Fordham University Press, 1997), pp. 36–44.

2. Gary J. Percesepe, "The Unbearable Lightness of Being Postmodern," *Christian Scholar's Review* 20, no. 2 (December 1990): 118–35.

3. Alvin Plantinga, *The Twin Pillars of Academic Scholarship*, the Stob Lectures of Calvin College and Seminary 1989–90, published as a pamphlet by Calvin College and Seminary, Grand Rapids, Michigan, pp. 16–17. Later in these same lectures, Plantinga cites structuralism, poststructuralism, and "deconstruction in literary studies" as prominent examples in the humanities of "the move from Enlightenment subjectivism to relativism" (p. 22). He then calls upon the Christian scholarly community to engage in what he calls "Christian cultural criticism," which he refers to as a "testing of the spirits": "Christian scholars have an obligation to discern and analyze these perspectives, to plumb the full extent of their influence, to recognize the way in which they underlie vast stretches of contemporary intellectual life, to note how they manifest themselves in the intellectual projects and pursuits that are currently fashionable. We have an obligation to point out what we see, to react to it, to comment upon it. . . . We need deep, penetrating, thoughtful, informed analyses of the various cultural movements and forces we encounter" (p. 28). In fairness to Plantinga, his Stob Lectures, intended primarily as talks to non–specialist Calvin undergraduates, is not the place to look for this "deep, penetrating, thoughtful, informed" analysis of structuralism, poststructuralism, and deconstruction. But I am not aware of any scholarly writings in which Plantinga *does* address himself to these issues. For a more developed treatment of Plantinga's rejection of humanistic "creative anti-realism" and his association of Kant with this view, see his 1982 Presidential Address to the Central Division of the American Philosophical Association, "How To Be an Anti-Realist," *Proceedings and Addresses of the American Philosophical Association* (1983). For Merold Westphal's response to Plantinga, which challenges Plantinga's interpretation of Kant and suggests important affinities between Kantian idealism and Christian theism, see Merold Westphal, "Christian Philosophers and the Copernican Revolution," in *Christian Perspectives on Religious Knowledge*, ed. C. Stephen Evans and Merold Westphal (Grand Rapids, Mich.: Eerdmans, 1993), pp. 161–79.

4. Jürgen Habermas, *The Philosophical Discourse of Modernity*, trans. Frederick Lawrence (Cambridge: MIT Press, 1987), pp. 161–84.

5. Jacques Derrida, *Memoires: For Paul de Man*, rev. ed., trans. Cecile Lindsay, Jonathan Culler, Peggy Kamuf, and Eduardo Cadava (New York: Columbia University Press, 1989), p. 260.

6. Richard Rorty, *Essays on Heidegger and Others: Philosophical Papers, Vol. 2* (Cambridge: Cambridge University Press, 1991), pp. 1–2.

7. Hans-Georg Gadamer, *Truth and Method*, trans. Joel Weinsheimer and Donald G. Marshall (New York: Continuum Publishing, 1994), pp. 366–67.

8. Ibid, p. 367; italics mine.

9. Ibid, p. 368.

10. Ibid, p. 369.

11. Ibid.

12. Richard J. Bernstein, *The New Constellation: The Ethical–Political Horizons of Modernity/Postmodernity* (Cambridge: MIT Press, 1993), p. 4.

13. See especially John D. Caputo, *The Prayers and Tears of Jacques Derrida: Religion without Religion* (Bloomington: Indiana University Press, 1997). See also Caputo's "Hermeneutics and Faith: A Response to Professor Olthius," *Christian Scholar's Review* 20, no. 2 (December 1990), pp. 164–70, and *Deconstruction in a Nutshell: A Conversation with Jacques Derrida* (New York: Fordham University Press, 1997), pp. 156–80.

14. Merold Westphal, "Deconstruction and Christian Cultural Theory: An Essay on Appropriation," in *Pledges of Jubilee*, ed. Lambert Zuiderwaardt and Henry Luttikhuizen (Grand Rapids, Mich.: Eerdmans, 1995), pp. 107–25; "The Transparent Shadow: Kierkegaard and Levinas in Dialogue," in *Kierkegaard and Post/Modernity*, ed. Martin Matustik and Merold Westphal (Bloomington: Indiana University Press, 1995), pp. 265–81; "Postmodernism and Religious Reflection," *International Journal for Philosophy of Religion* 38, no. 1–3 (December 1995): 127–43.

15. Merold Westphal, "The Ostrich and the Bogeyman: Placing Postmodernism," in *Christian Scholar's Review* 20, no. 2 (December 1990): 114–17. This essay was written to introduce my essay "The Unbearable Lightness of Being Postmodern," published in the same issue, pp. 118–35.

16. Merold Westphal, *Suspicion and Faith: The Religious Uses of Modern Atheism* (Grand Rapids, Mich.: Eerdmans, 1993).

17. The excerpt given in text is from an unpublished interview I conducted with Westphal. A much shorter version of this interview appears in *Books and Culture* (May/June 1997): 24–25.

18. Gilles Deleuze and Felix Guattari, *What Is Philosophy?*, trans. Hugh Tomlinson and Graham Burchell (New York: Columbia University Press, 1994), pp. 28–29.

19. Ibid.

20. Gary J. Percesepe, *Future(s) of Philosophy: The Marginal Thinking of Jacques Derrida* (New York: Peter Lang, 1989).

21. Jacques Derrida, *Limited, Inc.*, ed. Gerald Graff (Evanston, Ill.: Northwestern University Press, 1988), p. 141.

22. Ibid.

23. Ibid, pp. 141–42.

24. Jacques Derrida, *The Ear of the Other: Octobiography, Transference, Translation*, trans. Peggy Kamuf (Lincoln: University of Nebraska Press, 1985), pp. 157–59.

25. Jacques Derrida, *Specters of Marx: The State of the Debt, the Work of Mourning, and the New International*, trans. Peggy Kamuf (New York: Routledge, 1994), p. 90.

26. Ibid, p. 54.

27. Jacques Derrida, *The Gift of Death*, trans. David Wills (Chicago: University of Chicago Press, 1995).

2. Theological Issues

5

The Hermeneutics
of Difference

*Barth and Derrida on
Words and the Word*

GARRETT GREEN

One can be excused for reacting with skepticism to any proposal linking the names of Karl Barth and Jacques Derrida. Even a serious
scholar familiar with the thought of both might understandably be
doubtful that significant convergences can be found between two such
unlikely bedfellows. Is not Barth—for whom the Bible represents the
criterion and touchstone of theology, the definitive witness to the Word
of God—an example of just what postmodernists mean by a "logocentric" thinker committed to a meta-narrative? And even theologians
devoted to the method of correlation are likely to find in Derrida's deconstruction a most unpromising candidate for correlation with theology. Yet three recent books, all by scholars with impressive credentials
for undertaking the task, find significant and positive parallels between
Christian theology and postmodern philosophy and suggest in particular that a comparison of Barth and Derrida is a promising project.
Walter Lowe, in *Theology and Difference*, uses Barth's *Römerbrief* to argue
that Barth's theology offers us not a dualism rooted in the kind of op-
positions that cry out to be deconstructed, but rather an "analogy of
difference" with striking similarities to central themes in Derrida.[1]
Kevin Hart's book *The Trespass of the Sign* attempts a more general reconciliation between theology and deconstruction but includes hints
that Barth's non-metaphysical language is a step in the right direction.[2]

Hart does not pursue this option, however, since he finds more promise for dialogue with deconstruction in the tradition of negative theology. The most recent book to explore the relationship between theology and deconstruction is also the one that devotes the greatest attention to parallels and convergences between Barth and Derrida: Graham Ward's *Barth, Derrida and the Language of Theology*.[3]

Ward's book has already provoked a spirited response by Bruce McCormack, who accuses him of an "illegitimate appropriation of Barth . . . for 'postmodern' concerns," based on a misunderstanding of Barth's doctrine of analogy and an insufficient knowledge of his life and thought generally. McCormack's resounding "*Nein!*" to Ward's attempt at "negotiation" between Barth's theology of the Word and Derrida's "economy of *différance*" concludes with an appeal for an "Either-Or" choice: either Barth's theology—on its own terms and without postmodern "supplement"—or what McCormack calls the "abyss of deconstruction."[4] Bracketing for a moment the question of who offers the more compelling case, we can use their interchange to focus attention on the key issue raised by the linkage of Barth's name with Derrida's. For however far apart they may be in their outcomes, Ward and McCormack agree on the central theological question. Ward identifies "the immediacy of the Word in the mediation of words" as "the theological *and* linguistic hub around which the whole of the *Church Dogmatics* circulates."[5] He speaks of the problem of "how the Word takes possession of human words and thoughts," or, put the other way around, the problem of "the capacity of language to communicate the Word."[6] As McCormack puts it succinctly, echoing Barth's own formulation in 1921,[7] the theological task is to provide "a coherent account of the Word in the words."[8] If we take this issue as our point of entry for a comparison of Barth and Derrida, we must admit at the very least that there are some striking similarities between them. Whether these parallels are indications of a deep commonality or merely superficial affinities of expression between otherwise heterogeneous thinkers is the question to be explored here.

In order to evaluate the apparent convergences between Barth and Derrida and then to consider to what extent they are significant, I want to bring three deconstructionist rubrics—signs, presence, and *différance*—into conversation with Barth's theology. Following Ward, I will focus the inquiry on Barth's treatment of the knowledge of God in Chapter 5 of his *Church Dogmatics*. In terms of McCormack's interests, this choice also makes sense, since McCormack argues that the final Christological shift in the development of Barth's theology "first makes itself felt in the treatment of the doctrine of God in *Church Dogmatics* II/I" starting in the summer of 1937.[9]

The Necessity of the Sign

At the heart of Barth's treatment of the knowledge of God is a dialectical relationship of revealing and concealing, unveiling and veiling. So accustomed are we to associating the name of Karl Barth with "revelation" that it is easy to overlook the second, or negative, side of this dialectic. But without it, we are left with an undialectical theology of the Word—one that would deserve the epithet "positivism of revelation." What saves Barth's theology from positivism is his attention to the play of differences within his concept of revelation, especially in the section on "The Limits of the Knowledge of God" (§27), where he stresses God's *hiddenness*. In a crucial passage, he locates the theological principle at stake: "Precisely in his *revelation*, precisely in *Jesus Christ*, the hidden God has in fact made himself comprehensible"—*faßbar* is his word: God has made himself available, "graspable," "tangible."[10] Barth goes on to qualify this assertion in three parallel ways: "Not directly, but indirectly. Not for sight, but for faith. Not in his being, but in sign." He then summarizes all three: "Not, then, by the sublation [*Aufhebung*] of his hiddenness—but comprehensibly [*faßbar*]." So directness, sight, and being are all identified—and rejected—as descriptions of our epistemic relation to God; and indirection, faith, and *signs* are identified—and affirmed. "Revelation means *giving signs*," he can write; therefore, "Revelation means *sacrament*" (*CD*, p. 56/52). Karl Barth's theology can thus be accurately described as a semiology, a theological semiotics.

This move brings him into the arena of Derrida's central concerns—though whether for similar reasons cannot as yet be determined. As Geoffrey Bennington points out, "not only does Derrida begin with the sign in the order of his published work, *he asserts, from the beginning, that the sign is at the beginning.*" The whole problematic leading to deconstruction can be derived from the differences implied in our use of signs: "The sign refers to the concept which refers to the world, allowing us a grasp of the world which is other than chaotic and evanescent." The sign, according to Derrida, makes possible a language that does not consist simply of proper names. Its difference from what it signifies allows us, in Bennington's phrase, to "call a cat a cat rather than Marmaduke."[11] But the difference between sign and signified also means that no sign ever succeeds in fully (i.e., unambiguously) identifying its intended object. Signs do not refer to things directly but instead to other signs, which in turn refer to still other signs, in an inconclusive and never-ending deferral of meaning. Since we nevertheless *want* unambiguous meaning and we *desire* closure, this hermeneutical situation represents a continual temptation to falsify meaning by devious, and ultimately unsuccessful, attempts at fore-closure.

The Question of Presence

All of this sounds very much like Barth, except for one possibly decisive difference: Derrida is describing the grammar of signs in general, whereas Barth is talking about a *particular* use of signs, namely, to designate God. But in fact, for Derrida "God" is not simply one more sign, subject to the vicissitudes and deferrals of all signs; rather, it holds (or we would like it to hold) a unique place in the hierarchy of signs. To understand the place of the signifier "God" in Derrida's account, we need to introduce a second major rubric: *presence*. Kevin Hart points out that "the concept 'sign' presupposes a concept of presence: a sign is always a *sign of* something present or presentable."[12] There is a polemical edge to Derrida's account of the distinction between sign and presence, for he is persuaded that the entire tradition of Western thought has been dominated by a quest for the illusory goal of complete presence and has consequently produced a long series of projects in what Derrida calls the "metaphysics of presence." Such misguided quests assume "the possibility of thinking a *concept signified in and of itself*, a concept simply present for thought, independent of a relationship to language, . . . to a system of signifiers."[13] This goal Derrida dubs a "transcendental signified," something "which in and of itself, in its essence, would refer to no signifier, would exceed the chain of signs, and would no longer itself function as a signifier."[14] Though there are examples of non-theistic, and even atheistic, metaphysics of presence, "God" has been the favorite nominee for the transcendental signified. Thus, how a particular thinker treats the concept of God will be, from Derrida's perspective, an important clue to the thinker's semiotic assumptions and commitments.

In the case of Barth's theology, it quickly becomes apparent that God is no transcendental signified and that dogmatics, properly conceived, cannot possibly be a metaphysics of presence. Indeed, much of the thrust of Chapter 5 of the *Church Dogmatics* is directed against any suggestion that our knowledge of God could be based on immediate experience, which is just what presence entails. Barth's distinction between the primary and secondary objectivity of God appears designed to head off any such conclusion. From our standpoint, God is objective only in this "secondary" way: indirectly, not directly; for faith, but not for sight; veiled under signs, not as being. To stress God's hidden-ness, after all, is surely to deny God's presence, at least in any usual or straightforward sense of the term. Hiddenness, of course, is not all that Barth has to say about God, or even the most important thing. But it is the first, the *terminus a quo* of our knowledge of God, and thus its limit: in this life, we know God not as a presence "face to face" but in his "enigmatic" indirection (1 Cor. 13:12), by which he offers himself to us "in, with, and under the sign . . . of other objects." This "clothed" knowledge of God is what Barth means when he says that our knowl-edge God is a knowledge of faith. As the very distinction between the terms "faith" and "sight" implies, the former is a relationship not of presence but of absence.

The Economy of *Différance*

But "absence" is not quite right either. For Barth does not say or imply that in faith we live in the *absence* rather than the presence of God. Faith is, after all, an analogical relationship, an *analogia fidei*—a rela-tionship, in other words, characterized by likeness or similarity. By re-jecting the "analogy of being" that Barth found operative in both Ro-man Catholic and Liberal Protestant theology, he was rejecting the thesis that our knowledge of God is based on a similarity of *being* shared by Creator and creature alike. His alternative, however, was not to deny the likeness, the analogy, but rather to deny that it is based on being. But that means that faith is itself an analogical relationship, one that involves both *Gleichheit* and *Ungleichheit*—equality and inequality, parity and disparity (as the English translation has it), identity and dif-ference. In faith the Word of God is *neither* simply like our words *nor* simply unlike them; alternatively, in faith God's Word is *both* like *and* unlike ours. Barth is not simply glorying in paradoxes, however much his rhetoric may sometimes leave that impression. The key to resolving the apparent paradox of identity and difference, presence and absence, lies in what George Hunsinger calls Barth's actualism, the most dis-tinctive trait of his theology. "It is present," writes Hunsinger, "when-ever Barth speaks . . . in the language of occurrence, happening, event, history, decisions, and act."[15] Barth's actualism is epitomized in his preference for *becoming* over *being*. At crucial points in the *Church Dog-matics*, he contrasts the two verbs to make his point. In terms of the divine/human analogy, Barth puts it this way: strictly speaking, there *is* no analogy between God's Word and ours; the word we speak *is* not the Word God speaks. But by the grace of God—that is, through God's

act—our words *become* his Word. The term "analogy," he writes, "*is* not
. . . correct in itself. . . . It [nevertheless] *becomes* correct" in the context
of revelation. So "in *our* thinking and speaking similarity *becomes* similar to the similarity posited in the true revelation of *God*" (*CD*, p. 255/
226; Barth's emphasis). Although we are powerless to restore to our
words their original divine authenticity, Barth writes, nevertheless "in
our knowing this analogy of truth *becomes* [or *comes to be*],[16] by means
of the decision of his grace" (*CD*, p. 260/230). The very same relationship, and the same contrast between the verbs *to be* and *to become*, is the
hallmark of Barth's theology of religion. The climax and turning point
of §17 ("God's Revelation as the *Aufhebung* of Religion") arrives with
these words: "No religion *is* true. A religion can only *become* true, i.e.,
correspond to that which it gives itself out to be and is taken to be."
The model for the relationship is the justification of the sinner, which
means that the analogy of faith is at bottom an analogy of grace: "The
true religion is, like the justified human being, a creature of *grace*."[17]
Precisely the same must be said of the relationship between the divine
Word and human words: although our words *are* not the Word of God,
they can *become* the Word of God—by God's grace.

Derrida, too, is wont to speak in terms not simply of presence or absence, but of some more complex relationship that is irreducible to the
one or the other. "We must not suppose," notes Bennington, "that because Derrida questions presence he must therefore be a thinker of absence, emptiness, nothing."[18] To explain why this is so, we cannot avoid
Derrida's elusive and exasperating "neographism"[19] *différance* (with an
a)—much as we might wish that we could! In fact, so far as I can see,
one of the best ways to understand the point of *différance* is to see that
Derrida introduces it as the alternative to *presence*. He proposes to replace the metaphysics of presence with the economy of *différance*. And
his reasons for doing so are once again related to the way signs function, to what he calls "the problematic of the sign."[20] "The sign," he
writes, "represents the present in its absence. It takes the place of the
present." Thus the "sign, in this sense, is deferred presence." But the
sign is therefore not simple absence either, since its very purpose is to
represent (re-present) the signified. It should now be clear why the goal
of every metaphysics of presence—namely, to discover a transcendental signified—is illusory, for "the signified concept is never present in
and of itself, in a sufficient presence that would refer only to itself."
About the closest Derrida ever comes to a formal definition of *differance* is this statement: "*Différance* is the non-full, non-simple, structured and differentiating origin of differences."[21] A sign, then, according to Derrida, is neither a presence nor an absence but what he calls
a *trace*. In Bennington's paraphrase, traces are not atoms or elements

of a system but rather are "traces of the *absence* of the other 'element,' which is moreover not absent in the sense of 'present elsewhere,' but is itself made up of traces. Every trace is the trace of a trace. No element is anywhere present (nor simply absent), there are only traces."[22]

Despite the evident congruence between what Barth says about the dialectic of presence and absence in revelation and Derrida's account of the trace in the economy of *différance* (which likewise involves a dialectic of presence and absence), one might reasonably conclude that Barth and Derrida are talking about quite different subjects. But such a conclusion, I think, would be premature, for sharing a common subject is not the only way in which two thinkers can be significantly related. Ward's claim—to return to the disagreement between him and McCormack—is not that Derrida is writing about the same subject as Barth but rather that he has developed conceptual tools more suitable to Barth's subject matter than the tools Barth had at his disposal. What their projects have in common is their involvement with what Ward calls "the same double nature of language"; and he maintains that Barth's theological concern with the Word in the words can be clarified with the help of Derrida's philosophical insights into the way linguistic signs function. "With Derrida's notion of *différance*," Ward claims, "the coherence of Barth's theology of language is clarified."[23]

A General Theory of Language?

McCormack's challenge to Ward's reading of Barth raises a number of fascinating and important questions, and I for one hope that Ward will respond publicly to the charges. For this debate promises to be uncommonly productive, since the opponents are in fact very close to one another in important ways and are dealing with an issue of major importance to theologians in the current cultural situation. Since Ward himself, so far as I am aware, has not responded to McCormack, I want to try my own hand at developing a couple of strategic points relevant to their controversy.

Let me first say what I think Ward has accomplished, even if many of McCormack's criticisms should turn out to be true. By recontextualizing Barth's theology of the Word in a postmodern setting (a move that obviously grates on McCormack's nerves), Ward illumines Barth's theological project from a fresh perspective, and one that turns out to be surprisingly revealing. As I have tried to show by looking at the rubrics of the sign, the dialectic of presence and absence, and the uniquely Derridean logic of *différance*, Barth turns out to have anticipated certain concerns that were picked up by others only much later. The very tones in Barth's theology that were most jarring to the ears of his contemporaries have an almost familiar sound in our age that has become accustomed to the dissonant tones of deconstruction. Theological attention to postmodern philosophy would be justified on these grounds alone, that is, by its raising of questions that direct our attention to aspects of the theological tradition we may have neglected and by doing so in a way that puts us into conversation with secular intellectuals of our own day. But I will make the stronger argument that there are convergences not only of question but also of method and even—if properly qualified—significant convergences in matters of substance. I want to make good on these claims by looking first at the point where Barth seems most in agreement with Derrida, and then at a point where he seems to diverge from him most radically.

McCormack's first "observation" about Ward's reading of Chapter 5 of the *Church Dogmatics* is a charge of misrepresentation: he maintains that "Barth's problematic was never, at any point that of a general theory of language."[24] He accuses Ward of forcing Barth into a philosophical discussion in which he in fact declined to participate; and this error is a major part of Ward's alleged "appropriation" of Barth for illegitimate postmodern purposes. Now McCormack is surely right that Barth was never engaged in the kind of general theoretical enterprise represented by *Redephilosophie* and *Sprachphilosophie,* and he offers compelling evidence that Ward exaggerates the connection of Barth with the Patmos Circle. Nevertheless, in his own way—and that means as a theologian—Barth surely *was* interested in a general theory of language. Buried in a footnote near the end of Ward's book is an important reference to something Barth says in the opening paragraph of Chapter 1 of the *Church Dogmatics:* "there is no genuinely profane speech. In the last resort, there is only talk about God." This statement, rendered somewhat freely by the translator, follows Barth's blunt opening assertion that "not all human talk [*Rede*] is talk about God," even though "it really could and should be [*könnte und müßte wohl so sein*]."[25] The reason it should be is simply that everything, all the possible objects of our speech, have their origin and destiny in God (*von ihm her und zu ihm hin sind*). For this reason (now translating Ward's passage more literally), "there should be and ought to be no profane talk but rather, understood in terms of its ultimate subject matter [*in letzter Sachlichkeit*], only talk about God." In a few broad strokes, Barth proceeds to lay out "a general theory of language"—not a *Redephilosophie* but rather a virtual *Redetheologie.* He does so by situating and grounding human language, what we could call the linguistic human condition, in the context of the biblical narrative of salvation. The subjunctive modalities of Barth's opening statements (*könnte, müßte, dürfte*) point to our actual present situation as "fallen, lost, and damned recipients of mercy" living not in the *regnum gloriae* but in the *regnum gratiae*, "the present [age] between the times of creation and redemption." Our speech is understood by contrast with the speech both of original humanity (*Menschen des Urstands*) and eschatological humanity (*Menschen des Reiches der Herrlichkeit*), for whom all talk "as such" can be interpreted as talk about God. We, on the other hand, dwell in a kingdom of unlikeness, whose linguistic "symptom" (Barth's preferred metaphor) is a division, separation, distinction, or divorce (*Scheidung* carries all those connotations) running right through the heart of our speech. Furthermore, this linguistic division is a "provisional" (*vorläufig*) indicator pointing toward "that final division, that event, in which God is the one who acts."[26]

Can we not say that here Barth and Derrida, from their very different perspectives and out of their very different interests, are dealing with the same subject—and even, up to a point, saying similar things about it? They are one in their conviction that human speech is not a transparent window on reality, that in some deep sense using language is a self-contradictory enterprise, one bound to fall short of its mark. As much as we would like to mean what we say, we seem condemned always to say both more and less. Seeking wholeness, we inevitably speak in fragments; intending univocity, we equivocate in spite of ourselves. (Not only the white man, as they say in the old Hollywood Westerns, "speak with forked tongue.") And both Barth and Derrida issue repeated warnings against the temptation to think that we can transcend the inherent ambiguities of human language. At one point, at least, they even agree on a name for the wrong way of thinking about language: metaphysics. If such a convergence exists, limited as it is to a narrow but important range of human experience, a dialogue between them is both possible and potentially fruitful. Viewed from the theological side, Barth's *Redetheologie* allows us to interpret Derrida's economy of *différance* as a philosophical description of what it means to be language-users in the age of grace. It allows us to hear the deconstructionist warning against the metaphysics of presence as a postmodern reminder of the dangers of trying to usurp the role of God in our human speaking and writing. Most important of all, Derrida's account of what it means to be users of signs offers new conceptual tools for restating in our own time what Barth in his day called the dialectic of "veiling and unveiling" in God's self-revelation of his Word in our words.

Barth's Christian Semiotics

The more difficult part of a conversation between Barth and Derrida comes at the point where they appear to diverge. I can imagine at least the possibility of convincing a deconstructionist that faith in the God of Jesus Christ does not commit one to the metaphysics of presence and does not presuppose a transcendental signified of any kind. I find it much harder to imagine Derrida accepting Barth's identification of Jesus Christ as the "sign of all signs" (*CD*, p. 233/199). If such is the case, what does it tell us about the relationship between Christian faith and postmodern philosophy?

Let us look at the context of Barth's comment about Christ as sign. To begin with, we should take note of what Barth does *not* say: he does not identify Jesus Christ as a transcendental signified, as a moment of pure presence that grounds our otherwise shifting system of signs; rather, he identifies him precisely as sign and thus subject to the vicissitudes of all signs (in Derrida's terms), to the conditions of "secondary objectivity" (in Barth's terms). To do otherwise, we should note, to attempt to exempt Jesus Christ from the linguistic human condition, would amount to semiotic docetism, to an implicit denial of the full humanity of the incarnate one. It might even imply that simply to name Jesus Christ would render him present—a move that would turn every theologian (indeed, every Christian) into a conjurer. At the very least, it would turn Jesus into a transcendental signified by presupposing that we had extralinguistic access to his presence. Barth contrasts the sign-character of Christ precisely with his essential being: in revelation Jesus Christ becomes *faßbar* "not in his *Wesen* but rather in sign" (*CD*, p. 223/199). Saint Paul, writing of "the gospel of the glory of Christ," says something similar: "We have this treasure in earthen vessels, to show that the transcendent power belongs to God and not to us" (2 Cor. 4:7). Signs, understood the way Barth—and Derrida—understands them, are thoroughly earthen.

Barth goes so far as to identify revelation itself with signification: "This *is* God's revelation: that God has given to the creature chosen and determined for this purpose the commission and the power to represent and depict him [*ihn zu vertreten und darzustellen*], to bear witness to him." There follows immediately the decisive sentence: "The Word became flesh: that is the first, original, and governing sign of all signs" (*CD*, p. 233/199). We should note first of all the qualifier "governing" (*regierend*).[27] Barth is saying that in the story of Jesus Christ we have the hermeneutical key that renders God's "secondary objectivity" intelligible to us. Without ceasing to be a sign, this sign nevertheless governs our use and interpretation of all signs. Because it does so as a sign (and not as a transcendental signified), it does not escape the economy of *différance*. In attempting to paraphrase Barth's theology of the knowledge of God, Ward comments that "without revelation we occupy a world of circulating semiotics."[28] But even *with* revelation, on Barth's account, we occupy such a world; for our signs do not somehow become fixed once we attend to revelation. In the final subsection of Chapter 5, where Barth examines the veracity or the truth-character (*Wahrhaftigkeit*) of the knowledge of God, his analysis culminates in a discussion of what it means that our knowledge of God is a knowledge in faith. Here he returns to a recurrent motif in his dogmatics, the circular logic of theology,[29] which is represented by the very structure of §27 ("The Limits of the Knowledge of God"). For that knowledge originates—has its *terminus a quo*, or originating limit—in the hiddenness of God; and it eventually returns, as its *terminus ad quem*, or ultimate limit, to the same divine hiddenness. In this way, our knowledge of God is circular; it runs its course from the divine mystery to the divine mystery. Barth faces up to the problem of circularity with disarming candor, acknowledging that it may be an indication that we have not understood our knowledge of God as *wahrhaftig*. In other words, the circular logic of the knowledge of God could turn out to be a vicious circle. Barth does acknowledge that there are also *circuli veritatis*, circles of truth, but refuses to take refuge in that notion, acknowledging that in our intention to trace the *circulus veritatis Dei*, we might be deluding ourselves by means of a mere "word play" or a "systematic *Deus ex machina*" (*CD*, pp. 278–79/246). Even our appeals to faith, revelation, and grace (right as they are) offer no ultimate insurance against the possibility of self-deception. Expressed in the postmodern language of Derrida, Barth is saying that there is an undecidability between the *circulus veritatis Dei* and the *Deus ex machina* that calls for the decision of faith or unfaith. We will return to the necessarily unsecured nature of the knowledge of faith, but first we must acknowledge another important aspect of Barth's identification of Jesus Christ as "governing sign."

Listen once more to the linchpin of Barth's Christian semiotics: "The Word became flesh: that is the first, original, and governing sign of all signs." Notice that, strictly speaking, Barth does not identify Jesus as sign—or rather, he does so in a particular way. The governing sign is not the man himself, not even the God-man, as a *being* (this is what Barth means when he says "not in *Wesen* but in sign"). Instead, Barth names an *event*, the becoming-flesh of the Son of God in Jesus. This event, and not any thing or being, is the "sign of all signs." In keeping with Barth's actualism, we may surely paraphrase here: Jesus Christ *is* not the governing sign; rather, he *becomes* the governing sign—by the grace of God! But what is this event of incarnation but the epitome of the whole story of Jesus—indeed, of the whole story of the world told from the vantage point of God's redeeming love of his lost creation? The sign of Jesus Christ governs our speaking and writing, not by conjuring up a pure presence that secures our use of signs against ambiguity, but rather by directing our attention to the constitutive pattern that renders the whole story of God's gracious intercourse with his creation apprehensible to us. Expressed in somewhat different conceptual terms, the narrative of Jesus Christ is the catalyst by which the paradigm or normative pattern of the Holy Scriptures snaps into imaginative focus. That paradigm becomes in turn the root metaphor (the *analogia fidei*) by which our own lives are brought into analogical relationship with the story of the incarnation of Jesus Christ at the heart of the story of God and the world. "The Word became flesh" functions for Barth as the epitome of that scriptural paradigm and hence as the "governing sign of all signs" because it orders all our signs according the analogy of faith. In this way, God utters the Word in, with, and under our words.

The Supplementary Logic of Grace

Much of the vehemence of McCormack's attack on Ward's reading of Barth appears to derive from his assumption that Ward accuses Barth of inconsistencies and contradictions in his account of how God speaks his Word in our words. To make matters worse, in McCormack's view, Ward then suggests that Barth stands in need of a Derridean "supplement." "There is no aporia in Barth's theory of theological language," McCormack declares testily, "needing to be filled by Derrida or anyone else."[30] But surely here it is McCormack who has misread Ward. Granted that Ward's prose could be clearer (a fault that seems endemic to admirers of Derrida), his penultimate chapter on "Barth and the Economy of *Différance*" is not a corrective but rather a highly sympathetic interpretation of Barth's theology in the light of Derrida's economy of *différance*. Far from accusing Barth of contradiction, Ward (with help from Derrida) seeks to demonstrate the "coherence" of Barth's theology of the Word, which "otherwise *has been seen* as a contradiction which logically flaws his Christology and the soteriological operation of the Trinity."[31] Ward appeals to Derrida in order to defend Barth against charges of inconsistency. Or perhaps it would be more accurate to say that Ward acknowledges inconsistencies in Barth while arguing that he is right to be inconsistent—right for reasons that Derrida has brought to light. Read as an example of Derrida's economy of *différance*, "Barth's theological discourse is understood as a rhetorical strategy presenting both the need to do and the impossibility of doing theology." McCormack claims that "Ward has not grasped Barth's particularism,"[32] but it would be more accurate to say that Ward uses Derrida to explicate the hermeneutical heart of that particularism, namely Barth's identification of Jesus Christ as "the first, original, and governing sign of all signs." Ward paraphrases Barth's principle as follows: "Jesus Christ is the name of the remembered promise of a future presence, which circulates within the economy of *différance*. He is the promised Word, inaugurating and endlessly promoting the chain of signifiers which defer its final, realized presence."[33] Theologians may surely differ on the question of whether this postmodern setting of Barth's theology is an advance over Barth's own way of making the same points, for example, by stressing the circular character of dogmatics, its continual exposure to both *Anfechtung* and comfort. But the discussion is worth having, if only because so many of our contemporaries appeal to Derrida, frequently using him to discredit or dismiss theology. We have a precedent in Barth's own ad hoc use of philosophy in the service of dogmatics. If he can harness even so volatile a notion as Hegelian *Aufhebung* (one of his favorites), surely we can be permitted an occasional theological appeal to *différance* without plunging headlong into the "abyss of deconstruction."

Derrida's notion of *supplément* offers one model for the conversation between Christian theologians and postmodern philosophers—one that I find particularly attractive because it dovetails so well with a Christian understanding of our common life together under grace. In what we can call vulgar postmodernism—the ideology that has so often poisoned our professional societies and polarized our faculties by politically correct but philosophically misguided appeals to Derrida—deconstruction is identified with refutation. This perversion of postmodernism leads to an academic form of "Gotcha!" that works like this: if I can expose the unacknowledged play of opposites lurking in your favorite texts, I win the game! But if I understand the logic of supplementarity correctly, its moral implications are quite different. The fundamental hermeneutical situation in which we all find ourselves as users of signs, which Derrida indicates by the word *différance*, means that no text can ever be complete or self-sufficient, which in turn implies that every text stands in need of a supplement. For a supplement expresses what *cannot* be said in the original text. Note well: not just what *is not* said, but what *cannot be* said without rending the fabric—the "textile," as Derrida calls it—of the text; in other words, what makes the text the text. That is not a failing of the original, but it does represent the inevitable limits to which all texts are subject. (An excursus on Jesus' parable of the wineskins would no doubt be in order here.) The logic of grace in Christian teaching (including, surely, Karl Barth's dogmatics) is a logic of supplementarity; it shows us why we need each other, since none of us is hermeneutically self-sufficient. As Christians, we attribute this situation not to the unfortunate but unavoidable limitations of finitude but rather to grace: God has so arranged things that we cannot say what needs to be said (ultimately, the Word of God) on our own—and what God has ordained is good! This supplementary logic of grace has a historical dimension as well: we need those who have preceded us in the faith; we need their texts and they need our interpretations. We can never forget them, for a supplement does not replace the text it supplements. In this way, we catch a glimpse of what might be called the hermeneutical communion of saints.

But the supplementary logic of grace, according to the Christian vision, is not confined to the saints. McCormack (who may have been exposed to too much vulgar postmodernism) takes umbrage at Ward's suggestion that "Derrida has provided Barth's theology of language . . . with a philosophical supplement." He neglects to note that Ward goes on to say, "Barth provides Derrida's economy of *différance* with a theological supplement."[34] In the long run, I suspect that secular deconstructionists will have greater difficulty accepting this mutual supplementarity than will Christian theologians, but that is a question the secularists will need to settle for themselves. From the theological side of the conversation, however, I see some promising openings, which I would like to mention in conclusion.

I want to return to the point of hermeneutical vulnerability that Barth reaches in the conclusion of his theology of the knowledge of God in Chapter 5 of the *Church Dogmatics* because it goes to the heart of the differences finally separating Barth from Derrida, and Christian theology today from postmodern philosophy. Immediately after acknowledging the impossibility of securing the truthfulness of our knowledge of God against its reduction to a vicious circle, Barth makes what is perhaps the most remarkable statement of the entire chapter. If we take seriously the claim that only God's grace distinguishes the *circulus veritatis Dei* from the *Deus ex machina*, Barth writes, "then we can surely wish to have it no other way than that we cannot in fact defend ourselves in the face of that question" (*CD*, p. 279/246). Not only *are* we defenseless as believers, Barth is saying, we should *want* to be! (Those critics of the "neo-orthodox" Barth, whom McCormack so effectively refutes, should pay closer attention to passages like this one.) Like Derrida, Barth embraces *différance* (though surely for very different reasons) and thus opposes every attempt at theological closure as a refusal to trust oneself wholly to the grace of God.

Let me cite some examples from the New Testament as exegetical support for the Christian refusal to seek security by evading *différance*. There is a remarkable resistance to closure in the final sentence of John's gospel: "But there are also many other things which Jesus did; were every one of them to be written, I suppose that the world itself could not contain the books that would be written" (John 21:25). (If Mark's gospel indeed ends at 16:8, it would be an even more dramatic instance; but I will stay out of that debate for now.) The ending of John's gospel manages to achieve a literary "sense of an ending" while at the same time indicating the supplementary logic of the narrative of Jesus Christ. A quite different sort of example is the recurrent theme of asking for a sign in the gospel narratives. The crowds repeatedly demand a sign from Jesus, and he repeatedly refuses—rather, he gives them a different kind of sign from what they desire: "And he sighed deeply in his spirit, and said, 'Why does this generation seek a sign? Truly I say to you, no sign shall be given to this generation.' And he left them" (Mark 8:12). In the fourth gospel, Jesus' withdrawal hints at a salvific purpose: "and I, when I am lifted up from the earth, will draw all men to myself" (John 12:32). Jesus withdraws from us to save us. "When Jesus had said this, he departed and hid himself from them" (John 12:36b)—which is followed immediately by the evangelist's comment, "Though he had done so many signs before them, yet they did not believe in him." They did not believe, we may surmise, because Jesus' signs do not deliver the security of complete presence; they are promises yet to be fulfilled. Jesus draws all people to himself by allowing himself to be "lifted up," crucified—"erased," we might even say with Derrida.[35] We know Jesus only "under erasure," because otherwise we might be tempted to hold onto him in the present—to force him to be present, to stay with us. But Jesus, now as then, does not come as fulfilling presence but as summoner: "Follow me!" is not the announcement of the end of the road but an invitation to travel. Presence, as a term of Christian theology, is always an eschatological term: *parousia*. The logic of grace is a logic of supplementarity. By means of the continually fulfilling but never fulfilled rhythm of our life in Christ, God draws us forward, draws us into the divine life.

It is not just individual New Testament books that have open-ended endings. Can it be mere coincidence that the Church's scriptural canon

itself ends with this prayer? "Amen. Come, Lord Jesus!" But wait—
there is still one more verse: "The *grace* of the Lord Jesus be with all
the saints. Amen."

Notes

1. Walter Lowe, *Theology and Difference: The Wound of Reason* (Bloomington:
Indiana University Press, 1993).

2. Kevin Hart, *The Trespass of the Sign: Deconstruction, Theology and Philosophy*
(New York: Cambridge University Press, 1989); see esp. pp. 257, 262–63.

3. Graham Ward, *Barth, Derrida and the Language of Theology* (New York: Cambridge University Press, 1995).

4. Bruce Lindley McCormack, Article Review of Graham Ward's *Barth,
Derrida and the Language of Theology*, in *Scottish Journal of Theology* 49 (1996): 97–
109. Quotations are from pp. 97 and 109.

5. Ward, *Language of Theology*, p. 14.

6. Ibid., pp. 21, 25.

7. Karl Barth, *Der Römerbrief (Zweite Fassung), 1922* (Zurich: Theologischer
Verlag Zürich, 1989), p. xix (p. xii in the 1922 ed.). The English translation (p. 8)
has conflated Barth's description of the hermeneutical task, which should read, "to
the extent possible, the relation of the words to the Word in the words must be
uncovered" (my translation). See also Bruce L. McCormack, *Karl Barth's Critically
Realistic Dialectical Theology: Its Genesis and Development, 1909–1936* (Oxford: Clarendon Press, 1995), p. 270.

8. McCormack, review of Ward, p. 101.

9. McCormack, *Karl Barth's Critically Realistic Dialectical Theology*, p. 22.

10. Karl Barth, *Die kirchliche Dogmatik*, vol. 2, *Die Lehre von Gott*, pt. 1 (Zurich:
Theologischer Verlag Zürich, 1940), p. 223; translated as *Church Dogmatics*, vol. 2,
The Doctrine of God, pt. 1, ed. G. W. Bromiley and T. F. Torrance, trans. T. H. L.
Parker, W. B. Johnston, Harold Knight, and J. L. M. Haire (Edinburgh: T. and
T. Clark, 1957), p. 199. Hereafter, I cite this text parenthetically in text as *CD*. The
first page number thereafter refers to the German original and the second to the
translation. I have freely altered the translation when appropriate, generally pre-
ferring to stay closer to the original German than is the practice in the published
translation. I have also restored Barth's emphasis by the use of italics to indicate
gesperrte Schrift in the original (Barth's frequent use of this typographic convention
is often an important clue to his meaning).

11. Geoffrey Bennington, "Derridabase," in Geoffrey Bennington and Jacques
Derrida, *Jacques Derrida*, trans. Geoffrey Bennington (Chicago: University of Chicago Press, 1993), pp. 24–25.

12. Hart, *Trespass of the Sign*, p. 5.

13. Derrida, *Positions*, trans. Alan Bass (Chicago: University of Chicago Press,
1981), p. 19.

14. Ibid., pp. 19–20.

15. George Hunsinger, *How to Read Karl Barth: The Shape of His Theology* (New York: Oxford University Press, 1991), p. 30.

16. My translation is deliberately more literal than ordinary English usage can bear; the published translation says that the analogy "comes into being," which is better English but obscures Barth's characteristic contrast between *sein* and *werden*. Eberhard Jüngel has captured this distinctive usage in the title of his book *Gottes Sein ist im Werden* (English translation: *The Doctrine of the Trinity: God's Being is in Becoming* [Grand Rapids, Mich.: Eerdmans, 1976]).

17. Karl Barth, *Die kirchliche Dogmatik,* vol. 1, pt. 2 (Zurich: Theologischer Verlag Zürich, n.d.), p. 356; cf. *Church Dogmatics,* vol. 1, pt. 2, ed. G. W. Bromiley and T. F. Torrance, trans. G. T. Thomson and Harold Knight (Edinburgh: T. and T. Clark, 1956), pp. 325–26. See Garrett Green, "Challenging the Religious Studies Canon: Karl Barth's Theory of Religion," in *The Journal of Religion* 75 (October 1995): 473–86.

18. Bennington, "Derridabase," in Bennington and Derrida, *Jacques Derrida,* pp. 75–76.

19. Derrida, "Différance," in *Margins of Philosophy,* trans. Alan Bass (Chicago: University of Chicago Press, 1982), p. 3. Derrida refers to his coinage as a "neographism" rather than a neologism because part of its point is to stress the priority of writing over speech (since the "difference" between *différence* and *différance* depends entirely on the written words, their pronunciations being identical). That's why, presumably, Bennington defines *différance* first of all as "a witticism of Derrida's" (Bennington and Derrida, *Jacques Derrida,* p. 70).

20. Derrida, "Différance," p. 9.

21. Ibid., 11.

22. Bennington and Derrida, *Jacques Derrida,* p. 75.

23. Ward, *Language of Theology,* p. 34.

24. McCormack, review of Ward. p. 101.

25. Barth, *Die kirchliche Dogmatik,* vol. 1, pt. 1 (Zurich: Theologischer Verlag Zürich, n.d.), p. 47. Ward takes his translation from *Church Dogmatics,* vol. 1, pt. 1, ed. G. W. Bromiley and T. F. Torrance, trans. G. W. Bromiley, rev. ed. (Edinburgh: T. and T. Clark, 1975), p. 47 (cited by Ward, *Language of Theology,* p. 244 n. 8).

26. Barth, *Die kirchliche Dogmatic.* vol. 1, pt. 1, p. 48 (in both German and English); my translation.

27. The use of "controlling" to translate *regierend* in the published translation lends a harshly authoritarian tone that is not present in Barth's diction. It is also theologically imprecise, since the God of Israel and the church *governs* the world in freedom rather than simply "controlling" it.

28. Ward, *Language of Theology,* p. 29.

29. See Green, "Challenging the Religious Studies Canon," p. 478, n. 11, for further references to the circular logic of theology in Barth.

30. McCormack, review of Ward, p. 106.

31. Ward, *Language of Theology,* p. 247 (my emphasis).

32. McCormack, review of Ward, p. 102.

33. Ward, *Language of Theology,* p. 248.

34. Ibid., 256.

35. Jean-Luc Marion sounds a similar note when he proposes to "cross out

God" (with the cross of Saint Andrew); Marion, *God without Being: Hors-Texte*, trans. Thomas A. Carlson (Chicago: University of Chicago Press, 1991), p. 46. The question I would like to ask Marion, however, is whether this "crossing out" is only a limitation forced upon us by our finitude or a manifestation of God's grace to be affirmed and celebrated. Like so many modern theologians, he sees the great danger to theology and faith in idolatry. For a discussion of the dangers of the iconoclastic bias in modern theology, see Garrett Green, *Imagining God: Theology and the Religious Imagination* (Grand Rapids, Mich.: Eerdmans), pp. 91–97.

6

The Bitterness of Cain

(Post)modernity's Flight from Determinacy

WALTER LOWE

This essay is offered as a critique of modernity, but a critique which aims to be internal and empathetic in character. To achieve this, it proceeds by way of a modern literary text. It seek to distance itself from certain assumptions which are commonly made by theological critiques of the modern; for it seems to me that the prospects for a postmodern Christian theology depend in considerable part on how such a theology handles the concept of *transcendence*. In a move which is perhaps unusual for a theologian, I shall decline to make the notion of transcendence or some experience of transcendence pivotal for theology. Rather, I shall treat the concept with reserve, linking it to what I call "determinacy" and arguing that for Christian theology, any concept of transcendence is found *in the determinate* and remains indissociably linked, not to say bound, to it. At stake is a classic issue: the irreducibility, for Christian theology, of the scandal of particularity.

The target of my criticism is a certain anti-intellectualism, specifically the longstanding penchant, shared by liberal and neo-orthodox theologians alike, and now by postmodernists as well, to allege that the human intellect is inherently an instrument of domination. The German term *"Begriff,"* which is allied to the word *"greifen,"* "to grasp," is commonly adduced as evidence that the mind always seeks to control.

A previous version of this essay appeared in *Literature and Theology* 12, no. 4 (1998): 379–389. It is reprinted with the permission of Oxford University Press.

Even apart from questions about what the speaker's own mind is doing in advancing this position, and apart from the reliance on a faculty psychology, there is the fact that such argument has the gnosticizing effect of conflating finitude and sin. Implicitly or explicitly, the mind—the mind as particular "faculty," not as *pars pro toto* representative of the person—is portrayed as inherently bent toward the demonic. Little wonder, then, if such theologies seek transcendence elsewhere, in experiences construed to be independent of, if not antithetical to, the mind.

The essay criticizes the postmodernism of theorists such as Mark C. Taylor, a postmodernism that tends to move along the lines indicated above. But it does so by making use of deconstruction and Derrida. I regard deconstruction as neither a new foundation for theology nor a gatekeeper controlling what theology can and cannot say; but I hope to show by way of a fairly rich example that it can be of use.

I. Modernity

My choice of text is affected by a conviction that modernity is too important to be left to the postmodernists. Modernity is too rich and fertile to be left to a prima facie postmodernism that would collapse modernity into the Enlightenment and the Enlightenment into the Newtonian worldview—all the while professing sensitivity to difference. By presuming to know in advance what modernity is and what the texts of modernity will say, a facile radicalism thinks to spare itself the labor of thought. But it does so at the cost of a deep and unacknowledged debt to that other face of modernity, romanticism. In choosing a text from the arch-romantic writer George Gordon, Lord Byron, I mean to stipulate that whatever claims to be postmodern must be "post-" the Byronic position. Byron's dramatic poem *Cain* is far from the traditional theism with which modernity is often identified; upon its publication in 1821, it was showered with abuse by traditionalists. The poem sets forth the modern brief against religion—the protest of the passionate critic rather than the skepticism of the cool critic—in a rhetorically potent and conceptually acute manner.[1]

When the text begins, the Fall has already happened. We are east of Eden, outside Paradise. The rising sun finds Adam, Eve, Abel, and Adam and Eve's two daughters, Adah and Zillah, at prayer. Their successive salutations to God, each ending in "all hail!", recall the traditional creation story. Thus the obeisant family bespeaks the orthodoxy of Byron's time. Cain, however, does not pray. He has nothing to ask of God and reckons that he has received nothing worthy of thanks. With this opening gesture, Cain asserts autonomy over against God and family alike. Adam presses him, "Dost thou not live?"; Cain counters, "Must I not die?" (1:27–28). Cain will give no thanks for his life because it does not come to him unalloyed; it admixes death. Cain's implicit desire is to overcome this mixed condition, to transcend the ambiguity, to extricate immortality. At the same time, however, the exchange by which the issue is introduced—"Dost thou not live?" "Must I not die?"—is not reassuring, for it presents the one as the obverse of the other.

Now Eve speaks:

> Alas!
> The fruit of our forbidden tree begins
> To fall.
> *Adam.*   And we must gather it again.
> Oh, God!   why didst thou plant the tree of knowledge?
> *Cain.*   And wherefore pluck'd ye not the tree of life?
> Ye might have then defied him. (1:29–34)

Eve's phrase "fruit of our forbidden tree" is used in an extended sense, as the consequences of the tree. Exile from the Garden was such a consequence; but Eve implies that Cain's rebellion is another. The prospect must weigh upon Adam, for he cries out in words which are presumably a pious lament but verge on a questioning of God: "Oh, God! why didst thou plant the tree of knowledge?" It is the very question Cain will reiterate as soon as he is alone, and in a tone of forthright challenge. For the moment, however, Cain's attention is seized by another matter, a regret quite different from that of his parents: "And wherefore pluck'd ye not the tree of life?" Cain's lament is not that his parents defied God but that they did not go all the way. The problem is not that they ate *but that they ate only in part.* Insofar as in him lies, Cain is determined not to repeat the mistake.

Adam would suppress the grievance, but Cain will have none of it. His response is a modern manifesto.

> Why not?
> The snake spoke *truth:* it *was* the tree of knowledge;
> It *was* the tree of life:—knowledge is good,
> And life is good; and how can both be evil? (1:35–38)

These are bold words, bolder perhaps than Cain's reflections the moment before about the co-implication of life with death should permit.

Implicitly, he is working with a distinction; his life is not (true) life
because it is punctuated by death. In this passage, Cain performs his
own act of punctuation. He judges; he cuts through any ambiguity—
life, knowledge are unequivocally good. And the cutting is to a purpose; for if life and knowledge are unambiguously good, then Cain has
grounds for an indictment of God. God would have denied, prohibited,
or at the very least constrained the human good.

Cain's family departs. Alone, he broodingly returns to the sense of a
life which is no life. "And this is / Life!—Toil!" (1:64–65). Cain protests
God's sentence: "and wherefore should I toil? . . . What had *I* done in
this?—I was unborn" (1:65, 67). The emphatic "*I*" is of course significant, the voice of modern autonomy. His protest intensifies what has
been in process since Cain's first words, a differentiating of himself over
against family, especially father, and of course the father's God. Cain
differentiates himself (over against God and family) by opposing God's
delimitation of the human, unleashing an adversarial dialectic of unpredictable consequence.

Now Cain turns full attention to the sensitive topic his father only
brushed against. Pressing beyond, behind, or before the issue of Adam's
sin, Cain, the voice of modernity, asks the logically prior question of
why a tree potentially so disastrous was set in Eden at all, and why so
fair? why placed at the center?

> What was there in this?
> The tree was planted, and why not for him?
> If not, why place him near it, where it grew,
> The fairest in the centre? They have but
> One answer to all questions, "'twas *his* will,
> And *he* is good.' How know I that? Because
> He is all-powerful must all-good, too, follow?
> I judge but by the fruits—and they are bitter—" (1:74–78)[2]

Before I comment on this passage, let me summarize a few of the
points which seem secure so far. First, we are dealing with interdiction
and individuation. Second, Cain is probing back behind Adam's act to
God's antecedent act. And third, Cain contends that his father's real
offense was that, once started, he failed to go all the way. I mark these
results of my thus far conventional reading because I am about to shift
into a literary–critical hyperspace and will need to recognize home
base when I eventually regain it.

For with the line "I judge but by the fruits—and they are bitter—",
the text sets in our lap a gift which is more than any aspiring decon-

structionist can resist. Note that Cain is asserting a right to judge for himself. Thereby he not only questions God's judgment, he indicts the Judge. He reverses the roles of judge and judged. And on what basis would he accomplish so radical a reversal? He judges "by the fruits." But he does so in a setting in which it is impossible to juxtapose fruit and judgment without recalling that other fruit already spoken of, "the fruit of our forbidden tree" (1:30), the fruit which Adam bit, incurring judgment.[3] But having linked judgment–fruit–fruit–judgment by conventional literary practices, one can hardly ignore another connection, also generated within the same line—namely, that where the one fruit was *bitten,* the other is *bitter.* About this mere "bit," language and logic intertwine.

Let me say at the outset that I do not propose to make any of my arguments solely on the basis of such lexical connections. In other words, I want to assure you, if I can, that I'm not just trying to be cute. But I do intend to follow these bits of language decomposed, to see how much of our composition they compost or cover.[4] So far, just playing by ear, we have linked "bitten" and "to bite" to "bitter." Etymology encourages that linkage; "bitter" would seem to have roots in the Old English "bitan," which C. T. Onions, in *The Oxford Dictionary of English Etymology,* specifically glosses as " '*cutting*', 'biting,' whence 'cruel', 'harsh', 'violent.' "[5] In the present context of judging the Judge, the shadow of "cruel" and "violent" can hardly be ignored. For not only does it link the bite of the father to the bitterness of the son; it goes to the specific moral judgment which Cain makes on a state of things which he increasingly regards as the fruit of God's own action.

The traditional response to such charges is to say that if circumstances are bitter or biting now, it is because Adam bit first. Ah, but did he? A few lines earlier in the poem, Cain began to question whether the "original sin" was indeed original by asking why the tree was placed so enticingly. In a recognizably gnostic manner, he was tracing the evil back before Adam and Eve. But if this is so, then we have to say that Cain's explicit reasoning stands in the closest relation to the behavior of the linguistic fragment itself. For "bit," which led from "bitter" back to "bite," itself leads further back. One common sense of "bite" is to bite as a fish does, "to take or be caught by any bait";[6] conversely, "to bait" may be *"to cause to bite."*[7] Lexical association itself seems to ask, was Adam baited?

And there is more. The Oxford English Dictionary notes an obsolete slang usage of the substantive. A "bite" may be "an imposition, a deception; what is now called a 'sell,' "[8] as in the expression, "to put the bite on" someone. (A venerable pun calls a bishop a "bite-sheep,"[9] one

who fleeces the flock.) Did someone put the bite on Adam? The traditional answer is of course the serpent; and nicely enough, "to bite" may
be "to sting as a serpent."[10] But before the serpent's question was that
which the serpent questioned—namely, *God's bidding.* God had bid, yet
Adam bit: there we have original sin in a nutshell. But how close together they lie, the "bid" and "bit."[11] Those attuned to such resonances
might well have a sense of foreboding about God's forbidding.

Could it be the forbidding was a fore-biting, and that Cain, in his
back-biting, is only biting back? This is the question the lexical network
poses—but does not resolve. We have here an instance of what Derrida
calls "undecidability," a crucial term to which we shall return. Was
God's commanding itself a temptation, his bidding itself a baiting? In
such a case, one would be compelled to say that God's bidding was bad.
Adam's "sin" would not be original. However bad Adam had been, God
would have been bad before—when God forbad.

II. Determinacy

So it is that on the one side as on the other, recto and verso, the poem
performs the gnostic gesture of pressing back before the presump-
tive *Arche.* But what lies beyond the arche? What is the gnosis Cain
achieves when he chooses Lucifer over the Adah, who is both sister
and wife, and thus, according to Lucifer, prefers knowledge to love?
The answer, which constitutes the entirety of Act 2, is an endless expanse of space and time—an expanse which ultimately exceeds Cain's
comprehension. *And there is the rub.* For Cain wishes to comprehend.
At the end of his journey, he is still restless, unsatiated; he wishes to
know the origin of God (the true God beyond the god he knew), and
of Lucifer. To which his guide replies:

> Thy human mind hath scarcely grasp to gather
> The little I have shown thee into calm
> And clear thought; and *thou* wouldst go on aspiring
> To the great double Mysteries! the *two Principles!*
> And gaze upon them on their secret thrones!
> Dust!   limit thy ambition;   for to see
> Either of these, would be for thee to perish! (2:2.401–7)

Cain exclaims in true romantic fashion, "And let me perish, so I see
them!" One could hardly ask for a more explicit expression of the desire
for pure Presence. But Lucifer knows the consequence—"There / The

son of her who snatch'd the apple spake! / But thou would only perish, and not see them" (2:2.408–10).

This discontent with the very limits of comprehension goes beyond the brief against God's bidding, and so we do well to address it first. We have already observed that the German *Begriff* links "to know" with "to grasp." And since the fruit was of the tree of knowing, it is hardly a leap to link "to grasp" with "to bite." Cain's grievance against his father, we may recall, was that having taken a bite, he did not take all, the fruit of the other tree as well. But now—and this is crucial—*Cain finds his own grasp is limited*, and that fact is maddening to him. Again, his life seems no life; the affirmer of life longs for Presence and death.[12] A person in this posture is apt to experience any bidding as a binding; but that would be for want of coming to terms with another "bind" which is surely inescapable, namely the fact that human comprehension is finite, that indeed it *proceeds by* finitude. Human understanding goes by way of *determinacy*. When we bite, we mortals get only a bit.

It is often said of modernity and of the Western tradition generally that it seeks to grasp and control. In fact, such a charge would seem an ingredient to the postmodern turn. For postmodernism attests to the collapse of (Western) ontotheology, to use Heidegger's term, or logocentrism, to use Derrida's. Postmodernists argue that for all its declarations of independence, the modern worldview exemplified by Newtonian science shares with traditional theology the conviction that reality could be captured by fixed concepts, that history could be assigned an *Arche* and a *Telos*, and that human reason could trace timeless verities, as if such verities were inscribed in a celestial book. In our time, that phantasm, which had once seemed to be reality, has come to grief. Postmodernism, for its part, professes to lie beyond both the fantasy and the grieving. It accepts and celebrates the free play of the signifier, the endless flux of surface and image, a life of bricolage.

Such is the argument of a certain postmodernism.[13] Now let us see whether this characterization corresponds to what one finds in Derrida. Logocentrism, as Derrida describes it, is the prioritization of speech over writing, the elevation of speech as "living" over writing as "dead."[14] It is perhaps significant that "to bite" is used in engraving; it is "to eat out the lines of an etching on metal with an acid."[15] Logocentrism may be said to eschew this bite, to be the elevation of speech-as-freedom over writing-as-determinacy. In short, logocentrism exhibits itself as a *disdain for determinacy*.

Like all bad faith, logocentrism's is twofold. It obscures the extent to which it is itself dependent upon the operations of determinacy (cf. structure) while simultaneously exaggerating the extent to which the other is wedded to the determinate. The great merit of Hegel is to have called the romantics on this: "Just as there is an empty breadth [cf. the Enlightenment], so too there is an empty depth."[16] The rational capacity Kant delineated as *Verstand*, Understanding, which is precisely the capacity to punctuate, to delineate, to cut, is deserving of the highest respect. It is a poor, empty, short-circuited sort of knowledge that would shirk the labor of Understanding by appeal to immediacy, some intellectual intuition.

It was a favorite gesture of the romantics to lump religious tradition and scientific analysis together as being simply alternative forms of literalism, the dead hand of scholasticism upon the human spirit. William Blake immortalized this move in the figure of Urizen, the brooding god who metes out creation with a draftsman's tool. One lumps traditional religion and modernity–Enlightenment together as both being literalist—cf. writing—and confined to knowledge-by-bits; and one does so in order to define oneself over against all that, to dissociate and free oneself from it, to sever the chains of association. That is the romantic gesture. Hegel critiques it; but then when it comes time for Hegel to confront his own "anxiety of influence" vis-à-vis Kant, the Kant whose *Verstand* Hegel praised, Hegel repeats the gesture himself. He asserts that Kant's position is ultimately no more than a philosophy of the Understanding, not finally a philosophy of Reason. In his effort to distinguish himself, Hegel would have us believe that Kant was somehow able to delineate the faculty of Understanding, more or less exhaustively, without having any transcendence of it.

Earlier, I spoke of a "prima facie postmodernism" which would confine modernity to the Enlightenment and the Enlightenment itself to "the worldview of Newtonian science." We can appreciate now that this diminishment of one's interlocutor was no happenstance. Postmodernism of this stripe survives by denial, by obscuring its own profound links to modernity, its repetition of the romantic gesture. But if this is true of a certain kind of postmodernism, what is one to say of the postmodernism sketched a moment ago which so stresses the free play of the signifier? Derrida's own response is found in the valuable "Afterword" to *Limited Inc.*

I never proposed "a kind of 'all or nothing' choice between pure realization of self-presence and complete freeplay or undecidability." I never believed in this and I never spoke of "complete freeplay or undecidability." . . . There can be no "completeness" where freeplay is concerned. Greatly overestimated in my texts in the United States, this notion of "freeplay" is an inadequate translation of the lexical network connected to the word *jeu*, which I used in my first texts, but sparingly and in a highly defined manner. Above all, no completeness is possible for undecidability.[17]

"No completeness is possible for undecidability." We might almost say that undecidability is determinate. Better would be to say that undecidability *consists of* determinacy. Better still, undecidability consists of *over*determinacy (cf. the multiple meanings of a dream) and that it is overdeterminacy (such as that of the lexical network "bit") which makes it undecidable.

To which it must immediately be added that undecidability is not the negation of decision; far from it. For the particular undecidability of which Derrida speaks

> opens the field of decision or of decidability. It calls for decision in the order of ethical-political responsibility. It is even its necessary condition. A decision can only come into being in a space that exceeds the calculable program that would destroy all responsibility by transforming it into a programmable effect of determinate causes. There can be no moral or political responsibility without this trial and this passage by way of the undecidable. Even if a decision seems to take only a second and not to be preceded by any deliberation, it is structured by this *experience and experiment of the undecidable.*[18]

To begin to parse this passage one must work with a three-part distinction. First, there is the notion of a predetermined decision made according to some "calculable program." This effort to transfer decision from moral act to (pre)determinate effect would "destroy all responsibility." The existentialists would have called it bad faith, a flight from freedom. From a somewhat different perspective, the Frankfurt School speaks of the desire for "ready-made Enlightenment," insight on the cheap. In Kantian terms, the ineluctable role of *judgment* cannot be reduced to a function of the understanding. Second, there is the (over)determinacy of the undecidable by which any decision, even the most spontaneous, "is structured." Derrida insists upon the necessary "trial" and "passage by way of" the determinacy, the being-structured-by the undecidable. In so insisting, he recalls Hegel's salutary dictum that any notion of the infinite must pass by way of, must endure the trial of, the finite or determinate. Finally, there is the determinacy effected by the decision itself. "Decision" is of the family of "incision." It cuts through, or at least into, the ambiguity; it construes and effects an either/or, a "this," not "that," for which it is then responsible. Thus ethics has its own form of the scandal of particularity, for to make so much of one particular may seem quixotic, susceptible to derision. But that, as Paul Goodman observed in the context of war resistance, is the necessary concomitant of "drawing the line."[19]

This three-part distinction may serve as a brief indication of what is lost when an over-hasty postmodernism identifies undecidability with indeterminacy and presumes to know, as if by a predetermined program, what tradition and modernity have to say.

The "bit" is "the part of a key . . . which grips the levers of the lock."[20] In seeking a key to the foregoing discussion, let us consult the lexical tea leaves one more time. "Bite" may be traced back to the Sanskrit, "to cleave, split."[21] Joining "bite" and "bitter" is the fragment "bi," the figure of division. And that does provide a key. For Cain is a paradigm of what Hegel called the unhappy consciousness, the self divided within itself. Now modern theology, the theology of modernity, has been concerned to sell itself; and so it has offered itself as an antidote—an antidote for division. First, as an antidote for sin, division from God; but then the culture disavowed the burdensome notion of sin. Another malaise had to be found, and if not found, then created. For inevitably the antidote participated of the poison: awareness of sin had to be heightened before it was addressed. And when it no longer seemed persuasive that we were exiled from Eden, there was still the fact that we were not in it. There was still the unhappy consciousness to be rendered more acute, so that promises of wholeness might appeal. Repudiation of such double dealing is, I take it, the vital nerve of Nietzsche's brief against the Christianity he knew, and it remains compelling.

It is in this context that I would argue that contemporary Christian theology must be very cautious about making any direct appeal to such notions as the experience of transcendence. It seems to me crucial that theology ceases to identify itself with the romantic gesture, that it renounce its dialectical dependence on the unhappy consciousness— in sum, that it stop encouraging disdain for determinacy. The all-pervasive contemporary search for some experience of transcendence, some way out of the iron cage of modernity, has its own logic and necessity which are by all means to be respected. But Christian theology, insofar as it is an incarnational theology, or even a theology of the Incarnation, has a calling to stand by determinacy, the concreteness of the creation.

In classic theological language, what's biting Cain is finitude. Toward the God who had the temerity to create him finite he bears an attitude of "*ressentiment.*" Here, the lexical associations of "bit" have assisted us in thinking finitude concretely. More importantly, they have assisted us in thinking finitude without using the word, which inevitably evokes the metaphysical pairing/opposing of "finite" and "infinite," "finite" versus "infinite." I take this to be indicative of the real theological promise of deconstruction. What deconstruction gives us is a way of thinking finitude without extrinsic bracketing, without presuming a metaphysical wall (which Lucifer would have every right to challenge). The gift of deconstruction is that it enables us to think finitude from the center, or, if the notion of "center" is too metaphysical, to think finitude from within.

I believe that a rethinking of finitude is the necessary passageway forward for a Christian theology too often rendered toothless, unfit for incision or decision, by *its own* unhappy consciousness, that is, by discomfort with its own determinacy; which is indeed a determinacy not just of incarnation, but of *the* Incarnation, the necessary scandal of particularity.[22]

Notes

1. For the full text and a series of valuable essays, see Truman Guy Steffan, ed., *Lord Byron's "Cain": Twelve Essays and a Text with Variants and Annotations* (Austin: University of Texas Press, 1968). See also Paul Cantor, *Creature and Creator: Myth-Making and English Romanticism* (Cambridge: Cambridge University Press, 1984), pp. 135–55. I am indebted to Cantor's book for drawing my attention to the romantic creation myth as a genre.

2. Compare, of course, Matt. 7:16, "You will know them by their fruits."

3. For simplicity's sake, I follow Cain's practice of stressing Adam's act over Eve's. On the symbolism of tree and fruit in *Cain*, cf. Steffan, *Lord Byron's "Cain,"* pp. 77–79.

4. My intention is to be equally as serious about the lexical chains as about the manifest, logical meaning, neither more nor less. This, I take it, is Derrida's practice as well. The warrant for this approach is ultimately one of fruitfulness: it is my impression that the effort to plumb modernity's quarrel with Christianity may learn as well from the one angle as from the other (cf. Freud), and most from the interaction of the two.

See Rodolphe Gasché's brilliant treatment of equiprimordiality and infrastructures in *The Tain of the Mirror: Derrida and the Philosophy of Reflection* (Cambridge: Harvard University Press, 1986), pp. 179–85. "Each infrastructure partakes in a chain or in several chains, but which it never dominates." Examples are *"marge/ marque/marche,* or reserve/remark/*retrait/resistance/retard"* (p. 184). "The system of the infrastructures cannot be formalized, idealized, or systematized because it is precisely its play that makes those projects possible" (p. 185).

5. *The Oxford Dictionary of English Etymology,* ed. C. T. Onions (London: Oxford University Press, 1966), p. 97; cf. Eric Partridge, *Origins: A Short Etymological Dictionary of Modern English* (New York: Greenwich House, 1958) and *The Compact Edition of the Oxford English Dictionary* (Glasgow: Oxford University Press, 1971), 1:885.1. Though I have worked with the *Compact Edition,* my references are to the

original Oxford English Dictionary, hereafter cited as *OED*, citing volume, page, and column.

Some of the lexical chains I will be tracing, e.g., "bitten" and "bitter," go by way of etymology; but others, e.g., "bit" and "bid," do not. By refusing to discount the latter as "illegitimate," I hope to counter the assumption that a putative etymological "origin" is somehow normative.

6. *OED*, 1:883.1.

7. For example, "to incite a dog to bite," Partridge, *Origins*, p. 36.

8. *OED*, 1:884.1.

9. *OED*, 1:884.2.

10. *OED*, 1:883.1, "To 'sting' as a serpent, or an insect that sucks blood."

11. The terms link resonantly in the opening monologue of Peter Shaffer's play *Equus* (London: Penguin, 1973): "I can't jump because the bit forbids it." Compare the closing line of the play: "There is now, in my mouth, this sharp chain. And it never comes out" (pp. 18, 109). The bit that controls domestic animals links to Cain's disdain for his family's docile obedience, which he regards as a sort of slave morality.

12. Steffan observes that Cain regarded the marvels exhibited in Act 2 as being "beyond his faculties, but still inferior to his desires and conceptions" (*Lord Byron's "Cain,"* p. 37). In a prouder moment, the emphasis fell upon the second clause; now it settles upon the first.

13. See particularly Mark C. Taylor, *Erring: A Postmodern A/theology* (Chicago: University of Chicago Press, 1984). For a fuller treatment of Taylor and related issues, see Walter Lowe, *Theology and Difference: The Wound of Reason* (Bloomington: Indiana University Press, 1993), pp. 127–45. Compare the response to Taylor in Rodolphe Gasché, *Inventions of Difference* (Cambridge: Harvard University Press, 1994), pp. 12–16.

14. See Jacques Derrida, *Of Grammatology*, trans. Gayatri Chakravorty Spivak (Baltimore: Johns Hopkins University Press, 1974), pp. 3, 6–26.

15. *OED*, 1:883.2.

16. G. W. F. Hegel, *Phenomenology of Spirit*, trans. A. V. Miller (Oxford: Clarendon Press, 1977), p. 6.

17. Jacques Derrida, *Limited Inc.* (Evanston: Northwestern University Press, 1988), p. 115.

18. Ibid., 116.

19. Paul Goodman, *Drawing the Line* (1946; reprint, New York: Random House, 1962). On all three points, cf. Rowan Williams' exposition of the thought of Gillian Rose: "Thinking is afraid to begin; or rather, it looks for a beginning that is not a risk, a beginning that already contains or controls its goal. It is therefore constantly in flight from the recognition of the 'already' that locates all our putative beginnings in an unsought and uncontrolled middle. The only honest beginning is with difficulty; that is to say, we cannot 'start thinking', but 'begin' only with the acknowledgment that what we say is already put in question, already involved in the fertile error or misperception that Hegel and Kierkegaard alike identify as, in the most intricate sense, natural to thinking" (Williams, "Between Politics and Metaphysics: Reflections in the Wake of Gillian Rose," *Modern Theology* 11, no. 1 [January 1995]: 11).

20. *OED,* 1:881.2.
21. *OED,* 1:882.3.
22. These reflections on finitude may be extended by reference to the treatment of the *coram Deo* and the reinterpretation of Karl Barth in Lowe, *Theology and Difference,* pp. 98–101, 136–45.

7

Sketch of a Phenomenological Concept of Gift

JEAN-LUC MARION

I. Revelation and Gift

It is not astonishing that, when we deal with the philosophy of religion, the question of "gift" comes to the forefront. Without doubt, the two issues are formally distinct and there is nothing to be gained by confusing them. Nevertheless, two lines of analysis provide essential links between them.

The first link derives from revelation itself. It is opposed to the phenomenon of common law, whose poverty in intuition—even its limitation in meaning—permits objective knowledge, production, prediction, and reproduction. The phenomenon of revelation—if it exists—is characterized by its excess of intuition, which saturates all meaning and which, because of this saturation, provokes an event, the unpredictability of which escapes all production or reproduction. This phenomenon thus takes on the status of a gift, appearing to emerge out of itself, free and sudden. Therefore, the phenomenon of revelation reveals itself from itself and appears in the mode of that which gives itself. In a word, the revelation only appears as a gift.[1]

The second link between revelation and gift derives directly from phenomenology. In effect, at least from the "principle of principles,"

Translated by John Conley, S. J., and Danielle Poe. The French original appeared as "Esquisse d'un concept phénoménologique du don," in *Archivo di Filosofia* 62, no. 1–3 (1994): 75–94. It is reprinted with permission.

phenomenology thinks through all phenomenality from the starting point of the "giving" intuition: in order to appear, a phenomenon must be able to give itself. The radicality of this demand, moreover, goes beyond the intuition alone, since Husserl argues for the extension of givenness to certain meanings and essences, right up to considering the constitution of objects as a givenness of meanings (*Sinngebung*). Givenness, therefore, does not limit itself to the very restricted case of the phenomena of revelation but defines in a universal way all phenomenality.[2] Therefore, rather than reflection abandoning revelation when it considers the gift, it is, on the contrary, possible that revelation so traces the only possible path toward it: givenness as the first level of all phenomenality, the gift as the final trait of every phenomenon revealing itself. But if, in order to accede to a concept of revelation, one must pass by the gift, one must have access to the concept of gift itself. The question which now becomes central is, "Do we have an appropriate, if not exact, concept of gift?"

II. The Economy of the Gift

The gift could be understood in a strict metaphysical sense—as a particular case of causal relation. The giver, under the title of active efficient cause, would then produce the gift, considered as an effect, for the benefit of the passive gift-recipient. Breaking with the schema is not easy, despite appearances, for a simple reason: the criticism itself can easily remain limited to the ground of metaphysics. In effect, the recourse—habitual, in this context—to the gratuity of the gift risks only modifying the framework of efficiency, without in any way suppressing or even budging it: to produce "for nothing" remains, all the same, "to produce." It is still tied to efficiency. Moreover, gratuitous efficiency makes it even more obvious. The question which truly impresses itself, therefore, is, "Can one accede to a concept of gift or does an essential aporia affect it?"

Because he has not feared to attack this last question, Jacques Derrida has been able recently to define what we would call the paradox of the gift. Following a convincing analysis, Derrida penetrates, in effect, the aporia of the gift and also of the act of givenness. We will follow this analysis, both because of its own merits and, perhaps, in order to find there the means to establish the paradox, even beyond criticism. Derrida begins by setting forth the whole conceptual chain of givenness, of which "all the anthropologies, indeed the metaphysics" make a "system." From the metaphysical point of view—from which

it is clearly a question of "departing in a peremptory and distinct fashion"³—the givenness articulates itself into a giver, a gift given, and a
gift-recipient which are tied together, in principle, by a link of reciprocity, since the gratuity on the part of the giver claims, although
tacitly, some restitution on the part of the recipient. This schema,
which dominates all the anthropologies of the gift (and, first of all, that
of Mauss) remains, let us underline it more than does Derrida, entirely
metaphysical: the giver gives the gift as an efficient cause, uses a formal
cause and a material cause (what the gift is like), following a final cause
(the good of the recipient and/or the glory of the giver). These four
causes permit the givenness to satisfy the principle of sufficient reason.
The reciprocity repeats this sufficient reason right up to the perfect
application of the principle of identity in bringing the gift back to itself.
It is also by reference to this model that one can measure all the apparently extreme or aberrant forms of givenness, which never put anything into question. Thinking through givenness always returns to
thinking about the system of exchange that rules, through these terms
of causality and the principles of metaphysics. Now, as Derrida firmly
demonstrates, this model not only enters into self-contradiction with
each of its elements, but it manages to make all of givenness disappear.
The very phenomenon of givenness collapses before our eyes.

The first argument is as follows: "For there to be a gift, there must
be no reciprocity."⁴ It should have seemed absolutely evident that the
gift—let us say more exactly, the givenness—disappears as soon as
reciprocity transforms it into a system of exchange. The fact that this
exchange repeats the givenness implicitly (and not explicitly, as in
commerce) changes nothing. To offer something (an invitation, a service, etc.) remains to offer, and thus to enter into an economy: the
counter-gift follows the gift, the payment the debt, the reimbursement
the loan. As soon as the economy absorbs the gift, it turns givenness
into the economy. By annexing givenness, the economy dispenses with
it. In its place, it immediately substitutes calculation, interest, utility,
measure, etc. No moral consideration must interfere here with a pure
difference between the regimes of different phenomena: if there is
givenness, it must break completely with the principle of sufficient reason, that of identity and of the quadriform causality, which the economy follows in its metaphysical regime.

The second argument follows immediately: "For there to be a gift, *it
is necessary* [*il faut*] that the donee does not give back, amortize, reim-
burse, acquit himself, enter into a contract, and that he never have con-
tracted a debt."⁵ This refusal must not be understood as simply a subjective ingratitude—ingratitude which intervenes precisely only in the
midst of an economy of exchange and reciprocity—but rather as the
"non-consciousness" of the recipient, who neither sees nor knows that

a gift comes to him. The recipient benefits from a gift—pure gratuity—only if he does not immediately interpret it as a gift that has to be returned, a debt to be reimbursed as soon as possible. Moreover, an authentic gift may exceed any knowledge about it by its recipient, thus dispensing him from recognition from what he does not know. In many cases, the most significant ones in fact, the gift remains unknown. Such are the life given (and perhaps also the death) and love (sometimes hatred). The slogan, "If you knew the gift of God" may here serve as a paradigm (but not theological here) for every phenomenology of givenness: the recipient does not know and does not have to know which gift comes to him, precisely because a gift can and must surpass all clear consciousness. The unconsciousness of the gift—that is, the bracketing of the recipient in the givenness—has, moreover, at least two irreplaceable functions: to permit the recipient to support its excess—because a gift scarcely known remains perfectly given—and to permit the gift not to depend on the recipient—because a mishandled gift remains a perfectly given gift. The givenness supposes, therefore, the *epokke* of the recipient.

The third argument may be stated thus: "Forgetting [of the gift] must be radical not only on the part of the donee, but first of all [. . .] on the part of the donor." The disappearance of the recipient implies reciprocally that of the giver. In effect, the simple awareness of giving awakens the consciousness of one's self as giving, thus "the gratifying image of goodness or of generosity, of the giving-being who, knowing itself to be such, recognizes itself in a circular, specular fashion, in a sort of auto-recognition, self-approval, and narcissistic gratitude."[6] The best illustration of this narcissistic return on oneself, the giver, is taken from Descartes. The *Passions of the Soul* demonstrated—in a sense which considers itself absolutely positive—that generosity, considered as self-esteem and as a good use of one's free will, not only provoked the first passion of self-contentment but repeated in the ethical order the self-certitude achieved by the *ego cogito* in the metaphysical order.[7] To consider oneself as gift-giver, *a fortiori* as the poorly known giver by the recipient, is sufficient to produce a self-consciousness and thus to reestablish an economic exchange: in exchange for my poorly known gift, I receive—from myself?—the certain consciousness of my generosity. In losing my gift, I give it to myself, or rather, I re-find myself in exchange for my lost gift. Loss becomes gain par excellence—the best business possible, because I gain from it infinitely more than I lose: my very self against a simple gift which was worth less than I. The givenness, therefore, only becomes thinkable if one succeeds in liberating it from the metaphysical thesis par excellence: the preeminence in it (and on the gift) of the ego, the transcendental and constituent "I." The obstacle in arriving at a givenness free of itself is not tied to some theological excess but to a foundation much more certain, absolutely known, and supremely solid—the *inconsussum quid* which Descartes inaugurated in metaphysics and which still guides us. As long as the ego remains, the givenness stops. It only appears once the ego is bracketed.

After reciprocity, the final implication of the framework of giver, recipient, and givenness is the immobilization of the gift given. This paradox can support itself if one returns to the reason of the displacement of the giver and the recipient: this results from the gift, which, by immobilizing itself in exchange, freezes the economy and, therefore, makes the giver and the recipient appear to be the agents of the gift. Thus, "the subject and object are arrested effects of the gift."[8] The economic interpretation of givenness as a system of exchange, such as the agents froze it, rests upon the perspective that the agents place upon the gift, which is seen as an object of exchange. Therefore, it is the apparition of the gift, reifying givenness in its objectivity, which provokes the system of exchange and which forbids givenness as such. The consequence immediately arises: *"At the limit, the gift as gift* ought *not appear as gift: either to the donee or to the donor."*[9] The apparition, the entrance of the gift in objective phenomenality, thus prepares it for economic exchange and, logically, removes it from givenness. Derrida recovers "the phenomenology of the inapparent," without any theological turn, simply by criticizing the supposed evidence of the gift. It is "supposed" because it is in fact taken into the system of economic exchange. The non-apparition of the gift, however, does not imply any renunciation of phenomenology. First, because if it appeared—and most of the time it appears quite massively—then it would be necessary to renounce the phenomenology of givenness, which nevertheless one seeks: if the gift does not appear, it is so that the givenness as such may appear. Next, the non-apparition of the gift does not imply a renunciation of phenomenology because the reason for such an inappearance remains phenomenological: if the gift becomes a phenomenon of economic exchange, it freezes itself in its presence, in the most metaphysical sense. "If he [the donee] recognizes it *as* gift, if the gift *appears to him as such,* if the present is present to him *as present,* this simple recognition suffices to annul the gift."[10]

That which forbids the gift to remain within givenness by reconducting it to the rank of an object of exchange, only consists—this is the right word—in presence, understood to be the preeminent subsistence in oneself of beingness. If presence undoes the present (the gift in givenness), it is then necessary, in order to accede to the present, to remove it from this presence. This perfect paradox definitely echoes the fourth argument: "if the present is present to him *as present,* this simple recognition suffices to annul the gift." Similarly, "It cannot be gift as gift except by not being present as gift." Or, "If it presents itself, it no longer presents itself."[11] This is a disturbing result. One must leave the path toward givenness in suppressing access to the gift by a double impossibility: either the gift presents itself in presence and it disappears from givenness in order to embed itself in the economic system of exchange or the gift does not present itself and no longer appears, thus closing all phenomenality of givenness.

III. The "Truth of the Gift"

Still, this is not perhaps the obligatory result of this fourth argument (even if that appears to be Derrida's conclusion), but only one of the possible readings left open by its paradox. Does the incompatibility between the gift thought as such, according to givenness, and the presence as permanence in subsistence mean that the gift cannot absolutely think itself and appear or does it mean that it can only do so outside the horizon (deeply metaphysical) of presence? If appearance implies fixation in one's substance, then obviously the gift, as soon as it appears in its presence, disappears as the gift given; that is, it is lost and never offered for the giver, never possessed, and always only conceded to the recipient. But it loses itself in this way: it loses a manner of being—subsistence, exchange, economy—which contradicts its very possibility to give itself. In losing presence, the gift does not lose *itself* but loses that which neither conforms to it nor returns to it. Or rather, it *loses* itself—in the sense in which it finally disconnects from self, abandons itself outside of self—outside of *self*—in order to fulfill its loss, fulfill itself as loss, but not in pure loss. Or rather, exactly as in pure loss, as a *pure* loss which, in order to give itself, it must in effect disappear, it thus appears at the price of pure disappearance in it of all subsistence. This reversal can be explained in another way: if the gift is not present, so that it can never appear in and as presence, one may obviously conclude that it is not or that it does not *have* to be and "to be" according to presence in order to give itself. The gift gives itself precisely to the strict degree to which it renounces to be, excerpted from presence, undone from itself by undoing the subsistence in it. The paradox of Derrida—the present cannot be present in the presence—may thus yield another paradox—*the present gives itself without its presence.* If one paradox hides another, this is related to the very ambiguity of the other name of gift: present. To make a present is not the equivalent, by definition (not always, not even nearly always), of producing a *present.* The *parousia* obviously regulates the *presence* but does not control the *present.* The present owes nothing to the presence, or, at least, can very well owe nothing to it. The question of givenness is not closed when the presence contradicts the gift; on the contrary, it opens to the possibility of the present without presence—outside of being.

The remarkable fecundity of Derrida's analysis is manifest not only by its explicit result but also by the counter-interpretation which it supports and even urges. With an exceptional rigor, it leads to an enigmatic formula, which we will use here as a paradigm: "Let us go to the limit: The truth of the gift [. . .] suffices to annul the gift. The truth of the gift is equivalent to the non-gift or to the non-truth of the gift."[12] How should we understand this game of negations? In arguing formally, we could distinguish here two senses: (1) if *or* has a conjunctive value, one has "non-gift" equals "non-truth"; therefore, as the negations annul each other, "gift" equals "truth"; (2) if *or* has a disjunctive value, one has "non-truth," or "non-gift"; therefore, as the negations annul each other, we will have "either gift or truth." Thus, we can understand the formula either as the equivalence between gift and truth or as the reciprocal exclusion of the two.

If it is necessary to choose, Derrida would probably support the second interpretation. I do not prefer the first, although it is possible, because the point resides in the very ambiguity of the formula, namely that truth is equivalent to gift but also contradicts it. That it contradicts the gift is not surprising: Derrida has demonstrated that the emergence in presence abolishes the gift as such. More astonishing, on the contrary, is the possibility that truth is proper to gift. The most elegant solution would ask, in such a case, that one distinguish between the two accepted meanings of gift, one equivalent to and the other the contrary of truth. Despite its artificiality, let's borrow this last path. From Derrida's viewpoint, does such a distinction have any meaning? Up until now the answer has been "no," because the gift, in its truth, always disappears. However, this thesis is not his last word: he clearly envisages (although at the level of a simple suggestion) that the gift is doubled: "There would be, *on the one hand,* the gift that gives something determinate (a given, a present in whatever form it may be . . .); and, *on the other hand,* the gift that gives not a given but the *condition* of a present given in general, that gives therefore the element of the given in general." The first accepted meaning corresponds exactly to the gift whose presence annuls its status as present, the gift taken into the system of exchange and economy. We need not return to this. The second accepted meaning remains: it introduces nothing less than a gift which gives, a gift elevated in power, a gift beyond gift. But, since this strange gift gives nothing (nothing real, not a thing), it frees itself in order to give the condition of the given, "the *condition* of any given in general."[13] It works itself, for example, into the case of "giving time," "giving life," "giving death," etc. In any case, this advance is not sufficient for our purpose. First, it is not sufficient because it recognizes that the new gift gives at least one "condition"; now any condition whatsoever and as such remains a typical metaphysical function, that of foundation. Moreover, here we have the foundation of a "present in general," which we may suspect is in presence, even identified with it. Next, this advance is not sufficient because the modification of the object of the gift (from "given" to the "condition of given") neither permits the passage of the gift to givenness as such nor frees givenness from the economic model of exchange. Finally, it is not sufficient because the doubling of a concept rarely indicates that we have deepened it. Very often, we simply juxtapose the elements of a contradiction in order to soften it. Still, such a doubling of gift might place us upon the path of givenness.

The two interpretations of the formula, "the truth of the gift is equivalent to the non-gift or to the non-truth of the gift" as well as the two accepted meanings of gift (giving a given or a condition) present a border, whose crossing would lead to an entirely different determination of the gift than that pushed to contradiction by Derrida himself. If the gift as such, as present, disappears as soon as it enters into presence; if presence defines the manner of being of the substance in itself, such as metaphysics has privileged it; if truth, taken in its unique metaphysical meaning only lets the present appear in presence; then one must conclude that the gift, if it is ever to be thought through, must come about (and, first of all, to itself) outside of presence, outside of self-subsistence, and outside of truth.

If truth is sufficient, in effect, to annul the gift, then the gift only comes about in dispensing itself from *this* truth. If the subsistence of the gift is sufficient to annul it in exchange, then the gift will only produce itself in delivering itself from this very subsistence. If the present as presence is sufficient to annul the gift, then the gift will fulfill itself only in liberating itself from *this* presence. But, we might object, can the gift only assume this "duty" or is this a question of a chimeric effort? How can this be understood, if the "conditions of the possibility of gift . . . simultaneously designate the conditions of the impossibility of the gift?"[14] Quite simply, we can note that this objection contains its own refutation: it only establishes the conditions under which the gift becomes impossible. It in no way establishes that that which thus becomes impossible merits the name of gift. We respond, therefore, that the conditions of impossibility only prove that that which was studied does *not* merit the title of gift and that, if it will ever have the status of gift, it will have necessarily other conditions of possibility than this— conditions of its impossibility. Positively, this means that the gift does not give itself in the system of exchange, taken in the reciprocity which links giver and recipient: in this supposed economy of gift, one literally makes economy on the gift by transforming it into a subsistent state, permanently present, accorded value (of use and/or exchange)—a state of finality (useful, without end, etc.) produced or destroyed by efficiency and calculation, inserted into the framework of its causes, quite simply into a common being. Such a common being can never appear as a gift, not because the concept of gift contradicts itself but because this being possesses nothing resembling a gift. Every effort to grasp the gift, an effort which tries to begin with a concept of "gift" already obvious and settled, in order to accede to the gift never analyzes anything under this name other than a common being. Hypothetically, it should not, therefore, be possible to accede to the least gift.

What's missing here? The renunciation of the economic horizon of exchange, in order to interpret the gift, beginning with the horizon of givenness itself. First, we must break with the metaphysical interpretation of the given as the effect of an efficient cause, that is to say, against Spinoza—exemplary metaphysician—"*ipsisus rei datam sive actuosam essentiam*"[15]—literally, the essence of a thing, and because it is given, is never active as such, but exactly, given. The gift comes about as a given, thus from and within a givenness. Now it remains to describe the givenness—no longer according to what it excludes—but as such, if such an *as such* is still appropriate to it.

IV. Givenness Reduced

Describing this givenness is a question of thinking through the gift under the rubric of givenness itself, without referring it to the economy, because the impossibility we just noticed does not concern the gift as such—but rather its economical interpretation.

In effect, such an economy destroys givenness. First, with the recipient and the giver interpreted as conscious agents, this economy defines a permanent circuit which generally authorizes not so much the gift without calculation but chiefly the return on the gift—that is to say, exchange; from then on, the permanent circuit permits the repetition of exchange, thus bringing about reciprocity, which might then take on the allure of business. At this step, the gift has already lost its gratuity (it disappears as such). Next, this exchange also confirms the gift in its status as an object: in order to be able to repeat itself, to exchange itself, and to appreciate, the gift must acquire the consistency of objectivity, and thus also the visibility and the permanence which make it accessible to all the potential partners of economic exchange. Now accessible to all potential givers and recipients, the gift becomes indifferent to the terms of its givenness. Stripped of its own secret by its objectivity, it also destroys the eventual secret of the partners who place it in action.

If, therefore, the economy of the gift only makes economy of the gift, the gift only becomes itself by breaking away from the economy, in order to let itself be thought through along the lines of givenness. Therefore, one must reconduct the gift away from economy and toward givenness. To reconduct it is to reduce it. How can we reduce the gift to givenness without falling either into tautology (Isn't the gift equivalent to givenness?) or into contradiction (Doesn't givenness necessarily imply some transcendence?). But if we must have reduction, it could only occur, even in the case of an eventual reduction to givenness, in the manner in which reduction always operates in phenomenology: by the bracketing of all transcendence, whatever it might be. Reducing the gift to givenness thus signifies: thinking the gift as gift, making abstraction of the triple transcendence which affected it until now—by the bracketing of the transcendence of the giver, the transcendence of the recipient, and the transcendence of the objectivity of the object exchanged. If the *epokke* happens to exert itself upon the gift, it will exert itself in liberating the gift from the terms and the status of object, all transcendent, of economic exchange. Thus, it will reconduct the gift to pure and simple givenness, if, at least, such a givenness may occur.

In this operation, the reduction of the gift to givenness does not come about *despite* the triple objection raised against the gift by Derrida but quite clearly *because* of it: here, in effect, the alleged "conditions of the impossibility of gift" (neither recipient nor giver nor gift) become precisely the conditions of the possibility of the gift's reduction to pure givenness, by *epokke* of the transcendent conditions of economic exchange. The objection then becomes its own response: the gift is reduced to givenness once the recipient, the giver, and the objectivity of the gift are bracketed, in order to thus extract the gift outside of the economy and to manifest it according to the lines of pure givenness. But can such a reduction of gift to givenness in fact occur? Once liberated from its transcendent conditions, does the gift remain identifiable as such or does it collapse into a vague cloud, the last breath of a collapsed concept?

V. The Bracketing of the Giver

When a gift occurs, just what, in fact, is given to me? In other words, in order to be able to speak of a gift, what experience of consciousness is required? It is necessary, of course, to distinguish here between the experiences of gift affecting a consciousness in someone playing the role of giver and those affecting a consciousness in someone in the role of recipient. Let us consider both of these respective situations. First, the viewpoint of the giver: when and how does a gift give itself (to consciousness)? When the giver gives it, evidently. But what exactly does it mean, for the giver, to give a gift? Would it be a transfer of a piece of property to another? Undoubtedly no, despite appearances— first, because the transfer does not always take the shape of ceding a property item (it could be a loan or a lease, etc.), nor does it always assume some juridical status (it could involve a private agreement or a tacit accord, etc.); next, because such a regimentation would be suffi- cient to threaten the very status of the gift in leading it back, as we have already seen, to the status of exchange. Finally, the gift sometimes does not consist in any object at all: in the cases involving a promise, a reconciliation, a blessing (or a curse), a friendship, or a love (or a hatred), the gift is not identical to an object but emerges only at the moment of its occurrence; rather than being identical with the gift, the object becomes the simple occasional support for the gift.

It is the interchangeable and optional support (evidence, promise, memory, etc.) for the true itinerary of the gift, far more precious and serious than the object which makes it visible. Moreover, the more a gift provides an immense richness, the less it can make itself visible in an object, or the less that the object rendering it visible corresponds to the gift in fact. Thus, giving up power involves, in the final analysis, giving up the insignia of power (the *pallium*, the crown, the pectoral cross, etc.); but precisely, the surrendered insignia do not give power, they symbolize it. The power does not give itself with an object or ob- jects, because—giving itself the summit of all the objects—it is neither an object nor in the mode of objects. To give back power, and thus to give power, is never equivalent to making a gift of an object but is rather to give, at the occasion of an object appearing, the gift of power upon objects. Even more, to give oneself to another obviously does not coincide with the gift of some object; the only object which perhaps might prove this gift, because it makes it visible, is the ring worn on the finger: it indicates that another has given himself or herself to me by giving me this ring. But this ring does not attest to the gift made by another, because it is not costly enough either to pay for my own com- mitment (as if this golden ring is worth my life, my fidelity, my own gift) or to confirm materially what the other has given me in self- giving. On the contrary, the ring attests to the gift I have become not by equaling it but by giving the gift a symbolic support, without any parity with what it nonetheless shows. Thus, the gift does not coincide with the object of the gift. Moreover, we can suggest the following fundamental rule: the more that a gift reveals itself as precious, the less it fulfills itself as an object, or, to say the same thing, the more the object reduces itself to the abstract role of support, decoration, symbol. Reciprocally, the gifts which give the most give literally *nothing*—no thing, no object; not because they disappoint expectations but because what they give belongs neither to reality nor to objectivity.

But if the gift, from the perspective of the giver, does not coincide with an object, just what is it made of? In order to see it, it is sufficient to consider how the object gradually becomes the object of a gift: it does not become such at the moment when the giver himself considers it, for the first time, as gift, or, more exactly, as givable. And if the object becomes givable, it does not owe this status to some intrinsic property or to a real predicate—the object stays the same, whether it is givable or not—but rather to the eventual giver's glance upon it. Thus, the giver might, in the extreme, operate this transformation into something givable even without real support in some object (if he gives his faith, if he gives himself, etc.). The gift does not arise when he gives himself but rather when givability arises. Givability arises around the potential giver when he, in relationship, first of all, to himself alone, recognizes that the principle "I owe no one anything" may (and must) admit at least one exception.

The gift begins and in fact ends as soon as the giver envisions that he owes something to someone, when he admits that he could be a debtor, and thus a recipient. The gift begins when the potential giver suspects that another gift has already preceded him, to which he owes something, to which he owes himself to respond. Not only does the gift reside in the decision to give, accepted by the potential giver, but the giver can only decide inasmuch as he recognizes that another gift has already obliged him. The gift decides itself—which means first of all that the gift comes about by the decision, on the part of the giver, to give but which also means that this decision implies that the giver feels himself obliged, and thus obliged by an anterior gift, which confirms in advance the decision to give. The adage "I owe no one anything" only suffers an exception inasmuch as I already recognize myself, in advance, as the beneficiary of a gift—and am thus obligated toward a givenness. The obligation to give thus results directly from the obligation toward an anterior gift. The decision to make a gift implies, first of all, the decision to make oneself a giver; but making oneself a giver cannot be decided without the obligation (weighing upon the giver) of the gift which he has first received. The gift decides the giver. The gift itself decides: it resides in the decision of the giver, but this decision itself rests upon the obligation motivated by an anterior gift. Thus, we will conclude that in the context of reduction, the expe-

rience of consciousness where the gift gives itself consists in the decision of the gift—the decision of the giver to give the gift, but especially
the decision of the gift itself in deciding the giver. The gift *itself* gives
in giving the giver.

VI. The Bracketing of the Recipient

Does this paradox find confirmation when, to define the experience of
consciousness of the gift in the context of reduction, we move from the
perspective of the giver to that of the recipient? What exactly does it
mean for the recipient to receive a gift? Would it be the transfer of an
object of property from someone else to the recipient? Undoubtedly
the answer is "no," despite the appearances: first, because such a transfer does not properly concern the gift—it defines first of all exchange
and its economy, wherein it climaxes selling and buying; next, because
so many gifts occur without property transfer, because they do not derive their reality from an object—the receipt of life, death, forgiveness,
confidence, love, or friendship from another is neither said nor done in
terms of property, nor in terms of disappropriation, because it lacks any
object, outside of some possible symbols.

Most importantly, the act of receiving a gift resides neither in the
transfer of property nor in the object received for an obvious reason:
it resides in the act of acceptance itself. Two circumstances illustrate
this point perfectly: ignorance and refusal. Let us suppose a case involving a gift perfect in all of its reality—an object intentionally proposed by a giver. Now, although made within the rules, this gift could
effectively cease to be a gift. First, it is sufficient that no one would
recognize the gift as such, either by purely and simply ignoring it (i.e.,
by walking by without seeing or taking it) or by treating it in terms of
economic exchange (i.e., by paying for it, selling it, stealing it). In such
a case, the gift could not fulfill itself perfectly, although it does fulfill
the real conditions of givability (objectivity, availability, etc.). What is
it missing? It is missing its acceptance, that is to say, the recipient's
decision to receive it. Next, let us suppose that the gift truly fulfilled
and recognized as such nonetheless meets a certain refusal—because
the recipient disdains it (i.e., by considering it to be "too little"), is suspicious of it (i.e., by questioning "Just what is it?"), is fearful of it (*"et
dona ferentes"*), or simply shows malice toward it (i.e., by claiming that
"This would give pleasure all too well")—hence, the gift finds itself
shunted aside or mocked. What is it missing? Obviously, nothing

real—everything, everything which has the rank of a thing, has already clearly been given—but here again the gift does not coincide with anything real. What it is missing is not anything real either: it is a question here of its acceptance, pure and simple; that is to say, it is a question of the recipient deciding to receive it.

The gift fulfills itself perfectly when I—the recipient—make up my mind to receive it. The performance of the gift is linked more to my decision to accept it than to its own availability; moreover, it is often my decision which decides that something is found to be accepted. If we reflect, for example, on the call, the reception of the call (the recognition that there has clearly been a call for me) and the response by me become the strongest confirmation of the availability of this call—that no one else perhaps has heard, to which no one (undoubtedly) has responded in the same manner as I have.[16]

If we reflect upon the business of love, it often happens that it is acceptance which provokes, in reality, the availability of the gift; acceptance often hinges not always on the banal duplicity of seduction but often on the evidence that I, I alone and more than another, affirm the capacity to let myself be seduced and freely consent to this seduction, like a call inversing the usual chronology. I consent to the possibility of a gift to me of this person and not of another, thus provoking his or her availability. From the perspective of the recipient, the gift consists ultimately in the fact of self-decision, exactly as is the case in the perspective of the giver.

VII. The Reduction of the Gift to That Which Itself Gives

We will not object that deciding to give differs radically from deciding to receive, because there is nothing easy about the former (who does not wish to receive?) and there is nothing difficult about the latter (who wishes to give?), so the two decisions can neither be compared nor assimilated with each other. In effect, there is nothing easy about even deciding to receive: first, because receiving might imply receiving what one did not expect or what one did not want, even what one feared the most (what is specific to a gift is the fact that often "it is not a present"); next, in order to decide to receive, it is necessary to have more than the desire to possess or the search for one's own interest—it is necessary to renounce clearly the independence which permits oneself to be convinced that "I owe no one anything."

To decide to receive a gift imposes the acceptance, with this gift, of the owing of something to someone. The gratuity of the gift is paid for with the recognition—of the gift and of its very gratuity. Note well that this is not primarily a question of a recognition of debt toward the giver, such that we would be led back from gift according to givenness to gift according to economy; because the giver remains unknown or absolutely missing (such as absent parents, nature, even the state, etc.), it is even possible that this recognition deepens inasmuch as it cannot be fixed upon any identifiable partner, because such a gratuity places in question nothing less than the autocracy of the self and its pretension to auto-sufficiency. To decide to receive the gift is equivalent to deciding to become obligated by the gift. The decision between the potential givenness and the gift does not operate so much from the giver on the gift as from the gift upon the giver; the gift, by its own allure and prestige, decides the giver to decide himself for it—that is to say, decides (or determines) him to sacrifice his own autocracy, the autocrat of what is his own, in order to receive it. The gift decides about its own acceptance by deciding about its recipient. Thus, we will conclude that in the regime of reduction, the experience of consciousness in which the gift gives itself consists of the decision of the gift—the decision to receive the gift by the recipient but especially the decision to decide the recipient of the gift by the gift itself. The gift *itself* gives by giving its reception.

The gift reduced to givenness gives itself to consciousness as that which gives of itself, as much from the viewpoint of the giver as from the viewpoint of the recipient, one and the other situating themselves in relationship to it. This first determination has nothing paradoxical or tautological about it. It indicates, in effect, that the gift remains impossible as long as one is not attached to it, either in giving it or in accepting it. The gift only exists from the moment when its protagonists recognize it in a being, an object, even in the absence of being and object, and an immediate relationship between them. So recognizing the gift implies a phenomenological perspective, strict and particular, that, in front of the fact (object, being immediate relation), sees it as a gift. It is a question, if we wish, of hermeneutics, but of a hermeneutics that less often gives the meaning than it receives the meaning for precisely seeing the gift; it involves less gift of meaning than meaning of gift—coming from the gift, or rather seeing the fact as a gift, because it is envisioned from the starting point of givenness. Seeing the gift implies seeing it from the starting point of givenness; if the gift decides *itself*, it decides from the power of givenness, which weighs equally upon the giver and the recipient. Both only attach themselves to the gift inasmuch as they yield to the moment of givenness. The instant power of givenness makes the gift determine *itself* as gift through the double consent of the giver and of the recipient, who are less often agents of the gift and are more often acted upon by givenness.

From this, one reaches two conclusions. The first is that the gift, as that which decides *itself* by itself, supposes nothing other than the moment of givenness and thus does not belong to the economy of exchange but fulfills itself even and mainly in a regimen of reduction. The second conclusion is that this gift, reduced to that which decides *itself*, takes its character of given from givenness alone, that is to say, from itself, without depending on any extrinsic relation—not upon exchange nor upon the giver nor upon the recipient. The gift gives "itself" intrinsically in its *self*-giving.

VIII. The Gift Reduced—Without Return

The gift finds itself thus reduced to that which decides *itself* by and for itself. It appears in the horizon of givenness, where properly it (by itself) gives (as all phenomena give) as that which (par excellence) *itself* gives. Such a reduction, however, could only have been conducted through the axis of the object taken in exchange, whose bracketing has placed into relief the gift as such. One still must confirm this reduction from the perspective of the two terms of exchange: is it possible to reduce the gift to pure givenness by bracketing the recipient and the giver? Obviously, it is not a question here of eliminating the recipient and the giver but rather of establishing that the gift occurs even if they find themselves suspended and, thus, that they must be thought about from the starting point of the gift—reduced according to givenness— which is quite different from the supposition that the gift depends upon the recipient and the giver in order to give itself. Only a positive result would authorize us to speak of a perfect reduction of the gift, in all its dimensions, to that which itself decides, thus a reduction to pure givenness.

May we, in the gift, bracket the recipient without suspending the gift itself? In fact, the bracketing of the recipient belongs intrinsically to the possibility of the gift. In fact, it manifests itself as being linked to the gift in a manner that is respectively indispensable, possible, and preferable: (a) the bracketing of the recipient belongs necessarily to the gift, since the gift would simply and purely disappear if the recipient remained. In effect, if the recipient preceded the gift and remained independent of its occurrence, it could condition, provoke, or even offer it. Then the gift would regress to the level of an exchange, wherein reciprocity (actual or desired) reestablishes a pure and simple commerce. The gift would thus lose all gratuity, all grace, if it is given to a recipient capable of "offering" or compensating for it. "If it is for recompense that you give, where then is your grace?" (Luke 6:33).

The love of enemies might appear, at first glance, to be an extreme and unresolvable paradox, a simple pedagogical method for marking the logic of the love of one's neighbor. In effect, loving one's neighbor, even if it is demonstrably pleasant, even affectionate, already presents a task so difficult, so far beyond simple reciprocal sociability, that the love of one's enemies seems an unlikely bet. In fact, for a phenomenology of gift, it is quite different. If, in effect, we understand *love* as *give* in a privileged sense, this gift can only remain itself inasmuch as it does not diminish itself in an exchange, wherein reciprocity would annul the gratuity; the gift requires, in order to give itself, that it decide *itself* as a gift beginning with itself alone, and that it give without return, without either responses or reimbursement. The recipient must not be able to "offer recompense," or, at least, the hope of some recompense cannot enter into the consideration by which the gift *itself* decides. Such a recipient, identifiable as the beneficiary of the gift but not capable of compensating it, defines itself precisely as the "enemy": the one who does not love in return and therefore permits one to love freely (without reservation, in other words) permits the gift to occur. The enemy places the gift in evidence precisely by its refusal of reciprocity—to the contrary of friends who "return in equal measure" (Luke 6:34) and who downgrade the gift to the status of a loan with interest. The enemy thus becomes the ally of the gift and the friend becomes the enemy of the gift. The enemy emerges exactly as the model recipient-reduced, who receives the gift without re-offering it. The psychological paradox manifests a phenomenological necessity: the gift requires the bracketing of the recipient.

However, one will object, does not such a bracketing of the recipient, even if it appears necessary to the reduction of the gift, also render it impossible? Because if the recipient (the enemy) does not recompense the gift, it is first because he refuses it (he does not want to be loved). Now, does a gift refused remain a clear gift? In other words, in the very minute in which he permits the gift to occur, doesn't the enemy annul it? In order to respond to this question, it is sufficient to show that a gift refused clearly remains a full gift and, therefore, that the bracketing of the recipient is not only necessary (a) but also (b) possible. So, what actually remains of a gift refused (seen and rejected, seen and criticized) or even ignored (not singled out, silently overlooked)? First, the gift given remains, as an act of abandon, with or without objective support, where the gift definitively decides *itself*; the gift that fulfills itself with neither return nor regret perjures with neither recognition nor reception. The simple fact that a gift is abandoned does not destroy it; on the contrary, it confirms it in its character of givenness—no reciprocity whatsoever; there is not even the recognition of this gift which would corrode its pure gratuity. The abandon indicates that the gift not only surpasses every counter-gift but that it surpasses every possible acceptance. The abandoned gift manifests, by its very disproportion, its givenness. Nonetheless, in the context of an abandoned gift that is without a recipient, another phenomenon becomes visible: the missing recipient appears through the very figure of its missing-ingratitude. "If you knew the gift of God" (John 4:10); it is possible that the recipient does not know and therefore disdains it. This disdain, theologically as inevitable as it is sinful, still remains phenomenologically fertile, since it permits us to designate the recipient at the very same time as it fails to fulfill this role.

The failure of the recipient, necessary for the occurrence of the gift, does not suppress the gift and its appearance. On the contrary, it makes the recipient appear in a figure perfectly proportional to givenness: no longer the one who recompenses the gift and destroys it (the friend), not the one who simply denies it (the enemy), but the one who does not support it (the ingrate). The ingrate, in effect, does not determine himself as much as someone who does not want or who cannot return like for like as much as he simply does not support debt—not the debt of returning *but* the debt of receiving, accepting, or even offering a gift. The ingrate suffers from the principle and the very possibility of a gift which affects him and comes to him. He does not refuse this or that gift with this or that objective support; he refuses the debt, or rather the self-avowal that one is indebted. In his obstinate effort to reestablish the principle that "I owe no one anything," he thus confirms *a contrario* the rising up of the gift which decides itself out of itself and which places in question this principle. By this principle, the ingrate reveals negatively, in all of its purity, the gift reduced to givenness. Through the same gesture, he thus determines the figure of the reduced recipient, absolutely governed by the pure givenness of the gift.

From here on, we can better understand why the bracketing of the recipient might finally appear (c) desirable. The recipient masks himself under the aspect of the enemy and the ingrate, whose negations permit the gift to manifest itself through pure givenness, without either return or reciprocity of exchange. But this bracketing of the recipient does not necessarily imply a similar negation of the gift; it can also occur with the reception of the gift. This situation finds its perfect illustration in one of the eschatological parables: when Christ returns at the end of time, he will separate the just from the evil according to the criteria of the gifts they would have made to Him on earth—thus situating Himself in the position of recipient. But the elected, like the damned, will be astonished to have never seen, met, or identified as hungry, thirsty, homeless, naked, ill, and imprisoned the recipient they have (or have not) nourished, refreshed, housed, clothed, healed, and visited. No one has ever seen the recipient—in this case, Christ. "Then they will respond to him and tell him: 'Lord, when have we seen you?'" (Matt. 25:37, 44). This invisibility manifests without discussion the bracketing of the recipient; still, far from forbidding or weakening the gift, this invisibility doubles it by universalizing it: every human being may discern the face of the recipient precisely because this face remains invisible—"in truth, I tell you, inasmuch as you have done something for the least of my brethren, that you have done unto me" (Matt. 25:40). The impossibility of identifying the recipient par excellence, Christ, permits us to let the gift emerge on every other human face; the retreat of Christ permits the "least of his brethren" to rise and offer himself to the gift as a recipient's face. Thus universalized by the absence of the recipient, or rather, by his retreat, which sets up the place for universalization of the function of the recipient, the gift, which reduces the recipient, acquires its perfect freedom: it gives without eliciting acceptance from anyone, in complete indifference to the recipient's merits or demerits, in perfect ignorance of any eventual reciprocity (in other words, in complete conformity with the gratuity of the givenness). So we will conclude that the recipient may and must be bracketed; this indispensable operation, possible and preferable, in one way reduces the gift to pure givenness.

IX. The Gift Reduced—Without Beginning

Now we must consider the second part of the question. It asks, "Is it possible, in the gift, to bracket the giver without suspending this gift itself?" In order to respond, we need to bring about such an authentic bracketing, as in the case of a gift whose giver remains unknown or unknowable—in other words, an anonymous gift. Does the gift remain in such a case? Yes, it remains.

The gift remains because the absence or anonymity of the giver permits the giver to exercise full responsibility in deciding whether there is a gift or not: it thus reserves for him the full exercise of his function of interpreter ("Is this a gift?") and of his decision concerning recognition ("Am I its designated recipient and, therefore, am I under obligation?"). The inquiry involved in searching for the absent benefactor permits the giver to execute without reservation the logic of the gift perfectly reduced to givenness, because it does not obliterate the preliminary evidence of the designated recipient from an eventual recognition or a possible recompense. The regression to an economy of exchange remains impossible from the moment that one of the two terms is missing. Far from forbidding the gift, the bracketing of the recipient powerfully contributes to reducing the gift to givenness—that is, to itself.

But it is necessary to go beyond this. In the case of an absent, unknown, or undecided giver, I find myself, as recipient, in the situation where returning the gift is, in principle, impossible, whatever my intention may be (even if I am among the best intentioned). This impossibility reinforces the evidence of givenness on two levels: first, it marks the fact that the gift gives *itself* here without limit, without return, outside of commerce; it marks the fact that here it is precisely a question of gift and not of a loan (thus of a future return). The giver who gives according to the mode of givenness does not know what he gives: "When you give alms, your left [hand] should ignore what your right [hand] does" (Matt. 6:3). Perhaps he does not even know if he is giving. Most importantly, he does not want to know if the eventual recipient knows that he is giving. He gives not in order to know nor to make it known nor to make himself seen—but rather in order to give. If the gift only absolutely gives (itself) by giving itself to the point of loss, the loss of the giver also contributes to the occurrence of the gift; the absence of the giver manifests the reduction of the gift to givenness. But the impossibility, in principle, of "making a return" also reveals the reduction of the recipient to givenness; unable "to make a return," he understands himself as definitively in debt. The debt is not something which is added here to a conscicusness already self-confident, like the consciousness of some object simply inscribed in a consciousness, originally self-consciousness. It is in recognizing its debt that consciousness becomes conscious of itself, because the debt itself precedes all consciousness and defines the self: the self, as such, the self of consciousness, receives *itself* right off as a gift (given) without giver (giving).

The debt brings about the self in order that the self itself discovers itself already there—that is, as a fact and thus given. The consciousness of knowing that one is indebted to the absent giver brings about an exact coincidence among the self, the debt, and the consciousness of the debt and the self. The recipient discovers himself primordially and definitely unsolvable—not only by his lack of will for reimbursement or by lack of the methods for reimbursement or even by the recipient's ignorance but, in the first place, by the irremediable anteriority of the debt before any response. The debt here does not designate an act or a situation of the self, but rather its state, its definition—ultimately, its manner of being.[17] The debt exercises the differance: the absence of the recipient precedes everything, so that even the consciousness of self-reception of the gift (self-consciousness) and of obligation as a gift given (consciousness of debt) definitively makes a late entrance vis-à-vis the indebting givenness. Every recognition of debt, and thus all recognition toward the absent giver, confirms rather than eliminates the differance. But such a differance, if it is exercised with the debt, ultimately makes manifest the givenness itself: the consciousness of debt defines the mode of manifestation of the recipient when it finds itself bracketed—that is to say, reduced in the horizon to the function of pure givenness.

We have reduced the gift to givenness in order to expose the fact that beyond all objective support and all economy of exchange, *the gift intrinsically gives itself from its* self *giving*. We also just bracketed, first, the recipient in the figure of *the enemy* (of the ingrate and of the anonymous one) and, then, the giver, in the figure of the unsolvable *debt*. This yields the following paradox: *the gift, reduced to givenness, decides to give* itself *as an unsolvable debt given to an enemy*. Thus, we may pretend to have also reduced them to givenness. This triple reduction obviously does not aim to abolish the gift, the recipient, and the giver. On the contrary, it makes them play freely according to the mode of pure givenness.

X. What the Gift Reveals about Givenness

From the outset, we recognized the narrow link in phenomenology between the questions of givenness (dimension of all phenomena) and revelation (as a particular case of phenomena). We just sketched a reduction of the gift to itself and thus to pure givenness. Does this analysis illuminate our starting point? It does without a doubt, because it establishes the possibility of a gift reduced to pure givenness by describing the gift without making it depend upon a cause of inscribing it within an exchange. Appearing in the manner of a gift does not depend on an ultimately efficient giver (nor even on a receptive recipient) but rather on the very mode of appearing in terms of what decides itself as a gift. The character of gift—givenness—intrinsically belongs to the gift and to its mode of appearance rather than to the process whereby givenness defines itself extrinsically in relationship to a giver, to a cause, or to a certain efficiency. Givenness is in no way equivalent to production, but it is tied to the phenomenality of that which only appears by deciding *itself* from itself. It belongs to the phenomenon of revelation, among all phenomena, to most radically accomplish this emergence from self and not from a cause. This is because for revelation, appearance is ceaselessly exhausted in givenness, because it gives of itself in the strict sense—it abandons itself. But with this abandon, another question opens up.

Notes

I have reshaped and fully developed the argument in this chapter in *Etant donné. Essai d'une phénoménologie de la donation* (Paris: P.U.F., 1997–98), Book II, §§7–12, "Le don."

1. See my *Reduction and Givenness: Investigations of Husserl, Heidegger, and Phenomenology,* trans. Thomas A. Carlson (Evanston, Ill.: Northwestern University Press, 1988). See also my essay "The Saturated Phenomenon," trans. Thomas A. Carlson, *Philosophy Today* 40 (spring 1996):103–24.

2. See my work dedicated to *Reduction and Givenness,* and also the commentary by M. Henry, "Quatre principes de la phénoménologie," *Revue de Métaphysique et de Morale* (Paris: A. Colin, 1991), vol. 1.

3. Jacques Derrida, *Given Time: I. Counterfeit Money,* trans. Peggy Kamuf (Chicago: University of Chicago Press, 1991), p. 13.

4. Ibid., p. 12.

5. Derrida continues, "this simple *recognition* of the gift *as* gift, *as such,* [suffices] to annul the gift as gift even before *recognition* becomes *gratitude*" (*Given Time,* pp. 13–14). And also: "There is no more gift as soon as the other *receives*—and even if she refuses the gift that she has perceived or recognized as gift" (*Given Time,* p. 14). This last point can be argued; in fact, it could be that the gift survives her refusal (by way of ignoring it), as Derrida seems to suggest in the logic of his third and fourth arguments.

6. Derrida, *Given Time,* p. 23.

7. See my study in *Questions Cartésiennes,* chap. 5, §5, "La dernière formulation du *cogito:* La générosité" (Paris: P.U.F., 1991), trans. by J. Kosky as *Cartesian Questions* (Chicago, Ill.: University of Chicago Press, 1999).

8. Derrida, *Given Time,* p. 24.

9. Ibid., p. 14.

10. Ibid., p. 13.

11. Ibid., pp. 13, 14, and 15, respectively.

12. Ibid., p. 27.

13. Ibid., p. 54.

14. Ibid., p. 12.

15. Spinoza, *Ethics III,* §7: Demonstration.

16. See my "The Final Appeal of the Subject," in *Deconstructive Subjectivities,* ed. Simon Critchley and Peter Dews (Albany: SUNY Press, 1996).

17. I am not returning here to a regulation of the consciousness of debt, eliminated, to be sure, by Heidegger—"*das Dasein ist als solches schulding*"—(*Sein und Zeit,* §58; Tübingen, Germany: Max Niemeyer Verlag, 1927; cited according to the 10th ed., 1963), but also we should not forget the work by C. Bruaire, *L'être et l'esprit* (Paris: Fayard, 1983).

8

Against Idolatry

Heidegger and Natural Theology

GEORGE CONNELL

> The religious instinct is indeed in the process
> of growing powerfully—but the theistic
> satisfaction it refuses with deep suspicion.
> —F. Nietzsche, *Beyond Good and Evil*

In the above passage, Nietzsche describes an ambivalence about religious faith that might seem surprising, given his reputation as the quintessential atheist. A careful reading of his most famous statement on atheism—the madman's declaration of the death of God in *The Gay Science*—reflects a similar ambivalence. In sharp contrast to the casual, mocking disbelief of the "many . . . who did not believe in God [who] were standing around,"[1] the madman agonizingly cries out about the desolation of a godless world and the dreadfulness of our responsibility as God's murderers. But set against and overwhelming such "religious instincts," as Nietzsche reveals, is a "deep suspicion" that causes him to refuse all "theistic satisfaction." And it is for this suspicion—for his remorseless examination of religious believers and institutions, for his eagle eye for every form of mendacity, weakness, and resentment, and for his aversion to seeing life pass itself off under cover of religious faith—that Nietzsche is rightly remembered.

While the opening quotation applies to Nietzsche, it finds its fulfillment in Heidegger. Though he refuses "theistic satisfaction" as consistently as Nietzsche, Heidegger powerfully encourages the growth of "religious instinct" at the level both of emotion and of thought. He elicits experiences of wonder, awe, joy, guilt, and boredom so effectively that he shows that his early training in homiletics didn't go to waste. In particular, Heidegger elicits experiences of cosmological wonder—wonder that what-is is, that the cosmos exists—and teleological wonder—wonder that what-is is meaningful, intelligible, significant. While these experiences seem to cry out for "theistic satisfaction," for articulation as arguments for the existence of God, Heidegger steadfastly and even dismissively denies such satisfaction. How are we to take this? The question has two distinct dimensions. First, why does Heidegger encourage our religious instinct, only to deny it satisfaction? To what end would one intensify a desire for God that could not or would not be satisfied? Is it to prepare the self more fully for a now-deferred union, or is it to force the self to confront brutely the nonexistence of the desired?

To answer this elusive question requires moving to a second, more directly answerable question: how should we construe Heidegger's consistently negative attitude toward the theistic arguments that seem to follow so naturally from the experiences he elicits? Is he specifically averse to the theistic arguments, or does his critique betoken a rejection of theism per se? That is, is his objection epistemological or is it metaphysical? Does he reject natural theology as a proper mode of coming to knowledge of God, or is his critique of the theistic arguments really a way of exposing and opposing the religious instinct itself? In sum, how should we trace Heidegger's lineage? Does he follow Kierkegaard and Karl Barth in denouncing natural theology as an unworthy avenue to knowledge of the true God, or does he follow Nietzsche in exposing the roots of religious instinct so as to kill that which grows from them?

In the following essay, I will first document Heidegger's encouragement of the "religious instinct." Second, I analyze Heidegger's objections to natural theology. And third, I place Heidegger in relation to the very different criticisms of natural theology offered by Kierkegaard and Barth on the one hand and Nietzsche on the other. Since all four thinkers state their rejections of natural theology in terms of a rejection of idolatry, that concept will play a key role in bringing them into dialogue and, ultimately, in comparing and contrasting them. Though my explicit focus will be natural theology, this discussion's significance will be broader, since natural theology frequently gives articulate expression to what Nietzsche calls the religious instinct. In placing Heidegger in reference to Kierkegaard and Barth on the one hand and to Nietzsche on the other, we will see that both theism and atheism can have their own distinct reasons for viewing such an instinct and its rational expression with deep suspicion. To locate Heidegger in reference to those distinctive suspicions is already to go far toward understanding the ultimate tenor and tendency of his thinking as it relates to God.

I. Heidegger's Evocations of Wonder

A. Heidegger and Cosmological Wonder

The unwavering intent of Heidegger's thought is to recall us from forgetfulness to a reawakened awareness of Being. What Heidegger has in mind by this "awareness of Being" is so maddeningly elusive, at least in large measure, because it is more experiential than conceptual. George Steiner writes: "It is not 'understanding' that Heidegger's discourse solicits primarily. It is an 'experiencing,' an acceptance of felt strangeness."[2] As Heidegger sees it, this astonishment, this experience of wonder, does not simply define philosophy but rather humanness itself: "Man alone of all beings, when addressed by the voice of Being, experiences the marvel of all marvels: that what-is is."[3] It is to awaken this experience that Heidegger repeatedly asks and meditates upon what he calls the widest, deepest, and most fundamental of all questions, "Why are there essents rather than nothing at all?"[4] Given the provenance of this question—Leibniz's statement of the cosmological argument—and given the immediate tendency of people in widely different times and cultures to answer it by reference to the divine,[5] it appears that Heidegger powerfully and persistently encourages "the religious instinct" to "grow powerfully."

Beyond eliciting an experience of cosmological wonder that cries out for "theistic satisfaction" as an itch cries out for a scratch, the conceptual terms in which Heidegger articulates this experience appear to place Heidegger in the camp of the proponents of the cosmological argument. In the early eighteenth century, Samuel Clarke fundamentally recast debates over the cosmological argument by disconnecting the argument from the issue of infinite temporal regression.[6] He argued that even if there were such an infinite temporal regression, the question remains: "Why does this particular infinite series exist as opposed to some other series or none at all?" The crucial claim here is that it makes sense to ask why of the cosmos as a whole in addition to asking that question of the individual entities and events that compose the cosmos. Opponents have argued either that it is a mistake to ask for an explanation of the whole in addition to the parts or that such an explanation is already provided when each of the parts is explained.[7] But the central thrust of Heidegger's philosophy is to contend, with as does Clarke, that the whole (Being) is not simply identical to the parts (beings): "We do not inquire into this and that, or into each essent in turn, but from the very outset into the essent as a whole, or, . . . into the essent as such in its entirety" (*IM*, p. 2). Therefore, both experientially and conceptually, Heidegger's philosophy powerfully sets the stage for a cosmological argument for the existence of God.

B. Heidegger and Teleological Wonder

Heidegger's philosophy is fully as evocative of teleological wonder—amazement that what-is is meaningful and intelligible—as it is of cosmological wonder—that what-is is at all. Familiarity may rob us of a sense of how audacious Heidegger was in adopting a hermeneutical approach to ontology in *Being and Time*.[8] Hermeneutics arose as the theory and practice of biblical interpretation, enlarged its domain to include the interpretation of texts generally, and, with Dilthey, established itself as the methodology of the human sciences. While Dilthey claims for hermeneutics a status in its own domain of persons and cultural artifacts that is equal to that of the natural sciences in the domain of the extra-cultural, Heidegger boldly employs hermeneutics to achieve an understanding of Being—"the totality of what-is." More accurately, Heidegger presupposes that we already exist in an understanding of Being, so that the project of ontology is the interpretation of what we obscurely understand already.[9] While it is all too easy to get lost in the details of Heidegger's interpretation of this dim, everyday understanding of Being, Heidegger himself calls us back to the fundamental question on the final page of *Being and Time:* "How is this disclosive understanding of Being at all possible for Dasein?" (*BT*, p. 488). He repeats and rephrases this very question in one of his latest writings, "The End of Philosophy and the Task of Thought":

> Does the title of the task of thinking then read instead of *Being and Time:* Opening and Presence?
> But where does the opening come from and how is it given? What speaks in the "There is / It gives"?[13]

In either form, (and in spite of Heidegger's asking "what" rather than "who speaks"), this question seems to call out for a theistic answer. To illustrate this, let us look to a type of teleological argument that has had a number of recent advocates. Such apologists as C. S. Lewis, Hugo Meynell, and Paul Davies have argued that the (presumed) human ability to make sense of the world strongly indicates that that world has an intelligent creator. This version of teleological argument takes its point of departure in a question and a corresponding amazement that is strikingly like Heidegger's. For example, Paul Davies describes what he calls "The Scientific Miracle":

> Throughout the ages all cultures have extolled the beauty, majesty, and ingenuity of the physical universe. It is only the modern scientific culture, however, that has made any systematic attempt to study the nature of the universe and our place within it. The success of the scientific method at unlocking the secrets of nature is so dazzling it can blind us to the greatest scientific miracle of all: *science works*. Scientists themselves normally take it for granted that we live in a rational, ordered cosmos subject to precise laws that can be uncovered by human reasoning. Yet why should human beings have the ability to discover and understand the principles on which the universe runs?[11]

Davies answers these questions by arguing that indeed there is a "deep and meaningful resonance between human minds and the underlying organization of the natural world."[12] He then goes on to argue that the most plausible account of that resonance is one in which a rational God creates both the intelligible cosmos and intelligent minds that "know" it.

There are clearly similarities between Heidegger's question, "How is this disclosive understanding of Being at all possible for Dasein?", and Davies' question, "Why should human beings have the ability to discover and understand the principles on which the universe runs?" First, unlike many other teleological arguments, Davies focuses on the universe as a whole rather than on some local phenomenon. In Heidegger's terms, Davies' question is ontological rather than ontic. Second, Davies' argument focuses specifically on intelligibility rather than on some other indication of design (resemblance to machines, conduciveness to life, etc.). Thus, like Heidegger, he raises the question of the meaning of Being, since Heidegger defines meaning as "that wherein the understandability [*Verstehbarkeit*] of something maintains itself" (*BT*, p. 370).

Despite these similarities, there are crucial differences between the approaches of Heidegger and Davies as well, predominantly that Heidegger does not construe understanding of Being in terms of comprehension of the laws of nature by the natural sciences. Rather, Heidegger speaks of science as "the legitimate task of grasping the present-at-hand in its essential unintelligibility [*Unverstandlichkeit*]" (*BT*, p. 194). To grasp what type of intelligibility Heidegger has in mind, we must remember the distinctive hermeneutic resonances of "understanding" [*Verstand*]." It is the significance of everyday experience, the meaningfulness of familiar places and things, the intelligibility of other persons, that Heidegger has in mind when he speaks of understanding. He openly models his inquiry into Being on the reader's relation to the text, as described by hermeneutic theory. To the extent that his efforts are successful, Heidegger gives us reason to believe that Being itself is text-like. As Otto Pöggler puts it, Being, for Heidegger, is "the all-encompassing occurrence of sense and truth."[13] And a meaningful, significant Being is at least as indicative, if not more, of intelligent creation than is the law-governed, scientifically intelligible reality of which Davies speaks. That is why Hume's Cleanthes invokes images of a significant voice from the clouds or of a botanical library (in part 3 of *Dialogues Concerning Natural Religion*) in order to supplement and strengthen his original imagery of the cosmos as a machine.

Although a hermeneutically meaningful (as opposed to a scientifically intelligible) cosmos might well be a stronger indication of the existence of God, especially of a personal God, it also seems a much more difficult claim to make. Even with the impressive predictive successes of the natural sciences, scientific realism—the view that science progresses toward a description of the way reality is—is a beleaguered view. But it is much more difficult to assert that the sorts of meanings with which hermeneutics is concerned—meanings that seem to vary according to culture, time, and even individual person—are written into the very fabric of Being. Nonetheless, in *Being and Time*, Heidegger repeatedly confirms just such a "hermeneutic realism" in according both epistemological and ontological priority to ready-to-hand entities over present-at-hand entities: "The circumspective de-severing of Dasein's everydayness reveals the Being-in-itself of the "true world"—of that entity which Dasein, as something existing, is already alongside (*BT*, p. 141). But to insist, as Heidegger does, that we know ready-to-hand entities as they are "in-themselves" raises immediate problems: one and the same entity can appear radically different to the "circumspective de-severings" of different *Daseins*. Heidegger admits this but tries to avoid the paradox it occasions by privileging one viewpoint.

> Over there, across the street, stands the high school building. . . . [T]his building's being does not by any means seem to be the same for everyone. For us, who look at it or ride by, it is different than for the pupils who sit in it; not because they see it only from within but because for them the building really is what it is and as it is. (*IM*, p. 33)

But what if the people intimately involved with the school have different experiences? What if the school's Being is experienced differently by Jewish as opposed to Christian students, by women as opposed to men, by janitorial staff as opposed to faculty members? Nonetheless, Heidegger's "hermeneutic realism" can be construed in such a way that it doesn't conflict with the rich variety of experiences. In *Being and Time*, Heidegger recognizes this issue of varied experiences and proposes a response:

> Is "world" perhaps a characteristic of Dasein's Being? And in that case, does every Dasein "proximally" have its world? Does not "world" thus become something "subjective"? How, then, can there be a "common" world "in" which, nevertheless, we *are*? And if we raise the question of the "world", *what* world do we have in view? Neither a common world nor a subjective world, but the *worldhood-of-the-world* as such. (*BT*, p. 92)

"The worldhood-of-the-world" designates the "primordial totality," the unity that precedes and underpins multiplicity, the Heideggerian analog to Kant's transcendental unity of apperception. As such, it plays a central role in Heidegger's project of awakening us from "fallenness," from a fascination with beings that eclipses Being. While Heidegger's strategy in *Being and Time* is to follow the chain of references, assignments, and significances out from individual ready-to-hand entities so as to reveal the wider context within which they occur, Heidegger insists that worldhood is primordial and the discovery of the ready-to-hand entity secondary. That is, Heidegger asserts that the worldhood-of-the-world and, specifically, *Dasein*'s Being-in-the-world are the preconditions of all encounters with meaningful, ready-to-hand entities.[14] The implications of this claim are stunning: Heidegger shifts the primary locus of meaningfulness from individual meaningful entities (instruments or words) to the world as a horizon of meaningfulness. George Kovacs writes:

> There-being's familiarity with meaningfulness (*Bedeutsamkeit*) is the ontological condition for the disclosure of meanings . . . and the foundation of the possible Being of word and language . . . There-being can disclose meanings by virtue of the familiarity with meaningfulness, with the World. This disclosure means that There-being lets beings be what they are.[15]

Rather than becoming bogged down in disputes over conflicting experiences of meaning, over whose experience reveals the entity as it is "in-itself," we need to take a step back—to ask about or, even better, to marvel at meaningfulness as the ontological condition of our existence. Teleological wonder should be directed at the way we live our lives, immersed in significance as a fish is immersed in the sea. Just as the teleological arguments stated by Davies and others focus on the intelligibility of the cosmos and not on the correctness of any particular scientific theory, so Heidegger's account of the meaningfulness of Being isn't tied to any one experience of a being. Once we stop taking Heidegger's "hermeneutic realism" ontically, as privileging one revelation of Being over another, we can see that its real aim is to assert that we don't project meaning but rather submit to it: "Dasein, in so far as it *is*, has always submitted itself to a 'world' which it encounters, and this *submission* belongs essentially to its Being" (*BT*, p. 120–1).[16] This sense of Being as the "all-encompassing occurrence of sense and truth" to which we submit stays with Heidegger throughout his career. He spends those years listening to and for the voice of Being to see what meaningful, articulate dispositions of Being were being sent as our epoch's destiny. His increased awareness of the historical convinces him that, indeed, Being shows itself in a rich variety of ways. But each of Being's "sendings" is significant, meaningful, and articulate. That is why Heidegger so consistently employs the image of Being speaking. According to Eliade, the experience of such an inherently meaningful reality differentiates the religious from the non-religious person.

[For the religious person,] the existence of the world itself "means" something, "wants to say" something, that the world is neither mute nor opaque, that it is not an inert thing without purpose or significance. For the religious man, the cosmos "lives" and "speaks".... [F]or the non-religious men of the modern age, the cosmos has become opaque, inert, mute; it transmits no message, it holds no cipher.[17]

By this standard, Heidegger is clearly not modern. It seems, indeed, that in this regard his thought is more pre-modern than postmodern. To whatever epoch he is assigned, his experience of the world is distinctly religious. And both this experience and its conceptual articulation lead naturally, almost irresistibly, to the question out of which the teleological argument emerges.[18] Once again, as stated by Heidegger, that question reads, "How is the disclosive understanding of Being at all possible for Dasein?" (*BT*, p. 488); "What speaks in the 'There is / It gives'?"[19]

II. Heidegger's Refusal of "Theistic Satisfaction"

Having looked at the ways in which Heidegger's thought reflects and encourages the "religious instinct," at the ways in which it evokes profoundly religious experiences of cosmological and teleological wonder, we must ask now why he steadfastly refuses "theistic satisfaction." Why does Heidegger tantalize and then frustrate? Why does he stimulate a religious itch only to forbid one to scratch it? I intend to approach this puzzling question by looking at Heidegger's criticisms of natural theology, since the locus of his refusal is the inference, from the elicited experiences, to the existence of God.[20]

Heidegger makes a number of explicit critical remarks about natural theology throughout his writings. Though these remarks are usually quite fragmentary, we can readily grasp their essential force by looking to the ways they fit together with each other and by looking to the ways in which they reflect Heidegger's broader philosophical concerns. In the following, I will identify five of Heidegger's specific objections to natural theology and show how each leads on to the next, until they form a circle. That is, the objections are not ultimately distinct, but instead, each state is an aspect of a single refusal of natural theology.

1.

Faith, for which the theistic arguments are at best useless, is the appropriate basis for human relation to God and for that relation's theological interpretation.

> Theology is seeking a more primordial interpretation of man's Being toward God, prescribed by the meaning of faith itself and remaining within it. It is slowly beginning to understand once more Luther's insight that the "foundation" on which its system of dogma rests has not arisen from an inquiry in which faith is primary, and that conceptually this "foundation" not only is inadequate for the problematic of theology but conceals and distorts it. (*BT,* p. 30)[21]

Though this passage doesn't comment explicitly on natural theology, the primacy it accords to faith as the proper basis of theology renders the project of natural theology moot, at best.

It is important to note that Heidegger's use of "faith" here does not designate an epistemically unsupported acceptance of the propositions of dogmatics. On the contrary, he regards dogmatic propositions with the same suspicion with which he regards propositional formulations of philosophical insight: they represent the ossification and degradation of once-living experiences. For Heidegger, faith is a distinctive mode of Being-in-the-world, a mode which he struggles to describe in the lectures of the early 1920s but which he simply sets aside in *Being and Time* and subsequent writings. Working out the relation between faith as a mode of Being-in-the-world and Being-in-the-world as Heidegger interprets it in *Being and Time* is difficult. How are we to take Heidegger's stated neutrality on theological issues? Is faith simply one of many concrete determinations of Being-in-the-world, while Heidegger restricts his attention (as a philosopher) to generic Being-in-the-world? If so, then Heidegger's philosophy is neutral as regards faith in the same way that it is neutral as regards Romanian as opposed to Japanese Being-in-the-world. But sometimes Heidegger speaks as if there is a fundamental disparity between the Being-in-the-world of faith and the Being-in-the-world out of which he asks the question of Being. We hear just such a claim in a second, closely related objection to natural theology.

2.

When offered by a believer, the theistic arguments represent acts of hypocrisy in that the believer only pretends to put in question the existence of God.

> One who holds to such faith can in a way participate in the asking of our question, but he cannot really question without ceasing to be a believer and taking all the consequences of such a step. He will only be able to act "as if . . . " (*IM*, p. 7)

Any number of apologists who have employed theistic arguments would agree with Heidegger that faith is the basis both of their Being-in-the-world and their relation to God, but they would go on to assert that natural theology remains legitimate as a way to convert others, as a way to answer objections (Plantinga's "defeater defeaters"), or as a way for faith to seek understanding (Anselm's Proslogion). Heidegger rejects such employments of the theistic arguments as deceptive and hypocritical, because true questioning must hold itself open to the outcome of the questioning and cannot predetermine its results. But Heidegger's focus here isn't so much on deception or hypocrisy as moral shortcomings as it is on the closed quality of faith. Heidegger describes believers as those excluded from asking the central philosophical question. He ironically reverses Paul by describing philosophy as foolishness to believers, since philosophy persists in asking the question, "Why are there essents rather than nothing?"—a question that can never arise for the believer, since it is already answered before it can be asked. In his next objection to natural theology, we get a further description of this closing off of the ontological question.

3.

The theistic arguments offer ontic responses to an ontological question.

> The Being of entities "is" not itself an entity. If we are to understand the
> problem of Being, our first philosophical step consists in not *muthon tina*
> *diegeisthai* in not "telling a story"—that is to say, in not defining entities as
> entities by tracing them back in their origin to some other entities, as if Being
> had the character of some possible entity. (*BT,* p. 26)[22]

These passages connect Heidegger's rejection of the theistic arguments
with the dominant concern of his thought, the thinking of Being. To
try to answer ontological questions—questions of why what-is is and
why it is meaningful—in terms of a particular entity, even when that
entity is God, is worse than useless. By giving the appearance but not
the substance of an answer, we simply cover over the question and
return to everyday fallenness and forgetfulness of Being.[23]

4.

The theistic arguments are causal arguments, which infer God's existence as the cause of observed effects. At times, this objection is identical to the previous one in that ontic explanation is simply causal explanation. One entity explains another by being identified as its cause.
Thus, Heidegger writes, "The question 'why' does not look for causes
that are of the same kind and on the same level as the essent itself"
(*IM*, p. 3). But this is really to say that Heidegger doesn't look for causes
at all, since he limits "cause" to the ontic level and uses "ground" to
describe the relation between Being and beings (see *IM*, p. 2–3). In
many of Heidegger's later texts, however, the critique of causal thinking
takes on an additional dimension and urgency in that causal thinking is identified with the technological vision of the world. Heidegger
specifically identifies the "Principle of Sufficient Reason"—the "mighty
principle" which Leibniz brought to explicit formulation in stating the
cosmological argument—as the power that dominates us in this technological age.[24] Heidegger's lament over the domination of technology
is not finally distinct from his concern over providing merely ontic answers to the ontological question: the ultimate tragedy of causal, cal-
culative, technological thinking isn't the despoilment of the earth or
the manipulation of human beings (which are ontic concerns) but
rather the obscuring of Being that they bring about.[25] Since the theistic
arguments are causal arguments, they contribute to and represent
symptoms of this obscuring of Being. What is more, the very god they
infer is part and parcel of this desolate condition.

5.

The god whose existence is inferred via the theistic arguments is an
unworthy, false god. Unlike many critics of natural theology, Heidegger

doesn't simply assert that the arguments fail. The ontic, causal thinking of the arguments does lead us to a god, but this god is the god of metaphysics, not "the divine God." The theistic arguments find only what they went looking for: a cause to explain observed effects.

Thought metaphysically, the place that is peculiar to God is the place of causative "bringing about" and the preserving of whatever is, as something created.[26] What is it that keeps Heidegger from joining Aquinas in saying of the first cause, of the *causa sui,* that "This all men call God?" In "The Onto-Theo-Logical Constitution of Metaphysics," Heidegger answers vividly,

> This ground itself needs to be properly accounted for by that for which it accounts, that is, by the causation through the supremely original matter— and that is the cause as causa sui. This is the right name for the god of philosophy. Man can neither pray nor sacrifice to this god. Before the causa sui, man can neither fall to his knees in awe nor can he play music and dance before this god.[27]

This sounds like Pascal's assertion that the god of the philosophers isn't the God of Abraham, Isaac, and Jacob—that the cold, bloodless abstraction of natural theology is distinct from the living God of Israel. But Heidegger's indictment isn't simply based on what is missing from the god of the philosophers, on the ways that that god is a drastically diminished version of the living God. His indictment relates fundamentally to the use to which that god is put.

> We can properly think through the question, How does the deity enter into philosophy?, only when that to which the deity is to come has become sufficiently clear: that is, philosophy itself. As long as we search through the history of philosophy merely historically, we shall find everywhere that the deity has entered into it. But assuming that philosophy, as thinking, is the free and spontaneous self-involvement with beings as such, then the deity can come into philosophy only insofar as philosophy, of its own accord and by its own nature, requires and determines that and how the deity enters into it. (*ID*, p. 56)

That is, the deity of ontotheology serves us. We call the shots. Intellectually, this god serves to tidy up our explanations of reality, just as ethically and politically, this god serves to validate whatever regimes we need validated. This reduction of God to an instrumental role, to our tool, Heidegger most vividly elucidates in "The Word of Nietzsche: God is Dead."[28] Heidegger does not read the death of God of which Nietzsche speaks as a statement of "vulgar atheism"—the simple denial of God. The true death of God, or better the murder of God, lies in our reduction of God to a value, to the status of a means to our ends.

To summarize Heidegger's critique, natural theology, in pursuing the wrong task, loses itself in ontic, causal, technological thinking, thereby divorcing itself from faith and from all sense of Being, so that it comes to degrade and debase the God it purportedly serves. To put it in biblical terms, natural theology is guilty of idolatry. Heidegger comes very close to saying this explicitly when he says that the god of on-totheology is not one before whom one can dance or sacrifice. This charge becomes explicit when we link the statement quoted above (that natural theology prevents us from thinking Being itself) with Heidegger's claim (in "What is Metaphysics?") that we will only be able to leap into an awareness of Being when we free ourselves "from the idols to which we have been wont to go cringing" (WM, p. 257). In light of this charge of idolatry, we can begin to understand Heidegger's apparently hyperbolic claim that atheism may be closer to the divine God than is that which passes for theism.

> The god-less thinking which must abandon the god of philosophy, god as causa sui, is thus perhaps closer to the divine God. Here this means only: god-less thinking is more open to Him than onto-theo-logic would like to admit. (*ID*, p. 72)

But let us cast a suspicious glance at Heidegger's "Here this means only": is Heidegger's critique of natural theology, specifically, and of belief in God as the highest value really, as this suggests, just a propaedeutic, just a smashing of idols, that will clear the way for faith? Is this endorsement of atheism really a token of an open waiting for God? Or is there more to Heidegger's valorizing of atheism than that would suggest? To answer that, we turn in our final section to the question of lineage. Should we see Heidegger's critique of natural theology as continuous with the critiques offered by Kierkegaard and Barth, or is Nietzsche not the more apt connection?

III. Heidegger's Lineage

Heidegger's critique of natural theology is so stunningly parallel to those of Kierkegaard and Barth that there is a strong suggestion of important, direct influence. One might even speak of the three thinkers as forming a tradition of "Kierkegaardian objections to natural theology" comparable to the tradition of Reformed objections to natural theology that Plantinga has identified. To document the parallelism between the three, let us review the five objections to natural theology identified in the previous section.

1.

"Theology is seeking a more primordial interpretation of man's Being toward God, prescribed by the meaning of faith itself and remaining within it" (*BT*, p. 30). That Kierkegaard and Barth also insist on the centrality of faith in religious existence is too familiar a point to belabor. But the passage quoted above isn't simply about the nature of religious existence. In the first instance, it is a statement about proper theological procedure. Kierkegaard and Barth share with Heidegger this sense of the importance of methodological clarity and, like Heidegger, distinguish theology from philosophy on the basis of the foundational significance of faith for the former. This shared sense that sharp boundaries (and perhaps even good fences) make good neighbors is noteworthy in that these three thinkers work those boundaries. While Heidegger clearly identifies himself as a philosopher, Barth clearly identifies himself as a theologian, and Kierkegaard clearly identifies which hat he is wearing at a given time; the tension between philosophical and theological inquiry profoundly shapes the thinking of all three.

2.

"One who holds to such faith can in a way participate in the asking of our question, but he cannot really question without ceasing to be a believer and taking all the consequences of such a step. He will only be able to act 'as if'" (*IM*, p. 7). Heidegger's sense that believers who propound theistic arguments are doing so in bad faith has clear echoes in Kierkegaard and Barth. In *Philosophical Fragments*, Kierkegaard charges that "The whole process of demonstration continually becomes something entirely different, becomes an expanded concluding development of what I conclude from having presupposed that the object of investigation exists."[29] That is, he believes the premises of the theistic arguments to contain hidden presuppositions of God's existence and thus to be begging the question. Plantinga made Barth's similar, if sharper, statement of this criticism familiar to the philosophical community in singling it out (questionably) as the basis of Barth's rejection of natural theology.

> Now suppose the partner in the conversation discovers that faith is trying to use the well-known artifice of dialectic in relation to him. We are not taking

him seriously because we withhold from him what we really want to say and represent. It is only in appearance that we devote ourselves to him, and therefore what we say to him is only an apparent and unreal statement.[30]

3.

"The Being of entities 'is' not itself an entity" (*BT,* p. 26). Finding parallels in Kierkegaard and Barth to such an idiosyncratically Heideggerian concern as the thinking of Being might seem unlikely, but a significant point of connection appears when we recall that Heidegger speaks of the ontological difference. Heidegger repeatedly tells us that Being is totally different from, utterly other than, beings. This motif of utter otherness is, of course, central to both Kierkegaard and Barth and is a substantial motivation for their rejections of natural theology. For if God is truly "*totaliter aliter,*" we won't be able to mount the logical "*scala paradisi*" implied ironically by Kierkegaard's pseudonym, Johannes Climacus. It is significant that Climacus identifies God as the unknown in Chapter 3 of *Philosophical Fragments,* the same chapter in which he offers his critique of natural theology. And Barth is unambiguous in drawing such a negative conclusion from the otherness of God.[31]

4.

The theistic arguments are causal arguments, inferring God's existence as the cause of observed effects. While all three thinkers object to the causal character of the theistic arguments, their reasons for doing so are somewhat diverse. Kierkegaard's objections are essentially epistemic. He denies that the observed effect (the world) unambiguously results from a divine cause.[32] But his objection here isn't to thinking of God as a cause. Rather, he explicitly affirms that God is a cause, specifically a freely effecting one, so as to preserve a sense of the contingency of the world and the freedom of the creator against the Hegelian endeavor to view reality as the product of a logical dialectic (and hence to see it in terms of ground-consequent relations). Barth agrees with Heidegger in vigorously rejecting the reduction of God to the status of *causa sui* and infers from God's otherness that God is outside the causal nexus. Interestingly, Barth describes the baleful consequences of ignoring God's otherness by thinking of God as an "exalted force," as natural theology does, in terms that are strikingly similar to Heidegger's concern that causal thinking will induce (cause?) us to see Being as a being.

We make of the eternal and ultimate presupposition of the Creator a "thing in itself" above and in the midst of other things, of that which is living and abstracted from all concreteness a concrete thing—no doubt the highest—in the midst of other things, of the Spirit a spirit. . . . Rather than see in His Light—eternal and which no man can approach unto—the Light, we allow Him to become a light. (*R,* p. 47)

5.

The god of natural theology is an idol. In Chapter 3 of *Philosophical Fragments,* after identifying God as the unknown and dismissing the attempts of natural theology to achieve knowledge of the divine, Kierkegaard describes the typical human response, "fantastical fabrication" and "capricious arbitrariness" (p. 45), whereby humans produce their own gods—that is, idols. He continues by describing a ghoulish doppelgänger of Christ, a human-invented notion of God become human—so human, in fact, that in no regard is this incarnate God discernible or distinctive from everyone else. Rather than denouncing a comfortably alien and untempting idol, such as a golden calf, Kierkegaard identifies idolatry with the obliteration of God's otherness and the validation of ourselves and our ways. The immediate proximity to the discussion of natural theology at least suggests that natural theology itself could be the means to such idolatrous self-deification. That suggestion is confirmed in Kierkegaard's assertion that it is the mark of an idol to be known directly, without the risks of offense and uncertainty.[33] And when, as in Christendom, the true God is worshipped complacently, without these risks, even that true God is worshipped as an idol, even as a person worshipping an idol truly actually worships God. Kierkegaard further radicalizes his critique of overt but complacent belief when he says that not only the devout heathen but also the impassioned atheist is closer to belief, a claim that either anticipates or inspires Heidegger's similar claim. With a characteristically paradoxical flourish, Barth offers a ringing denunciation of natural theology as idolatry on the basis of the biblical passage, in Romans, most frequently cited in support of natural theology:

> For what can be known about God is plain to them. Ever since the creation of the world his invisible nature, namely his eternal power and deity, has been clearly perceived in the things that have been made. So they are without excuse. (Rom. 1:19–20)

The key to Barth's radical reinterpretation of these lines is his emphasis on what follows in verses 21–23:

> for although they knew God, they did not honor him as God or give thanks to him, but they became futile in their thinking and their senseless minds were darkened. Claiming to be wise, they became fools, and exchanged the

glory of the immortal God for images resembling mortal man or birds or animals or reptiles.

Why does Paul, like Kierkegaard, place a discussion of idolatry so close to his discussion of the natural knowledge of God? As Barth sees it, it isn't that people ignore natural evidence of God and thus fall into idolatry. Rather, to relate to God on the basis of that evidence as opposed to on faith leads to (or may be) idolatry.

> The whole world is the footprint of God; but in so far as we choose scandal rather than faith, the footprint in the vast riddle of the world is the footprint of His Wrath. (R, p. 43)

For Barth, "Wrath" has a special significance over and above God's appropriate anger; it designates "the questionableness of life in so far as we do not apprehend it" (R, p. 42). How, precisely, does natural theology subject us to wrath—that is, hide from us our "questionableness?" In the first instance, it does so by placing us on the same level as God, even though it apparently assigns God the most honorific status:

> Our relation to God is ungodly. We suppose that we know what we are saying when we say "God." We assign to him the highest place in our world: and in so doing we place Him on one side with ourselves and with things. (R, p. 44)

Once the qualitative difference between God and humans is obscured, the way is open for us to use God to our own ends, and this invariably takes the form of idolatry.

> We are not concerned with God, but with our own requirements, to which God must adjust himself. Our arrogance demands that, in addition to everything else, some super-world should also be known and accessible to us. Our conduct calls for some deeper sanction, some approbation and remuneration from another world. Our well-regulated, pleasurable life longs for some hours of devotion, some prolongation into infinity. And so, when we set God upon the throne of the world, we mean by God ourselves. In "believing" on Him, we justify, enjoy and adore ourselves. (R, p. 44)
> Wherever the qualitative difference between men and the final Omega is overlooked or misunderstood, that fetishism is bound to appear in which God is experienced in birds and fourfooted things, and finally, or rather primarily, in the likeness of corruptible man—Personality, the Child, the Woman—and the half-spiritual, half-material creations, exhibitions, and representations of His creative ability—Family, Nation, State, Church, Fa-

therland. And so the "No-God" is set up, idols are erected and God, who dwells beyond all this and that, is "given up." (*R*, pp. 50–51)

This grim picture leads Barth to affirm atheism over idolatrous belief in terms that are very similar to Heidegger's: "The cry of revolt against such a god is nearer the truth than is the sophistry with which men attempt to justify him" (*R*, p. 40).

There are, then, striking parallelisms between the critiques of natural theology offered by Kierkegaard, Barth, and Heidegger. But the question remains open as to the fundamental meanings of those critiques. Kierkegaard and Barth criticize natural theology, in the name of faith, as the proper mode of relation to God. In contrast, Heidegger criticizes natural theology (and ontotheology, generally) in the name of awareness of Being. Thus, placing Heidegger in reference to Kierkegaard and Barth requires determining the relation between faith in the "divine God" and awareness of Being. Heidegger's standard response is to keep the two separate, leaving the former as the legitimate province of theology and the latter of philosophy. But is this compartmentalization an evasion? Does Heidegger's commitment to the question of Being ultimately lead him to a negative judgment of faith parallel to his negative judgment of ontotheology? Earlier I quoted a passage from *An Introduction to Metaphysics* that says that believers can only act "as if" they are asking the ontological question. The continuation of that passage confirms that Heidegger believes that faith, just as much as natural theology, closes off the question of Being.

What we have said about security in faith as one position in regard to the truth does not imply that the biblical "In the beginning God created heaven and earth" is an answer to our question. Quite aside from whether these words from the Bible are true or false for faith, they can supply no answer, because they are in no way related to it. Indeed, they cannot even be brought into relation with our question. From the standpoint of faith, our question is "foolishness."

Philosophy is this very foolishness. A "Christian philosophy" is a round square and a misunderstanding. There is, to be sure, a thinking and questioning elaboration of the world of Christian experience, i.e. of faith. That is theology. Only epochs that no longer fully believe in the true greatness of the task of theology arrive at the disastrous notion that philosophy can help to provide a refurbished theology if not a substitute for theology, which will satisfy the needs and wants of the time. For the original Christian faith philosophy is foolishness. To philosophize is to ask "Why are there essents rather than nothing at all?" Really to ask the question signifies: a daring attempt to fathom the unfathomable question by disclosing what it summons us to

ask, to push our questioning to the very end. Where such an attempt occurs
there is philosophy. (*IM*, pp. 6–8)

Given that Heidegger speaks in that passage of the "true greatness" of
theology (a compliment rather tarnished by the fact that in the same
lecture course he speaks of the "inner truth and greatness" of Nazism
[*IM*, p. 199]), it is initially implausible to suggest that Heidegger here
delegitimizes faith. But Heidegger says that faith, true faith and not just
idolatrous faith in the causa sui of ontotheology, occludes the question
of Being. But why should it? If the question of Being essentially involves wonder that what-is is, then why shouldn't faith essentially involve grateful wonder at God's gift of creation? Heidegger's overt response here is that one cannot truly ask a question (in this case, "Why
are there essents?") if one already has an answer (in this case, God).
But the issue here isn't really one of when one finds an answer but
rather of whether one does. Heidegger presses his question not to get
an answer but to make us feel the absence of an answer. His motivation for denying an answer is, in part, psychological, since anxiety is
uniquely the mood to which Being shows itself. Just as comforting
assurances about an afterlife can stifle proper anxiety in the face of
death, so belief in God as our creator can tranquilize a proper sense of
our thrownness.

Heidegger zealously protects the mystery of both our whence and
whither and thus views with suspicion theistic reassurances on both
counts. But beyond the psychological agenda of protecting anxiety
from tranquilization, is there an ontological dimension to his refusal of
faith? In the passage above, Heidegger describes philosophy as "a daring attempt to fathom this unfathomable question." I take his use of
"unfathomable" not as a hyperbolic way of saying "very difficult" but
as indicating that there is no answer, that we find no bottom in this
deep, that Being, the ground of beings, has no ground and so hangs
suspended in the abyss. Heidegger presents this as a possibility in *An
Introduction to Metaphysics* (where he says our search for a ground may
only find an abyss or non-ground [*IM*, p. 3]), but it is a possibility he
had already confirmed in *Being and Time*: "'In-itself' it is quite incomprehensible why entities are to be uncovered, why truth and Dasein
must be" (*BT*, p. 271; See also *BT*, p. 194, and WM, p. 258).

Note that he says here that the event of Being, the disclosure of
truth, is incomprehensible in itself and not simply for us. Whereas the
Kierkegaardian abyss—the 70,000 fathoms—is an epistemological
abyss, an abyss of uncertainty resulting from our finite and fallen condition, it is plausible to take Heidegger's abyss to be ontological, to be a
description of the way things are ultimately. As such, the abyss Heideg-

ger describes is more like the empty space described by Nietzsche's madman.[34] And just as Nietzsche's madman precedes his proclamation of empty space by purportedly seeking God, so Heidegger's evocations of teleology and cosmological wonder, his asking of questions that seem to cry out for theistic answers, ultimately serve to make his readers feel that absence all the more deeply. Thus, Heidegger's critique of natural theology, though very like the critiques of Kierkegaard and Barth in terms of detail, is arguably more like Nietzsche's announcement of the "Twilight of the Idols" in terms of substance. But only arguably. It remains possible to read Heidegger's abyss as an epistemological abyss—like Kierkegaard's 70,000 fathoms. After all, Heidegger expresses due phenomenological modesty when he writes, "[Our investigation] asks about Being itself in so far as Being enters into the intelligibility of Dasein" (*BT*, p. 194). Since "a 'ground' becomes accessible only as a meaning" (*BT*, p. 194) and meanings are within our world of experience, that which is the transcendent(al) condition of that world would necessarily be available only as an abyss. At least unless and until that transcendent(al) condition decided to make itself known.

While Heidegger's description of a thoroughly contingent world of meanings hanging unsupported in an abyss of meaninglessness provides the guiding ontological vision for his postmodern heirs (e.g., Foucault, Derrida, Rorty), Heidegger himself cannot resist projecting religious veneration out into the abyss: "For hard by essential dread, in the terror of the abyss, there dwells awe (Scheu). Awe clears and enfolds that region within which man endures, as at home, in the enduring" (WM, p. 261). The religious character of this awe is unambiguous, given that Heidegger speaks of responding to the object of that awe, Being, with sacrifice and thanks.

So we end where we began—with ambivalence. Heidegger's thought both stimulates "the religious instinct" and suspiciously resists "theistic satisfaction." What has been accomplished in tracing this circuit? First, we have seen that Heidegger's critique of natural theology is part of a tradition that begins with Kierkegaard and includes Barth. Given the fragmentary, obscure, and sometimes hyperbolic character of each of these three thinkers' critiques of natural theology, viewing them as a group can be quite useful in determining the proper readings of those critiques. But beyond this essentially historical finding, I believe this essay shows us something about the ambiguous relations of theism and atheism today. While in the past theism and atheism faced each other with clearly drawn battle lines, the situation we have surveyed is far less definite. On the one hand, we have seen Kierkegaard and Barth, who criticize theism from within (in the name of faith), praise atheism as preferable to theism. While they meant this as a shocking call back to true faith, their critiques are readily appropriated by Heidegger, whose position on faith is unclear, and thereafter by less ambiguously atheistic philosophers. On the other hand, the prophetic zeal with which those atheistic philosophers denounce our theistic idols is itself borrowed from the life of faith. Those thinkers dwell under the threat of inadvertently or at least un-self-consciously serving the very God they deny. And while it might be thought an evasion, a failure to complete the task of deciding Heidegger's proper filiation, this ambiguous conclusion, like the dying Lessing's ambiguous answer to Jacobi that Kierkegaard so enjoyed,[35] is actually quite Kierkegaardian and in sharp contrast to the unambiguous if still ambivalent atheism of Nietzsche and that of his postmodern heirs, who join him in proclaiming the death of God.

Notes

1. Friedrich Nietzsche, *The Gay Science*, trans. Walter Kaufmann (New York: Random House, 1974), p. 181.

2. George Steiner, *Heidegger*, (Chicago: University of Chicago Press, 1987), p. 11. "It is the unique and specific business of philosophy, therein and at all times referential to its Greek inception, to be incessantly astonished at and focused on the fact that all things are; that there is a universal and totally determinant attribute to things, which is that of existence. This astonishment and the meditation it entails—what Heidegger would call 'the thinking of Being', 'the endeavor to think Being'—sets philosophy on the way toward the question of what it is that is, of what indwells in all extant things, of what it is that constitutes beingness" (p. 27).

3. Martin Heidegger, "What is Metaphysics?", in *Existentialism from Dostoyevsky to Sartre*, revised and expanded edition, ed. Walter Kaufmann (New York: New American Library, 1975), p. 261. Hereafter referred to parenthetically in text as WM.

4. Martin Heidegger, *An Introduction to Metaphysics*, trans. Ralph Manheim (New Haven, Conn.: Yale University press, 1959), p. 1; hereafter referred to parenthetically in text as IM.

5. See Michel Foucault, *The Foucault Reader*, ed. Paul Rabinow (New York: Pantheon, 1984). Foucault, in discussing Nietzsche, gives a vivid if jaundiced view of this tendency when he writes, "History also teaches how to laugh at the solemnities of the origin. The lofty origin is no more than 'a metaphysical extension that arises from the belief that things are most precious and essential at the moment of birth' (Nietzsche, *Wanderer*, no. 3). We tend to think that this is the moment of their greatest perfection, when they emerged dazzling from the hands of a creator or in the shadowless light of a first morning. The origin always precedes the Fall. It comes before the body, before the world and time; it is associated with the gods, and its story is always sung as a theogony" (p. 79). Foucault's parenthetical citation

is from Friedrich Nietzsche, *The Wanderer and His Shadow* (1880), in *Complete Works* (New York: Gordon Press, 1974), no. 3.

6. A short passage from Samuel Clarke's *A Demonstration of the Being and Attributes of God* (1705) is anthologized in Baruch Brody, ed., *Readings in the Philosophy of Religion: An Analytic Approach* (Englewood Cliffs, N.J.: Prentice Hall, 1974), pp. 66–67.

7. See David Hume, *Dialogues Concerning Natural Theology*, part 9, and Paul Edwards, "The Cosmological Argument," in Baruch Brody, ed., *Readings in the Philosophy of Religion*, pp. 71–83.

8. Martin Heidegger, *Being and Time*, trans. John Macquarrie and Edward Robinson (New York: Harper and Row, 1962). Hereafter referred to parenthetically in text as *BT*.

9. Ibid., p. 25, which states, "Inquiry, as a kind of seeking, must be guided beforehand by what is sought. So the meaning of Being must already be available to us in some way. As we have intimated, we always exist in an understanding of Being. Out of this understanding arise both the explicit question of the meaning of Being and the tendency that leads us towards it conception." See also *BT*, p. 62.

10. Martin Heidegger, *Basic Writings*, ed. David Farrell Krell (New York: Harper and Row, 1977), p. 392.

11. Paul Davies, *The Mind of God* (New York: Simon and Schuster, 1992), p. 20. Meynell summarizes his version of the argument thus: "(1) that knowledge is possible; (2) that the world is nothing other than what knowledge, actual or potential, is of; (3) that the world's capacity to be known entails something about its overall nature and structure; (4) that the fact that it has such an overall nature and structure is best accounted for on the supposition that it is due to the fiat of some one entity analogous to the human mind; which is roughly what is commonly meant by 'God'" (p. 118). See also C. S. Lewis, *Miracles* (New York: Macmillan, 1947), in which Lewis summarizes his version of the argument thus: "This [the belief that God created Nature], and perhaps this alone, fits in with the fact that Nature, though not apparently intelligent, is intelligible—that events in the remotest parts of space appear to obey laws of rational thought. Even the act of creation itself presents none of the intolerable difficulties which seem to meet us on every other hypothesis" (p. 41).

12. Davies, *Mind of God*, p. 20.

13. Otto Pöggler, *Heidegger's Path of Thought*, trans. Daniel Magurshak and Sigmund Barber (Atlantic Highlands, N.J.: Humanities Press International, 1987), p. 3.

14. See George Kovacs, *The Question of God and Heidegger's Phenomenology* (Evanston, Ill.: Northwestern University Press, 1990), p. 63. Kovacs glosses Heidegger's point: "The World is a network (matrix) of relations (*Bezugszusammenhang*) of purposefulness, an existential of There-being as to-be-in-the-World. There-being is the ontic condition of the possibility of discoverabilty of being encountered as 'being-destined' (*Bewandtnis*) in the World. Through this encounter the 'in-themselves' (*An-sich*) of beings can be disclosed. There-being is already referred to an ontic World to be encountered. Here appears the basic referential dependence (*Angewiesenheit*) of There-being on other beings (instruments). The World is a horizon, a 'wherein' (*Worin*), within which the instrument is encoun-

tered by There-being. The World is the network of relations that renders possible the purposefulness (the Being) of an instrument. There-being, by comprehending its own Being, comprehends the ultimate term of references (of instruments), and this disclosure of the 'whereunto' is ontologically prior to the ontic encounter (with an instrument)."

15. Ibid. Sartre's claim that all specific, ontical experiences of nausea are dependent on ontological nausea is interestingly parallel to Heidegger in its meaning.

16. Karl Löwith writes, "Consciousness is the necessary condition for the emergence of meaning and objects, but it does not create them" (quoted in Kovacs, *Question of God*, p. 29).

17. Mircea Eliade, *Sacred and Profane*, trans. Willard Trask (New York: Harcourt, Brace, and World, 1959), pp. 165, 178. Derrida makes much the same point: in discussing the distinctively religious view of reality, he writes, "The nonquestion of which we are speaking is the unprecedented certainty that Being is a Grammar; and that the world is in all its parts a cryptogram to be constituted or reconstituted through poetic inscription or deciphering; that the book is original, that everything belongs to the book before being and in order to come into the world; that any thing can be born only by approaching the book, can die only by failing in sight of the book; and that always the impassable shore of the book is first." Jacques Derrida, "Edmond Jabes and the Question of the Book," in *Writing and Difference*, trans. Alan Bass (Chicago: University of Chicago Press, 1978), pp. 76–77. This serves as an admirably concise statement of the view that I have been seeking to show is Heidegger's.

18. See Edmund Husserl, *Ideas Pertaining to a Pure Phenomenology and a Phenomenological Philosophy*, trans. F. Kersten (Dordrecht: Kluwer, 1982), p. 134. There is no doubt that Heidegger was quite aware that a teleological argument could be formulated on the basis of the world's intelligibility, since Husserl does just that in *Ideas*. "Reduction of the natural world to the absolute of consciousness yields factual concatenations of mental processes of consciousness of certain kinds of distinctive regular orders in which a morphologically ordered world in the sphere of empirical intuition becomes constituted as their intentional correlate, i.e., a world concerning which there can be classifying and describing sciences. At the same time, precisely this world, with respect to the material lower level, admits of becoming determined in the theoretical thinking of mathematical natural sciences as the 'appearance' of a Nature as determined by physics, subject to laws of Nature which are exact. In all this, since the rationality made actual by the fact is not a rationality demanded by the essence, there is a marvelous teleology." Note that Husserl's statement of "rational grounds for [believing in] the existence of an extra-worldly 'divine' being" (p. 134) resembles that of Paul Davies more closely than it resembles that of Heidegger in that Husserl focuses on the success of the natural sciences.

19. Heidegger, *Basic Writings*, p. 392.

20. Even before turning to his explicit objections to natural theology, a reflection on the two experiential indications of theism just surveyed shows that theism may be on unsteady footing in Heidegger's thought. While many apologists see the different theistic arguments as working together to form a "cumulative case," Heidegger's two types of quasi- or proto-religious experience undercut each other.

On the one hand, cosmological wonder—wonder that what-is is—emerges precisely in the experience of the collapse of meaning and the defamiliarization of the world, thus calling into question the sense of the world as a domain of preexistent significance. On the other hand, the experience of the world as meaningful and significant breeds a familiarity and an "at-homeness" that Heidegger labels fallenness, the fascination with beings that abolishes the awareness of Being, the sense of cosmological wonder.

21. Martin Heidegger, *The Question Concerning Technology*, trans. William Lovitt (New York: Harper and Row, 1977), pp. 3–21. Heidegger gives a much fuller development of this view of faith as the proper basis of theology in the contemporaneous essay, "Phenomenology and Theology." This essay is especially significant in that it spells out the way Heidegger sees philosophy serving as a "corrective" to theology despite the fact that, as he sees it, theology should appeal to faith as its ultimate basis and not to rational demonstrations of the existence of God.

22. According to Heidegger, "Every entity which is not God is an *ens creatum*. The Being which belongs to one of these entities is 'infinitely' greater than that which belongs to the other; yet we still consider creation and creator alike as entities" (*BT*, p. 125).

23. In this regard, Heidegger's rejection of natural theology is very like Socrates' challenges to the all-too-ready answers his partners give to his questions in dialogue. Only by taking away those answers could Socrates lead his partners into really hearing and really thinking about his questions.

24. Martin Heidegger, *The Principle of Reason*, trans. Reginald Lilly (Bloomington: Indiana University Press, 1991), p. 121.

25. See Martin Heidegger, *The End of Philosophy*, trans. Joan Stambaugh (New York: Harper and Row, 1973), p. 104. "[T]he 'world' has become an unworld as a consequence of the abandonment of beings by Being's truth. For 'world' in the sense of the history of Being (cf. *BT*) means the nonobjective presencing of the truth of Being for man in that man is essentially delivered over to Being. In the age of the exclusive power of power, that is, of the unconditional pressing of beings toward being used up in consumption, the world has become an unworld in that Being does presence, but without really reigning. As what is real, beings are real. There are effects everywhere, and nowhere is there a worlding of the world and yet, although forgotten, there is still Being." Heidegger makes the same point in "The Question Concerning Technology": "The rule of Enframing threatens man with the possibility that it could be denied to him to enter into a more original revealing and hence to experience the call of a more primal truth" (Heidegger, *Question Concerning Technology*, p. 28).

26. Heidegger, *Question Concerning Technology*, p. 100.

27. Martin Heidegger, *Identity and Difference*, trans. Joan Stambaugh (New York: Harper and Row, 1969). Henceforth referred to parenthetically in the text as *ID*.

28. In *QT*, pp. 53–112.

29. Søren Kierkegaard, *Philosophical Fragment*, trans. Howard Hong and Edna Hong (Princeton, N.J.: Princeton University Press, 1985), p. 40.

30. Quoted by Plantinga in Alvin Plantinga and Nicholas Wolterstoff, eds., *Faith and Rationality* (Notre Dame: University of Notre Dame Press, 1983), pp. 68–69.

31. "God is the unknown God and precisely because He is unknown He bestows life and breath and all things. Therefore the power of God can be detected neither in the world of nature nor in the souls of men. It must not be confounded with any high exalted force known or knowable. The power of God is not the most exalted of observable forces nor is it either their sum or their fount. Being completely different it is the krisis of all power that by which all power is measured and by which it is pronounced to be both something and nothing, nothing and something." Karl Barth, *The Epistle to the Romans*, trans. Edwyn Hoskyns (Oxford: Oxford University Press, 1980), p. 36. Hereafter referred to parenthetically in the text as *R*.

32. Kierkegaard, *Philosophical Fragment*, p. 42.

33. Søren Kierkegaard, *Concluding Unscientific Postscript*, trans. Howard Hong and Edna Hong (Princeton: Princeton University Press, 1992), vol. 1, p. 246.

34. See Nietzsche, *Gay Science*, p. 181.

35. Kierkegaard, *Concluding Unscientific Postscript*, vol. 1, p. 70.

9

Yearning for Home

The Christian Doctrine of
Creation in a Postmodern Age

STEVEN BOUMA-PREDIGER

"Gee but it's great to be back home, home is where I want to be." So sing Simon and Garfunkel in the opening lines of their song "Keep the Customer Satisfied." This yearning for home, as they tell it, is occasioned by being "on the road so long, my friend" that "if you came along I know you couldn't disagree." Road weary, our peripatetic traveling salesman—always striving to keep the latest customer satisfied—voices a common desire: to be at home. This longing for home is evident not only in music but also in movies. For example, in one of the all-time American movie favorites, *The Wizard of Oz*, Dorothy, having returned to her Kansas farmhouse and family, to musical crescendo exclaims "There's no place like home, there's no place like home!" Like Simon and Garfunkel's first line, this famous last line articulates an apparently common longing of the human soul—to come home.

This yearning for home is by no means limited to secular settings. Religious folk, too, not infrequently speak of home. Many strands of Native American spirituality, for example, are infused with language about the land and earth as home. Judaism is incomprehensible without attention to Israel as homeland. And Christian worship in its many expressions often speaks of home, as is evident in the words of a famous Isaac Watts hymn:

> Our God, our help in ages past,
> Our hope for years to come,
> Be thou our guard while troubles last,
> And our eternal home.

Augustine's restless heart yearning for a home of solace and serenity has a seemingly universal resonance.[1]

Home. Longing for home. Coming home. This theme (or set of themes) lies deep within our psyche. Indeed, many observant culture watchers have concluded that this motif is especially characteristic of contemporary Western culture. For example, Richard Middleton and Brian Walsh claim that "a profound homelessness" pervades modern/postmodern culture.[2] For an increasing number of us today, "the experience of the world as our home, in the sense of a place where we know the rules and responsibilities of the house, is lost and a nomadic homelessness dominates the ethical horizon."[3] In this paper, I intend to explore this theme of postmodern homelessness. More exactly, I aim to show two things. First, such claims about the homelessness of our postmodern age are in fact correct. That is, in many ways and for many reasons, we—as late-twentieth-century Westerners—do not feel at home in the world. Second, the Christian gospel, and particularly the doctrine of creation, properly understood, can offer healing and wholeness to people anxiously adrift in the flux and degradation of the postmodern world. In short, the Christian doctrine of creation can provide needed resources for redemptively addressing the hopes and fears of our postmodern age.

In what follows, I first, ever so briefly, sketch some of the postmodern terrain and in so doing will seek to redeem my claim that our age is aptly described as an age of homelessness. More precisely, I argue that there are three features of our time which give rise to our feelings of homelessness. I then engage in a phenomenological analysis of home and its near equivalents. For the purposes of more deeply understanding both our time and the Christian gospel, we must achieve greater purchase on the experience and the concept of home. Third and last, I attempt to show how the Christian doctrine of creation—the Christian community's storied response to the questions of where we are and who we are as humans—can fittingly and redemptively address our contemporary homelessness. These remarks, too, will of necessity be brief. This endeavor, it should be admitted, is more a programmatic essay than a detailed discussion of a particular argument or line of thought—more like a Monet landscape than a Cézanne still life.

I. Awhirl Is King: The Homelessness of Postmodernity

"I get it. Zeus is dead, and now Awhirl is the new king." So exclaims the old farmer Strepsiades in Aristophanes' comic social commentary, *The Clouds*. Persuaded by Socrates that Zeus has been driven into exile by the new god Awhirl, Strepsiades himself persuades his son Pheidippides that Awhirl is king, and they together seek to flaunt the moral and legal order of ancient Athens for personal gain. Only too late does Strepsiades regretfully realize that his embrace of Awhirl as king has set his mind awirl and thus caused him to reap the bitter consequences of "making love to evil crookery."[4] Awhirl is king. So exclaim many in the postmodern world. Witness contemporary philosopher John Caputo, who describes his hermeneutic project as "a set of reflections aimed at 'coping with the flux,' at learning to get along in the concrete without the guardrails of metaphysics."[5] Our time is often and rightly characterized as a time of ever-accelerating change, motion, flux. As in *The Clouds*, everything seems up in the air, and finding one's way is for many a dizzying and confusing endeavor. Living in a whirlwind is disorienting. All the familiar landmarks are gone or, at best, only vaguely perceived.

This sense of coping with the flux is related to a pervasive sense of rootlessness. Awhirl has uprooted many of our common means of forming and fostering identity and has rendered us homeless wayfarers. As astute observer of American culture Francis Fitzgerald puts it, commenting on communities as vastly different as Liberty Baptist Church, Sun City, Florida, and Rajneeshpuram: "rootlessness and the search for self-definition" are "characteristic features of American life."[6] Or as psychologist Paul Wachtel observes, in his tellingly titled *The Poverty of Affluence:* "We are not only restless but rootless. In the pursuit of more, in the effort to better ourselves, we must leave behind what we previously had."[7] In the poignant words of one young postmodern nomad: "I have no beliefs. I belong to no community, tradition, or anything like that. I'm lost in this vast, vast world. I belong nowhere. I have absolutely no identity."[8] For many today, all the guardrails are gone. They feel rootless and homeless. Like it or not, awhirl is king.

A. Epistemological Constructivism and the Suspicion of Truth

There are at least three reasons for this sense of homelessness. First, there is the widespread belief that all truth claims or claims about reality are merely social constructs. To use the expression made popular by Peter Berger and Thomas Luckmann, reality is a social construction.[9] Or to quote Trudy the bag lady in *The Search for Signs of Intelligent Life in the Universe*, reality is "a collective hunch."[10] As many authors have noted in recent years, the personal features of all knowing, to use Michael Polanyi's language, are ineliminable.[11] This has, of course, been a truism for the hermeneutical tradition for some time, whether evident in Heidegger's notions of *Vorhabe*, *Vorsicht*, and *Vorgriff* or in Gadamer's concepts of *Vorurteile*, *Horizontverschmelzung*, and *Wirkungsgeschichte*.[12] This perspectivalism, in the minds of many, necessarily leads to a strong version of epistemic relativism, illustrated in Richard Rorty's now-famous claim that "truth is what our peers will, *ceteris paribus*, let us get away with saying."[13] Since all claims to truth are merely social constructions, truth is simply an honorific term used to describe our best guess at the way things are, or, in Rorty's more pragmatist reading—in which every whiff of truth as correspondence is banished—simply a term to describe what works.[14]

Related to this epistemological constructivism is a profound and pervasive suspicion that all claims to truth—indeed of all narratives—are nothing more than disguised attempts to control and dominate the other. Perhaps influenced (knowingly or not) by Ricoeur's three "masters of suspicion"—Marx, Nietzsche, and Freud[15]—or, more likely, driven to suspicion and cynicism by devious advertising, corrupt politics, and scandalous religion, a great many people today distrust all theories, stories, worldviews—at least insofar as they imply any sort of universal scope—as simply the will to power of a particular historically situated person, community, or both. In the philosophical literature, this hermeneutics of suspicion is powerfully presented by Nietzsche and, more recently, Foucault.[16]

For example, Foucault the genealogist relentlessly displays "the endlessly repeated play of dominations" in the history of the West, arguing that "humanity installs each of its violences in a system of rules and thus proceeds from domination to domination."[17] Whether in sexual mores or the penal system or the organization of knowledge, the various social practices of Western civilization are nothing more than the will to power. Put in other terms, each society has its "regime of truth" which legitimates certain beliefs and practices, and in so doing inevitably sanctions the domination of those on the margins.[18] Hence, for Foucault, "everything is dangerous."[19] Anything can be (mis)used to do violence to the other. And so, to borrow the language of Merold Westphal, to a hermeneutics of finitude must be added a hermeneutics of faultedness, in which sin becomes an epistemological category.[20] Our claims to truth are not only situated but sinful, and hence we have a double rationale for our suspicion.

The deconstructive scalpel cuts even deeper, however, for it is not just claims to truth which are called into question but also certain common assumptions about meaning, namely that meaning is (or ever can be) fixed. In other words, in our postmodern age there is a kind of semantic homelessness underlying the above-mentioned epistemic homelessness, as Derrida—"the philosopher of the flux par excellence"[21]—especially makes clear. For example, in his important early essay, "Différance," Derrida argues that because words are "irreducibly polysemic," there is an ineradicable undecidability to meaning.[22] In contrast to both Descartes and Hegel, for Derrida there is no "Eden of originary presence" or any "Eschaton of organic totality," and thus meaning is always on the way and never at home.[23] We never stand at the *archê;* nor will we ever reach any *teios.* In short, "displaced presentation remains definitively and implacably postponed," and so we are always already exiles from any permanent semantic resting place.[24] We are all homeless hermeneuts, exiled exegetes, yearning for a homeland that never was and never will be. Indeed, as Caputo insightfully notes, for Derrida any distinction between home and exile disappears since there is no home—"there never was anything originary, primeval, undistorted."[25] *Différance* is originary. So Derrida counsels that we should give up any nostalgia for "a lost native country of thought."[26]

As Middleton and Walsh cogently argue, epistemic and semantic perspectivalism wedded with a hermeneutics of suspicion is powerfully acidic to any secure sense of home for two reasons. First, the recognition that one's own meaning-giving worldview is arbitrary can easily produce anomie and terror. "Since it is precisely the function of a social construction of reality to shield us from the abyss of meaninglessness by providing us with a 'sacred canopy' of meaning and order, the realization that this canopy is humanly constructed (not an inevitable given) leaves us with a sense of vertigo, unprotected before the abyss."[27] In other words, "becoming aware of our worldview *as a worldview,* of its particularity, subjectivity, and limitations, can have a profoundly anomic effect."[28] One feature of being-at-home is having a sense of order and safety. Home is a place made familiar and secure by the recognition and imposition of order. Anomie, as the loss of meaningful order, thus represents a profound kind of homelessness.

Second, the acknowledgement that one's sacred canopy is violent elicits a sense of complicity and guilt. As Middleton and Walsh put it: "If reality is socially constructed, then we have to admit that we have participated (whether actively or by acquiesence) in the construction of what is often a nightmare."[29] As many African Americans will readily and powerfully attest, the sacred dream of "life, liberty, and the pursuit of happiness" has been for them a brutal nightmare.[30] As many women will easily and tearfully declare, the dominant androcentric sacred canopy still disempowers and often abuses them.[31] And, to take only one more of many possible examples, we wealthy members of the so-called "developed nations" are only recently, if at all, waking up to the ecological nightmare no longer merely looming on the horizon but frighteningly real for those with the eyes to see.[32] The disorienting deconstructive therapy of postmodernism, if taken seriously, is, as Middleton and Walsh put it, "profoundly painful."[33] We realize that our home is a house of pain.

B. Socio-Psychological Anomie and the Nomadic Self

Mention of pain leads to the second reason for the homelessness of postmodernity, namely, the experience of self as nomad. In addition to epistemological constructivism, with its suspicion of all stories, another feature of our contemporary age is the socio-psychological anomie produced by the rootlessness of the nomadic self. As many perceptive culture watchers have noted, in the absence of many traditional means of identity formation and given assumptions about the social construction of reality (including the self), postmoderns find that they are multiple selves on an endless quest for stable identity and lasting fulfillment. For example, Walter Truett Anderson claims that we often feel like refugees because we have been "deeply dispossessed" of "old bases of personal and social identity," and so he finds extensive evidence of what he calls the three A's: alienation, anxiety, and anomie.[34] Albert Borgmann speaks of this phenomenon as "the expatriate quality of public life," whereby "we live in self-imposed exile from communal conversation and action."[35] And Paul Wachtel perceptively notes that the changing view of Faust (from villain to hero) well illustrates the claim that restlessness and rootlessness have become modern virtues. As Wachtel observes:

> The rift in community and continuity that so characterizes our lives and the tendency to throw things away—whether possessions, relationships, or ties to a particular place or community—account in substantial measure for why we are so preoccupied with our "identities." In the modern world we must make an identity for ourselves; we do not inherit one.[36]

Unlike the heroic self-construction of modernity, however, the selves under construction in the postmodern age have an identity crisis. For as Anthony Thiselton succinctly puts it, "postmodernism implies a *shattering of innocent confidence in the capacity of the self to control its own destiny.*"[37] Prometheus is no longer the accurate symbol of our age—Sisyphus is. Given the violence perpetuated on human and non-human alike by the modern culture of heroic individualism, our confidence in our ability to control the world is waning, if not extinguished altogether. For example, in our attempts to master ourselves, we find ourselves instead caught in Weber's iron cage. In our schemes to manage "human resources," we dehumanize our sisters and brothers. In our efforts to subdue the natural world, we discover a degraded creation whose wounds cry out for healing. As Middleton and Walsh assert, the "anthropological self-assuredness" of modernity is "difficult to sustain in a postmodern world."[38]

In addition, many people today suffer from what could be called "the Zelig syndrome." Faced with the daunting challenge of creating oneself ever anew—of constructing a self in a world largely devoid of familiar rules or normative guideposts, they grope or dance (depending on one's judgement of the situation) to achieve some semblance of a self. Like Woody Allen's Zelig—who literally changed shape and identity depending on his personal circumstances—postmoderns metamorphose, chameleon-like, into a nearly endless string of identities to conform to the latest fashion or to cope with the unceasing flux. The postmodern self, in short, is an "infinitely malleable self" who takes on the constructed identities proffered by the carnival of contemporary culture.[39]

Of contemporary philosophers, Richard Rorty perhaps most clearly champions this Zelig-like postmodern self. Like Kierkegaard's aesthete, for Rorty the supreme compliment is that something is interesting and, correlatively, the lowest blow is that it is boring. For example, "getting the facts right . . . is merely propaedeutic to finding a new and interesting way of expressing ourselves, and thus of coping with the world."[40] Thus, "edifying philosophy," as Rorty describes it, is characterized by "the poetic activity of thinking up such new aims, new words, or new disciplines."[41] Truly good philosophy is interesting philosophy,[42] and the philosopher should be the poet—"the maker of new words, the shaper of new languages" who is "the vanguard of the species."[43] Indeed, for Rorty, a kind of postmodern redemption is possible only through the project of self-creation exemplified in the work of the poet and in the creation of a "poeticized culture," where the goal is "the creation of ever more various and multicolored artifacts."[44] This making of a self is an endless process in which we "redescribe ourselves, our situation, our past, in those terms [the terms of past heroes like Hegel, Kierkegaard, and Nietzsche] and compare the results with alternative redescriptions which use the vocabularies of alternative figures," thereby hoping "by this continual redescription to make the best selves for ourselves that we can."[45] Such is the postmodern vision of the human and its task: the plastic self always on the prowl.

But how exactly does this view of the human person produce a sense of homelessness? Wherein lies the pain? The Zelig-like nomadic self is homeless for at least two reasons. First, a malleable self always under construction is not easily able to make commitments or enter into lasting relationships, since such relationships necessarily require some relatively stable self to do the relating.[46] As Middleton and Walsh nicely put it, "Who would the *I* be in the *I do?*"[47] The postmodern view of the human person as a series of multiple selves offers precious few psychological resources for making and keeping authentic and satisfying commitments. Because we are a plethora of selves, we do not know who we are; and because we do not know who we are, we are unable to decide what to do. We are not at home with ourselves, for our "selves" are constantly in flux. A Foucaultian reading of the world as the endless play of domination combined with this view of the self as nomad makes it easier to understand why some people maintain that the most prudent course of action to take in making one's way in the world, to use an image from one of my past undergraduate students, is to become an M-1 tank—impervious to all attempts by others to gain intimacy with you and able to steamroll over anyone who dares to stand in your way. The pain and isolation in such a self-image are not difficult to discern. Nor is the sense of homelessness.

Second, the sense of anomie is not only internal but external. That is, the radical undecidability characteristic of the nomadic self is also seen as an inextricable feature of the socially constructed world. So, for example, in the face of moral undecidability and the perceived absence of any moral standards which exist independently of the (all too human) will to power, there are no norms for action. As Alasdair MacIntyre has displayed so persuasively, human action is seen merely as an expression of individual preferences.[48] In sum, "deconstructive patterns of thinking may have therapeutically served us well by uncovering our biases, interests, assumptions and reifications, but they leave us in a normless universe."[49] In a migrancy culture—in which "neither the points of departure nor those of arrival are immutable or certain" and in which identities "are constantly subject to mutation" so that "the promise of a homecoming . . . becomes an impossibility"— there is little or no sense of order, of *nomos*, to be found.[50] Without such *nomos*, we feel homeless.

C. Global Ecological Degradation and Deafness to the Earth

This sense of anomie leads to the third reason why postmodernity can accurately be described as an age of homelessness. Increasingly in our time we learn, often first-hand, of the despoilation of our earthly home. Our planet—this blue-green earth—is being rendered inhospitable, and we, its inhabitants, made to feel not at home in the only house available to us. It is a rare day when we do not learn of some new ecological degradation. Global warming, holes in the ozone layer, toxic wastes, oil spills, acid rain, drinking water contamination, overflowing landfills, topsoil erosion, species extinction, destruction of the rain forests, leakage of nuclear waste, lead poisoning, desertification, smog—such is merely a partial litany of ecological worry and woe.

If our non-scientific observations need any confirmation, there are plenty of more highly trained earth watchers ready and willing to speak out about the current state of the planet. For example, after surveying 700,000 articles in the literature, biologist Calvin DeWitt concludes that "the magnitude of environmental abuse is overwhelming."[51] He lists seven major degradations brought on by our assault on creation: (1) land conversion and habitat destruction (e.g., land lost due to deforestation or human "development"); (2) species extinction—at the rate of three species per day; (3) land abuse (e.g., loss of topsoil to wind and water erosion); (4) resource conversion and waste and hazard production (e.g., manufacture of pesticides and herbicides); (5) global toxification (e.g., chemical and oil spills); (6) alteration of planetary energy exchange (e.g., the greenhouse effect and ozone depletion); and (7) human and cultural degradation (e.g., the displacement of agriculture by agribusiness).[52] Such, unfortunately, is the plight of the earth, our home.

Our sense of the degradation of the earth is shaped not only by books and news reports about far away places but perhaps more powerfully by our own firsthand experience with various forms of ecological dis-ease. For example, Kent County, Michigan, along with Muskegon and Ottawa Counties to the west, are currently out of compliance with the federal clean air standards. In short, there is too much ozone in the air too often in the summer, and so the air is unhealthy to breathe. While much of the problem is traceable to Chicago and Milwaukee—smog, after all, knows nothing of state or national boundaries—these counties have burgeoning populations (200,000 people in Ottawa County alone), and it is clear that much of the problem resides with those of us who live in them. Try as we might, we cannot shake shouldering at least part of the blame. We drive gas-guzzling cars (which cause 60% of the air pollution in most cities) when we could and should walk or bicycle. We mow our lawns and plow our drives with machines which emit various hydrocarbons, carbon monoxide, nitrogen oxides, and lead. In short, we live in a way which renders our own home less than optimally habitable.

It is not only our air but also our water that tells us that our home is despoiled. For example, after most thunderstorms, the Grand River, which runs through the center of Grand Rapids, Michigan, is a veritable sewer. Unable to handle the influx of water, the city dumps millions of gallons of raw sewage into the river—much to the obvious displeasure of those who live downstream, not to mention the non-human creatures who live in or around that body of water. Prospects are not much better in Holland, Michigan, where I reside (thirty-five miles to the west). Our local lake—Lake Macatawa—is second to last (in one survey of ninety lakes tested) in the state in terms of water quality. And Lake Michigan is beset with a variety of problems—from toxic waste to zebra mussels. And these comments pertain to an area of the country—indeed, of the world—that is reasonably healthy, ecologically speaking. Though some are oblivious to the groaning of creation, many people have an inchoate if not visceral sense that all is not well at home on planet earth. Given even a minimal awareness of the problems in our *oikos*, it is not surprising that we feel homeless.[53]

Of the cast of postmodern suspects (at least of the philosophical ilk), it is Heidegger who is most helpful in shedding light on this issue.[54] For example, in his discussion of modernity as the unconditional will to power, Heidegger explains how our objectification of the earth is in fact an assault on the earth. As he puts it:

> In this revolutionary objectifying of everything that is, the earth, that which first of all must be put at the disposal of representing and setting forth, moves into the midst of human positing and analyzing. The earth itself can show itself only as the object of assault, an assault that, in human willing, establishes itself as unconditional objectification. Nature appears everywhere . . . as the object of technology.[55]

In other words, modern Western culture is so suffused with a technological habit-of-being or attitude that everything becomes an object to be used in the service of our own individual or collective human will. Everything becomes "standing reserve"—valuable only as a means to our human ends.[56] But, avers Heidegger, "what a thing is in its Being is not exhausted by its being an object."[57] There is so much more to reality than our objectifying attitude can capture or ever know. As Hamlet insists to Horatio: "There are more things in heaven and earth than are dreamt of in your philosophy."

Elsewhere, Heidegger points to this enthrallment of technique when he decries the "circularity of consumption for the sake of consumption" which so characterizes our technologized culture—"a world which has become an unworld."[58] Unlike the birch tree or the honeybee, which never overstep their possibilities, humans, whose *modus vivendi* is a "technology that devours the earth" in "exhaustion and consumption," transgress their proper limits and drive the earth beyond its own possibilities.[59] According to Heidegger, it is as if "the being of pain were cut off from man under the dominance of the will, similarly the being of joy," and only by means of a stewardly shepherding of Being will our deafness to the pain and the joy of the earth be overcome.[60] In other words, we are, most of us, most of the time, deaf to the groanings of the earth and its creatures, and our deafness is rendering our earthly home increasingly uninhabitable. These insights both illuminate our present creational autism[61] and emphasize the need to learn how the world works, and in so doing, to develop the requisite skills and virtues[62] to fulfill our divine calling to be earthkeepers, so that we can regain a sense of being at home on earth.

In summary, postmodernity is an age of homelessness. Given the suspicion of all stories, generated by various forms of constructivism; given the rootlessness and nomadic nature of the self, fostered by a kind of socio-psychological anomie; and given the unknowing deafness to the non-human other, which has in large measure produced the growing ecological crisis—given all these features of our contemporary world, it is no surprise that many of us feel homeless. But what exactly is it to be homeless? And what does it mean to be at home? What precisely is a home?

II. There's No Place Like Home: A Phenomenology of Home

Dorothy's joyful exclamation, not to mention the above exploration of the postmodern terrain, raises the immediately preceding questions. There is no place like home. But what is a home? A promising start to a better understanding of the phenomenon called home can be made by following the *via negativa*—that is, by contrasting home with some of the things it is not. Home, for example, is not merely a place to stay. We sometimes stay in motels or hotels, perhaps even for relatively long periods of time, but we typically do not consider or call such places home. Motels and hotels signify transience and unfamiliarity, while home is a place of permanence and familiarity. No matter how long we have been there, in a motel we are always a guest. Home, by contrast, signifies a certain degree of spatial permanence—a kind of enduring presence or residence in the same place.

But home is not just a place of permanence, for home is not the same as house. The common expression "Make a house a home" points not only to the denotative but also to the connotative difference between house and home. A house is a residence, whereas a home is an abode.

A house is a domicile, while a home is a dwelling. In a house one occupies space; it is one's legal resting place. It is where the bills come. In a home, one takes a mere place (house) and creates a psychological space in which more than the bills come to rest. It is that to which friends and family come. A house is made of brick or wood or sod or thatch. A home is made of memories and stories and relationships: a place of (mere) residence versus a place of (in)dwelling.

Heidegger both confirms and sharpens this analysis. For example, in his essay "Building, Dwelling, Thinking," he distinguishes building from dwelling. Buildings house us, but "not every building is a dwelling."[63] We inhabit buildings, but we do not dwell in them. And this is so, Heidegger asserts, because "dwelling and building are related as end to means."[64] In other words, a building, while not itself a dwelling, nevertheless is a means to the end of human dwelling. Yet, Heidegger insists, this way of putting it is misleading, for "building is not merely a means and a way toward dwelling—to build is in itself already to dwell."[65] He backs this claim by tracing the etymology of the German verb *bauen* to recover the meaning of building as dwelling (*wohnen*). In sum, "genuine building" is dwelling, and to dwell is "to cherish and protect, to preserve and care for."[66] This, in fact, is the meaning of being human: "To be a human being means . . . to dwell."[67] And for Heidegger, "to dwell" is "to be set at peace."[68] And like the biblical term "shalom," to be at peace implies more than merely the absence of conflict; it means to set free or to spare. Being at peace "takes place when we leave something beforehand in its own essence, when we return it specifically to its essential being."[69] In other words, dwelling is a being at peace in a particular place which involves a "letting be" of the other. Dwelling is, in short, a form of hospitality.

David Orr also insightfully describes this important distinction between residing and dwelling, between being a resident and an inhabitant, with particular attention to matters ecological.

> The resident is a temporary and rootless occupant who mostly needs to know where the banks and stores are in order to plug in. The inhabitant and the particular habitat cannot be separated without doing violence to both. . . . To reside is to live as a transient and as a stranger to one's place, and inevitably to some part of the self. The inhabitant and place mutually shape each other.[70]

Elsewhere, Orr expands on this distinction:

> A resident is a temporary occupant, putting down few roots and investing little, knowing little, and perhaps caring little for the immediate locale be-

yond its ability to gratify. . . . The inhabitant, by contrast, "dwells," as Illich
puts it, in an intimate, organic, and mutually nurturing relationship with a
place. Good inhabitance is an art requiring detailed knowledge of a place,
the capacity for observation, and a sense of care and rootedness.[71]

And so while residents require only "cash and a map," inhabitants
"bear the marks of their places," and when uprooted, they get homesick.[72] And this is so because for the inhabitant, there is a place of
dwelling in which one finds identity and from which one derives
meaning and apart from which one feels a bit lost and lonely.

Reflection on homesickness can further elucidate the meaning of
home. What is it to be homesick? Think of children away from home,
perhaps at a summer camp. Or call to memory the first week or two
at college or university. Or the first months living in a foreign country.
In the case of children, homesickness often has physical symptoms—
upset stomach, loss of appetite, insomnia. Common to almost all such
experiences is a kind of disorientation. When we are homesick, we feel
emotionally out of sorts, out of balance, out of kilter. We more quickly
and easily get lost, turned around, mixed up. The familiar is now un-
familiar—different places, customs, language. The habitual ease with
which we once negotiated much of everyday life is gone: When does
the mail come? Where do I get the car repaired? How do I make a long-
distance call? We no longer feel "at home," because home functions as
a (more than merely physical) point of orientation around which our
world is rendered meaningful. There is a geography of home which
consists of more than the lay of the land. Our unique topography involves more than merely our *topos* as a point on a map, important as
that is.[73] Home is an *axis mundi*.[74]

Such reflection reveals another important ingredient in our experience of home, namely, a sense of belonging. Think of the resonances of
home team, hometown, homeland. Home is where we belong, where
we find a place, where we gain identity. Just ask any long-suffering
Cubs fan or a proud Bostonian or a persecuted Palestinian. Not only
a point of orientation, home is a locus of acceptance and affiliation.
Jürgen Moltmann states it well: "I am 'at home' where people know
me, and where I find recognition without having to struggle for it."[75]
When we are homesick, we long for the familiar and familial bonds
of affection derived from membership in our clan or group. We long
for that place where we belong. Even if those affectional bonds are
strained or absent, we nevertheless find ourselves returning to that
place where we know we will find refuge. To recall Robert Frost's famous words in his poem "The Death of the Hired Man": "Home is the
place where, when you have to go there, they have to take you in."

At a minimum, home is where you are taken in, even if neither you nor your family find the prospect pleasant. More positively, home is "a place where you feel you belong, and which in some sense belongs to you."[76] Home is necessarily interpersonal, essentially intersubjective.

Related to the experience of homesickness is that of homecoming. In times of war, when soldiers return from places of conflict, we speak of homecoming. Many high schools and colleges, usually once a year, have a homecoming for their graduates. And we often refer to Christmas as a time of homecoming for faraway family members who venture home. Here, too, our language discloses that home has to do not primarily with place but with indwelt and intimate space. The home to which we, as soldiers or alumna/ae or family, come when we participate in a homecoming is a webbed network of relationships—with shared stories and memories—that may or may not be fixed to a particular place. For example, while the homecoming of college graduates almost always involves visiting the alma mater—and perhaps reliving one's youth through the smells of the old science building or the feel of Old Main—a return to visit the parents at Christmas may not mean stepping inside the old homestead. Indeed, returning "home" when your parents' home is no longer the address you grew up reciting in school is often a strange and unsettling experience. Home simply does not feel like home. And yet it is a homecoming of sorts, for despite the different place, there is still a space intimately and peculiarly shaped according to the life projects and unique identity of your family. Your picture, after all, hangs on the wall or rests atop the piano.

So what is home and what does it mean to be at home? What insight has this ever-so-brief phenomenology attained? First, home is a place of permanence. Whether connected to a stable locale or not, home signifies that which endures vis-à-vis the transient and the fleeting. Second, home is a dwelling made familiar by the memories and stories and projects which have shaped it as the particular space it is. We are at ease at home because we know the way around, the family customs and quirks and jokes, the rules of the house. Third, as a dwelling (as opposed to a domicile), home is where we are at rest, because there is mutual respect for the integrity of the inhabitants. At home we let each other be. Home is a place of contentment. Fourth, home is a place of hospitality. At home, family is taken in if not welcomed. Ideally, the *Ausländer* too is received. The stranger is welcomed and her needs cared for because one is at home, at ease, without fear. Fifth, more than merely a residence, home is what we inhabit. Ecologically understood, home is our habitat, and as such, it includes the non-human world. Home roots us in a place, embeds us in the sights and smells and sounds of a particular piece of earth. Sixth, home is a point of orientation, according to which our world is made meaningful. It is that *topos* from which our *graphê* makes sense. It is that the absence of which causes us to become sick. Seventh, home is a locus of affiliation. It is where we belong. It is, minimally, where they have to take us in, like it or not. It is, ideally, where we are loved and cherished even though we are known. It is where we have a shot at being forgiven.

In sum, home is a place of shared memories and high hopes, of old traditions and new dreams, of a present enfolded by a sometimes only dimly remembered past and an unforeseen yet awaited future. As the eloquent Frederick Buechner puts it, we are suspended between "the home we knew" and "the home we dream," and so we long for that place "where you feel that all is somehow ultimately well even if things aren't going all that well at any given moment."[77] Home is that familiar place where you can truly be yourself, because you are known and valued and loved. Forgiveness abides at home, for home is a place of grace. Home is that for which, when away, we yearn.

III. All of Our Yearning Only Comes Home to You: Redemptive Homecoming

"Lord of the starfields, Sower of life, / Heaven and earth are full of your light; / Voice of the nova, / Smile of the dew, / All of our yearning only comes home to you." So sings Canadian singer–songwriter Bruce Cockburn. And after this confession of mystery and praise to the creating–sustaining God of the Bible, in a powerful refrain he prays: "O Love that fires the sun keep me burning." In a culture of incredulity toward meta-narratives, of rootlessness and isolation, of deafness to the groaning of creation—in a culture such as this, is it possible that the Christian gospel could speak words of healing and shalom? Can the Christian story and the Christian community redemptively address the hopes and fears of suspicious postmodern nomads living homeless on an increasingly fouled earth? If it can, how exactly will it do this? These questions, among others, are the focus of this section. To recall, my contention is that the Christian gospel, in particular the doctrine of creation, can indeed speak redemptively to the postmodern condition. For as Cockburn asserts, a central claim of the Christian faith is that the Love which fires the sun is our true home. Suffice it to say that here I can only (barely) begin to defend this claim.

Let's take stock. If in modernity certain meta-narratives are taken as true and benign, in postmodernity, all meta-narratives are seen as violent even if partially true. Is it possible to acknowledge the danger of grounding stories and yet affirm a non-violent meta-narrative of God's love affair with the cosmos?[78] If in modernity one finds the false homes of complacency and naïveté, in postmodernity there are the false homes of cynicism and suspicion. Is it possible to move beyond cynicism to the risk of faith as trust, and beyond suspicion to a second naïveté, a home of refined faith?[79] If in modernity there is nostalgia for the Eden of originary presence and hope for the Eschaton of organic totality, in postmodernity there is stern rejection of both nostalgia for the immediacy of pure presence and hope for the totality of absolute knowledge.[80] Granted the full weight of the postmodern critique, is it nevertheless possible to foster authentic hope for the home of which we dream based in part on remembrance of the past actions of that Love which fires the sun?

If modernity is populated with Cartesian/Hegelian epistemic home-boys, postmodernity is rife with Derridean epistemic nomads. Is it possible that a postmodern Christianity might discover an alternative to both—namely, Kierkegaardian epistemic knights of faith?[81] If in modernity human finitude is (falsely believed to be) overcome and we humans declared de facto divine, in postmodernity, human finitude is (rightly seen to be) ineradicable, and the judgement is rendered that there is no God. Is it possible to acknowledge our inescapable finitude as humans but, in so doing, to rejoice that though we are not God, God is?[82] If in modernity we have the individual, rationally superior, inflated self, in postmodernity we find the socially constructed, historically conditioned, deflated self.[83] Is it possible to speak cogently of the person-in-relation, gifted and called by God, neither the measure of all things nor the prisoner of all things?

If modernity gives us the endless possession of the other, postmodernity gives us the endless play of the other. Is it possible to envision and enact genuine receptivity to and care for the other—to offer healing hospitality to the Stranger?[84] If in modernity God was either a projection or a useful fiction (or perhaps real but on holiday), in postmodernity God is either dead or unknowable. Is it possible to affirm a living God—a trinitarian God who is a family of excessive, overflowing love[85]—known preeminently in that crazy carpenter from Nazareth whose *raison d'être* was to suffer with? In sum, if in modernity we are always at home, in postmodernity we are never at home, because there is no home, or at least no permanent home.[86] Is it possible to speak coherently of home, but with the recognition that all homes this side of God's good future fully realized are provisional?

These questions not only situate the challenge of articulating a postmodern version of Christian faith but also point in the direction I wish to proceed. For at the heart of the Christian gospel is the message that we, all of us, are homeless—we are pilgrims—but that there is a home in which our yearning hearts can and will find rest, because "the whole creation is a fabric woven and shot through with the efficacies of the Spirit."[87] Creation is a place of grace, as surely as God is a God of unfathomable love.[88] The Christian story, in other words, is a grand story of redemptive homecoming that is at the same time grateful homemaking.[89]

First, two caveats—call them Westphal's warnings—about speaking of creation. First, taking seriously Foucault's claim that "everything is dangerous," Merold Westphal rightly warns that the doctrine of creation by itself has no defense against being used to render God safe and harmless. In his words, "the creation motif is labile and Janus faced"; though "it does not posit the identity of the human and divine . . . by itself it has no defenses against being absorbed into a philosophy of identity that provides ontological guarantees against the possibility of our being separated from God." Hence, the creation and fall motifs must be united, so that "the mild otherness of the former is preserved in the wild otherness of the latter."[90] In short, any doctrine of creation must include some attention to the fall, lest the doctrine of creation itself be (mis)used to domesticate God and to subvert authentic and honest worship.

Second, following a cue from Kevin Hart, Westphal reminds us that speech about God as creator does not provide and is not intended to provide anything like a full explanation of the world. As Westphal insists:

> If we had an adequate knowledge of who God is and what it means to create, such a statement [In the beginning God created the heavens and the earth] could count as an explanation; but we could have such knowledge only if we had seen God naked and had been present when God created the world, i.e., only if we had radically transcended the human condition.[91]

In other words, echoing Heidegger's criticism of ontotheology, a proper understanding of the doctrine of creation reminds us that "God does not enter into philosophy on the latter's terms"—that is, as a philosophical explanation.[92] Much discussion of creation and evolution notwithstanding, the doctrine of creation is not so much an explanation of how things came to be as a portable story which tells us, in part, who we are and where we are.[93] Enough of warnings; on to the matter at hand. Where to begin? For now, we begin with two affirmations.

A. Creation as Gift

Central to the Christian understanding of creation is the claim that creation is the sheer gift of a gracious creator. That is, God did not have to create any world at all, and God was not obligated or forced to create this particular world. Creation is both ontologically and existentially contingent.[94] Creation need not be. It is, rather, a gracious act of a loving God. For example, neither a Platonic cosmogony, in which the creator is externally limited by recalcitrant matter, nor a neo-Platonic cosmogony, in which a principle of plenitude necessitates that God create, adequately describes the nature of creation or creator.[95] Creation exists only because of God's gracious decision.[96] God is not only an agent able to freely intend and effect action—unconstrained by anything except the divine nature itself—but more importantly, God is the epitome of self-giving love. As Middleton and Walsh assert:

> God's love is not only at the root of the divine decision to create the world (answering the question *why* God created) but also describes the most fundamental character of reality (*what* God created). Creation is wrought by the extravagant generosity of God's love.[97]

Indeed, the Christian confession of God as triune affirms that God is a perichoretic family of love—a community of mutually indwelling love characterized by overflowing generosity.[98] This understanding of God—and of divine power and divine love—is strikingly portrayed in the gospel accounts of Jesus. Langdon Gilkey puts it well:

> To the amazement of all, the disciples and enemies of Christ alike, the divine power reveals itself in precisely that which is most vulnerable and powerless: self-giving love. Truly here was one of the most radical transformations of values in all historical experience: not the avoidance of suffering, but its willing acceptance in love, became the deepest clue to divinity.[99]

Or, as Jean-Luc Marion affirms, "a properly Christian name of the God who is revealed in Jesus Christ . . . is agape."[100] Given this name, predication "must yield to praise," for, as Marion reminds us, "Love is not spoken, in the end it is made."[101]

That love to be love must move beyond words to action indicates an important feature of any adequate response to postmodern homelessness. Ultimately, in an age of cynicism and suspicion—when all is seen as a covert bid for power by competing self-interests—the only truly credible witness will be flesh-and-blood, non-manipulative regard for the other. So, in response to the Nietzschean presumption that all Christian claims to truth (and all actions) are but disguised attempts to control and dominate, Anthony Thiselton insightfully turns to Dietrich Bonhoeffer, since it was Bonhoeffer who, by example as well as by word, powerfully railed against cheap grace and testified to the way of the cross. As Thiselton puts it, "It is as if Bonhoeffer said to

Nietzsche from his Nazi prison: 'But not all Christians are as you suggest.'"[102] So, Thiselton concludes, "A love in which a self genuinely *gives* itself to the other *in the interests of the other* dissolves the acids of suspicion and deception."[103] Any hope of a hearing for a Christian message of healing rides on the shoulders of those of us who, like Bonhoeffer, resist the temptation to use God and others for our own advancement. In other words, the claim that all meta-narratives are violent will be shown to be false only if and when we Christians embody the non-violent meta-narrative of the cruciform Christ.

To summarize, by affirming that creation is wrought (and redeemed) by the God of extravagant grace, the confession of creation as gift both bursts the bubble of modernity, which rests comfortably at home in the supposed security of its violence-producing stories, and also casts the light of postmodern suspicion onto suspicion itself. With regard to claims to truth, if in modernity there is overweening Promethean presumption and in postmodernity there is unremitting Sisyphusian suspicion, affirmation of creation as the gift of that Love that fires the sun and freely tented among us renders it possible to wed trust and suspicion and to forge a hope which looks the sharp and bent edges of reality full in the face but nevertheless clings to the God of grace.

The theme of creation as gift also addresses the postmodern view of the self as malleable and homeless nomad for two reasons. First, the phenomenology of gift and giftedness suggests that when given a gift, the appropriate response is gratitude to the giver and care for the gift. In other words, the experience of gracious provision readily and rightly evokes a response of gratitude and care. Christians from the Reformed tradition ought especially to find this analysis familiar, since gratitude is one of the theological themes emphasized within that tradition. For example, commenting on the most loved of the Reformed confessions, the Heidelberg Catechism, with its triadic structure of guilt/grace/gratitude, Henry Stob affirms:

> What drives the Christian to love and obedience is thankfulness. This gives to the moral life a characteristic note of joy. Appreciative of God's mercy, thankful for his unspeakable gift, happy in his gracious conferments, the Christian seeks with might and main to show forth his praises and to do his will.[104]

Creation as gift thus implies an identity: we humans are *homo gratus*. More exactly, we are grateful caretakers of God's gift of creation. We find our identity not in endless Zelig-like permutations but in responding to God's bountiful and gracious provisions with humble gratitude and joyful care. We care for God's creatures because it is a fitting response to God's providential care for us. We are grateful because God is gracious. Grace begets gratitude and gratitude care.

Second, we express that gratitude and exercise that care on this blue-green earth. We are not rootless and homeless, for this is our home. As the Genesis creation narrative states, we are earth creatures (*'adâm*) made from the earth (*'adâmâh*)—humans from the humus. We are kin with all other creatures. We are not independent, isolated, autonomous selves but rather persons-in-community, including our biotic community. We know who we are not only because we know where we are but also because we know with whom we are. As Joseph Sittler clearly states, "I am constituted by my relationships [within the human world]. . . . But I am also constituted by my encounters with the nonhuman world."[105] And so, declares Sittler, "I am stuck with God, stuck with my neighbor, and stuck with nature (the 'garden'), within which and out of the stuff of which I am made."[106] We humans are thoroughly relational, bound up not only with God and not only with other humans but also with the plants and animals and oceans and mountains of this exquisitely complex and beautiful planet.

In short, by affirming that we are persons-in-relation at home on planet earth—called to respond to God's provisioning grace with gratitude and care, the confession of creation as gift challenges the modern self-image of the human as autonomous rational individual—"man the measure"—and also calls into question the postmodern image of humanity as hopelessly unstable and isolated. With respect to the nature of the human, if in modernity we have the heroic self and in postmodernity we find the resigned self, acknowledgment of creation as gift makes it possible to posit the responsive and responsible self—gratefully loving God and faithfully serving the neighbor in need.

This affirmation of creation as gift also speaks to our deafness to the earth's creatures and our despoilation of creation. For the giftedness of creation, as the Bible reminds us, includes the conviction that all creatures exist to praise God, their maker. For example, Psalm 148 calls upon all created things to praise God: the angels and hosts of heaven, the sun and moon and stars, fire and hail, snow and frost, water and wind, mountains and hills, fruit trees, wild animals, creeping things, kings and princes and rulers, women and men. All creatures are invited to sing a symphony of praise to the God of unsurpassing glory.[107] Albert Borgmann refers to this speaking non-human other as "eloquent reality."[108] Creation is eloquent, if only we have the ears to hear. Creation as gift calls us to acknowledge the ways we have muffled the voices of our non-human neighbors and challenges us to listen for the groaning of creation so that we might work for its redemptive flourishing.

Moreover, creation as gift implies not only that creation is eloquent but also that the plethora of non-human creatures are valuable regardless of human utility. In the effusiveness of divine grace, God has created and continues to create and sustain a profusion of beings whose value extends beyond their usefulness to humans. Psalm 104, for example, speaks not only of all things as being created by God but of the world as a cosmos in which all creatures—wild asses, cedars of Lebanon, storks, marmots, young lions—depend upon God for their existence and their flourishing. And these creatures are valuable not only because of their usefulness to humans—some are useful, indeed essential, to us—but because they are valuable to each other (e.g., the cedars are valuable as places for birds to nest and the mountains are valuable as places of refuge and rest for the wild goats), and, most importantly, they are valuable simply because God made them. In brief, instrumental value to humans is only one of several values that non-human creatures have.[109] God is a generous giver of that which evokes joy and delight.[110] No miserly or Scrooge-like deity, as diffusive goodness God is magnanimous in creating a world both bountiful and beautiful. The Christian doctrine of creation has no room for any anthropocentric utilitarianism which finds non-human creation valuable only insofar as it serves human needs.

In sum, by affirming that creation is eloquent and valuable above and beyond human usefulness, the confession of creation as gift repudiates both the modern view of "nature" as a mere mute resource to be pillaged and the postmodern reenchantment of nature as divine. With regard to the world, if modernity is characterized by an unbridled anthropocentrism and postmodernity by an uncritical biocentrism, recognition of creation as gift makes it possible to embrace a theocentrism, in which one properly acknowledges both the eloquence of reality and the grace of its creator and thus overcomes our creational autism by attending to "the dearest freshness deep down things."[111]

B. Creation as Good

One of the distinguishing features of Christian theology is the belief that creation is essentially good.[112] The fall is contingent, not necessary. Evil is a perversion of God's intentions for creation—an adventitious quality rather than an essential property. Evil is all too real, but it is an alien intruder which has no legitimate place in God's good creation. Evil is not intrinsic to creation; it is, rather, a defect.[113] So, for example, neither a Manichean cosmology, in which evil is seen as a cosmic principle or power equal to good, nor a Babylonian cosmogony, in which creation is the product of a violent battle, accurately conveys the way things are. In the biblical view, God wages no war in creating but rather speaks creation into existence. As Middleton and Walsh perceptively note:

> Rather than beginning with a conflict amongst the gods, the Scriptures begin with the effortless, joyous calling forth of creation by a sovereign Creator who enters into a relationship of intimacy with his creatures. Therefore, creatureliness qua creatureliness is good. . . . This means that a biblical worldview will grant no ontological standing or priority to evil or violence. Indeed, violence is seen, in this worldview, as an illegitimate alien intruder into God's good creation. In contrast to an ontology of violence, then, the Scriptures begin with of an ontology of peace.[114]

God is good. Indeed, God is overflowing Goodness. And so creation is good. Violence is not originary. Peace is primordial.

These claims are extremely significant given the postmodern suspicion of all stories as necessarily violent and manipulative. Over against the common assumption that chaos is primary, the claim that goodness—a good God and a good creation—is fundamental is good news. For those who believe that violence is woven into the warp and woof of reality, the assertion that evil is real but not ontologically necessary is gospel. As Pedro Trigo puts it:

> God creates out of free will, out of love. God creates out of the divine word of benediction. What exists, then, is blessed, good, primordially good, only good, transcendentally good: not only good in principle, for the creative word of blessing resounds everlastingly.[115]

Because this is so, we can move "from ambivalent experience to faith in goodness."[116] That goodness is primordial implies grace and the God of grace. Lewis Smedes says it well:

> Grace does not make everything right. Grace's trick is to show us that it is right for us to live; that it is truly good, wonderful even, for us to be breathing and feeling at the same time that everything clustering around us is wholly wretched. . . . Grace is rather an amazing power to look earthly reality full in the face, see its sad and tragic edges, feel its cruel cuts, join in the primeval chorus against its outrageous unfairness, and yet feel in your deepest being that it is good and right for you to be alive on God's good earth.[117]

Suspicion is often necessary, but it need not be the only posture. Violence is painfully real, but love endures to the end.

In short, by affirming that evil is a surd which has a beginning but no origin in God's good world, the confession of creation as good rejects as naive any modern notion of unhindered human perfectability while also refusing to accept the postmodern presumption that violence will always have the last word. Concerning the stories we tell, if in modernity there is creation without the fall (and thus little need for redemption) and in postmodernity there is the fall without creation (and hence little hope of redemption), assent to creation as the good gift of a gracious God makes it possible—indeed shows it necessary—to hold creation and fall together (with redemption) in a grand story which tells how the Maker of heaven and earth willingly absorbs evil in order to bend a warped world back to its intended harmony and to prod it forward to its God-desired destiny.

This motif of creation as good also speaks to postmodern self-understanding. An implication of the goodness of creation is that finitude is good. Human finitude in particular is not evil, not something to be escaped. We have, however, a penchant for forgetting this central feature of our existence. Indeed, we have a deep desire to avoid looking our finitude, especially our mortality, straight in the face.[118] For to acknowledge the temporally limited nature of our existence raises the question of whether death is the end of life or whether there is Someone who is sufficiently able and willing to preserve our life beyond biological death and in whom we can rest in spite of our fear and anxiety. Not surprisingly, the Bible speaks often of human finitude. For example, Psalm 8—which refers to humans as having been created a little lower than God and crowned with glory and honor—also reminds us that humans are mortal and hence finite.[119]

But we are not just finite; we are faulted. Though often confused, the two are not the same. Finitude is a good feature of human existence. It is simply how God made us—a feature of our humanity to joyfully accept. Faultedness, however, is not God's intention. The brokenness we know in ourselves and all around us is something we acknowledge with regret and something we seek, with God's grace, to overcome. This feature of human existence is also powerfully depicted in the Bible. For example, in Genesis 3 we learn that Adam and Eve desired to transcend their creaturely finitude and become like God in knowing good and evil. But in this attempt, they fail to trust in God, and, thus, they experience alienation. Their relationship with God is broken, they become estranged from each other, they lose touch with their own true and best self, and they are out of joint with the earth. In these four ways they, and we, are alienated. Our lives are tainted with a contagion called sin. The Bible confirms what we know in our hearts: the world and our own lives are not the way they are supposed to be.[120]

To sum up, by affirming that we are finite and faulted creatures but that human finitude in itself is not part of our brokenness, the confession of creation as good unmasks the pretensions of modernity, which would like to believe in the godlike capabilities of human power (technology) and ingenuity (creativity), and also provides an awareness of *nomos* when we are facing the abyss of postmodern anomie. With regard to human nature, if the modern self is an epistemic homeboy and the postmodern self is an epistemic nomad, acknowledgement of creation as good implies that because we are situated and sinful, our claims to truth must be put forward with genuine humility and self-critical honesty, and also that in faith we can trust in the God whose grace hounds our guilt and in whose loving embrace we can rest when facing our own mortality.

Finally, the theme of creation as good addresses our deafness to the degradation of the earth. That creation is good means not only that goodness is more primordial than evil and that finitude is good; it also means that difference is good and that harmony need not be purchased at the price of dominating the other. Otherness is okay. Difference is built into creation itself. For example, the Genesis 1 creation story speaks of a great diversity of creatures. Through God's "let there be," the earth brings forth living creatures of every kind: birds, fish, animals both domestic and wild, flying and creeping things, even sea monsters. God sees this plethora of creatures and declares it to be good. Indeed, God sees everything created (not just humans) and declares that it is very good (verse 31). Creation is a place of beauty and blessing and delight. Because of God's wise creative activity, the diverse kinds of creatures fit together into a harmonious whole. As John Milbank states:

> Christianity, however, recognises no original violence. It construes the infinite not as chaos, but as a harmonic peace which is yet beyond the circumscribing power of any totalizing reason. Peace no longer depends upon the reduction to the self-identical, but is the *sociality* of harmonious difference. Violence, by contrast, is always a secondary willed intrusion upon this possible infinite order (which is actual for God).[121]

As any basic biology course will confirm, the world certainly knows radical difference, including predation and parasites and pathogens. But not withstanding nature red in tooth and claw, biology and theology concur in affirming that creation is a place of flourishing fittedness.

Furthermore, God calls us to serve and protect the garden which is the earth, and for its own sake (Gen. 2:15). We are to offer hospitality to the other—including the non-human other—in a way which gives evidence of genuine openness, receptivity, and attentiveness.[122] Rather than blindly or knowingly seeking to dominate, we are to exercise the kind of stewardly care which befits us as God's image-bearing representatives.[123] Care, not wanton disregard or ignorant misuse, should characterize our way of life.[124] And as many attest, we need the wild otherness of wild places to foster our own sense of humility and joy.[125] In other words, our serving and protecting the earth and its creatures is fostered by spending time in places where our own sense of control is diminished and our sense of dependence is magnified.

In short, by affirming that difference is good and that harmony need not be gained by the reduction of the other to more of the same, the confession of creation as "good" shows the lie to the modern project of the technological totalization of the other just as surely as it points beyond the hopelessness of much postmodern thought, which either merely celebrates the play of difference or finds difference necessarily inimical to authentic community. With regard to the world, if in modernity the fearful flight from otherness leads to the hubris of ecological degradation and in postmodernity the recognition of otherness occasions despair concerning our earthly home, reflection on creation as good renders meaningful an embrace of difference which prompts not despair but faith and the kind of joyful "keeping" of creation that is fitting of creatures grateful for God's gracious provisions.

IV. Homeward Bound

We are all of us pilgrims and wayfarers. But the stories we tell of our earthly pilgrimages are not all the same. Many today describe their sojourn as one of perpetual homelessness. Suspicious of all claims to truth, restless and anxious about the future, fearfully aware that we are despoiling our earthly home, many people feel awhirl in the postmodern world. The home they knew is at best a happy memory, and the home they dream is a chimera. As Simon and Garfunkel attest, in their hauntingly beautiful song "Homeward Bound," these postmodern nomads, despite claims that there are no homes, find their hearts longing to be:

Homeward bound, I wish I was,
Homeward bound.
Home—where my thought's escaping.
Home—where my music's playing.
Home—where my love lies waiting silently for me.

These folk long for that familiar place where they belong, where they will be loved, where the home they dream might just be real. Like

Simon and Garfunkel, in the last line of the last verse, these sojourners sing "I need someone to comfort me."

Christians, too, yearn for home. They, too, are pilgrims. But their tale of home seeking is a story about a sojourning people at home in creation because of a good God who gifts them for the journey and who comes in person to comfort them. The Love that lies waiting for us, to hear Christians tell it, is that fierce Love which fires the sun and that self-emptying Love who pitched his tent among us. Our Redeemer is our Creator. We are not yet at home, and so we, like our forebears, walk by faith and not by sight; but the day is coming when God's glory will fill heaven and earth, all tears save those of joy will disappear, and our mourning will turn to dancing. We will experience a heaven-on-earth homecoming of comfort and belonging and delight. Shalom will prevail, and our yearning hearts will find their home in the heart of God—a God who makes a home among mortals. Such a story, to postmodern ears, is good news.[126]

Notes

1. Augustine, *Confessions*, Book 1.

2. Richard Middleton and Brian Walsh, *Truth Is Stranger than It Used To Be* (Downers Grove, Ill.: Intervarsity, 1995), p. 145.

3. Ibid., p. 61.

4. Aristophanes, *The Clouds,* trans. Alan Sommerstein (New York: Penguin, 1973), pp. 129, 146, 171–72.

5. John Caputo, *Radical Hermeneutics* (Bloomington: Indiana University Press, 1987), p. 239.

6. Frances Fitzgerald, *Cities on a Hill* (New York: Simon and Schuster, 1986), p. 390.

7. Paul Wachtel, *The Poverty of Affluence* (Philadelphia: New Society, 1989), p. 95.

8. Walter Truett Anderson, *Reality Isn't What It Used to Be* (San Francisco: Harper Collins, 1990), p. 51.

9. Peter Berger and Thomas Luckmann, *Social Construction of Reality* (Garden City, N.Y.: Doubleday, 1966).

10. Jane Wagner, *The Search for Signs of Intelligent Life in the Universe* (New York: Harper and Row, 1985), p. 18.

11. Michael Polanyi, *Personal Knowledge* (Chicago: University of Chicago Press, 1962). The literature is vast, but for a narrative of the recent developments in philosophy of science, see Harold Brown, *Perception, Theory and Commitment* (Chicago: University of Chicago Press, 1977), and Del Ratzsch, *Philosophy of Science* (Downers Grove, Ill.: Intervarsity, 1986).

12. Martin Heidegger, *Being and Time* (New York: Harper and Row, 1962), §32;

Hans-Georg Gadamer, *Truth and Method* (New York: Continuum, 1975), 2nd part, §2. See Anthony Thiselton, *The Two Horizons* (Grand Rapids, Mich.: Eerdmans, 1980) for a clear and insightful discussion of these (and other) issues.

13. Richard Rorty, *Philosophy and the Mirror of Nature* (Princeton, N.J.: Princeton University Press, 1979), p. 176.

14. Richard Rorty, *Consequences of Pragmatism* (Minneapolis: University of Minnesota Press, 1982), chap. 9.

15. Paul Ricoeur, *Freud and Philosophy* (New Haven, Conn.: Yale University Press, 1970), p. 32.

16. For example, in his assertion that "linguistic legislation" properly describes our "enigmatic urge for truth," Nietzsche claims that truth is merely that which conforms to conventions, and thus, to be truthful is simply to use the customary metaphors. Given that language cannot adequately express reality, for Nietzsche truth is "a mobile army of metaphors, metonyms, and anthropomorphisms—in short, a sum of human relations, which have been enhanced, transposed, and embellished poetically and rhetorically, and which after long use seem firm, canonical, and obligatory to people." Hence, "truths are illusions about which one has forgotten that this is what they are," and so to be truthful necessarily involves "the obligation to lie according to fixed conventions." Even without explicit attention to Nietzsche's more famous claims about the human will to power, suspicion of seemingly firm customs is called for. See Friedrich Nietzsche, "On Truth and Lie," in *Portable Nietzsche*, ed. Walter Kaufmann (New York: Penguin, 1982), pp. 44–47. For a lucid explanation of the kind of postmodern suspicion informed by Nietzsche's understanding of the will to power, see Merold Westphal, *Suspicion and Faith* (New York: Fordham University Press, 1998), chaps. 35–36.

17. Michel Foucault, "Nietzsche, Genealogy, History," in *The Foucault Reader*, ed. Paul Rabinow (New York: Pantheon, 1984), p. 85.

18. Michel Foucault, "Truth and Power," in *Power/Knowledge*, ed. Colin Gordon (New York: Pantheon, 1980), p. 131.

19. Michel Foucault, "On the Genealogy of Ethics," in *Foucault Reader*, p. 343.

20. See, e.g., Merold Westphal, "Positive Postmodernism as Radical Hermeneutics," in *The Very Idea of Radical Hermeneutics*, ed. Roy Martínez (Atlantic Highlands, N.J.: Humanities Press, 1997): "Taking St. Paul Seriously," in *Christian Philosophy*, ed. Thomas Flint (Notre Dame: University of Notre Dame Press, 1990); and "Christian Philosophers and the Copernican Revolution," in *Christan Perspectives on Religious Knowledge*, ed. C. Stephen Evans and Merold Westphal (Grand Rapids, Mich.: Eerdmans, 1993).

21. Caputo, *Radical Hermeneutics*, p. 116.

22. Jacques Derrida, "Différance," in *Margins of Philosophy*, trans. Alan Bass (Chicago: University of Chicago Press, 1982), pp. 8–9.

23. Westphal, "Positive Postmodernism," p. 56. Or, as Richard Bernstein puts it in *The New Constellation* (Cambridge, Mass.: MIT Press, 1982): "Derrida seeks to show us that we never quite are or can be at home in the world" (p. 179).

24. Derrida, "Différance," p. 20. As Caputo states: "the hermeneut is an exile longing for the native land" (*Radical Hermeneutics*, p. 117).

25. Caputo, *Radical Hermeneutics*, p. 118.

26. Derrida, "Différance," p. 27. Derrida offers a similar argument in "Struc-

ture, Sign, and Play in the Discourse of the Human Sciences," in *Writing and Difference*, trans. Alan Bass (Chicago: University of Chicago Press, 1978), pp. 278–93.

27. Middleton and Walsh, *Truth Is Stranger*, p. 36.

28. Ibid., p. 37.

29. Ibid.

30. See, for example, Cornel West, *Race Matters* (New York: Random House, 1994).

31. See, for example, Rosemary Radford Ruether, *Sexism and God-Talk* (Boston: Beacon, 1983).

32. See, for example, Bill McKibben, *The End of Nature* (New York: Doubleday, 1989).

33. Middleton and Walsh, *Truth Is Stranger*, p. 37.

34. Anderson, *Reality*, pp. 36–37. See also Robert Bellah, Richard Madsen, William Sullivan, Ann Swidler, and Steven Tipton, *Habits of the Heart* (New York: Harper and Row, 1986), chaps. 3, 6.

35. Albert Borgmann, *Crossing the Postmodern Divide* (Chicago: University of Chicago Press, 1993), p. 3.

36. Wachtel, *Poverty*, pp. 93–94, 99.

37. Anthony Thiselton, *Interpreting God and the Postmodern Self* (Grand Rapids, Mich.: Eerdmans, 1995), p. 11.

38. Middleton and Walsh, *Truth Is Stranger*, p. 49.

39. Ibid., p. 52.

40. Rorty, *Mirror of Nature*, p. 359.

41. Ibid., p. 360; cf. pp. 364–65, 370, 389.

42. Richard Rorty, *Contingency, Irony, and Solidarity* (Cambridge: Cambridge University Press, 1989), p. 9.

43. Ibid., p. 20.

44. Ibid., pp. 53–54.

45. Ibid., p. 80.

46. See, e.g., Lewis Smedes, *Caring and Commitment* (San Francisco: Harper and Row, 1988), chap. 5, and Margaret Farley, *Personal Commitments* (San Francisco: Harper and Row, 1986), chap. 2.

47. Middleton and Walsh, *Truth Is Stranger*, p. 57.

48. Alasdair MacIntyre, *After Virtue*, 2nd ed. (Notre Dame: University of Notre Dame Press, 1984).

49. Middleton and Walsh, *Truth Is Stranger*, p. 60.

50. Ian Chambers, *Migrancy, Culture, Identity* (New York: Routledge, 1994), p. 5.

51. Calvin DeWitt, *Earthwise* (Grand Rapids, Mich.: CRC, 1994), p. 30. Elsewhere, DeWitt declares that "a crisis of degradation is enveloping the earth." In DeWitt, "Seven Degradations of Creation," *Perspectives* 4, no. 2 (February 1989): 4. See also "The State of the Planet," in *Earthkeeping in the 90's*, ed. Loren Wilkinson (Grand Rapids, Mich.: Eerdmans, 1991); McKibben, *The End of Nature*; and any recent *State of the World*, published by the Worldwatch Institute.

52. DeWitt, *Earthwise*, pp. 30–35.

53. As many note, this sense of ecological homelessness—of not feeling at home in our *oikos*—will in the future most likely increase. For example, Wachtel speaks of "pollution and the problem of environmental limits" as "the weightiest

of all the denied realities of the consumer life" (*Poverty*, p. 48); and Anderson lists "massive environmental change" as one of two "mega-issues" facing us as we enter the twenty-first century (*Reality*, p. 262).

54. Most of the others implicitly if not explicitly endorse the dominant anthropocentrism and utilitarianism which underwrite much of the ecologically destructive Western worldview. For example, in Derrida's move from "We are not God" to "There is no God," he betrays not only a logical fallacy (*non sequitur*) but also his anthropocentric assumption that since we as humans cannot do *x*, therefore no one can. As Borgmann accurately observes: "The postmodern theorists . . . have failed to see their own anthropocentrism" (*Crossing*, p. 117).

55. Martin Heidegger, "The Word of Nietzsche," in *The Question Concerning Technology and Other Essays* (New York: Harper and Row, 1977), p. 100. For discussion of the causes of current ecological degradation, see James Nash, *Loving Nature* (Nashville, Tenn.: Abingdon, 1991), chap. 3; Steven Bouma-Prediger, *The Greening of Theology* (Atlanta, Ga.: Scholar's Press, 1995), chap. 1; and Steven Bouma-Prediger, "Is Christianity Responsible for the Ecological Crisis?", in *Christian Scholar's Review* 25, no. 2 (December 1995).

56. Heidegger, "The Word of Nietzsche," p. 103. And this objectification process, Heidegger insists, degrades not only the earth but God. Indeed, it is, ironically, Christians themselves who deliver "the heaviest blow against God" when they "discourse on the being that is of all beings most in being without ever letting it occur to them to think on Being itself, in order thereby to become aware that, seen from out of faith, their thinking and their talking is sheer blasphemy if it meddles in the theology of faith" (p. 105). In short, we all too easily turn not only the earth but God into an object and a means to our own ends.

57. Martin Heidegger, "Letter on Humanism," in *Basic Writings*, ed. David Krell (San Francisco: HarperCollins, 1977), p. 228.

58. Martin Heidegger, "Overcoming Metaphysics," in *The End of Philosophy* (New York: Harper and Row, 1973), p. 107.

59. Ibid., p. 109. In contrast to such hubristic attempts at mastery, Heidegger suggests that our proper role is shepherd. "It is," he asserts, "one thing just to use the earth, another to receive the blessing of the earth and to become at home in the law of this reception in order to shepherd the mystery of Being and watch over the inviolability of the possible" (p. 109). That is to say, being at home on the earth requires a rare kind of receptivity to the goodness and blessedness of the earth and its creatures—a kind of attentiveness and openness which inspires proper care for creation.

60. Ibid., p. 110.

61. Thomas Berry, *The Dream of the Earth* (San Francisco: Sierra Club, 1988), pp. 16–17.

62. For one explication of the ecological virtues, including receptivity and respect, see Steven Bouma-Prediger and Virginia Vroblesky, *Assessing the Ark* (Philadelphia: Crossroads, 1997), part 1.

63. Martin Heidegger, "Building, Dwelling, Thinking," in *Basic Writings*, p. 323.
64. Ibid., p. 324.
65. Ibid.
66. Ibid., p. 325.

67. Ibid.

68. Ibid., p. 327.

69. Ibid. Heidegger ends this 1951 essay with the question, "what is the state of dwelling in our precarious age?" He concludes that "the *real plight of dwelling* does not lie merely in a lack of houses" but rather in the fact that, having forgotten how properly to dwell, we mortals "*must ever learn to dwell.*" In this, insists Heidegger, lies the true origin of "man's homelessness" (p. 339). With this claim, Heidegger presciently identifies a signal feature of our postmodern homelessness. And insofar as authentic dwelling requires us, as he affirms, to serve and protect creation (Gen. 2:15) and respect the integrity—the essential being—of the non-human Other, he prophetically points the way forward to authentic homecoming.

70. David Orr, *Ecological Literacy* (Albany: SUNY, 1992), p. 102.

71. Ibid., p. 130.

72. Ibid.

73. See, e.g., Belden Lane, *Landscapes of the Sacred* (New York: Paulist, 1988).

74. Mircea Eliade, *The Sacred and the Profane* (New York: Harcourt Brace Jovanovich, 1959).

75. Jürgen Moltmann, *God in Creation* (San Francisco: Harper and Row, 1985), p. 46.

76. Frederick Buechner, *The Longing for Home* (San Francisco: HarperCollins, 1996), p. 7.

77. Ibid.

78. Middleton and Walsh, *Truth Is Stranger,* chap. 5.

79. Paul Ricoeur, *Symbolism of Evil* (Boston: Beacon, 1967), pp. 349, 351.

80. Westphal, "Positive Postmodernism," p. 56.

81. Caputo, *Radical Hermeneutics*, pp. 33–35.

82. Westphal, "Postmodernism and Religious Reflection," *International Journal for the Philosophy of Religion* 38, no. 1–3 (December 1995): 135.

83. Thiselton, *Interpreting God and the Postmodern Self,* chaps. 12, 19, 20.

84. Emmanuel Levinas, *Totality and Infinity* (Pittsburgh: Duquesne University Press, 1969), pp. 158, 171.

85. Jürgen Moltmann, *The Trinity and the Kingdom* (San Francisco: Harper and Row, 1981), chaps. 2, 5.

86. Westphal, "Positive Postmodernism," pp. 53–54.

87. Moltmann, *God in Creation*, p. 212.

88. Joseph Sittler, *Gravity and Grace* (Minneapolis, Minn.: Augsburg, 1986), chap. 1.

89. For these terms, thanks to Brian Walsh, "Homemaking in Exile: Homelessness, Postmodernity, and Theological Reflection," unpublished paper.

90. Merold Westphal, "Faith as the Overcoming of Ontological Xenophobia," in *The Otherness of God*, ed. Orrin F. Summerell (Charlottesville: University of Virginia Press, 1998), p. 162. See also p. 165, where he speaks of these motifs as "intertwined."

91. Westphal, "Postmodernism and Religious Reflection," p. 133.

92. Ibid.

93. On the notion of doctrines as portable stories, see N. T. Wright, *The New Testament and the People of God* (Minneapolis, Minn.: Fortress, 1992), chap. 5.

94. Robert Russell, "Cosmology, Creation, and Contingency," in *Cosmos as Creation*, ed. Ted Peters (Nashville, Tenn.: Abingdon, 1989), p. 195.

95. Thomas Morris carefully distinguishes between the principle of diffusiveness of goodness and the principle of plentitude. See Morris, *Our Idea of God* (Downers Grove, Ill.: Intervarsity, 1991), pp. 146–49.

96. For a more extended presentation of this notion of decision, as one of what I call "The Seven D's of Creation," see Steven Bouma-Prediger, "Creation as the Home of God: The Doctrine of Creation in the Theology of Jürgen Moltmann," in *Calvin Theological Journal* 32, no. 1 (April 1997).

97. Middleton and Walsh, *TruthIs Stranger*, p. 149.

98. Articulations of a social or interpersonal theory of the Trinity abound; for one influential statement, see Moltmann, *The Trinity and the Kingdom*. See also Cornelius Plantinga, "Social Trinity and Tritheism," in *Trinity, Incarnation, and Atonement*, ed. Ronald Feenstra and Cornelius Plantinga (Notre Dame: University of Notre Dame Press, 1989), for an argument in favor of such an understanding of God as triune.

99. Langdon Gilkey, *Maker of Heaven and Earth* (Garden City, N.Y.: Doubleday, 1959), p. 217. See also "Creation, Being, and Non-Being," in *God and Creation*, ed. David Burrell and Bernard McGinn (Notre Dame: University of Notre Dame Press, 1990), p. 233, where Gilkey states that it is no surprise that most theologians in this century have questioned the priority of the definition of God as Absolute Being and have, rather, "empathized with Moltmann's effort to understand the divine nature also in terms of the divine suffering present in and revealed through the crucifixion." For an eloquent, profound, and poignant expression of the truth that suffering love is the deepest clue to divinity, see Nicholas Wolterstorff, *Lament for a Son* (Grand Rapids, Mich.: Eerdmans, 1987).

100. Jean-Luc Marion, *God without Being* (Chicago: University of Chicago Press, 1991), p. 82.

101. Ibid., pp. 106–7.

102. Thiselton, *Interpreting God and the Postmodern Self*, p. 23. The locus classicus for Bonhoeffer's treatment of "cheap grace" is *The Cost of Discipleship* (New York: Macmillan, 1963), chap. 1. See also Bonhoeffer's *Letters and Papers from Prison* (New York: Macmillan, 1971).

103. Thiselton, *Interpreting God and the Postmodern Self*, p. 160.

104. Henry Stob, *Ethical Reflections* (Grand Rapids, Mich.: Eerdmans, 1978), p. 78; see also Allen Verhey, *Living the Heidelberg* (Grand Rapids, Mich.: CRC, 1986), chaps. 8–9.

105. Joseph Sittler, "The Sittler Speeches," in *The Center for the Study of Campus Ministry Yearbook* 1977–78, ed. Phil Schroeder (Valparaiso: Valparaiso University Press, 1978), p. 45.

106. Joseph Sittler, "Evangelism and the Care of the Earth," in *Preaching in the Witnessing Community*, ed. Herman Stuempfle (Philadelphia: Fortress, 1973), p. 102.

107. Similar examples of the praise offered to God by non-human creatures are found in Isaiah, chaps. 42–44, 55, and in many other psalms, e.g., Psalms 96 and 98.

108. Borgmann, *Crossing*, pp. 117–19.

109. Holmes Rolston III, *Environmental Ethics* (Philadelphia: Temple University Press, 1988), chap. 1. Reformed folk, again, have good reason to feel at home with this affirmation, since John Calvin speaks of creation as "this magnificent theatre of heaven and earth, crammed with innumerable miracles"—valuable for its own sake as well as for its provisions to humans. See *Institutes*, 2.6.1, and 3.10.2; cf. 1.6.2 and 1.14.20. For an excellent exposition of Calvin's view of nature, see Susan Schreiner, *The Theatre of His Glory* (Grand Rapids, Mich.: Baker, 1991).

110. This theme of delight is the last of my "Seven D's of Creation" and is developed in my "Creation as the Home of God." See also Nicholas Wolterstorff, *Until Justice and Peace Embrace* (Grand Rapids, Mich.: Eerdmans, 1983), chap. 7.

111. Part of a line from Gerard Manley Hopkins' poem "God's Grandeur."

112. Gilkey, *Maker of Heaven and Earth*, chap. 7.

113. Another one of my seven D's. For an explication, see "Creation as the Home of God."

114. Middleton and Walsh, *Truth Is Stranger*, p. 153.

115. Pedro Trigo, *Creation and History* (Maryknoll, N.Y.: Orbis, 1991), p. 87.

116. Ibid. This quotation is the title of chapter 3.

117. Lewis Smedes, *How Can It Be All Right When Everything Is All Wrong?* (San Francisco: Harper and Row, 1982), p. 3.

118. For a powerful and insightful analysis of the human tendency to deny mortality and in so doing create and perpetuate evil, see Ernest Becker, *Denial of Death* (New York: Macmillan, 1973) and *Escape from Evil* (New York: Macmillan, 1975).

119. The finitude of humanity is also powerfully portrayed in the book of Job. In the deluge of questions put by God from the whirlwind (chaps. 38–41), Job is, among other things, forcibly reminded of his finitude. Job has not commanded the morning or entered the storehouses of the snow or provided prey for the ravens. He does not know when the mountain goats give birth or who let the wild asses go free. That the hawk soars and the eagle mounts up is not Job's doing. Job's power and knowledge are finite. He is creature, not creator.

120. Two recent books which illuminate the phenomenon of sin very clearly are Ted Peters, *Sin* (Grand Rapids, Mich.: Eerdmans, 1995), and Cornelius Plantinga, *Not the Way It's Supposed To Be* (Grand Rapids, Mich.: Eerdmans, 1995).

121. John Milbank, *Theology and Social Theory* (Oxford: Basil Blackwell, 1990), p. 5. As Middleton and Walsh put it (*Truth Is Stranger*, p. 154): "This [ontology of peace] is not, however, the peace of an imposed homogeneity. That would be violence all over again. Rather, the biblical worldview perceives in the world a wonderful variety of different *kinds* of creatures living together in fundamental harmony. . . . There is, therefore, a *sociality* of difference."

122. See, e.g., Merold Westphal's suggestive essay, "Existentialism and Environmental Ethics," in *The Environmental Crisis*, ed. Edwin Squiers (Mancelona, Mich.: AuSable, 1982). For another attempt to spell out virtues like these, with specific reference to endangered species, see Bouma-Prediger and Vroblesky, *Assessing the Ark*.

123. See, e.g, Douglas John Hall, *Imaging God* (Grand Rapids, Mich.: Eerdmans, 1986).

124. For example, in *Caring for Creation* (New Haven, Conn.: Yale University

Press, 1994), leading ecological philosopher Max Oelschlaeger advocates this term as the centerpiece of his "ecumenical approach to the environmental crisis."

125. Many classic wilderness writers make this claim, e.g., Henry David Thoreau, John Muir. For a recent defense, see Bill McKibben, *The Comforting Whirlwind* (Grand Rapids, Mich.: Eerdmans, 1994), chap. 4.

126. Many thanks to Hope College colleagues Allen Verhey and Andrew Dell'Olio for reading and commenting on earlier versions of this paper.

10

Toward a Postmodern
Theology of the Cross

Augustine, Heidegger, Derrida

JOHN D. CAPUTO

In this age of the death of God, it is of no little interest and significance that two of the major European philosophers of this century, two of the masters of postmodernity, if this is a word we still can use, have chosen (at different points in their work: one very early on, the other only later) to comment on the ageless power and beauty of Augustine's *Confessions*. In the summer semester of 1921, at the very beginning of his work, when he was still thinking within a Christian context, the young Heidegger (then thirty-two years old) devoted a lecture course to the tenth book of the *Confessions;* the course is a remarkable anticipation of the main lines of *Being and Time*, arguably the major work by any continental European philosopher written in this century. In 1989–90, at the age of fifty-nine, an age when he says he was learning the meaning of the word "dying," Derrida, supposedly a very secular and anti-traditional philosopher, wrote a beautiful autobiographical piece entitled *Circonfession*, which, like the famous narrative of his North African "compatriot" Saint Augustine, tells the story of his life, including the story of his dying mother, by grafting it upon numerous and sometimes lengthy citations of Augustine's Latin text.

Heidegger and Derrida produce very different texts and find strikingly different Augustines. Heidegger's Augustine is mediated to him by Luther and Kierkegaard—this lecture course was held two years after his formal break with Catholicism—while Derrida's Augustine seems indebted to Levinas and is hence a much more Jewish Augustine. Heidegger's *Confessiones* recount a battle with concupiscence, while Derrida's tell the story of his circumcision, of the cut in his flesh which also signals a deep cut or severance from which all his thinking originates. Heidegger's Augustine is a very Pauline Christian soldier, fighting the good fight of faith, outfitted in the breastplate of hope and the helmet of faith, one for whom the Christian faith spells battle and trouble, so that his "confessions" read like a war journal. Derrida's Augustine is a man of prayers and tears, a much more womanly man, weaving together womanly tears and a manly circumcision, a man for whom confession is a matter of asking pardon, of confessing one's faults, of concern for the other.

Interestingly enough, and at the risk of shocking devout and orthodox readers of Heidegger, Derrida, Augustine, and the Scriptures (both Jewish and Christian), I would say that Heidegger and Derrida offer different renderings of the cross—two different, let us say postmodern, versions of what Luther called the *theologia crucis*—and it is around this thematic of a postmodern theology of the cross that I will organize my remarks here.

Heidegger's reading of the *Confessions*, while it is quite brilliant in its own right and though it provides a fascinating glimpse of the genesis of *Being and Time*, is extremely one-sided and very much held captive by the spiritual militancy of Paul, Luther, and Kierkegaard. Inspired by Luther's *theologia crucis*, Heidegger singles out the trials and tribulations by which factical life is buffeted in fighting the good fight of faith. But the phenomenon of the cross admits of another and significantly different emphasis, for the cross stands for suffering flesh and for the solidarity of Jesus with everyone who suffers. Seen thus, the cross points in the direction of an ethics of compassion rather than to an existential analytic of authentic self-possession. As I have argued elsewhere, that is a direction which Heidegger never took and, indeed, to which he seems endemically, systematically blind. When he read the New Testament, he found there only a *Kampfsreligion*, a Pauline battlefield with a self that wills what it does not and does what it wills not.[1] Heidegger seems never to have noticed the widows and the poor, the lame and the lepers, the young man raised from the dead, the blind and the crippled, and the systematic work of *therapeuein*, of healing, of *cura* as healing, around which the ministry of Jesus was organized. That, in turn, explains why Heidegger was so defenseless against the *Kampfsphilosophie* of the Nazis and against the bizarre extremes to which *Kampfsphilosophie* was taken by Jünger and Jünger's strange version of Nietzsche, which cleared the way for Heidegger's embrace of National Socialism. Had Heidegger a little more care for *cura* as healing, had he cared more for the cross as a symbol of solidarity with the suffering other, and had he cared less for a heroic freedom that stares into the abyss—out there all alone in the dark night of *Eigentlichkeit, coram morti*—he might have been less inclined to lend his good name and considerable genius to the Nazi nightmare. *Qui amat periculum, incidet in illum.*

What interests me in the present study is the entirely different reading of Augustine's *Confessions* to be found in Derrida's *Circonfession*. Without trying to undermine or simply jettison Heidegger's provocative gloss upon the *Confessions*, I maintain that Derrida provides the more sensitive rendering of Augustine, indeed, one that is quite sensitive to the *theologia crucis* and, let us say, more generally, to the biblical theology of suffering, Christian or Jewish. The spirit of Derrida's rendering of the *Confessions* is nicely captured in Daniele da Volterra's *Woman at the Foot of the Cross,* a stunning drawing of a weeping woman that Derrida includes in *Memoirs of the Blind* (the text accompanying his Louvre exhibit). This magnificent figure of a woman bent by grief, of a woman of sorrow, is not narrowly Christian but more broadly biblical, and not narrowly biblical but a broader figure of the human condition generally. That is why Derrida can say—this is the hope, the risk, the wager—both that *Circonfession* is a story of something that happens only once, with him, "It only happens to me" (*Circ.*, p. 282/*Circum.*, p. 305), and that this is "Everybody's Autobiography" (*Circ.*, p. 288/ *Circum.*, p. 311).

Augustine, Heidegger, and the Hermeneutics of Facticity

Qui amat periculum, incidet in illum.

(He who loves danger, perishes by it.)
—Eccles. 3:27; Augustine, *Confessions;* Derrida, *Circonfession*

In a remarkable footnote in *Being and Time*, Heidegger says that the analysis of "care" (*Sorge*) "is one which has grown upon the author in connection with his attempts to interpret the Augustinian (i.e., Helleno-Christian) anthropology with regard to the foundational principles reached in the ontology of Aristotle" (*SZ*, p. 199, n. 1; *BT*, p. 492, n. vii).[2] With the recent appearance of Heidegger's 1921 lecture course on Augustine's *Confessions*, it is at last possible to make sense of this fascinating remark.

Heidegger's reading of the *Confessions* is important for two reasons.

In the first place, Heidegger undertakes there an existential phenomenological *Destruktion* of Augustine's work,[3] that is, he attempts to break through, or read back past, the heavy overlay of Neoplatonic metaphysics in Augustine in order to find the concrete, historical experience of life, what he calls in the early Freiburg period the "factical life" that pulsates beneath it. For the *Confessions* are not a metaphysical tract but a *confiteri*, a distinctive way of interpreting things that is rooted in Augustine's experience of Christian life (GA 60, p. 212). The distinction between the "metaphysical" and the "factical" thus amounts to a distinction between the Greek and Christian, a distinction which is also an indistinction inasmuch as Heidegger thinks that by the time of Augustine, it is not possible perfectly to distinguish Greek and Christian, the two having become already inextricably intertwined in the Patristic period. In order to find the authentically Christian, one would need to return to the early Christian, to primitive Christianity (*Urchristentum*), of which the only record is the New Testament, an effort undertaken by Heidegger during the preceding semester, in which he offered a commentary on Paul's letters to the Thessalonians, the earliest documents in the New Testament.[4] In the second place, Heidegger seeks to formalize Augustine's account of factical life—that is, to raise it to the level of an existential–phenomenological formality, a structural generality, or what in the 1920s he calls a "formal indication," so that what results from the analysis is broader than its specifically Christian contents and could stand as an indicator of factical life in general, rather like the distinction in *Being and Time* between the existential and the existentiell.

Heidegger's lecture course, entitled "Augustine and Neoplatonism," focuses on Book 10 of the *Confessions*. The heart of the *Destruktion*—that is, of the hermeneutic retrieval of Christian facticity from the *Confessions*—is the analysis of the soul as a *terra difficultatis* (*SZ*, pp. 43–44; *BT*, p. 69), a land of difficulty (*Confessions*, bk. 10, chap. 16) and struggle (*Kampf*), a being that has become a question to itself (GA 60, p. 247), beset by *molestias et difficultates* (*Confessions*, bk. 10, chap. 28). The analysis focuses on the phenomenon of *tentatio*, the life of the soul as trial and temptation. In its mode of *confiteri*, the soul is not a stable self-identity, a substance at rest and at one with itself, but rather a being that has become a question unto itself, at odds with itself and pulled in opposing directions. *Ecce ubi sum*, Augustine says. See in what a state I am, in what turmoil and unrest. *Flete mecum et pro me flete*. Weep with me and weep for me, all you who feel within yourselves that goodness from which good actions come. *Tu autem, domine deus meus, exaudi et respice et vide et miserere et sana me*. But do thou O Lord my God hear me and look upon me and see me and heal me, *in cujus oculis mihi quaestio factus sum*, in whose eyes I have become a question to myself (*Confessions*, bk. 10, chap. 33). Life is through-and-through insecure, and "no man ought to be oversure that though he is capable of becoming better instead of worse, he is not actually becoming worse instead of better" (*Confessions*, bk. 10, chap. 32). This phenomenon of the questionability of the self to itself, of the insecurity of the self, is what organizes Heidegger's reading of the *Confessions*.

To be sure, the question of the self for Augustine is inseparable from the question of God. As Kierkegaard, whom Heidegger cites at this point, says: "The greater the conception of God, the more self there is; the more self, the greater the conception of God" (*SUD*, e.t., 80). What constitutes the self *as* a self, Kierkegaard says, is that in the face of which the self takes its measure, that before which it stands face to face, and what "an infinite accent falls on the self by having God as the criterion" (*SUD*, 79; GA 60, p. 248). The more immediately the soul stands before God, *coram deo*, taking God as its measure, the more deeply it enters within itself. Heidegger emphasizes that struggle is thus the measure of life *coram deo*. "God is there," Heidegger comments, "in troubling over the life of the self" (GA 60, p. 289). The life of the soul before God, the very facticity of factical life, is struggle (*Kampf*), difficulty (*Schwierigkeit*), burden (*onus*), trouble (*molestia*) (*Confessions*, bk. 10, chap. 28). *Vita . . . tota tentatio [est]* (*Confessions*, bk. 10, chap. 32).[5] Life is all trial and temptation, an "inner *Kampf*" (GA 60, p. 275) of the self with itself. To take the easy way out (*leichtnehmen*), to give into the drift into the "world," to "fall" into the world—that is to decline the invitation to Christian life. The dynamics, or better, the "kinetics," of *tentatio* are described in terms of a pull (*Zug*) and a counter-pull (*Gegenzug*) having to do with the force of "concupiscence," the pull or lure that worldly things exert over our heart's affections, dragging us into the world and turning us away from God. A *moles* is not to be understood as it ordinarily is, as a natural thing, like a stone, Heidegger comments, but rather as a suction or a pull that draws me away from myself (GA 60, p. 267). [C]*adunt in id quod valent* (*Confessions*, bk. 10, chap. 23): some men fall in among what they prize while others resist, fighting the good fight against the "concupiscence of the eyes, the concupiscence of the flesh, and the pride of life" (1 John 2:16), the famous tripartite division of the spiritual battleground around which Augustine has organized Book 10.

In short, for Heidegger, the life of the soul before God is *cura*, a condensation of Augustine's text in transparent anticipation of the central claim of the existential analytic, that the Being of *Dasein* is care. But Heidegger translates *cura* in 1921 as *Bekümmerung*, being troubled, anxious, or disturbed, and not yet as *Sorge*, as in *Being and Time*. "The end of care is delight (*delectatio*)" (*Ennarationes in Psalmos*, bk. 7, chap. 9); the goal and telos of care is the delight it takes in that for the sake of which it has troubled itself. Augustine says that we "are scattered abroad in multiplicity" and dispersion (*in multa defleximus*), dissipated by many worldly cares, but by "continence we are collected and bound up into unity within yourself" (*Confessions*, bk. 10, chap. 29), turned back to the one thing necessary. Just so, in *Being and Time*, "everyday" *Dasein* is scattered and disseminated (*zerstreut*) in the world of the "they," and by resolutely projecting upon death, it is brought back to itself. *Tentatio*, Heidegger adds (GA 60, pp. 248–49), is not a property of something objectively present, not something that may or may not accompany experience, but rather it is the very stuff of experience, the fabric of which factical life is woven. For factical life is not a thing with properties but a possibility—with the freedom either to fall into the world or to gather itself together before God. To exist is to live radically in possibility (GA 60, p. 249). The possibility and the counter-possibility, the movement toward God/self and the counter movement, are not isolable psychic events but co-given tendencies, each constituted by its strife and contention with the other. So, Augustine says, I am made a burden to myself because I weep over sorrows in which I should rejoice and rejoice in pleasures over which I should sorrow. Again, when I am in adversity, I desire prosperity; but when I am in prosperity, I fear adversity. Each is what it is over and against the horizon of the other, in an interplay of desire and fear, rejoicing and sorrowing. The pull and the counter-pull, the tendency to scatter and regather, belong together in a unity of opposing tensions.

Tentatio has what Heidegger calls a "*Vollzugsinn*," translated by Kisiel as "actualization-sense" and by van Buren as "fulfillment sense," meaning, as van Buren says, "the sense of enacting, performing, actualizing, or fulfilling the horizonal prefiguration of the whole intentional relation."[6] The notion is perhaps best seen as an existential adaptation of Husserl's distinction between an intention and its fulfillment, the difference being that a *Volizugsinn* is sense that demands not intuitive but actional or actualizing fulfillment. A *Vollzugsinn* is grasped *in actu exercitu*, in the very doing of it, actionally and existentially. *Tentatio*, accordingly, is not to be understood as signifying a constative or theoretical content but as a formal indication of a disturbance in life that is understood only if is undergone. "Weep with me and weep for me," Augustine says, "all you who feel within yourselves that goodness from which good actions come. Those of you who have no such feeling will not be moved by what I am saying" (*Confessions*, bk. 10, chap. 33). My life will be alive (*viva erit vita mea*), Augustine says, when I will adhere to you with all of myself (*Confessions*, bk. 10, chap. 28). My life is authentic (*eigentliches*), Heidegger comments, I truly exist, when I let the whole of my facticity be permeated and transfixed by You, when my life is "so actualized (*vollzug*) that every action is carried out before You" (*so vollzogen, daß aller Vollzug vor Dir vollzieht*) (GA 60, p. 249).

The three directions of concupiscence, of the *defluere*, the three directions in which the soul's life may run off, are three "dangers" (*Gefahr*) (GA 60, p. 211) to the soul not "objectively" (bringing about its metaphysical destruction) but "factically" (confessionally, concretely, existentially, having to do with a corruption of its *cura*, the ruination of that which the heart treasures). They are not to be taken as objective items on a list, but "in their full factical 'how,' in which I have and am the world and my life" (GA 60, p. 214). They cannot be analyzed in terms of metaphysical distinctions like body and soul, reason and senses, but rather in terms of the *quotidianum bellum* (*Confessions*, bk. 10, chap. 31), of the daily war the soul wages against the tendencies that pull it apart and scatter it abroad, *malitia diei et nocti*, the evils of the day and night, the little skirmishes of everydayness, whether waking or sleeping. Thus, as I am pulled off course by the flesh (*caro*), so that I eat not in order to nourish myself but in the disorder of taking delight in food instead of God, so I must counter this tendency with fasting (*Confessions*, bk. 10, chap. 31). Again, the eyes (the cognitive sphere, generally) are disordered by *curiositas*, by the desire for something novel (*Neugier*), by a throng of endless vanities, and this under the pretense of seeking knowledge, an excess carried to the point of "morbid" curiosity, which takes a perverse delight in seeing a mangled corpse (*Confessions*, bk. 10, chap. 35). Augustine's analysis of the three tendencies of concupiscence makes an explicit appearance in *Being and Time* in the analysis of the way that everyday *Dasein* "falls" into the world (§35–38): a generous citation of the text of *Confessions*, Book 10, chapter 35, on the *curiositas occulorum*, appears in §36.

The first two forms of concupiscence, Heidegger comments, are "*umweltlich*," having to do with our worldly commerce with things (*weltliches Umgehen*)—with people and things in which we seek sensual gratification. But the third struggle—with worldly pride and ambition (*ambitio saeculi*)—has more directly and explicitly to do with the self, with being a self (*Selbstsein*), with how the self "is there" (GA 60, p. 228), because in it we take delight in the validity and importance of the self in the world. Here the energies of *cura* are spent in winning ourselves standing in the with-world (*Mitwelt*), in winning "with-worldly validity" (GA 60, p. 229). This war is conducted on the battlefield of language: *quotidiana fornax nostra est human lingua;* "*we are tried daily in the furnace of the human tongue*" (*Confessions*, bk. 10, chap. 37). Here, language is conceived as a battlefield—not as a medium of expression or communication but as the medium in which the soul strives with itself, with its vanity, with the regard in which it is held in the *Mitwelt*. I make my way around the world *emendicato*, like a beggar, in search of words of praise and approval from other people (*Confessions*, bk. 10, chap. 37). More insidious still (*intus etiam*), I am inclined by pride to make myself important in my own eyes, to be secretly pleased with myself in the interior of my own heart. After all, I am doing things for which I should indeed be praised; am I supposed to do evil in order to avoid praise? The fault is to regard my good deeds as my own doing, not God's in me.

When Augustine writes "[i]n all these and other similar perils and toils, You see the trembling of my heart," Heidegger comments, "Augustine clearly sees the difficulty and the ultimately anxiety-producing character (*beängstigende*) of Dasein in such having-of-the-self (in full facticity)" (GA 60, p. 241). Still, captured as he is by Neoplatonic metaphysics, Augustine lacks the full methodological resources, lacks the conceptuality adequate to the demands of factical life that could articulate fully the land of difficulty he has discovered, the hidden regions of the self he would explore (GA 60, p. 230). The most one can do at this point is to stake out the direction that a factical interpretation would take, a direction that tends finally toward *Being and Time* itself.

For Augustine, the whole of life is trial and temptation, and it is only in temptation that a human being knows of what sort (*qualis*) it is. Life is hard and beset by difficulty, tending by an inner momentum to fall away from itself, transfixed by the *possibility* of being drawn away from its own inner course. This possibility grows more intense, Heidegger says, "the more life is lived," that is, the more intensely our *cura* is directed into the world of our concerns (*umweltlich*), into the with-world (*mitweltlich*), and toward oneself (*selbstweltlich*). Again, this possibility of falling grows more intense "the more life comes to itself," that is, the more the very being of life as a concern about itself is intensified, which means the more life takes itself as its own measure. Life grows as *molestia* grows; conversely, as *molestia* increases, we become increasingly aware of the full determination and genuine sense of life. *Molestia* was misunderstood by Greek asceticism and by Christian asceticism, too, insofar as it had come under the spell of the Greek, as if it were some sort of objective thing that could be simply cut off or detached by *apathia*. The Greeks failed to see that life is trial and trouble all the way down. Life would not be life, would not be living, were it not shot through with the possibility of falling, were not the task of winning oneself back from the pull of *Abfall* dangerous all the way down (GA 60, pp. 244–45). To work all this out, Heidegger says, a radically new categorical determination of "life" is required (GA 60, pp. 243–44). To be sure, this project of thinking through factical "life" was ultimately superseded for Heidegger—life (*vita, Leben*) would be regionalized as a "biological" category in *Being and Time* (§10)—by the problematic of "Dasein," whose "essence" is *"Existenz."*

Theologia Crucis

The distinction Heidegger makes between the Neoplatonic metaphysics of Augustine and the experience of factical life draws heavily upon Luther's distinction between the *theologia crucis* and the *theologia gloriae*, something which is made clear in the Oscar Becker manuscript that appears as appendix 2 in *Phänomenologie des religiösen Lebens*. Augustine's neo-Platonism turns on what Heidegger calls Augustine's "axiology," a schema for rank ordering higher and lower values, from the lowest objects of use (*uti*) to the highest objects of enjoyment (*frui*). As the fundamental characteristic of life, *cura* is itself distributed into *uti*, a care for the temporal things we need to use, and *frui*, the ultimate and irreducible enjoyment of unchangeable things (GA 60, p. 273). The *vita beata*—the highest, happiest, most blessed life of all—is to enjoy the highest value, God, the *summum bonum*, while the worst and lowest life—one in which care is set adrift by the pull of concupiscence—is to use the invisible and unchanging things of God in order to enjoy the changeable things of this earth. When Augustine says that God is *"decus meum,"* "my pride and glory," Heidegger comments that "this is a Neoplatonic thought" (GA 60, p. 286). The good life is a well-ordered life: you obey God, and the flesh obeys you! A good man is a good valuator (*"integer aestimator,"* De doct. Christiana, bk. 1, chaps. 27–28; GA 60, p. 279). Heidegger emphasizes that this axiology has a fundamentally "aesthetic" sense—the beautiful belongs to the essence of Being" (GA 60, p. 271)—for *frui* means to take delight in beauty and in the good, too, insofar as it is also beautiful. Heidegger claims that the *fruitio dei* is a "specifically Greek" conception—going back not to Paul but to Plato (GA 60, p. 277), to Greek conceptions of *nous* and *theoria*—which is decisive for the subsequent history of medieval theology and mysticism. Nonetheless, *frui* is redirected by Augustine away from its Greek orientation to "intuitive" enjoyment and is "rooted in the characteristically Christian conception of factical life" (GA 60, p. 272). Thus, while we live in hope of eternal rest and enjoyment, the present, temporal life remains one of labor and difficulty.

Heidegger questions the suitability of this Greek metaphysical hierarchy to the "phenomenon" of factical life. The *Confessions* clearly reveal to us the interweaving of the authentically Christian problematic—the question of *tentatio*, of the *deflux in multum*, and of the *quaestio mihi factus sum*—with an axiology that is fundamentally Greek and metaphysical in origin (GA 60, pp. 280–81). They freely intermingle the contemplation of eternal and unchangeable being, which Heidegger suggests is a way that "Greek philosophy plays itself into Augustine's thought" (GA 60, p. 279),—with the dynamics of factical life. The Christian and the Greek constitute not only different historical epochs but phenomenologically different ways of making God accessible, resulting in different determinations of God's *Gegenständlichkeit*, the way God comes to stand in experience (GA 60, pp. 179–80, 292–93). It is one thing to make God accessible as *summum bonum* or *summa pulchritudo*, which is to treat God, in Hellenic and neo-Platonic terms, as the summit of a desire for intuitive vision and unity. But it is a radically different thing to approach God in fear and trembling, with a chaste and pure fear, what Augustine calls a *timor castus*—a loving, even trusting, fear of separation from God—as opposed to the more slavish fear (*timor servilis*) of eternal punishment (GA 60, pp. 293–97).[7] Augustine arrived at this distinction by way of resolving the seeming contradiction between the psalmist's cry that the fear of the Lord is pure, enduring forever (Ps. 19:9) and John's reminder that perfect love casts out fear (1 John 4:18) by saying that love casts out servile fear while loving fear lives forever. The God given in chaste fear, on the battlefield of *tentatio*, is the living God, the biblical and Pauline God, who competes for attention throughout Augustine's texts with a neo-Platonic *summum bonum*, a being of peace and light, of rest and beauty:

> But on the whole, the explication of the experience of God in Augustine is specifically "Greek" (in the sense in which indeed our whole philosophy is "Greek"). It never comes to a radically critical posing of the question and consideration of origins (destruction). (GA 60, p. 292)

And what is true of God is no less true of the "self," treated alternatively by Augustine as spiritual substance and as a land of difficulty, and the "world," which is not only an aggregate of entities for him but a phenomenological region of lure and temptation. Augustine's texts oscillate between metaphysics and facticity, on the verge of a conceptual and categorical revolution of which they are never quite capable, which both invite and require a *Destruktion* that would transform the three great themes of metaphysics—God, the self, and the world—around which Descartes and Kant organized modern philosophy. Today, Heidegger laments, we read Augustine through the lens of modern and especially of Cartesian philosophy, mistaking the factical

life of the self that is astir in Augustine for a Cartesian *cogito* born of
Descartes' epistemological problematic of doubt and certitude (GA 60,
pp. 298–99).

The conflation of Greek and Christian thematics in Augustine, perhaps even the inundating of the Christian by the Greek, was authorized
and made possible, Heidegger points out, by the reading of Romans
1:20 that prevailed from the patristic period throughout medieval
philosophy, according to which the invisible things of God are seen
through the visible things he has made. This text was taken to be a
Pauline confirmation of the Platonic ascent of the soul from the sensible to the supersensible world (GA 60, p. 281). It is only in Luther,
Heidegger contends, that the meaning of this text is properly elucidated. "Only *Luther* in his earliest works has opened a new understanding of primal Christianity (*Urchristentum*)," Heidegger says (GA 60, pp.
281–82), an understanding which, it is not too much to say, fundamentally shaped Heidegger's conception of a hermeneutics of facticity,
particularly in the mediation of Luther to Heidegger by Kierkegaard,
although later on, Heidegger laments, even Luther fell into a scholasticism of a peculiarly Protestant kind.

Luther's conception is most clearly articulated in three theses from
the Heidelberg Dissertation of 1518: "No. 19: 'The man who looks
upon the invisible things of God as they are perceived in created things
does not deserve to be called a theologian.'" Upon which Heidegger
comments, "The initial giving (*Vorgabe*) of the object of theology is not
attained by way of a metaphysical consideration of the world" (GA 60,
p. 282). The second thesis reads thus: "No. 21: 'The theologian of glory
calls evil good and good evil, while the theologian of the Cross says
what a thing is.'" Upon this, Heidegger says, "The theologian of glory,
who amuses himself aesthetically with the wonders of the world, calls
the sensible God. The theologian of the cross says what things are" (GA
60, p. 282). The third thesis follows: "No. 22: 'The wisdom that looks
upon the invisible things of God from His works, inflates us, blinds us,
and hardens our heart'" (GA 60, p. 282).

As Alister McGrath explains, "[t]he 'theologian of glory' expects
God to be revealed in strength, glory and majesty, and is simply unable
to accept the scene of dereliction on the cross as the self-revelation of
God."[8] The theologian of glory looks to sensible things to embody in
their beauty the surpassing beauty of God, hoping to find the majesty
of God in a majestic mountain and to find the glory of God in a sunrise.
This is dangerously close to paganism for Luther, to a Greek and neo-
Platonic ascent from the sensible to the supersensible. Above all else,
it ignores the distinctively Christian message of the cross. For in the
cross, contrary to the expectations of human reason, God reveals himself not by analogy and by an approximate ascent through similitudes,

but, *per contaria,* through his opposite, and *per posteriora* (Thesis No. 20), through his back or "rearward" parts (Exod. 33:23). In the cross, God reveals himself not through the order of the natural world, which is a common and natural revelation, but through Christ, through the perversity and disorder of his death, *per passiones et crucem.* In the cross, God is revealed not through the glory of natural manifestations but is revealed in the concealment of death and ignominy.

Thus, God reveals his power through weakness, his heights through lowliness, his wisdom through foolishness. He has revealed his power and justice by concealing it in the humiliation and death of Jesus on the cross. He has chosen for his own the least among men, those whom the world counts as *me orta,* the nothings and nobodies, who are not wise or powerful by the world's standards, and these he employs "to reduce to nothing the things that are" (1 Cor. 1:28). The defining feature of Christianity, that which sets it apart from paganism and a merely natural knowledge of God, is the cross, something that is neither visible to the senses nor understandable to reason but that is accessible only to faith. "*Crux sola est nostra theologia.*" So he is "worthy to be called a theologian" (*dignus dicitur*), a genuinely Christian theologian, who relies not on reason but faith and who proceeds not from the visible manifestations of God's glory but from the scenes of ignominy and distress that beset the human condition under which God has paradoxically revealed himself precisely by concealing himself from human wisdom.

What Luther calls the *theologia gloriae* lies unmistakably behind what Heidegger calls Augustine's "axiology." that is, his Neoplatonic scale of lower and higher, his metaphysics of ascent to the *summum bonum,* his ordering of human life to the enjoyment of self-sufficient and all-fulfilling goodness and beauty. By the same token, Luther's *theologia crucis* lies no less clearly behind Heidegger's valorization of struggle and difficulty, trial and trouble, and his insistence that what is distinctively *Christian* in Augustine, the still detectable traces of *Urchristentum* in Augustine, is his narrative of the life of *tentatio,* which goes to the essence of what Heidegger means by "facticity" or "factical life."

Indeed, Heidegger sketches the "dimensions" of factical life, let us says its factical spatiality (anticipating the existential spatiality of *Dasein* discussed in §22–24 of *Being and Time),* in terms of Augustine's account of the "symbolism" of the cross in Sermon 53. When Augustine speaks of "interiority," Heidegger warns, we must avoid every "cosmic-metaphysical reification of the concept of God" (GA 60, p. 290). God is found in the inner man, in the heart, but only so long as we understand the dimensions of interiority—the proper dimensionality of the heart—whose measure is to be taken from the cross. When we turn within, we do not find an inner nook of the world from which everything else is excluded but rather the infinite length and breadth of God's infinity. We do not lose everything else but find everything anew "*in te*." The inner life and spatiality of the heart does not have the sense of a *res extensa* but of a *Vollzugssinn*, an actional or operative sense, a sense that is grasped or understood only in the doing, *in actu exercitu*, in the very act and action of concrete life.

Thus, according to Augustine, the breadth (*Weite, latitutdo*) of the inner world, symbolized by the outstretched hands of Jesus nailed to the cross, is the richness and fullness of good works. Its length (*Länge, longitudo*), symbolized by that part of the upright post of the cross extending from the transversal that tends toward the ground, upon which Jesus' body is stretched out, is its patience and perseverance. Its height (*Höhe, altitudo*), symbolized by the upright from the transversal to the sky above (*supernus*), is its expectation of what lies above it, to which the heart must lift itself (*sursum corda*). Finally, its depth (*Tiefe, profundum*), symbolized by that part of the cross which is sunk into the ground, is the hidden grace of God, which itself unseen is that from which what is seen rises up (GA 60, p. 290, n. 25).[9]

Odd as it may sound to secular ears, this Pauline theology of the Cross, of Christ and of Him crucified, which so captured Luther (and after him, Kierkegaard), lies behind what Heidegger called in the early Freiburg lectures the "hermeneutics of facticity"; it lies also behind the famous account of *Dasein* as a being of "care" (*Sorge*) in *Being and Time*, from which it issued. Thus, is it possible to understand what Heidegger meant when he said, in that remarkable footnote, that the analytic of *Dasein* as a Being of care is "one which has grown upon the author in connection with his attempts to interpret the Augustinian (i.e., Helleno-Christian) anthropology with regard to the foundational principles reached in the ontology of Aristotle" (*SZ*, p. 199, n. 1; *BT*, p. 492, n. vii). To understand the reference to Aristotle we would need to follow a separate lecture course on the *Nicomachean Ethics*, in which Heidegger focused on the Aristotelian demand to hit the mark of *arete*, which is but one, neither overshooting nor undershooting it, as a task of particular "difficulty" (GA 60, pp. 108–10), while there are many ways to miss it, which is, accordingly, "easy" to do (*Nicomachean Ethics*, 1106 b 28 ff.).

Circumfession: The Prayers and Tears of Jacques Derrida

The issue of Derrida's reading of the *Confessions* is not a "hermeneutics of facticity" but a deeply personal meditation on the passion and death of his mother, not a war journal but a journal of her death agony. The Confessions, Derrida tells us, are the place that he "discovered the prayers and tears of Saint Augustine" (*Circ.*, 12/*Circum.*, p. 9)—not the dynamics of authentic *Dasein*. He does not write a commentary *on* the *Confessions* in the third person; rather, he identifies with the *Confessions*, with Augustine, "my compatriot" (*Circ.*, p.19/*Circum.*, p. 18)—he, the son of these tears (*filius istrarum lacrymarum*) (*Circ.*, p. 126/*Circum.*, p. 132), whose mother is dying, like Monica, on the other side of the Mediterranean. He does not write *on* the *Confessions*, but he confesses, in the first person, like Augustine. "[F]or like SA [Saint Augustine] I love only tears, I only love and speak through them" (*Circ.*, p. 95/*Circum.*, p. 98). He confesses with tears and prayers—"not only do I pray, as I have never stopped doing all my life" (*Circ.*, p. 57/*Circum.*, p. 56)—asking for pardon, addressing You, or God. But what is there for him to confess? He confesses by writing his Judaism and his breach with Judaism, his circumcision and his "de-circumcision," a divided spirit which suffers both the guilt of being Jewish and the guilt of having bid farewell to Judaism. But that cut in his flesh, that divided self, is creative, constituting the passion of his life and work.

He writes of his bodily fluids, of the flow of his tears, of his blood, of semen and menstrual blood, too, and of the running bedsores (*escarres*) of his dying mother, all circulating in the image of circumcision, in a flowing, fluid paratactical prose whose fifty-nine chapters (one for each of his fifty-nine years of life) constitute the flow of a single sentence or *phrase* (*Circ.*, pp. 110–11/*Circum.*, p. 115). If the Christian Augustine confesses the winding path by which he was drawn to faith in Christ, Derrida, the "little black and very Arab Jew," confesses the cut in his flesh, his circumcision—"Circumcision, that's all I've ever talked about" (*Circ.*, p. 70/*Circum.*, p. 70)—about which all his writings on limits, margins, marks, cuts, incisions, inscriptions, the ring of economy and the gift, etc., turn.

The counterpart to the *theologia crucis* in *Circonfession* is not the robust vitality of *Selbstbekümmerung* but the flowing blood and wounded body of his dying mother, which stands in for the death of every other, in connection with which he cites a line from Celan: "It was blood, it was, that you shed, O Lord" (*Es war Blut, es war, was du vergossen, Herr*) (*Circ.*, pp. 99–100/*Circum.*, p. 103). He lives with "the terror of an endless crucifixion, a thought for all my well-beloved Catherines of Siena," who wrote about the blood of Christ shed in his circumcision and on the Cross. In his texts, Derrida says, he is always shedding his own blood, tearing at his skin until he hits blood, although he does so by writing about others, so that we will be indebted to them, not him (*Circ.*, pp. 222–23/*Circum.*, pp. 239–40). *Circonfession* is a remarkably

Derridean *theologia crucis*—*sans* the theology, a deconstructivist *theologia crucis*.

So, unlike Heidegger, Derrida's interest is not confined to Book 10, but he is drawn to the preceding autobiographical books, to the narratives of Monica and Augustine's youth. Still, like Heidegger, Derrida is also fascinated by Book 10: *Ecce ubi sum;* See in what a condition I am. *Flete mecum et pro me flete;* Weep with me and weep for me. But when this text is cited, it refers not to the athletic robustness of factical life, but to his dying mother—once a lovely young woman who loved to play card games and stayed up late playing poker the night before Derrida was born—now unable to drink from a cup, the water running down her chin, and to his own condition when he suffers a facial paralysis that is eventually identified as a form of Lyme disease (*Circ.*, p. 95/*Circum.*, pp. 98, 115, 120). *Tu autem, domine deus meus, exaudi et respice et vide et miserere et sana me;* But do thou O Lord my God hear me and look upon me and see me and heal me—*in cujus oculis mihi quaestio factus sum*—in whose eyes I have become a question to myself (*Confessions,* bk. 10, chap. 33). But for Derrida, the questionability of life does not signify the insecurity of the self, the battle the self wages with itself for authenticity, but rather the longing of love and desire, the question of what I love when I love my God, of what I desire when I love and desire what is "to come" (*à venir*), which is what Derrida calls "*the* impossible"—"having never loved anything but the impossible" (*Circ.*, p. 7/*Circum.*, p. 3).

For Derrida, Augustine's *Confessions* are the occasion of a prayer, of revealing the "secret" of his prayers and tears—"I wonder if those reading me from up there see my tears . . . if they guess that my life was but a long history of prayers" (*Circ.*, p. 40/*Circum.*, pp. 38–39)—not of an analysis of the formal structure of factical life. Derrida finds in Augustine not the virile militancy of a spiritual battlefield but bodies bent by sorrow and grief, not the brawny bravado of *Eigentlichkeit* but the woman weeping at the foot of the cross, not the combative strength of a Christian soldier but the weakness of a suppliant begging for God's help, not a masculinized *Kampfsphilosophie* but love, not a soul whose mettle is fired by a war with concupiscence but saintly eyes blinded by tears.

For Heidegger, the hermeneutic presupposition of *confiteri*, of the confessional mode, is that the soul is the scene of battle, turmoil, and unrest. But for Derrida, confession reduces us to tears and to asking for pardon, and it is linked with the flow of blood. *Cruor, confiteor:* to confess is to let my blood flow, to draw my blood with a syringe/pen, and to store my confession of faith (*cru*) in a labeled bottle like wine (*cru*) (*Circ.*, p. 13/*Circum.*, p. 10). To confess is to mix the outpouring of blood with the outpouring of tears. "I owe it to autobiography to say that I have spent my life teaching so as to return in the end to what mixes prayer and tears with blood" (*Circ.*, p. 22/*Circum.*, p. 20). Blood is the color of mortal life, of "desire, history, or event" (*Circ.*, p. 82/*Circum.* p. 80). Circumfession is the confession in writing, *in litteris*, of Derrida's circumcision, the confession of his Jewish/Arab provenance and of his lack of a language, for the Christian/Latin/French in which he writes these confessions is and is not his, and that is brought home by the generous citations of Augustine's lush Latin. I am the last of the Jews (*Circ.*, p. 145/*Circum.*, p. 154), he says, like his namesake Elijah, the last of the prophets—a philosopher, who, having left Judaism, revisits or is revisited by his Jewishness, in this age after the death of God. Confession means for him to make a gift without return, like a last will and testament, beyond the circle (*Circ.*, p. 221/*Circum.*, p. 238), leaving behind a secret that everyone understands but him.

Monica never makes an appearance in Heidegger's lecture course. Like Kierkegaard, this Heideggerian Augustine seems to have no mother. But *Circonfession* is, from the first page on, all about Monica/ Georgette Safar Derrida, dying in her emigrant home, on the other side of the Mediterranean in Nice (having emigrated from what is today Algiers), like Monica dying in Ostia (*Circ.*, p. 20/*Circum.*, p. 19). Derrida looks like his mother, favors his mother's side, resembling perhaps an ancestor on the mother's side who emigrated from Portugal to Algeria at the beginning of the nineteenth century (*Circ.*, pp. 232–34/*Circum.*, p. 253). When he weeps, he never knows who is weeping, he or his mother (*Circ.*, p. 243/*Circum.*, p. 263). There is no evading death and dying in *Being and Time*, but that always means *my* death, while *Circonfession* is a journal of the death of Derrida's mother, of the other, of what Mark Taylor calls the "(m)other," and of my death insofar as it concerns the other. In *Circonfession*, at fifty-nine years of age, Derrida says, he is learning how to die, but that is always seen from the point of view of the other. He tries to give himself death, *se donner la mort*, not in the sense of committing suicide but in the sense of seeing himself dead and of seeing others "seeing me lying on my back," gathered around his grave, "and I weep like my own children at the edge of my grave" (*Circ.*, p. 41/*Circum.*, p. 40). He fears for his life, not for himself but for her, from her fear for him, so that he fears too that perhaps, after her death, he will no longer fear death (*Circ.*, p. 198/*Circum.*, p. 212).

As Augustine's *Confessions* (though they are addressed to God) do not tell God anything God does not know (bk. 9, chap. 1), so Derrida's circumfession consists not in disclosing the truth, in communicating some secret truth to anyone, to G(eoffrey), God, or us. Derrida has no truth to tell but is making the truth, doing the truth, *facere veritatem*, confessing in writing, *confiteor in litteris*, with prayers and tears, as much religion as literature. But what then is confessed? The "essential truth of avowal" has "nothing to do with truth, but consist[s] . . . in asked for pardon," because to write is to ask pardon (*Circ.*, pp. 47–50/*Circum.*, pp. 46–49). As Augustine is not trying to give God some information that God otherwise lacks but rather "to arouse my feeling of love toward Thee, and that of those who read these pages" (bk. 10, chap. 1), Derrida, who does not know the secret, who has no secret Truth to tell, is trying to arouse his love of life and ours, to transform himself through and through (*Circ.*, pp. 75–76/*Circum.*, pp. 76–77), and to learn how to die (*Circ.*, p. 193/*Circum.*, p. 208). He walks around with a secret unknown to himself, in a sealed text, which he is always commenting upon, which others will open and read (*Circ.*, pp. 238–39/ *Circum.*, pp. 257–58).

If Heidegger identifies the formal structure of *Vollzugsinn*, Derrida actually carries it out, enacts a confession, performs it, *in litteris*. *Circonfession* is written with the personal passion of the *Confessions*, as a work of "memory and heart" (*Circ.*, p. 85/*Circum.*, p. 87). Of his dying mother, Derrida writes, "a little while ago she pronounced my name, Jackie, in echo to the sentence from my sister passing her the receiver, 'hello Jackie,' something she had not been able to do for months and will perhaps do no more, beyond the fact that through her whole life she scarcely knew the other name" (*Circ.*, pp. 80–82/*Circum.*, p. 83). "Jackie," we learn, is his given name, "Jacques" a pen name, and "Elie" a Hebrew name given to him at birth, a name so secret that it was unknown until recently even to him, a *"given* name that I received without receiving . . . a sign of election (*on élit*)" (*Circ.*, p. 82/*Circum.*, p. 84). He thought of calling a notebook on circumcision that he had been keeping the "Book of Elijah," Elijah being the prophet guardian of circumcision. Like Monica weeping for Augustine when he set sail for Europe, Georgette weeps over the nineteen-year-old Jackie setting sail for France (*Circ.*, p. 16/*Circum.*, p. 177). He remembers feigning illness one day as a child when, holding his mother's hand, she walked him to school; when later in the afternoon she returns to pick him up, he reproached her for leaving him "in the world, in the hands of others," having forgotten that he was supposed to be sick. "She must have been as beautiful as a photograph" (*Circ.*, p. 250/*Circum.*, p. 271). These are secrets of the heart that he communicates to us, *in litteris*, in a personal memoir.

There is pain in *Circonfession*, not the pain of factical life struggling for authenticity but the pain emblematized in circumcision. That, of course, is a pain I do not remember but whose trace is unmistakable, hence a "phantom pain," a pain we think, presumptuously, that the infant does not much mind. We assure and comfort ourselves with the thought, possibly the fantasy, Derrida says that the orange flower water with which the child is bathed immediately after the rite of circumcision has an anesthetic virtue. The phantom pain I cannot remember, with which I try to identify, is the pain of the mother who is kept in a separate room, in tears, while the rite is enacted; or the pain of the mother, Monica/Georgette, dying on the other side of the Mediterranean. The unmistakable trace of pain left by circumcision is the pain of the other—"a threat which returns every time the other is in pain, if I identify with him, with her, even" (*Circ.*, p. 66/*Circum.*, p. 66), whose pain is always a phantom for me, for, like the trace of circumcision, I see it but do not feel it and can only try to remember it.

The lively kinetics and spiritual athleticism of the hermeneutics of facticity that Heidegger finds in the *Confessions* stand in remarkable contrast to the dominant motifs of *Circonfession*: a dying woman confined to bed, her running bedsores, fading memory and speech; and Derrida's facial paralysis, finally diagnosed as Lyme disease, which appears as a filial counterpart to the mother's terminal illness. The cause of Derrida's facial paralysis was at first unknown, an alarming symptom of a stroke perhaps and perhaps the prelude to a more massive stroke and an untimely death. Might Derrida's death overtake and precede his mother's? Would he be dead before her, before he finished these confessions? He sees himself dead before her, while she, her memory gone, does not see his death. *Ecce ubi sum:* a twisted mouth, a disfigured face, a cyclops: "my left eye fixed open like a glass-eyed cyclops" (*Circ.*, p. 98/*Circum.*, p. 95), an invisible scar to match the visible *escarres* of the dying mother, an invisible scar to match the visible scar of circumcision, a "scarface . . . the monocular warning light of his [God's] evil" (*Circ.*, p. 101/*Circum.*, p. 104; cf. *Confessions*, bk. 7, chap. 5), a punishment perhaps for any of many faults—*Ecce ubi sum:* the dying mother, increasing blindness, distorted speech, inability to recognize her children, living, dead or dying—if that is what is happening to Jackie.

There is a conversion, a *metanoia*, in *Circonfession*, but it is not the self-recovery of authentic Christian freedom from the sway of sin that Heidegger reads in Augustine but a conversion brought about in Derrida from without—"I am no longer the same since the FP [facial paralysis], whose signs seem to have been effaced though I know I'm not the same persona" (*Circ.*, p. 117/*Circum.*, p. 123). Derrida is learning how to die and what his death means for others.

One of the surprises that is in store for us in *Circonfession* is Derrida's love of God. "What do I love when I love you," "my God," Augustine asks (*Confessions*, bk. 10, chaps. 6–7). For Heidegger, the name of God is the name of struggle (*Kampf*): to love God is to love difficulty (*Schwierig-*

keit), burden *(onus),* and trouble *(molestia) (Confessions,* bk. 10, chap. 28). *Vita . . . tota tentatio* [*est*] *(Confessions,* bk. 10, chap. 32): "God is there," Heidegger says, "in troubling over the life of the self" (GA 60, p. 289). Struggle gives the measure to life, and the life of the soul before God, *coram deo,* raises struggle *(Kampf)* to its highest pitch and to its most exuberant vitality. But for Derrida the name of God is mingled with tears. Where is God? *In memoria mea.* Where in my memory?

> Well, I'm remembering God this morning, the name, a quotation, something my mother said . . . to quote the name of God as I heard it perhaps the first time, no doubt in my mother's mouth when she was praying, each time she saw me ill, no doubt dying like her son before me, like her son after me . . . I hear her say, *"grâce à Dieu, Dieu merci"* when the temperature goes down, weeping in pronouncing your name . . . I'm mingling here the name of God with the origin of tears. *(Circ.,* pp. 112–13/*Circum.,* pp. 117–18)

For "Jackie," this weepy, pusillanimous little child whom the adults love to tease and reduce to tears, the name of God commingles with tears; for the internationally known philosopher, for "Derrida," the name of God remains the question of all questions. Unlike Heidegger, for whom this name spells the end of questioning, Derrida asks again and again, confesses that he has been asking all his life, *quid ergo amo cum deum* [*meum*] *amo:* What do I love when I love my God? "Can I do anything other than translate this question by SA into my own language?" *(Circ.,* p. 117/*Circum.,* p. 122), having slightly altered the position of the *meum* in the text of *Confessions* (bk. 10, chap. 6). The emphasis in this very biblical expression "my God" is on the *my,* not in the sense that this is merely some sort of subjective fabrication on his part but in the sense of a God who belongs to him even as he belongs to his God, to this most personal God who knows the secrets of his heart and to whom he confesses; a little like, in the beginning of Genesis, the God "of Abraham" and "of Jacob" had such a personal sense that it needed to be made plain that these are the same God. This preoccupation with Judaism and God: "that's what my readers won't have known about me," he says, "like my religion about which nobody understands anything" *(Circ.,* p. 146/*Circum.,* p. 154).

Even Monica/Georgette, worrying over the faith of the son of these tears, knows nothing of this religion. She had been afraid to ask Jackie whether he still believed in God, even though she might have known that "the constancy of God in my life is called by other names, so that I quite rightly pass for an atheist" *(Circ.,* p. 146/*Circum.,* p. 155). God is omnipresent for Derrida, in this "absolved, absolutely private language," not in the form of a eyewitness who sees everything he does nor of a transcendent law regulating every moment of life but in the sense of being "the secret I am excluded from," the "open secret" (*secret de Polichinelle*), which is known to others but not to him. The name of God is the name of the secret that penetrates and suffuses everything he does and writes, where the secret is not a deep and hidden *magnum mysterium* in the sense of a negative theology but rather the secret that there is no secret, that there is no deep Truth to which only a few initiates have access. The secret is that there is no Secret Truth, which is why there is no Truth or Secret to confess but only texts. To be sure, this is no cause for despair for Derrida but rather a source of passion, what he calls elsewhere *la passion du non-savoir*, the passion which arises from non-knowledge, from the un-truth, which does not condemn but enjoins the endless play of interpretation. That is why the secret is known to everyone but him, why it is an open secret, for it is precisely in the ear of the other, or in their counter-signatures to come, that the secret of Derrida will be laid bare. His secret is nothing he knows and nothing he can confess, so that his God "circulate[s] among the unavowables" (*Circ.*, pp. 146–47/*Circum.*, pp. 155–56), God being the name of the secret, of I know not what, of the passion of not knowing that drives writing.

For Heidegger, language is the furnace in which authentic *Dasein* is tried, the chatter of the "they" which distracts and dissipates authentic resolve. But for Derrida, language is a mark of dispossession: "I'm reaching the end without *ever* having read Hebrew" (*Circ.*, pp. 264–65/ *Circum.*, pp. 286–87), the notorious convolutions and learned circumlocutions of his texts being, thus, the way he constantly gropes with the unknown grammar of Hebrew in "Christian Latin French," "a language made a present to me by its colonization of Algeria in 1830" (*Circ.*, pp. 263/*Circum.*, p. 285). Even circumcision, the thing itself, has been relayed to him in the word "*circoncision*," which is Christian/ Latin/French; indeed, even that word was dropped among Algerian Jews who, "through fearful acculturation," preferred to speak of their "baptism" and to call Bar-Mitzvah "communion" (*Circ.*, pp. 71–72/ - *Circum.*, pp. 71–73). Derrida speaks the language of the outside, an outsider's language, the Latin of the *numerus clausus*. He took flight from Hebrew when they tried to make him learn it as a child, even as French could never be his (*Circ.*, p. 267/*Circum.*, p. 289). That exile, that loss, engendered his taste for words and letters and became the passion that would make his whole life a *confiteri in litteris*. That is a profoundly different conception of language than is to be found in Heidegger's thought, where language is the language of the *Heimat*, Germany's or

Being's, where speaking is empowered by autochthony, by the gathering together of the essential power of the *Volk* or *Sprache* from which one speaks.

In *Being and Time,* Heidegger speaks of a primordial and ontological guilt, of a finitude which it is the whole point of authentic *Dasein* to assume, to appropriate and take over, to make one's own. In the Heideggerian analysis of guilt, the idea is to refine guilt into the fine point of authentic resoluteness so that authentic *Dasein* is pointed into the definite, finite, refined finitude of its own singlemost *Seinkönnen*, the *Seelenfünklein* of authentic freedom. Primordial or ontological guilt for Heidegger is thus the scene of freedom, but for Derrida, guilt is the scene of confession. Derrida, too, writes of a guilt for which he can remember no fault: "scenes of guilt in some sense faultless, without any deliberate fault, situations in which the accusation surprises you," scenes that constitute a paradigm for a whole life, scenes he must not precisely "assume," since they are older than freedom (Levinas) but which he must allow to become productive, for they "play in their Confessions an organizing and abyssal role" (*Circ.*, p. 278/*Circum.*, p. 301). This incomprehensible fault is "all Hebrew [not Greek] to me" (*Circ.*, p. 279/*Circum.*, p. 302), the fault of being all Hebrew, or not quite all, "for I am perhaps not what remains of Judaism." But then again, "what else am I in truth, who am I if I am not what I inhabit and where I take place, *ich bleibe also Jude,* i.e., today in what remains of Judaism to this world," a fragment of Judaism, a broken shard and remainder (*Circ.*, pp. 279–80/*Circum.*, pp. 302–3). This faultless guilt, which is to be Jewish and then again to have broken with Judaism, is like the scar of circumcision for which he can remember no pain, or like Augustine's notion of original sin, that which we inherit but do not commit (which Kierkegaard, whose lead Heidegger followed, felt compelled to rewrite in *The Concept of Anxiety* so as to give freedom a place), or like Kafka (another prisoner of Prague), or like Isaac (whose fate on Moriah was even more incomprehensible than father Abraham's).

Derrida speaks of the "despair" that stretches from "the innocent child who is by accident charged with a guilt he knows nothing about, the little Jew expelled from Ben Aknoun school" to "the drug-factor incarcerated in Prague, and everything in between" (*Circ.*, p. 282/*Circum.*, p. 306). "I always thought," he writes, "the other must have good reason to accuse me" (*Circ.*, p. 277/*Circum.*, p. 300), and he did not then see that "it was enough to seek to track down the event by writing backward, never seeing the next step"—about the future, always to come (*à venir*), he is essentially blind—in order to prepare "the moment when things turn round, the moment at which you will be able to convert and see your sacrificer face on," not in order to continue the cycle of persecution but to "make the truth," *facere veritatem*, to confess in writing. His fault is the crime of being Jewish, the guilt of being the hated other, which is compounded by his own unfaithfulness to being Jewish, his breach with, his crime against, Judaism. He is chosen from of old to be Jewish, but he has abandoned the chosen (*élu*) people, the people of *élu/Élie*, abandoned (*aban-donné*) his givenness, himself, so that by marrying outside Judaism and by not circumcising his sons, he too is one of those who persecutes the Jews, who does nothing to save the Jews, in Christian/Latin/French.

Circonfession ends on May 1, 1990, in Laguna Beach, California, not far from Santa Monica, California (Derrida's mother still lay dying in Nice—she would not succumb until December 5, 1991), on the occasion of the "Final Solution" conference at the University of California–Los Angeles. After his address, a "young imbecile," apparently unaware that Derrida is Jewish, asks Derrida what he did to save the Jews during the war. Still, the youngster might be right, the other is always right, for he did not do enough to save one Jew, himself, *for* his Jewishness, this being an alliance mostly honored in the breach, or *from* his Jewishness, this lack of continuity with his Jewishness also amounting to a lack of rupture. His circumcision signifies his cut from the covenant cut in his flesh, from the community of the covenant, but a cut that is not clean.

Sero te amavi, pulchritudo tam antiqua et tam nova (*Confessions*, bk. 10, chap. 27), Augustine writes: Too late have I loved thee, o beauty so ancient and so new. Too late, Derrida writes, you are too late (*trop tard*), you (*toi*), the counterpart of me (*moi*), for this secret which is withheld. "You have spent your life inviting calling promising, hoping sighing dreaming, convoking invoking provoking, constituting engendering producing, naming assigning demanding, prescribing commanding sacrificing"—so that you, the witness and the counterpart of me, will attest this "secret truth, severed from truth, that you will never have had any witness" (*Circ.*, pp. 290–91/*Circum.*, p. 314).

The truth is that there is no Truth; the secret is that there is no Secret, no Secret Truth to which we have some secret access or witness. Unlike Heideggerian *Denken*, which is steered by a mighty *Geschick*, a destiny and *moira*, our destiny on Derrida's account is "destinerrance," destiny gone errant, cut off from destiny and the Truth of Being. The cut of circumcision in *Circonfession* comes down to being cut off from truth, *sevrée de la vérité*, from the Truth of Being or of the Book. "You alone, whose life will have been so short, the voyage short, scarcely organized, by you with no lighthouse and no book, you the floating toy at high tide and under the moon, you the crossing between these two phantoms of witnesses that will never be the same," where *toi* and *moi,* the witness and the one to whom witness is given, can never be one, where both the witness and the one to whom one gives witness are both in the blind, where no Truth, no Truth of truth, no Secret Truth can ever be testified to and secured. But this destinerrant condition, the blindness of eyes blinded by tears, these prayers and tears, are for Derrida not a paralyzing and immobilizing despair but the passion of non-knowing, the prayers and tears of a somewhat Jewish, avant-garde Augustine, who has in his own unrepeatable way found a way to repeat the *Confessions* of Augustine and even to repeat, in a slightly postmodern beat, the *theologia crucis.*

Notes

1. John D. Caputo, *Demythologizing Heidegger* (Bloomington: Indiana University Press, 1993), chaps. 2–3.
2. The following abbreviations are used in this study: *SZ,* Martin Heidegger, *Sein und Zeit,* 15. Aufl. (Tübingen, Germany: Niemeyer, 1979); *BT,* Martin Heidegger, *Being and Time,* trans. John Macquarrie and Edward Robinson (New York: Harper and Row, 1962); GA 60, *Phänomenologie des religiösen Lebens,* 1, "Einführung in die Phänomenologie der Religion" (Wintersemester 1920–21), ed. Matthias Jung and Thomas Regehly; 2, "Augustinus und der Neuplatonismus" (Sommersemester, 1921); 3, "Ausaurbeitung und Entwürfe," ed. Claudius Strube, Gesamtausgabe, B. 60 (Frankfurt: Klostermann, 1995); *SUD, Kierkegaard's Writings,* vol. 19, *Sickness unto Death,* trans. Howard and Edna Hong (Princeton, N.J.: Princeton University Press, 1980); *Circon., Circonfession: Cinquante-neuf périodes et périphrases,* in *Jacques Derrida,* Geoffrey Bennington and Jacques Derrida (Paris: Éditions du Seuil, 1991); *Circum., Circumfession: Fifty-nine Periods and periphrases,* in *Jacques Derrida,* Geoffrey Bennington and Jacques Derrida, trans. Geoffrey Bennington (Chicago: University of Chicago Press, 1993).

For excellent accounts of the matters discussed in the first part of this article, see Theodore Kisiel, *The Genesis of Heidegger's "Being and Time"* (Berkeley: University of California Press, 1993), and John van Buren, *The Young Heidegger: Rumor of the Hidden King* (Bloomington: Indiana University Press, 1994).

3. As van Buren shows in *Young Heidegger* (pp. 162–67), the very term *Destruktion,* first appearing in Heidegger's early Freiburg lectures, in the winter semester 1919–20 course, seems to have been taken from Luther's use of the Latin *destructio,* which describes the "right" attitude a Christian theology should take to that "blind pagan Master Aristotle." The Lutheran destruction became for Heidegger the paradigm of the task of the destruction of Greek and scholastic metaphysics, down to its sources in primal Christianity. See Heidegger, *Gesamtausgabe,* vol. 58, *Grundprobleme der Phänomenologie* (Frankfurt: Klostermann, 1993), pp. 139 ff., 61–62, 205.

4. Indeed, Heidegger was early on interested in the work of theologian Franz

Overbeck, who had declared that even by the time of the New Testament, the primitive Christian experience was beginning to be turned over to theological *objectification* because of contamination by Greek philosophy. See Istvan Féher, "Heidegger's Understanding of the Atheism of Philosophy," *American Catholic Philosophical Quarterly* 69 (1995): 189–228 (appendix 2).

5. "Ecce unde vita humana super terram tota tentatio est." Augustine, *Epistulae*, bk. 95, chap. 2; cf. GA 60, p. 241 n. 1.

6. Van Buren, *Young Heidegger*, p. 29. It is distinguished from the content-sense or intentional content; and the relational-sense, or meaning of the way we are related to the content. See van Buren, *Young Heidegger*, pp. 29–32.

7. See Augustine, *In Epist. Joannis ad Parthos.*, bk. 9, chap. 5, and *In Psalmos*, bk. 19, chap. 10. In a note to the analysis of *Angst* in §40 of *Being and Time*, Heidegger draws our attention to Augustine's distinction between *timor castus* and *timor servilis* and treats it as a predecessor of the distinction between *Angst* and *Furcht*, on which latter distinction, he says, the most headway has been made by Kierkegaard (*SZ*, p. 190n; *BT*, p. 492, n. iv). This is a not entirely generous way of saying that he has taken this distinction over, in all of its phenomenological particulars, from Kierkegaard and then reinscribed it within his own project, the "existential analytic." Pure fear, Heidegger says in 1921, is self-fear, a salutary troubling about one's own being, while servile fear is world-fear, a concern directed at things or other persons (GA 60, pp. 296–97).

8. Alister E. McGrath, *Luther's Theology of the Cross* (Oxford: Blackwell, 1990), p. 167. My characterization of this distinction is greatly indebted to McGrath, pp. 148–75. See also van Buren, *Young Heidegger*, pp. 159–67, 187–90, 196–202, 376–82.

9. See Augustine, *Sermones*, bk. 53, chaps. 15–16.

3. Ethical and Social Issues

11

Emmanuel Levinas
and Hillel's Questions

EDITH WYSCHOGROD

"Philosophy is in crisis," says the postmodern thinker. "Yet," she continues, "We are forced to comport ourselves within its ambit, forced to dance its dance, to use its concepts and to unsay them even before they are said." But what is meant by philosophy, and how are we to unsay it if we have at our disposal only *its* notions? Can philosophy provide its own critique without lapsing into self-referentiality? Is there an exteriority, an outside of philosophy that speaks otherwise than philosophically, that can call into question philosophy's hierarchy of constructs? And if there is, what boots it if this exteriority must enter into conversation with philosophy so that it is once again trapped by philosophy?

Emmanuel Levinas treats these questions in terms of a relation of languages, by which are meant discursive practices: "Greek," the language of philosophy, is that nexus of concepts that constitutes Western thought; "Hebrew," whose square script, *les lettres carrées,* is the vehicle for the interpretive approaches deployed by the Sages of Jewish tradition, strategies that speak without speaking and are the language of an ethics that is prior to philosophy. This claim is not meant to imply that ethics is an apophatics, a language of silence, but rather that ethics is spoken otherwise than ontologically. Philosophy for Levinas is an ontology, a thinking of the meaning of being. It is self-enclosed, offering only an internal *point d'appui* for ethical reflection, that of a subject that is construed either as a consciousness in the manner of German Idealism and Husserlian phenomenology or as Heideggerian being-in-the-world. To be sure, Heidegger criticizes a material ethic and the positing of conscience as bound up with taking action, but he fails, from Levinas' perspective, to contest the subject as a freedom and thus to check the violence endemic to political and economic life. Rather than proclaiming the demise of ethics, Levinas sees ethics (freshly interpreted) as a challenge to ontology and to a philosophy of the subject. "Philosophy is an egology," says Levinas, in a terse formulation; it must be called to order from outside itself. Judaism will provide postmodernity's thorn in philosophy's side, perpetually remonstrating with philosophy, accusing it not because of any specific infraction but simply for being what it is, the arena of cognition at best and of politics at worst.

But the matter does not end here. If Judaism is to do its job, it must be understood; it must somehow enter into this universal language that it cannot do without; philosophy, in turn, must become Judaized. Each is, as it were, both contaminated and rescued by the other. Although early interpretations of Levinas' philosophical thought often cordoned off his Jewish writings, their essential reciprocal relations have recently come under close scrutiny.[1]

In what follows I presuppose the bond between philosophy and Judaism without attempting to develop this line of analysis in detail. Nor do I wish to consider any particular Talmudic text as the inspiration for some aspect of Levinas' thought (for example, the Talmudic invocation to supreme obedience, to do before hearing), as it bears upon his own account of alterity. Instead I hope to expose a deep and unmanifest connection between a specific rabbinic text and the structure of *Totality and Infinity*,[2] such that the former provides a homologue of the latter as an exposition of egology and alterity. The rabbinic text will be seen as a miniature (in a sense yet to be specified) of Levinas' work. The apothegm to which I refer is one of the most celebrated sayings, virtually a commonplace, of Jewish Talmudic wisdom from Tractate *Aboth*, 1:14, of the *Mishnah*. *Aboth* is a compilation of contemplative and folkloric sayings, or *Agadah*, that contrast with the legal writings or *Halakhah* of the *Mishnah* as a whole. The chapters of *Aboth* were set aside, ultimately published under the title *Pirke Aboth*—the term *Pirke* simply means chapters, not ethics, and the title was misleadingly translated as *Ethics of the Fathers*.[3] The saying in question reads, "He [Hillel] used to say: —If I am not for myself who is for me? and when I am for myself what am I? And if not now, when?"[4]

I shall turn first to the meaning of miniaturization, then to some traditional interpretations of Hillel's seminal maxim that are widely separated in time, that of Rabbi Nathan (possibly dating to the third century) and that of the nineteenth-century rabbi, Samson Raphael Hirsch. Finally, I shall consider the way in which the structural articulation of *Totality and Infinity* both conceals and reveals its homologue, Hillel's saying and the commentaries upon it in *Pirke Aboth*. Because Hillel's words are known to anyone with even a rudimentary knowledge of rabbinics, it can be assumed that it was not only conceptually available but subliminally operative in Levinas' thought. It is also highly likely that he was acquainted with the famous commentary of Rabbi Nathan on *Pirke Aboth* but less certain that he was conversant with Samson Raphael Hirsch's neo-Kantian gloss on *Pirke Aboth*. However, Levinas' familiarity with the more famous Hermann Cohen's neo-Kantian Judaism would render the philosophical underpinnings of Hirsch's interpretation familiar.[5]

The World of the Very Small

The cultural understanding of the small has been dominated by the view of the infinitesmally minuscule: the atom, the gene, and, more recently, the bytes and pixels of the information culture. Whether envisioned as visible when enlarged by optical instruments or as transportable fragments that can be expanded into actual language and images, the small is understood as a part of a larger whole.

A miniature, however, is not a part but a homologue of a whole. Although little has been written recently on this subject, the miniature was a matter of considerable interest to earlier structuralist and phenomenological thinkers. Thus, Levi-Strauss contends:

> To understand a real object in its totality we always tend to work from its parts. The resistance it offers us is overcome by dividing it. Reduction in scale reverses this situation. Being smaller, the object as a whole seems less formidable. By being quantitatively diminished, it seems to us to be qualitatively simplified. . . . This quantitative transposition extends and diversifies our power over a homologue of the thing, and by means of it the latter can be grasped, assessed and apprehended at a glance.[6]

One could object that Levinas' view of rabbinic hermeneutics has been clearly stated by him, that is, that the gloss of a rabbinic passage entails an expansion of text in a lengthening chain of signifiers, one that is justified by the polysemy of Hebrew words. "Words co-exist rather than being immediately co-ordinated or subordinated to one another,"[7] thus opening associative rather than logical sequences. The quest for meaning goes beyond the putatively plain (*pshat*) sense of the text, so that Levinas is led to conclude, in what might seem like a Derridean gesture of dissemination, that "There is not one verse, not one word of the Old Testament— . . . read by way of Revelation—that does not half-open on to an entire world."[8]

But this manner of interpretation cannot be imported into a philosophical work. All too often the term "midrash," now become fashionable, is used to describe the expansion of texts of vaguely rabbinic inspiration. But a midrash is a rabbinic commentary upon Scripture, often narrative but also legal, a description that fails to depict Levinas' philosophical work even in a stretched sense. Nor can the genre of Levinas' philosophical writings be identified with *Gemara*, the Talmudic commentary upon the *Mishnah* (rather than upon Scripture), for the *Gemara* is a corpus of largely juridical texts. What is more, the associative character of rabbinic interpretation veers radically from any given text that prompts it, whereas Levinas hammers away insistently upon the originary themes of self and Other that guide his analysis in *Totality and Infinity* and which, I argue, are those of Hillel's apothegm.

Miniatures are neither diagrams nor blueprints. They are not, as Levi-Strauss contends, "passive homologues" of objects, but rather, they "constitute a real experiment with the object."[9] The miniature is seen as a solution to a particular problem, one in which the interpreter is not a passive observer; instead, her act of contemplation is, even if only subliminally, already one in which possible permutations are envisaged. A greater richness of the minature's intelligible dimensions supplants its diminished sensible dimensions.[10]

Yet, it can be objected, the relation of text to miniature is contrived in that what is to be miniaturized is something palpable or visualizable, whereas what is modeled by a miniature of a Levinasian text are aniconic *echt* Levinasian tropes: pure exteriority, the infinite, diachrony, and temporal transcendence. This objection is valid only if the miniature is construed as the result of a simple process of mechanical shrinkage or as a representation, in an undeconstructed sense of the term. But Gaston Bachelard, originally a philosopher of science who came to envision a poetics of space, claimed that imagination enters into miniaturization, claiming that

> Values become condensed and enriched in miniature. Platonic dialectics of large and small do not suffice for us to become cognizant of the dynamic values of miniature thinking. One must go beyond logic to experience what is large in what is small.[11]

In support of his account, Bachelard offers this citation from Rostand's *Cyrano de Bergerac*, one that would be difficult to surpass as an analogue for the relation of Hillel's maxim to Levinas' text:

> "This apple is a little universe in itself, the seed of which being hotter than the other parts, gives out the conserving heat of its globe; and this germ . . . is the little sun of this little world, that warms and feeds the vegetative salt of this little mass."[12]

Bachelard points to the seed's concentrated heat as moving from visual to lived image and to the seed as genetrix of the apple, upon which it bestows its own properties. He concludes that the imaginative process that generates miniatures is the inverse of observation that ends in a diagram. Rather than summarizing, it multiplies images. The difference between "an absolute image that is self-accomplishing," that of the apple seed, for example, and "a post-ideated image that is content to summarize existing thoughts" is condensed in Bachelard's remark; "Bohr's planetary atom, the little central sun *is not hot.*"[13]

One could also argue against the view that Hillel's adage is a miniature, that miniatures are the products of *techne* (or making), and that texts are not material artifacts with spatial dimensions. But Levinas refers to revealed texts as "living spaces" and to reading as a mode of inhabiting these spaces. The book, for Levinas, is the habitation of Israel as a people of the Book.[14]

Finally, one might object that to think of Hillel's adage as a miniature is to conceive of it as a plan. Like the architect's model or computer simulation, it would then anticipate a work that remained to be constructed. But, as we have seen, the miniature is not stable but rather shifts with each interpretive move so that it is as much an afterthought as a forethought. Not only do texts interact, but, for the traditional interpreter, the text, as Levinas reminds his readers, is

> lost in signs . . . illuminated by the thought that comes to it from outside or from the other end of the canon, revealing its possibilities which were awaiting its exegesis, immobilized in some way in the letters.[15]

Hillel's Adage: Some Expatiations

It is impossible to grasp the way in which Hillel's maxim functions within Judaic tradition without seeing it in the context of the study of

Torah—as the effort to grasp what is divinely revealed in the sacred texts of Scripture and Talmud. To render vivid to Christians the affective register in which such study is conducted, R. Travers Herford speaks of it as "the Pharasaic form of the Beatific vision" and (citing Kepler) as "the effort to think God's thoughts after him."[16] Levinas' account of Torah study takes this paradigm for granted. He writes:

> The statement commented upon exceeds what it originally wants to say; . . . contains more than it contains; perhaps . . . an inexhaustible surplus of meaning [is] locked . . . in its actual words, phonemes and letters. . . . Exegesis would come to free . . . a bewitched significance that smoulders beneath the characters or coils up in all this literature of letters.[17]

Aboth de Rabbi Nathan, The Fathers According to Rabbi Nathan, the oldest commentary on *Pirke Aboth*,[18] based upon an earlier version of the text, presupposes this framework. In Rabbi Nathan's text, the saying that begins, "If I am not for myself" is placed in conjunction with two other logia attributed to Hillel, both of which can be read as "seeds" of *echt* Levinasian themes, peace and the critiques of polity and egology.

A detailed excursus into Rabbi Nathan's elaboration of Hillel's logia would extend beyond my concern with the ground plan of *Totality and Infinity*. It is nevertheless significant that in the chapter that contains the saying of Hillel upon which I principally focus, an ancillary passage reads: "Be of the disciples of Aaron, loving peace and pursuing peace, loving mankind and drawing them to the Torah" (*ARN*, p. 63). Rabbi Nathan interprets the figure of Aaron as the peacemaker who encourages forgiveness. An additional gloss reads: "[Aaron] would sit with [a man] until he had removed all rancor from his heart. And when the two men met each other, they would embrace and kiss each other." Aaron reconciles them by enacting a remarkable ruse. When two men quarreled, Aaron would come to each and recount how the other had repented, an event that had not yet occurred but which, when envisioned by the angry parties, would generate forgiveness. Thus, Aaron says to each: "My son, mark what thy fellow is saying! He beats his breast and tears his clothing, saying 'Woe unto me! How shall I lift my eyes and look upon my fellow! . . . I am ashamed . . . for I it is who have treated him foully'" (*ARN*, p. 64). The theme of peace already announced in Levinas' Preface is, of course, a key theme in the conceptual repertoire even if it is not in the structure of *Totality and Infinity*.

The next saying in Rabbi Nathan's work that is contiguous with the passage that is the focal point of my thesis reads, "A name made great is a name destroyed. And he that does not increase, ceases. And he that does not learn, deserves to die. And he that puts the crown to his own use shall perish" (*ARN*, p. 63). Rabbi Nathan's gloss suggests, first, that one should avoid the attention of government, a thieving institution; second, that not adding to the study of Torah means one will lose what has already been learned; and, finally, that using the crown, which here refers to the tetragrammaton (the unpronounceable name of God), for one's own ends assures that one will perish utterly (i.e., have no place in the world to come).

Consider, now, Rabbi Nathan's gloss of the passage that I have suggested is a homologue for *Totality and Infinity:* "If not I for myself, who then is for me, And being for myself, what am I" (*ARN*, p. 69); this passage is interpreted not in terms of the dyad self/other which reflects the duality of the modern subject and the other as an other self but rather in the context of laying up merit. Thus, the self is one who is under the mandate of Torah, both in terms of *who* is to obey it, only I myself, and *when* such obedience is demanded, only in the here and now. Merit can only be laid up in this lifetime, for, as scripture asserts, "A living dog is better than a dead lion" (Eccles. 9:4). This life and this life only is the venue for repentance; even the righteous cannot store up merit when they are dead. One may infer that the living process of gaining merit rather than the product, merit itself, is the higher good.

Yet how is one to explain that *merit* is bound up with profit for *myself?* Rabbi Nathan's gloss does not cordon off an egology in the manner of Levinas because, in the absence of the modern subject, there can be no egology. This gloss would seem, therefore, to offer an unpromising homologue for a Levinasian account of the self. Yet the text is open to another interpretation, to which I shall recur: the self of Rabbi Nathan is already fissured by Torah, by merit as the fostering of peace and as repentance both in one's heart and in one's deeds. Moreover, "If not now, when" conveys the sense of urgency reinforced by the comparison of a dead lion with a live dog.

It is no surprise that *Ethics of the Fathers* should prove a lure and a seduction for Samson Raphael Hirsch (1808–88), a leading figure of German orthodox Jewry. Influenced by the *Aufklarung* and especially by Kant, Hirsch writes a commentary on the work replete with the language of duty and of the fellowman. In regard to 1:14, Hirsch's gloss reads,

It is only through his own efforts that a man can attain spiritual fitness and moral worth, which are the most essential attributes to which he can aspire. Similarly it is primarily upon himself, his own efforts . . . that man must depend in the process of acquiring and . . . preserving the worldly goods he needs. . . . But a man must never say "Since it is solely by my own efforts

that I have become what I am, I will use my attainments for myself alone."
For it is only in selfless devotion, [when] he actively works to create, . . . and
to increase the prosperity and happiness of his fellowman that a man begins
to become truly human in the image of God. . . . To this task every moment
of your life should be devoted. Do you know whether indeed you will still
have another moment to do this work?[19]

On the face of it, this reading would appear to offer rough-and-ready
analogies for Levinas' text: the necessity for a self and the total dedi-
cation of self to the Other. This is indeed the "plain sense" that may be
attributed to the ground plan of *Totality and Infinity*. But I shall argue
instead that the plain sense is challenged by the more recondite reading
of Rabbi Nathan, in which alterity shadows egology from the outset,
and in which the two remain in a deliberate and unresolved tension,
one that persists in the Levinasian scheme.

Totality and Infinity: Some Readings

One of the received views of *Totality and Infinity* interprets Levinas as
the critic of Heidegger's subsumption of alterity by ontology but as
himself, following many of the phenomenological leads suggested by
Being and Time. On the one hand, Levinas concedes that philosophy
cannot escape ontology; on the other, despite Heidegger's account of
the difference between Being and the beings and his critique of the
modern subject, Levinas contends that Heidegger does not transcend
the totalizing and egological impulses of Western thought. Heidegger's
account of the *es gibt* as evidence for Being's generosity is overturned
to become the *il y a* in Levinas' thought, a trope for the indeterminate,
the murky, the heaviness of being without form. More importantly, for
Levinas, Heidegger's treatment of the *Mitsein,* the sphere of being-with-
others, regards the Other merely as one who is alongside myself but
whose existence does not weigh upon me as a moral force. For Heidegger, ethics, as dominated by modern ontology, treats the being of the
subject as will. But this, for Levinas, is a misunderstanding of ethics,
which must be an Ethics of ethics, prior to ontology and thus first philosophy. This reading of Levinas generally concedes that the mark or
trace of rabbinism must be incised across the history of philosophy as
critique, but maintains that *Totality and Infinity* remains principally a
conversation with Heidegger's thought.[20]

The genealogical relation of Levinas to Franz Rosenzweig does not
so much challenge the received view just described but rather provides

another reading, an account of how Rosenzweig furnished the resources for undermining both Heideggerian ontology and the Hegelian conception of the state. Rosenzweig's quarrel with German Idealism is replicated in Levinas' encounter with Heidegger's fundamental ontology. Whereas for Rosenzweig it is the unique self that breaks into the globalizing tendencies of the Fichtean ego and the Hegelian polity, for Levinas it is *autrui*, the other person, who disrupts Heideggerian ontology.[21] Levinas' double indebtedness is summed up by John Llewelyn: "If *Totality and Infinity* is a section-by-section dissection of *Being and Time*, it is also a running commentary and critique of infinite totality that is meant to be replaced by the idea of a finite wholeness," a strategy for which Rosenzweig is responsible.[22]

Robert Bernasconi's analysis of the relationship between empiricism and transcendence offers yet another reading of *Totality and Infinity*. For Levinas, he argues, the face-to-face relation is both a concrete experience and a transcendental pre-condition for ethics. But if experience is a *prior* condition for ethics, does it not disrupt the possibility of a *transcendental* condition? What is more, Levinas thinks that the beyond of the totality must be reflected within it, so that totality and infinity are not opposed in such a way as to mean "totality versus infinity," both because they could be reintegrated in a Hegelian synthesis and because transcendence must be *enacted* and therefore requires the world. Thus, "the conditions for the possibility of the experience of totality are the conditions for its impossibility."[23] The relation with alterity unfolds within the historical conditions of economic and political existence. Only through this anterior/posterior strategy can a way be negotiated beween the discourses of both experience and transcendence. On this reading, "the rupture with the totality shows that there never was a totality."[24]

From Hillel to Levinas

To see the complex relation between the apothegms of Hillel and Levinas, four pre-conditions that I have tried to adumbrate in the preceding sections must now be presupposed: first, if Hillel's saying is to be seen as a miniature, the process of miniaturization itself must be understood as dynamic; a miniature is neither a blueprint nor a copy. Second, the saying of Hillel must be discerned not only in its context of other rabbinic sayings in *Pirke Aboth* but as it is appropriated in certain later traditional interpretations. Third, although Heidegger and Rosenzweig provide indispensable languages for the development of

the argument of *Totality and Infinity*, the relation between self and Other
must also be seen otherwise than in the terms provided by these philosophical predecessors. For Levinas, experience and transcendence perpetually reinstate and undo one another,[25] so that egology is interrupted by alterity, and alterity requires an egology. There is, to be sure,
a linear phenomenological progression from self to Other in the unfolding of *Totality and Infinity*, but each is infiltrated, virtually sabo-
taged, by its other.

For Levinas, a key question is, "Who must the I be if it is to be affected by the Other while resisting subsuming or being subsumed by
that Other?" Does Hillel's question, "If I am not for myself, who is for
me?" allow for an adumbration of this doubleness? Levinas contends
that the I is not a static identity but a being whose very existence consists in reidentifying itself through the happenings of its life (*TI*, p. 36).
Lived as a sequence of such returns to itself, this I is called into question
by the Other, a process that Levinas calls Ethics (*TI*, p. 43). But such a
calling into question presupposes a separate self, one who is a cognitive
subject (although not only such) and who reduces the otherness of
the object to what Levinas calls "the same" by representing it. In fact,
the other person cannot be rendered as an object because she or he
is the Other, always already given as uncontainable in thought, as
an excess refractory to representation, or in Levinasian terms, as the
Cartesian infinite, whose ideatum exceeds any idea we can have of it.
The Other is not another "myself for myself" (*TI*, p. 33), perhaps a reference not only to Levinas' negative view of Husserl's contention that
the self can be given empathically and thus as another me, but also as
a covert reference to Hillel's text.

After the ground plan, the forecourt, as it were, of *Totality and Infinity*
as a whole, is laid out in Section 1, Section 2 provides a phenomenological account of the separate self that is opposed both to the Kantian
subject and to the Heideggerian *Dasein*. This separateness is produced
as inner life or psychism arising through thought in its opposition to
totality: "The original role of psychism . . . is already a way of being . . .
resistance to the totality. Thought or the psychism opens the dimension this way requires," Levinas writes (*TI*, p. 54). As separate, the self
breaks with Being and lives outside of God, in a manner Levinas designates as atheism—a position that is not a negation of God but rather
one that defines a being who, without existing as its own cause, nevertheless exists as an independent will.

But before it can exist as a subject of will or cognition, it must exist
in a more primordial relation to the world, as enjoyment, as a *zoon* or
vital being who "lives on" the world, relishes and finds satisfaction in

it. Such a being is immersed in the density of a medium, a formless space, the elemental (e.g., earth, air, street, and the like). At the same time, a vantage point, a site that is one's own, one's home, is needed as a point of entry, return, and security. The world thus understood is not, as for Heidegger, a nexus of things as objects of utility. "To enjoy without utility, in pure loss, gratuitously . . . in pure expenditure—this is the human," he contends (*TI*, p. 133). Life thus understood is existence not as cognition but as sensibility. Although Levinas does not hesitate to celebrate the love of life, one might object that need thwarts such simple happiness. Yet for Levinas, without indigence or need there would be no satisfaction (*TI*, p. 146). But need and satisfaction exact a price: one who has needs is concerned for the future, a worry that can only be overcome through human labor. In sum, for Levinas the lived modalities of self,

> egoism, enjoyment, sensibility and the whole dimension of interiority—the articulations of separation—are necessary for the idea of Infinity, the relation with the other which opens forth from the separated and finite being. (*TI*, p. 148)

The separated self prior to the advent of the Other just described signals a break with the epistemological and moral subject of German Idealism and would seem to preclude any connection with Samson Raphael Hirsch's neo-Kantian gloss of Hillel's words, "If I am not for myself who will be for me?" For Hirsch, ethics arises through human action as the result of human effort, so that ethics is, as it were, a labor. Yet Hillel's apothegm reins in Hirsch's Kantianism in that the "for myself" cannot mean the Kantian self that is universalizable as a moral agent. Hirsch sees that there must be a self of economy, "acquiring and preserving the worldly goods [that humans] need,"[26] if there is to be a functioning ethical self, a self that, in his terms, can assist the fellowman. For Hirsch, as for Levinas, generosity presupposes the acquisitive self that can, by dint of its labor, satisfy its needs.

Hillel's second question, "If I am for myself only, what am I?", implies a challenge to the view that I see the telos of my life as the satisfaction of my needs and interests without regard for others. For Levinas, the advent of the Other is in and of itself a critique of the I: "The Other—the absolutely other—paralyzes possession, which he contests by his epiphany in the face" (*TI*, p. 171). As an insistent and commanding presence, not only does the Other proscribe violence, but the Other comes to me as from a height, contests what I possess, mandates donation, self-divestiture, decrees that I become hostage for her or him. The face as an ethical datum is not given visually but discursively: the face addresses me. In a dense passage, Levinas writes:

> Absolute difference inconceivable in formal logic, is established only by language. Language accomplishes a relation between terms that breaks up the unity of a genus. . . . [and] is perhaps to be defined as the very power to break the continuity of being and history. (*TI*, p. 195)

In sum, the Other's relation to the self is interlocutory, contesting her or his absorption in discursive content, yet it remains bound to language.

The relation to the Other renders secure the singularity of each and every other but in no way addresses the question of *all* the others. The assurance of singularity is contrary to the notion of each subject as the fellowman who always already exists as a universal subject. Thus, for Samson Raphael Hirsch, ec-centricity in the etymological sense is to be avoided. The *imago dei* is actualized only through "increasing the happiness and prosperity of one's fellowmen." But for Levinas, the totality, the domain of economy, polity, and history, cannot remain untransformed by alterity. Thus, Levinas insists, "Everything that takes place here between us concerns everyone. . . . The face places itself in the full light of the public order," (*TI*, p. 212) a concern that Levinas calls justice. "The epiphany of the face qua face opens humanity," he maintains (*TI*, p. 213).

The "correction" supplied by a Levinasian approach (i.e., an insistence upon singularity) to Hirsch's neo-Kantian gloss of Hillel's saying precludes any easy identification of Hirsch and Levinas. Yet the developmental account of *Totality and Infinity* as a progression from self to Other reenacts the movement from man to fellowman, a movement that, for Levinas, must pass through a chain of experiences from enjoyment, labor and cognition to the disruption of the self by the face of the Other. Yet there is an alternative view suggested by the gloss of Rabbi Nathan that unsays this progression and suggests a more profound connectedness of Levinas to Hillel.

Recall that Rabbi Nathan speaks of Hillel's being for oneself in terms of acquiring merit. "If I do not lay up merit in my lifetime, who will lay it up for me?" Even as a separated self, therefore, one is already bound up in a relation with transcendence in that merit consists in obedience to God's commands. Levinas too insists upon the primordiality of the relation with infinity:

> The idea of infinity (which is not a representation of infinity) sustains activity itself. Theoretical thought, knowledge, and critique, to which activity has

been opposed, have the same foundation. The idea of infinity, which is not in turn a representation of infinity, is the common source of activity and theory. (*TI*, p. 27)

In addition to mentioning merit, Rabbi Nathan adds the words "in my lifetime," a phrase that would seem to be appropriate only after the coda or concluding phrase of Hillel's apothegm, that is, after the sentence "If not now, when?". But Rabbi Nathan leaps ahead and deploys "in my lifetime" as an adumbration of the sentence about laying up merit for oneself. His gloss continues: "'For a living dog is better than a dead lion' (Eccles. 9:4) better even than Abraham, Isaac and Jacob: for they dwell in the dust" (*ARN*, p. 69). This astonishing claim reflects not an atheological hedonism but rather points to life as the deferring of death, the time span in which repentance is still possible. For Rabbi Nathan, the words "living dog" may refer to the sinner who is alive: "If he repents, the Holy One, blessed be He, receives him; but the righteous, once he dies, can no longer lay up additional merit." Even the righteous can no longer acquire merit once dead. Yet, paradoxically, Rabbi Nathan speaks in praise of life but says also that it is precisely in the interest of the world to come that prayer and study are undertaken.

For Levinas, the temporalization opened up by death converges remarkably with Rabbi Nathan's interpretation. Death, says Levinas, is imminent but not yet, and, as such, it is postponed or delayed. Unlike Heidegger, for whom existence is an ec-stasis towards death, for Levinas (as for Sartre), death puts an end to my possibilities. But death is also, for Levinas, feared as a hostile other. What is crucial is that death opens an aperture, an interval that *is* temporalization: on one's way to death, "one has time to be for the Other" (*TI*, p. 236). As long as there is time, one can stand away from the present, maintain a distance toward it, and change one's thoughts and actions, repent, and do otherwise. By switching to Rabbi Nathan's trope, one can store up merit, not for an afterlife but for the instantiation of Goodness.

In/conclusions

It is by now widely attested that Levinas' appeal to Jewish sources derives largely from a desire to avoid the pitfalls of what he regards as a unitary tradition of Western philosophy, in which Ethics is subordinated to ontology. If Ethics is to be first philosophy, as Levinas argues, it must proceed otherwise than ontologically. Recent interpreters of Levinas' Jewish writings have paid careful attention to them in terms of the manner in which they provide inspiration for this new articulation of Ethics. The independence of these discursive arenas, of philosophical and Jewish thought, maintained by Levinas himself has been broken by his interpreters, a "contamination" that has yielded fruitful results. It now behooves Levinas' readers to look beyond his explications of specific Talmudic passages to the conceptual and structural affinities between his major works and certain rabbinic texts, affinities that offer still another perspective on writings that have heretofore (and with good reason) been examined as meditations, principally upon Husserl, Heidegger, or Rosenzweig.

The relation between one of Levinas's major works, *Totality and Infinity,* and Hillel's apothegm about being for oneself exclusively is not merely one of historical influence but, more significantly, of homology, in the sense that one is a miniature of the other, "a little universe in itself." A long hermeneutical tradition has already endowed the apothegm of Hillel with numerous meanings. The ancient and well-known reading of Rabbi Nathan and the less familiar neo-Kantian gloss of Samson Raphael Hirsch have become part of a catena of interpretations that enter into the construction of the miniature I have attempted to sketch and constitute, as Bachelard would have it, "a real experiment with the object." Levinas' conception of the separated self and its disruption by alterity must be seen in the light of this chain of transmission. Hillel's saying together with Hirsch's gloss is homologous, in part, with the diachronic unfolding of *Totality and Infinity,* its phenomenological trajectory that proceeds from self to Other. Yet for Levinas, the Other disrupts the antecedent life of a satisfied self, a self that cannot, as Hirsch would have it, simply pass from man to fellowman.

The dimension of alterity is more subtly revealed in Rabbi Nathan's account of Hillel's saying: for Rabbi Nathan, the self is always already imbricated in a transcendence that transforms life into a matter of extreme urgency, an absent presence that is solicited and that solicits. Does not God say, Rabbi Nathan asks: "If thou wilt come to my house, I shall come to thy house; to the place my heart loves, my feet lead me?" (*ARN,* p. 69). This question is interpreted by Rabbi Nathan to mean that those who go to meet God by attending the house of study, the synagogue, or who, in earlier times, went up to the Temple in Jerusalem, leaving gold and silver behind, are blessed by Him (*ARN,* pp. 69–70). Real time becomes for Rabbi Nathan the alloted span of human life in which transcendence comes to pass, because in that interval alone, merit can be acquired and repentance undertaken. What is miniaturized in this complex of texts, especially that of Rabbi Nathan, is the urgency of the phrase "in my lifetime," an interval that in Levinas' elaboration of time is the period during which good deeds may be done. Death is the enemy not because it terminates my activities as such but because it puts an end to my being for the Other, to that post-ponement that is one's life as the interval during which Goodness can come to pass.

Notes

1. See the excellent analysis of Judaism's relation to philosophy as one of cor-relation, the transformation of a term through its relation to another term, in Robert Gibbs, *Correlations in Rosenzweig and Levinas* (Princeton, N.J.: Princeton University Press, 1992). Gibbs argues that not only does Levinas aver in his philosophical works that ontology is non- or even anti-ethical, therefore requiring Judaism as its other, but that Levinas' Hebrew writings are infiltrated by the Greek—that Judaism needs philosophy. See especially pp. 155–75. Susan Handelman, in *Fragments of Redemption: Jewish Thought and Literary Theory in Benjamin, Scholem and Levinas* (Bloomington: Indiana University Press, 1991), pp. 263–305, argues powerfully that, for Levinas, the Jew is not an abstraction, a trope for alterity, but an essential event of being. For this reason, the Jew must be understood philosophically. If this is the case, Levinas is suggesting a postmodern inside/outside relationship. The connections of philosophy with non-philosophy in a general context in Levinas' thought has been made thematic in numerous quarters. See especially articles by Paul Davies, Theo de Boer, Merold Westphal, and myself in *Ethics as First Philosophy: The Significance of Emmanuel Levinas for Philosophy, Literature and Religion*, ed. Adriaan T. Peperzak (New York: Routledge, 1995).

2. Emmanuel Levinas, *Totality and Infinity*, trans. Alphonso Lingis (Pittsburgh: Duquesne University Press, 1969). Hereafter cited in the text as *TI*.

3. R. Travors Herford, in his introduction to *The Ethics of the Talmud: Sayings of the Fathers* (New York: Schocken Books, 1962), notes that *aboth*, a term meaning "fathers," refers to the name of the tractate and not to persons specified as fathers. When the tractate was singled out for commentary as an individual text, the term *pirke* (the plural of *perek*, or chapter) was added so that the tractate came to be known as *Pirke Aboth*. The titles "Sayings of the Fathers" or "Ethics of the Father" can be misleading if they are thought to translate *pirke*. The teachers mentioned represent a historical chain of transmission of the tradition and determine the organization of the tractate, while its content consists of ethical maxims. The sixth chapter of *Pirke Aboth* is not part of the Mishnah, generally agreed to have been compiled in the early part of second century, and was assembled after the closing of the Talmud (pp. 3–6). *Aboth* is included in the prayer book as a text that is studied between the afternoon and evening prayers on certain Sabbaths.

4. The translation of Herbert Danby, *The Mishnah* (London: Oxford University Press, 1933), reads: "He used to say: If I am not for myself who is for me? and being for mine own self what am I, and if not now, when?" (p. 447). I have cited

R. Travers Herford's more contemporary rendering, although Danby's translation, despite its somewhat archaic language, implies a certain hardening, when one is for oneself, that more clearly suggests Levinas' account of egoity.

5. The relevant source is Hermann Cohen's *Religion of Reason out of the Sources of Judaism*, English edition, trans. Simon Kaplan (New York: Fredrick Unger, 1972). For a comparison of Levinas and Cohen, see my "The Moral Self: Emmanuel Levinas and Hermann Cohen" in the Israeli journal *DAAT: A Journal of Jewish Philosophy and Kabbalah* 4 (winter 1980): 35–58.

6. Claude Levi-Strauss, *The Savage Mind* (Chicago: University of Chicago Press, 1966), p. 23.

7. Emmanuel Levinas, *Beyond the Verse*, trans. Gary D. Mole (Bloomington: Indiana University Press, 1994), p. 132.

8. Ibid.

9. Claude Levi-Strauss, *Savage Mind*, p. 24.

10. Ibid.

11. Gaston Bachelard, *The Poetics of Space*, trans. Maria Jolas (Boston: Beacon Press, 1969), p. 150.

12. Ibid., p. 151.

13. Ibid., p. 153.

14. Levinas, *Beyond the Verse*, p. 130.

15. Ibid., p. 103.

16. Herford, *Ethics of the Talmud*, p. 15.

17. Levinas, *Beyond the Verse*, p. 109.

18. According to the introduction by Judah Goldin to his translation of *The Fathers According to Rabbi Nathan*, Yale Judaica Series, vol. 10 (New Haven, Conn.: Yale University Press, 1955), pp. xx–xxi (hereafter cited in the text as *ARN*), the work was probably compiled between the seventh and ninth centuries, whereas its date of composition may go back to the third century. The identity of Rabbi Nathan remains obscure. He may have been an older contemporary of Rabbi Judah the Prince, compiler of the Mishnah.

19. *Chapters of the Fathers*, trans. and commentary by Samson Raphael Hirsch (New York: Philipp Feldheim Inc., 1967), p. 17.

20. Adriaan Peperzak, *To the Other: An Introduction to the Philosophy of Emmanuel Levinas* (West Lafayette, Ind.: Purdue University Press, 1993), especially pp. 11–14, 138–41. Peperzak writes: "Levinas's philosophy cannot be separated from its polemical connections with Western ontology and its greatest contemporary representative [Heidegger] in particular" (p. 14). John Llewelyn, in *Emmanuel Levinas: The Genealogy of Ethics* (London: Routledge, 1995), argues that Levinas sees himself in continuity with Heideggerian ontology but calls into question the primacy of fundamental ontology, of the ontological difference, and turns instead to the concrete realm of the ontic (p. 108). The genealogical relation of Levinas to Franz Rosenzweig does not so much challenge the received view as show how Rosenzweig provided the resources for undermining Heideggerian ontology. By shattering the all, Rosenzweig demonstrates the uniqueness of each human. Thus Gibbs writes in *Correlations*, "Even Heidegger's ontology subordinates the being of each person to the question of Being. Levinas finds in Rosenzweig the requirement that each person is an infinite end" (p. 24). Stephane Moses, "Rosenzweig

et Levinas: Au dela de la Guerre," in *Philosophie et la religion: Entre Ethique et l'ontologie*, Proceedings of the Colloque "E. Castelli," University of Rome, 1996, ed. Marco M. Olivetti (Milan: CEDAM–Casa Editrice Dott. Antonio Milani, 1996), shows that for both Rosenzweig and Levinas, the totality is the realm of war, one that for Levinas is bound up with ontology. The question for both is "how to get out of the totality . . . beyond being . . . [to] a place of pure transcendence, where man can mean outside all context?" (p. 796); translation mine.

21. See Gibbs, *Correlations:* "Even Heidegger's ontology subordinates the being of each person to the question of Being. Levinas finds in Rosenzweig the requirement that each person is an infinite end" (p. 24). See also Moses, "Rosenzweig et Levinas."

22. Llewelyn, *Emmanuel Levinas*, p. 105.

23. Robert Bernasconi, "Rereading *Totality and Infinity*," in *The Question of the Other: Essays in Contemporary Continental Philosophy*, ed. Arlene B. Dallery and Charles C. Scott (Albany: State University of New York Press, 1989), p. 24.

24. Ibid.

25. This relation anticipates that of the Saying (*le dire*) and the said (*le dit*) and their unsaying by way of the *dedire* in Levinas' *Otherwise than Being and Beyond Essence*, trans. Alphonso Lingis (The Hague: Martinus Nijhoff, 1981).

26. *Chapters of the Fathers*, p. 16.

12

Love's Reason

From *Heideggerian* Care
to *Christian* Charity

NORMAN WIRZBA

> He who says he is in the light and hates his
> brother is in the darkness still. He who loves his brother
> abides in the light, and in it there is no cause for stumbling.
> —1 John 2:9–10)

Among the many elements that inspire and invigorate postmodernism, surely one of the more prominent has to be the acute awareness of reason's fall from innocence. By this "fall," I mean the acknowledgment that reason, though it may claim as its origin something like the wonder Plato and Aristotle talked about, could just as well be inspired by boredom, anxiety, evasion, pride, or the drive for power. Thinking is not a benign activity. It is, as many postmodern writers insist, an activity in the service of interests. The idea of a pure, objective thought is not only an illusion but also a confusion about the nature of the activity of thinking. Thinking is an activity performed by human beings immersed in unthematized, pre-philosophical commitments, both personal and social, that shape and constrain thought's productions throughout. In the shorthand of Emmanuel Levinas, "*Esse* is *interesse;* essence is interest."[1]

We should not be surprised, then, that the major philosophers within the postmodern canon emphasize reason's underside, its less than innocuous past. Nietzsche, for instance, made it his business to confront the metaphysical/moral/religious-minded people of his time with their own resentment, fear and weakness.[2] Heidegger, throughout the many turns of his thought, sought to draw our attention to a supreme forgetfulness of Being which, among other things, led to a technological age that treated everything as "standing reserve," as fodder for narrowly conceived human interests. Foucault, in his genealogical readings, gives us a vivid portrayal of how power structures play into the very formation of what counts as reasonable and what does not, and thus what will bear the stamp of legitimacy (and all the protection and privilege that accompanies such legitimacy). And Derrida, to complete the representative sample, uncovers the strategies of text producers that would fulfill the nostalgic longing for cohesion, closure, and comfort.

In their own way, each of these thinkers shows the naïveté of a pure, objective reason. Philosophical life has, from the beginning, been infiltrated by elements of "subjective experience" such as the emotions or affections, or deep-seated desires. Even those who would argue most vigorously (where does this vigor come from?) for a dispassionate reason are deeply passionate about being dispassionate. We can understand this, I think, by recognizing that the activity of thinking is only one dimension in the flow of a personal life. Over and above thought are desire and interest, both of which are vital for the inspiration and form of thought. Levinas again makes this point succinctly: "Speculation is subordinate to action. There would be no thought if speculative reason were without interest. Speculative reason is not deployed in an impersonal serenity. In the beginning was the interest."[3] In short, it is within the domains of interest and desire that the activity of thinking occurs.

What this suggests is that any exploration or analysis of reason must pay careful attention to what we might call the affective dispositions of the ones engaged in the reasoning process. What we should be asking is, "How is reason shaped, inspired, directed by the interests, that is, the concerns, worries, and expectations of the ones doing the thinking?" This line of questioning will clearly exasperate those who think of reason as a purely disinterested activity. One of the aims of this essay, however, is to show that we fall into a trap when we believe that a self-critical or self-satisfied reason is readily within our grasp.

Although attention to affective dispositions makes an explication of the life of reason more complicated, it yields several important benefits. First, we discover that the idea of reason that emerges has more depth and gives us a richer context from which the work of critique and construction can emerge. Second, it gives us a better indication of the limits of reason, what it can or cannot claim for itself. Third, it enables us to establish richer points of contact between the activity of thinking and other human activities (feeling, doing, perceiving) necessary to the flow of life. And finally, an understanding of the interests of reason forces us to be more honest about who we have been, who we are, and what we would like to become. In short, what I am suggesting is that attention to pre-philosophical life is a crucial part of philosophical life itself. One cannot adequately discuss the nature of philosophical work if one does not at the same time place this work within the context of human activity conceived more broadly.

In the first part of this essay, I turn to the early Heidegger's recovery of the dispositional character of philosophizing, a recovery made possible by the deconstruction (*Abbau*) of inherited patterns of philosophizing.[4] Heidegger sought to restore philosophy to the life out of which all philosophizing grew. This life he called "facticity." To help us gain access to the dimension of facticity, he had to develop a radical phenomenology that would take us beyond the transcendental, theoretical standpoint he inherited from Husserl and the neo-Kantians. The courses he delivered at Freiburg from 1919 through the early 1920s were all attempts to clarify the nature of this task. By analyzing this period, especially the phenomenology of religion course of 1920–21,[5] and his programmatic 1922 essay "Phenomenological Interpretations with Respect to Aristotle: Indication of the Hermeneutical Situation,"[6] we will begin to appreciate how important it is for philosophy to bring to light reason's pre-theoretical and theoretical life.

In the second part of this essay, I elaborate more fully the framework of Christian facticity, the elements that guide Christians in their relatedness to life. I show that a certain reading of theological texts proved immensely helpful to Heidegger as he tried to put philosophy on a new path, but that in pursuing this path, he did not go far enough. I will argue that love (*agape/caritas*), the dimension that Heidegger for the most part ignored in his reading of Saint Paul, and then forgot in his attachment to Aristotle, sits at the center of Christian facticity as its inspiration, means, and goal. My concern will not be simply to chronicle examples of love as we find it in the gospels. Rather, my goal is to make explicit the structures of love, to lay bare its interests and desires, and then proceed to an elucidation of how the interests of love might transform the ideas of reason we might have. My thesis is that insofar as the activity of charity informs the activity of reason, we are presented with a transformation of reason no less dramatic than the transition from darkness to light expressed in John's letter.

It is remarkable, as Max Scheler once suggested (his judgment, for the most part, stands even today), that Christian philosophers have not yet developed their philosophizing from out of this distinctly Christian understanding of charity. Scheler writes:

> it is precisely the *structure of experience* of the world, of one's neighbor, and
> of divinity, which the Christian conception has most changed. Yet just on

this point, on this unique revolution of the human spirit, the Christian idea has, for unfathomable reasons, failed to be *intellectually* and *philosophically* expressed. This is only part of a much more universal fact. Christianity has never, or only in weak ways, come to a philosophical picture of the world and of life, a picture that sprang *originally* and *spontaneously* out of *Christian experience*. There never was and is not now a "Christian philosophy," unless one understands by this an essentially Greek philosophy with Christian ornamentation. But there is a system of thought that, springing from the *root* and *essence* of Christian experience, observes and discovers the world.[7]

My essay represents a first step in articulating a uniquely Christian conception of reason, a conception informed by Christian facticity, especially the Christian experience of charity.

Facticity, Phenomenology, and Philosophy

When Heidegger returned from the war, he proclaimed that philosophy was at an end. Clearly he did not mean this in the sense that philosophy departments would close or that books bearing the word "philosophy" in their titles would cease to be written. Rather, he thought that philosophy as the discipline that was rooted in and spoke to life as it was lived concretely could no longer be practiced, at least not if the models of philosophy then in vogue were to be taken as guides. What passed for philosophy was, in Heidegger's eyes, a theoretical practice that divorced the thinker from life. Rather than staying close to life in all of its indeterminacy, ambiguity, and difficulty, philosophers tended to ossify and simplify. The categories of thought, which were supposed to bring life into clarity, had the effect of dissimulating it. Hence Heidegger spoke of the need to tear down or strip away (this is what *Abbau* literally means) the accretions of a series of philosophical mistakes.

One of these mistakes was *Weltanschauungsphilosophie*, the philosophy of worldviews. In his 1919 lecture course "The Idea of Philosophy and the Problem of Worldviews," Heidegger noted that the idea of a worldview is an idea that rests upon abstraction and distance from concrete life, even as it purports to shed light on life. In the closing hour of the course, Heidegger told his students: "Phenomenology is the investigation of life in itself. Despite the appearance of a philosophy of life, it is really the opposite of a worldview. A worldview is an objectification and immobilizing of life at a certain point in the life of a culture. In contrast, phenomenology is never closed off, it is always provisional in its absolute immersion in life as such."[8] Clearly, here Heidegger is attempting to redefine philosophy, to give it a new inspiration; and to do so, he will develop a phenomenology that is adequate to the task. This is what much of the work of the early Heidegger is concerned with.

The immediate question, of course, is how shall philosophy "immerse itself" in concrete, factical life and still remain as philosophy? Is not mediation the heart of philosophizing (via categories, definitions, structures of the understanding, etc.), and insofar as reality is mediated, is it not already distanced or cut off from its original movement? Heidegger recognized that this was a serious problem. But as he sees it, this is the sort of question to which we must always return if we want philosophy to remain close to life as we experience it. As George Kovacs puts it, "For Heidegger, philosophy is not a theoretical, speculative science at all; it is a way of disclosing (living) experience. It is a primordial, pretheoretical science that is able to reach and describe (phenomenologically in hermeneutic intuition) lived experience prior to its disruption and deformation by the theoretical attitude."[9]

How shall we approach the pre-theoretical as pre-theoretical? This is an important question to consider, for it would seem that every approach would already be theoretical; that is, in trying to "make sense" of the pre-theoretical, we would, perhaps unwittingly, have organized life according to an alien schema or theory. Heidegger's response to this problem was to say that every approach to reality (here he simply repeats Husserl's first principle of phenomenology) must accept that reality as it gives itself to us. To accomplish this approach, however, Heidegger required of phenomenologists a non-transcendental posture he called *Hingabe*, the dedicative submission or self-abandonment of the phenomenologist to personal life. What is required of phenomenology if it is to attend to concrete experience as it is lived is the sort of listening or attunement which resists the urge to quickly organize or formalize experience in objective or theoretical terms.

Heidegger thought that if phenomenologists could perform this "hermeneutic intuition," pre-theoretical experience would not reveal itself as a mute chaos. Instead, we would find that the pre-theoretical already exhibits meaningful structures that enable people to get around in their worlds. Factical life-experience (*Faktische Lebenserfahrung*) is not a jumbled mess. Rather, there is always a meaning-giving context that encompasses our dealings with the world. Heidegger says: "The meaningful is the primary, [for] it gives itself immediately, without any detour of thought across the apprehension of a thing. Overall and always, it signifies to me, who lives in an environing world, it is wholly world-like, 'it worlds' (*Es weltet*)."[10] A theoretical posture would suggest that we first need to interpret things so that we can contextualize them in a meaning framework. Attunement to the pre-theoretical, however, reveals that things are already meaningful or are of significance to us apart from any theoretical posture, any posture that requires us to step back and look at them from an "objective" perspective (*PRL*, pp. 13–14). The path that would later lead to *Being and Time*'s description of *Zuhandenheit*, as things being ready-to-hand, has already come into view.

In order to get at this non-objectifying, pre-theoretical meaning, Heidegger developed a method called "formal indication" (*formale Anzeige*). Crucial to this method and its success was the requirement that the phenomenologist not import an alien framework with which to model or schematize the reality that presents itself. Reality must show itself from itself, from out of its own meaning-context. This is why the method is purely formal. It is open-ended, not having a specifiable content that would limit the process of description. Formal indication resembles a pointing to reality without that pointing compromising or dissimulating what is indicated.

It is, of course, an important question whether or not an entirely prejudice-free description is possible. I, with Heidegger, am inclined to think it is not. Every description is a description from out of a situation which, in certain ways that are not always clearly noticed or acknowledged, constrains and conditions our viewing. This does not mean, however, that one cannot attempt, as far as this is possible, to put these prejudices in check, or as I (without Heidegger) will later argue, allow another to teach us about our prejudices.[11]

What Heidegger above all wanted to do with the method of formal indication was resist the urge common to the philosophy of his day, which simply assumed that the knower must take an active (aggressive) posture with respect to the reality in question. He wanted to resist the tendency exhibited by Kant who, in the preface to the second edition of the *Critique of Pure Reason*, says: "reason has insight only into that which it produces after a plan of its own, and that it must not allow itself to be kept, as it were, in nature's leading-strings, but must itself show the way with principles of judgment based upon fixed laws, constraining nature to give answer to questions of reason's own determining" (Bxiii). One of the assumptions at work in this Kantian, transcendental posture is that reality becomes meaningful as a consequence of the thinker's theoretical activity. This is precisely the assumption Heidegger denies. The task of formal indication, then, is to transcribe a pre-theoretical meaning-context that is operative prior to the tribunal of reason so that a rough sketch in terms of philosophical concepts can be made.[12] Notice that formal indication does not try to order pre-theoretical experience. It does not need to do this because the order is already there. Rather, it must accomplish the more difficult task of patiently allowing the things to speak for themselves; hence the importance of a posture of submission and self-abandonment on the part of the philosopher. Hence also the perpetual need for the deconstructive moment, the moment in which old assumptions and prejudices are stripped away. Heidegger, as quoted by van Buren, describes philosophy as the "infinite process of radical questioning that holds itself in questioning."[13]

We have already suggested that "hermeneutic intuition" and "formal indication," if successful, would reveal a lifeworld that is not mute or chaotic. This is because life in its concrete facticity is not aimless or arbitrary but follows rhythms and patterns: "life always lives in a world, it always has a tendency toward a certain content, it does not run its course in the void."[14] One might want to say that this directedness of pre-theoretical life is the result of a self-contained ego having made certain decisions about what it wants in life and now is actively pursuing them. But this understanding assumes too much. To view the self as a being standing over and against objects that it then orders according to its own plan assumes that the self from the start distances itself from the world—that is, that the self lives only in a theoretical mode.

In his two religion courses of 1920–21, especially the course entitled "Introduction to the Phenomenology of Religion," Heidegger is careful to note that formal indication reveals a particular experience of the self, an experience not of a self standing outside of the world but as thoroughly immersed within it. He says that as I encounter myself in factical life, as in the interrelatedness of my experiences or the collection of my experiences, I do not meet a separable "I-object" (*Ichobjekt*). Rather, I meet an I thoroughly bound up (*verhaftet*) with an environing world (*Umwelt*) in which I suffer and endure, perform and accomplish, feel depression and elation. Heidegger is explicit: "this self-experience (*Sich-Selbst-Erfahren*) is not a theoretical 'reflection'" (*PRL*, p. 13). The world is not met here as an alien, theoretical object that I then manipulate according to some prevenient plan. Rather, the world already concerns me as the sphere in which I move and live, and in my interaction with it, my dealings with it, I and the world participate in a context that gives meaning to both. Heidegger's phrase "it worlds" tries to indicate this reciprocal movement. The world does not stand "there" apart from the me who is "here" because this assumes that the two are clearly separable, when in fact they are always intimately joined in their movement. In other words, Descartes' concern about the existence of an external world and my knowledge of it represents a fundamental mistake. The error resides in the assumption that knower and known are separated and need to be brought together. Heidegger's point, however, is that the two are already united in the movement called "worlding," a movement that is shot through with meaning and sense. He summarizes this by saying, "The 'world' is something within which one can *live* (whereas one cannot live in an object)" (*PRL*, p. 11).

It was Heidegger's contention that much of the philosophical tradition had overlooked or dissimulated this feature of existence. It was also his conviction that the early Christian community retained a sense for this worlding in its understanding of the Christian life. Christian facticity as it was understood by the apostle Paul in his letter to the Thessalonians was above all temporal existence. By this, Heidegger meant that the early Christians had a pre-theoretical understanding of time that focused on the moment of decision. Time is not a theoretical construction that floats above the Christian's life and neatly compartmentalizes it into a past, present, and future. Rather, the Christian experience of time is such that the past (namely, the event of God's love to humanity demonstrated in Christ) carries into and through the present as that which guides and informs all that one does now and into the future. Being a Christian is about having-become something (*Gewordensein*): "The having-become is not merely occasionally known; knowing makes up its very being, and it makes up the very being of that knowing. This knowing differs radically from any other kind of knowing and remembering, defying the usual scientific psychologies; it emerges directly from the situational context of the Christian life experience."[15] In other words, in having-become a Christian, a past decision is routinely undergone anew such that one's decision accompanies past, present, and future—that is, one's entire being. This decision, or more appropriately decisiveness, provides a meaning-context, gives a directedness to life, which exhausts and exceeds theoretical categories.

The description of early Christian experience that Heidegger gives in this course is repeated by many of the theologians Heidegger was reading at the time, people such as Augustine, Luther, and Kierkegaard. What united them was the sense of Christian life as "repetition," as the perpetual beginning again and moving forward from out of one's past. Van Buren summarizes this position in the following: "The 'way to God,' as well as human life in general, is a constant circular *kinesis* and becoming (*genesthai*), since what one has become and is in actuality (*energeia*) is never cut off from the lack, privation (*steresis*), not-yet, and non-being of possibility (*dynamis*), in terms of which life is to be repeated and renewed."[16] Seekers of God never arrive. They are, as Heidegger often put it, perpetually "on the way," traveling a path that is broken and fractured rather than smooth and straight (*PRL*, p. 120).

Heidegger understood the task of a phenomenology of religion to lie precisely in the explication of this being on the way. When we return to the text of 1 Thessalonians, we see a description of the "how" of Christian facticity (*das Wie des Erfahrens*). Christians are above all those who have turned away from false gods and have turned to God in service and waiting (1 Thess. 1:10). In order to be a Christian, one must have adopted a posture, namely the posture of turning toward God. Paul describes the Christian disposition as "standing fast in the Lord," which, according to Heidegger, means wakefulness and uncertainty. Hence the "how" of Christian existence is permeated by vigilance, by the sense that every decision and every move takes place before the presence of God.[17] Moreover, the god to whom Christians devote their lives is no anchor (*Halt*) who calms and makes Christian life comfortable or easy. Heidegger goes so far as to say it is blasphemous to claim such security when the life of the Christian is throughout characterized by "immense difficulty" (*ungeheure Schwierigkeit*) (*PRL*, pp. 122–24). What we see here is that the Christian life is not first and foremost a theoretical understanding of the content of religion, its "what," but rather a pre-theoretical disposition, or "how," characterized by vigilance, disquietude, trust, and hope.

Paul's letter to the Thessalonians thus reveals a unique response to what Christians should do as they await their Lord's return. They should not try to calculate the hour of his arrival (that, after all, is something that remains hidden, having no objective, graspable referent). Instead, they should focus their form of life such that the here and now is informed, even afflicted (*Bedrängnis*), by the future return (*PRL*, pp. 93–105). As John D. Caputo puts it, "Time and history are transfixed with urgency, pushed to an extreme of tension, radically energized by an apocalyptic sense which demands complete existential vigilance."[18] In short, the early Christians, rather than speculate or theorize about the times, that is, assume a posture of dispassionate reflective distance, lived temporality.

What Heidegger discovered in early Christian experience, then, was an unthematized understanding of the phenomenon of facticity. By this, he meant that Christians understood that religious life was not lived in the theoretical mode, which would then lead to questions about the whatness of God and world. For Christians, the "objective" world did not suddenly become something else as a result of their becoming Christians. What changed in Christian experience was the "how" of one's existence, a how governed by a new sense of temporality as repetition. Though Christians lived in the same world as non-Christians, they lived in it very differently. The sense of being before God is the pre-theoretical meaning-context that governs all Christian dealings with the world. One can well imagine Heidegger's dissatisfaction with the many forms of theology prevalent in his time, as well as throughout the tradition, which rushed to provide a theoretical statement of the content of faith, and in so doing invariably lost touch with this originary meaning-context.

If we turn briefly to his 1921 course entitled "Augustine and Neoplatonism," we can see that Heidegger develops the fundamental posture of the Christian in terms of care understood as *Bekümmerung* (which has the sense of disquietude, of being troubled) rather than *Sorge* (a more practical care, as it would be defined with reference to Aristotle). Reading Augustine and Luther, Heidegger would interpret care primarily in terms of trial and travail. The life of the Christian is a constant struggle of renewal before God (*PRL*, pp. 205–10). What keeps it on the go and what gives it its directedness is the sense of the "not yet," the sense of one's fallenness and distance from God. In other words, Christian life is not held together by a *Wissenschaftstheorie* but by a fundamental disposition or comportment to God. Christian facticity derives its sense and direction not from a theoretical "what" but from a pre-theoretical "how."

After 1921, the religious texts we have talked about recede into the background of Heidegger's work and writings and Aristotle moves to the foreground. This is an important shift, and it is reflected in the transition from *Bekümmerung* to *Sorge*. When dealing with religious themes, it is quite natural that disquietude would be highlighted because the life of faith is a life lived in fear and trembling before God. But if one assumes, as Heidegger did in 1922, when he wrote "Phenomenological Interpretations with Respect to Aristotle: Indication of the Hermeneutical Situation," that philosophy is "fundamentally atheistic" (AI, p. 367),[19] then the anxiety of being before God disappears. One's dealings with the world can be more relaxed and certainly less urgent; Christ's imminent return ceases to play any determinative role. Care as *Sorge* is, in effect, a naturalized and domesticated form of care as *Bekümmerung*.

The Aristotle that emerges in Heidegger's hands is not the theoretician he is often made out to be. Rather, he becomes one of the first phenomenologists to have caught sight of the thinker's primordial attachment to the world, his or her originary "having" of the world. Philosophy is less about the articulation of things in the world and more about the comportment or posture one has within one's world. Heidegger thought he found confirmation for his thesis in the fact that Aristotle, in the *Nicomachean Ethics*, spoke of no less than five modes of such comportment: making, doing, seeing, knowing, and understanding. These are not five theoretical postures but five ways of being, five ways of comporting oneself or getting on with the world. They exhibit what is now beginning to develop in Heidegger's mind as the fundamental posture of the concretely living being: care (*Sorge*). Armed with this new sense of what philosophy ultimately is, we are now in the position to retranslate the famous lines from the opening of the *Metaphysics* not as "All men by nature desire to know," but as "The urge to live in seeing (*eidenai*), the absorption in the visible, is constitutive of how the human being is."[20] What needs to be observed here is Heidegger's emphasis on the "how" of life and his translation of *eidenai* not as theoretical knowing but as circumspective (*Sichumsehendes*) seeing, the kind of seeing that notices what is of concern to oneself.

In the 1922 text on Aristotle, we see Heidegger reiterating that "philosophical research is the explicit actualization of a basic movement of factical life and maintains itself always within factical life" (AI, p. 361). In other words, we need to be careful not to import from outside the sorts of philosophical prejudices we are routinely taught in "philosophical" books. The task before us is to render explicit the basic movement of factical life from out of itself. "The basic sense of the movement of factical life is *caring* [*Sorgen*] (*curare*). In the directed, caring 'Being-out-toward-something' ['*Aussein auf etwas*'], the That-with-respect-to-which [*das Worauf*] of life's care, the world at any given time, is there, present. The movement of caring has the character of *dealings* [*Umgang*] which factical life has with its world" (AI, p. 361). We see here that *Sorge* turns out to be the fundamental posture of factical experience, for it is in terms of care that the basic directedness of experience is to be grasped and understood. How does care reveal itself? In my dealings with the world, in the way that I comport myself to the world. Heidegger says care is "the care of livelihood, of profession, of enjoyment, of Being-undisturbed, of not dying, of Being-familiar-with, of knowing-about, of making life secure in its final goals" (AI, pp. 361–62). There are, in other words, many ways in which *Dasein* deals with the world: tinkering, utilizing, producing, possessing, "holding in truthful safe-keeping," etc. Each of these dealings presupposes familiarity with and a particular sort of knowing of that with which it deals. Notice that this familiarity is not of the theoretical sort. It is better understood as a practical know-how (savoir faire, perhaps). Notice too the absence of the Christian sense of urgency. From now on, Heidegger's account of facticity and care will be much more Aristotelian; it will be governed by *Dasein's* appropriative negotiating with the world rather than a standing firm before God.

Heidegger develops his description of care by saying that it is a circumspective having of the world. Circumspecting (*Sichumsehen*, literally looking after and around oneself) is the sort of concern (*Besorgen*) that seeks to safeguard and increase the sort of know-how, the sort of familiarity one has with the world. We can surmise that this is because

Dasein is driven by the need to maximize dealings, that *Dasein* is only insofar as it does deal with a world.[21] *Dasein's* dealings with the world are thus governed by this circumspective having, and it is in terms of such having that the world has significance or meaning. Heidegger writes, "Circumspection gives to life its world as interpreted according to those respects in which the world is expected and encountered as the object of concern, in which the world is put to tasks, in which the world is sought as refuge" (AI, p. 363). In other words, the world is meaningful because it is an integral part of my life which aims to take care of itself. The remainder of Heidegger's essay prefigures very nicely many of the themes we will find in 1927 in *Being and Time*, themes like "falling," death, *das Man*, and authentic/inauthentic life.

These analyses of facticity show us, then, a meaningful world that is fundamental and pre-theoretical. Before we talk about the world in terms of subject and object, in terms of its whatness, there is a "how" to existence which entails a meaning-context more originary than the meaning-context provided by a theoretical appropriation of the world. In fact, laying bare these pre-theoretical structures may give us an important clue as to the origins of theoretical discourse by showing us how the form and matter of theoretical discourse is constituted and constrained by pre-theoretical life (one should consider, for instance, how *Dasein's* intention to "fall," its tendency to make things easy for itself, plays into the development of instrumental and technological reason). Heidegger thinks that a careful reading and reinterpretation of various Aristotelian texts will bear out this hypothesis. Aristotle is thus a major philosopher who thinks of *Dasein* in terms of its care-ful dealings with the world. Heidegger notes,

> Thus the That-with-respect-to-which towards which the primordial experience of Being is directed is not the Being-field of *things* as of a kind of object which is grasped in a *theoretical* and fact-like manner, but rather the world which is encountered in the dealings which produce, perform, and make use of. . . . Being means *Being-produced* and, as something produced, it means something which is significant relative to some tendency of dealings; it means Being-available. (AI, pp. 374–75)

The inspiration for instrumental/technological reason is to be found in the structures of care.

What we see, then, in the early Heidegger's radicalizing of phenomenology is that the philosophical gesture is a gesture which moves from out of a primordial meaning-context governed by care. In the phenomenon of care basic tendencies, what we at the start of this essay called interests, are always already at work. To pay attention to these

interests, to observe these dealings (what Heidegger called our "hermeneutic situation"), is to perform the task of radical phenomenology.

Christian Facticity Revisited

The picture of Christian existence that Heidegger drew in these early
years depended heavily on Pauline texts that stressed vigilance before
Christ's imminent return. The focus was on the mode of temporal existence evident in this vigilance. What I would like to suggest is that
this is a one-sided emphasis and that it does not go far enough as a
description of Christian facticity. John D. Caputo has also criticized
Heidegger for failing to adequately represent other themes within the
New Testament canon. Caputo notes that Heidegger, for instance, was
so eager to give a reading that highlighted the life of the Christian as
a life of struggle and battle (*Kampf*) that he "left out the whole thematics of the ethics of mercy, of the cry for justice, the appeal that issues
from flesh and pain, from afflicted flesh."[22]

Caputo is certainly correct in this criticism. The range of human experience witnessed and thematized in the Scriptures is not adequately
treated in Heidegger's analysis. One finds in Heidegger little talk of forgiveness, of service, of illness and pain. In fact, one wonders, as does
Caputo, whether or not Heidegger, though he often expressed his dis-
like of Hellenizing tendencies within Christianity, is reading these biblical texts through Greek eyes. Signs of this Greek influence can be
seen in his elitist sense of the wise and prudent person to the exclusion
of the person in need of mercy and care. But we must be careful here,
because Heidegger did not intend to give a complete description of
Christian facticity. The course he gave did not attempt to treat more
than the texts written to the Galatians and Thessalonians, where the
themes he stresses are certainly apparent. In any event, I would like to
suggest that if Heidegger had not abandoned his project of developing
a description of Christian facticity, he might have discovered a conception of reason that, while somewhat at odds with an Aristotelian conception, nonetheless is as rich and deep as the Greek facticity he did
eventually develop.

We can locate the point of alteration in the choice Heidegger made
to stress care as *Bekümmerung* and then *Sorge*, rather than *Liebe*. *Bekümmerung*, as indicated above, has the sense of being troubled, of experiencing oneself in the mood of disquietude. This understanding corresponds well with the theme of working out one's faith in fear and
trembling before God. But should Christian existence be governed pri-

marily by *Bekümmerung?* This is a difficult question to answer, for it
depends on how one understands this disquietude. Clearly, there are
ways of being troubled that can get in the way of Christian living, and
this is why John's epistles speak of love as casting out fear (1 John
4:18). Christians, in other words, are to live confident lives before God,
knowing that God cares for their needs even before they are spoken.[23]
But at the same time, Christians must not take the fulfillment of needs
as a foregone conclusion, as something to be taken for granted. In a
fundamental sense, Christian life is governed by thankfulness and
praise, by the reflecting of God's glory in us back to God.[24] Gratitude
is a fundamental disposition that governs Christians' lives in their dealings with the world. This element is missing in the early Heidegger
when he discusses Christian facticity.[25]

How about *Sorge?* We saw earlier that Heidegger interpreted care as
Sorge to be the basic movement of factical life, a care manifested in the
circumspective concern one has for the world. Circumspective concern
is concern for oneself, is a looking after oneself (*sehen-um-Sich*). I do
not mean this in a selfish sense, as though *Dasein* is by nature focused
only upon itself. This interpretation would be to misunderstand the
"worldly" character of *Dasein*'s existence. In other words, *Dasein* is not
some Cartesian self cut off from the world, figuring out how to bend
reality to its own designs. But what is not to be overlooked in circumspection (*Sichumsehen*) is the centrality of the self. From this centrality,
there follows quite naturally Heidegger's emphasis upon authentic existence as the existence that is properly one's own (*eigentlich*), an existence which holds before itself its own death. One cannot help but get
the sense that for all Heidegger's talk about the decentering of the self,
self-clarity still remains the ultimate goal.

Christian facticity attuned to the activity of love (*Liebe*) resists this
Heideggerian tendency. If we turn to New Testament portrayals of love,
we discover that the love we are commanded to exhibit is always patterned on the prior love exhibited by God in Christ. In fact, it grows
out of and is a response to the gratitude Christians feel before the marvel of love that they have themselves experienced. Christ's new com-
mandment is that we love one another as Christ first loved us (John
13:34). What does this love reveal to us in the way that Christians deal
with the world?

The example of Christ exhibits, among other things, a life formed
by a single disposition, the disposition or inclination of the "one-for-
the-other." This disposition is expressed throughout the life and death
of Christ as his service to the other. What makes this a disposition and
not merely a command or theoretical stance is that the command to
love another, to put another before oneself, must not remain at the level

of command; that is, if one is merely following a command, then one's actions are not governed by love. Love functions according to its own logic, if we can put it this way.

What I mean by this "logic of love" can be elucidated by the parable of the Good Samaritan (Luke 10), a parable in answer to the question, "Who is my neighbor?" How is it that the ones who traveled past the wounded man failed to be charitable and help him? Clearly it was not a matter of an incapacity on the part of the priest and Levite to see this person as wounded and in need of attention. Nor could their evasion stem from an ignorance concerning the teachings of love or an inability to understand, at least in some minimal sense, religious doctrine. Rather, the incapacity resided in an inability to "see" in a certain way and thus make the automatic connection between a perceived need and the required response of addressing that need. This different sort of seeing, the sort of seeing informed by the disposition of love, cannot be learned by merely memorizing its precepts. To be informed by love is to see automatically that the perception of distress (to even recognize another person as in distress is already part of the disposition) entails a readiness to help. It is this automatic entailment that allows us to speak of a logic of love.

What distinguished the Samaritan from others was his capacity to see the world differently. On an objective level, the world was the same for all who encountered the suffering traveler. But the Samaritan was governed by a different "how" of existence; hence his seeing went beyond theoretical seeing. The how of his existence was permeated by a disposition to love which from the start views the world through the needs of the other rather than the needs of the self. This is a case in which Christians' dealings with the world are governed primarily by what we might call *Ihnenumsehendes* concern, concern for the other, rather than *Sichumsehendes* concern, concern for the self. Christian facticity and care, in other words, are patterned after an existence which finds its inspiration and its goal in the other. Christians are like the grain of wheat which first dies and then is literally opened up so that true life can begin (John 12:24). Crucial to this metaphor is the vulnerability and exposure of the self to the point of death so that new life can begin. It is as though the self which truly loves must first, as Levinas puts it, be turned inside out. Without this prophetic conversion, the self maintains the posture of the *solus ipse*, the self which lives first and foremost from out of itself.

One of the ways for us to characterize the exteriorization of the self formed by love is to use the metaphor of dwelling. There are numerous ways in which to dwell. One can, for instance, dwell in isolation, cut off from the world as much as possible. One effect of this mode of dwelling is that the self becomes insulated. In being cut off, or in having sealed itself off from all that would be disturbing, the self does not encounter an otherness which would cause it to alter its being. To be sure, the isolated self goes out into the world and deals with it so as to secure its dwelling, but it carries its insulation with itself. This self is entirely at home with itself.

What is not to be overlooked, however, is that the self can be comfortably at home with itself even as it lives in community with others. Our dwelling together can be such that we form what Levinas called an "intimate society," a collection of like-minded folks who in their like-mindedness secure their dwelling in such a way that no outsider can disturb or force a reconsideration of the legitimacy of their dwelling.[26] In this case, because the self lives in a closed community, the primary form of relatedness to the world is still circumspective, perhaps an *Unsumsehendes* concern, concern for ourselves. The move to exteriorization has not yet been broached because each self finds in its community members a reflection of itself and its needs and wants.

Christian concern or love marks the turn toward exteriorization. It begins when the walls which would secure our comfortable dwelling begin to be dismantled or deconstructed (*Abbau*) so that the claims of the other upon our lives can be seen and felt. In other words, the mode of dwelling characteristic of Christian concern would be governed by hospitality, a manner of existence ruled by welcome and responsiveness. Clearly, in order to be maximally hospitable requires a transformation of the sense of home and dwelling as we have so far seen it.

In a certain respect, Christian dwelling will be nomadic insofar as the walls of home that are used to shield us from the other must become temporary, flexible, more permeable. Notice that the sense of home is not obliterated, for that would make it difficult to serve the other in his or her need. Nor does the self which has undergone prophetic conversion amount to the extinction of the self (Nietzsche), for such extinction would preclude the possibility of our having something to give to the other. Rather, concern for the other demands the sort of existence which refuses to claim any place as our own privileged place (consider Christ's comment that his followers will have no place to lay their heads). Walls do not confer personal rights or exemptions. They must not serve as the barricade that will protect us from the stranger who passes by, nor as the guarantee of our lordship in a specified terrain. Considered from a domestic perspective, the Christian must admit that everyone, even one's kin, is in an important sense a stranger (consider Christ's remark in Mark 3:31 that he has no brothers or sisters other than the ones who do the will of God). Love understood as concern for the other does not try to obliterate the difference be-

tween self and other. It adores the distance (Weil), maintains the soli-
tude (Rilke), as a sign of the integrity and sanctity of the other, and in
so doing makes possible the responsive movement characteristic of the
works of charity.

What is not to be overlooked in this description of dwelling, this
account of how one deals with the world, is the conception of the self
it entails. Christian identity, much like Heidegger's account of *Dasein*,
requires a being thoroughly immersed in the world rather than standing over and against it. But unlike Heidegger, the self formed by love
is not only immersed in the world, and so ready to appropriate it, but
also responsible and attentive to the claims of others. Christian identity
is formed through vigilance *and* compassion. In this alteration we find
the movement from *Bekümmerung* through *Sorge* to *Liebe*.

Having begun to articulate the structure of love in terms of the
transformation of one's concern-ful dealings with the world, we must
now try to sketch in schematic fashion how the love which animates
Christian existence also informs the activity of reason. If we take different forms of reason (contemplative, instrumental, and enframing,
for example) to represent the thematic articulation of ways of relating
to the world, ways of dealing with the world (in the modes of enjoyment, use or classification), then it is clear that to the disposition of
love there should correspond a distinct form of reason. This form of
reason I am calling "love's reason." How shall we identify it?

As we have already seen, when love governs facticity, the presence
and claim of the other becomes the prism through which all seeing
takes place; the structure of love provides the conditions for the possibility of seeing. Love correlates here with light. The New Testament
witness makes this clear when it repeatedly states that insofar as one
loves, one walks in the light and thus truly sees, whereas when one
fails to love, one walks in the darkness (cf. 1 John 2:9–10 and 1 John
3:19–21). Without love, one stumbles, does injury to oneself and others. With love, on the other hand, one seeks the advantage of the other
and in the process finds one's true self. The form of reason which
would correspond to this love must therefore be a reason which is first
and foremost for-the-other, that is, not immediately governed by con-
siderations of enjoyment, use, or classification.

To speak of love's reason as a reason for-the-other rather than a reason for-the-self requires that we be clear about the transformation in
the very structure of reason implied by this shift. The forms of reason tied to circumspective concern are for the most part synchronous,
meaning that the inspiration, means, and goal for this reason find a
rallying point around the self. If we take instrumental reason as our
example, it becomes clear enough: the goal of instrumental reason,

which might be the procurement of some result, is determined by the same one who will also set the means by which that goal will be achieved. What inspires the whole process is again the one choosing and pursuing the goal. What ensures the synchronous flow of instrumental reason is the absence of any claim upon the knower from outside. Reason, in other words, is autonomous.

Reason which is for-the-other exhibits a different structure, a diachronous structure, because it is from the start attuned to the claim of the other. Love's reason has a goal which responds to the other's distress or need (in this respect, the reasoner is fundamentally out of control). Its means are always the means that are conducive to the other's well-being. And its inspiration is the other, because when one sees the other through love, an alteration of the psyche has taken place in which the psyche from the first is claimed by the other.[27] Love's reason, because it is so attuned to the other, is heteronomous. It is governed by the modality of waiting and vigilance for the other (Heidegger had some helpful things to say here), just as it is governed by a fundamental responsibility to the other (Heidegger had little to say about this dimension). It is a dia-chronous reason, or as Paul would call it, a "foolish wisdom," because it lives through the cross of Christ.

We can characterize the heteronomous nature of love's reason by noting its availability, its non-indifference. Reason formed by love is governed and punctuated by the postures of attentiveness and humility, which means that reason perpetually prepares itself for the reception of otherness. To be receptive means to get oneself, one's own agendas and projects, out of the way. It is a spiritual activity of purification in preparation for welcome. Love's reason thus moves between the poles of suspicion and fidelity, criticism and response, acknowledgment and knowledge, attunement and assertion. It keeps the deconstructive moment alive in the form of self-questioning and being put into question.[28] But it also fosters the drive to break up the autonomous structures through which I might otherwise live. In other words, the reason that is put in question is liberated to serve.

As with all forms of reason, it is important to remember that love's reason cannot be adequately understood if it is abstracted from the personal and social forms of life that support and nourish it. To speak of love's reason without at the same time speaking of love's activity is to assume that reason is an abstraction that floats above the temporal sphere of human activity,[29] whereas our foregoing analysis of the hermeneutics of facticity in the early Heidegger, as well as the scriptural witness, argue that this is not the case. The Apostle Paul reminds us that it is not those who speak eloquently about the mysteries of love who have understood the truth (1 Cor. 13). Rather, it is those who follow in the paths of Christ, that is, those who do what Christ has commanded, who will come to know the truth that makes people free (John 8:31–32). Here disposition and thought interpenetrate.

If love correlates with light, then the way one sees and understands the world is fundamentally transformed. Autonomous reason meets the world in terms set by the thinker. In essence, this means that the autonomous thinker continually meets him- or herself in others and thus does not really see at all. Love's reason, on the other hand, because it is heteronomous, is, for the first time, truly free to meet the other as other, as more than the projection of my needs, desires, or fears. To be inspired and informed by the disposition of charity is thus to engage in the deconstructive labor of detaching the autonomous "I" from what it knows. Love's reason loosens the grip on the world we would like to have (for purposes of security and comfort) and instead enjoins us to walk lightly, attentively, and compassionately. Love's reason recognizes that insofar as I clear the ground of myself, God can appear and the other be genuinely welcomed.[30]

In short, reason chastened by love issues forth in service and praise. The way to love's reason is through the conversion of heart and mind. It is always provisional in nature, given that it is governed by repentance and confession. But insofar as we are capable, or better yet, are made capable of, this reason, we bear witness to the light that enlightens all of creation.

Notes

1. Emmanuel Levinas, *Otherwise than Being or Beyond Essence*, trans. Alphonso Lingis (The Hague: Martinus Nijhoff, 1981), p. 4.

2. I have developed this aspect of Nietzsche's work in Norman Wirzba, "The Needs of Thought and the Affirmation of Life: Friedrich Nietzsche and Jesus Christ," *International Philosophical Quarterly* 37, no. 4 (1997): 385–401.

3. Emmanuel Levinas, "The Primacy of Pure Practical Reason," trans. Blake Billings, *Man and World* 27 (1994): 451.

4. Our understanding of this formative period in Heidegger's thought has been greatly enhanced by the two excellent books: one by Ted Kisiel, *The Genesis of Heidegger's "Being and Time"* (Berkeley: University of California Press, 1993), and the other by John van Buren, *The Young Heidegger: Rumor of the Hidden King* (Bloomington: Indiana University Press, 1994). My understanding of this period in Heidegger's career draws from the helpful summaries and analyses provided by these texts.

5. This lecture course, along with his course on Augustine and neo-Platonism and notes for a course on medieval mysticism (a course Heidegger never actually

offered), has recently been published as volume 60 of the *Gesamtausgabe* as *Phäno-menologie des religiösen Lebens* (Frankfurt am Main: Vittorio Klostermann, 1995). References to this volume (my translation) will be cited in the text using the abbreviation PRL.

6. Martin Heidegger, "Phenomenological Interpretations with Respect to Aristotle: Indication of the Hermeneutical Situation," trans. Michael Baur, in *Man and World* 25 (1992): 355–93. References to this essay are cited in the text using the abbreviation AI (for "Aristotle: Introduction"). This essay was not intended by Heidegger for publication. He wrote it quickly for the benefit of obtaining a teaching position at either Göttingen or Marburg. It is in many ways a pivotal essay, summarizing paths his thought had taken since at least 1919 and foreshadowing the direction his thought was about to take.

7. Max Scheler, "Love and Knowledge," in *On Feeling, Knowing, and Valuing: Selected Writings,* ed. Harold J. Bershady (Chicago: University of Chicago Press, 1992), pp. 157–58. This essay was originally published in 1916 and was among the texts Heidegger was reading with some care.

8. Kisiel, *Genesis,* p. 17. Kisiel drew this quote from student notebooks not included in the *Gesamtausgabe* edition of the lectures.

9. George Kovacs, "Philosophy as Primordial Science in Heidegger's Courses of 1919," in *Reading Heidegger from the Start,* ed. Theodore Kisiel and John van Buren (Albany: SUNY Press, 1994), pp. 95–96. As we will see, the term "pre-theoretical" does not mean some kind of special, mystical experience. Rather, the pre-theoretical simply refers to common, everyday experience that is meaningful before a theoretical meaning structure is imposed upon it.

10. Kisiel, *Genesis,* pp. 45–46.

11. I have developed the nature of a philosophical conception of teaching in Norman Wirzba, "Teaching as Propaedeutic to Religion: The Contribution of Levinas and Kierkegaard," in *International Journal for Philosophy of Religion* 39 (April 1996): 77–94.

12. See John van Buren's "The Ethics of *Formale Anzeige* in Heidegger," in *American Catholic Philosophical Quarterly* 69, no. 2: 164.

13. Ibid., p. 168.

14. Kisiel, *Genesis,* p. 118.

15. Ibid., p. 182.

16. John van Buren. "Martin Heidegger, Martin Luther," in *Reading Heidegger from the Start,* p. 169.

17. Ibid., p. 163. See also Kisiel's summary: "The ultimate message of First Thessalonians is that the *kairos* (moment of opportunity, insight, decision) is maintained by, and so contains, a steadfast persistence, 'to stand fast in the Lord' (1 Thess. 3:8), to hold out and endure not only in absolute 'fear and trembling' but also in and through the everyday works of faith and labors of love" ("Heidegger [1920–1921] on Becoming a Christian: A Conceptual Picture Show," in *Reading Heidegger from the Start,* p. 183).

18. John D. Caputo, "Reason, History and a Little Madness: Towards a Hermeneutics of Christian Historicality." in *American Catholic Philosophical Quarterly* 68 (1994, annual supplement): 29.

19. Heidegger would reiterate this fundamental and methodological atheism in

several early texts, including *The History of the Concept of Time: Prolegomena* (1925) and *The Metaphysical Foundations of Logic* (1928). Philosophy does not (should not) decide the question on whether or not God exists. Heidegger is simply suggesting that philosophy must not proceed along, and thus be conditioned by, belief in God. See the excellent article by István Fehér on precisely this point: "Heidegger's Understanding of the Atheism of Philosophy: Philosophy, Theology, and Religion in His Early Lecture Courses Up to *Being and Time*," in *American Catholic Philosophical Quarterly* 69, no. 2 (1995).

20. Kisiel, *Genesis*, p. 239.

21. I say "surmise" because Heidegger wants to insist that formal indication does not bring into the description of factical life some view of human nature or the like. It wants to understand life from within itself, meaning it wants to be purely descriptive. Whether or not this is finally an impossibility, and whether or not Heidegger heeded his own advice, is an important question to consider. Perhaps all we can say is that formal indication will reveal tendencies which we are then free to interpret as we wish. We must be careful, however, not to let these interpretations prejudice the description itself.

22. John D. Caputo, *Demythologizing Heidegger* (Bloomington: Indiana University Press, 1993), p. 57. Cf. chapter 10 above.

23. One can compare Matt. 6:25–34 and the comments of Caputo: "The right way to be in time is to trust God, about tomorrow, about today, from day to day, from moment to moment, because time is God's rule, not man's" ("Reason, History," p. 34). Heidegger, in his early appropriation of the New Testament, made a fateful choice to stress *merimna* (anxiety) over trust and love.

24. For a fuller description of Christian virtue in terms of divine glory, see the essay on Gregory of Nyssa entitled "The Force of Identity" in John Milbank's work *The Word Made Strange: Theology, Language, Culture* (Oxford: Blackwell, 1997). Milbank notes: "Whereas for the world, virtuous deeds *result* in praise, for Gregory virtuous deeds are *only*, in themselves, the praise of another, attribution to God as their source, which is at the same time an offering of the deeds *back* to God as return of gratitude" (p. 196). We will return to this theme when we examine the heteronomous nature of love's reason.

25. It is true that the later Heidegger will say *Denken ist danken* (thinking is thanking), but it is unlikely that the sense of thankfulness here expressed grows out of a uniquely Christian sensibility.

26. Emmanuel Levinas. "The Ego and the Totality," in *Collected Philosophical Papers*, ed. Alphonso Lingis (Dordrecht: Martinus Nijhoff, 1987).

27. My analyses here are informed by Emmanuel Levinas' *Otherwise than Being or Beyond Essence*, particularly chap. 5: 1–2.

28. I develop these themes in detail in Norman Wirzba, "From Maieutics to Metanoia: Levinas's Understanding of the Philosophical Task," in *Man and World* 28 (1995): 129–44.

29. Pierre Hadot, in his *Philosophy as a Way of Life* (Oxford: Blackwell, 1995), has made this point forcefully and more generally with respect to the idea of the philosophical life in the pre-modern period. Michel Foucault says something very similar when he writes: "Even if it is true that Greek philosophy founded rationality, it always held that a subject could not have access to the truth if he did not

first operate upon himself a certain work which would make him susceptible to knowing the truth—a work of purification, conversion of the soul by contemplation of the soul itself" ("On the Genealogy of Ethics: An Overview of Work in Progress," in *The Foucault Reader*, ed. Paul Rabinow [New York: Pantheon, 1984], p. 371). In the case of love's reason, we would say that one becomes susceptible to the truth of Christ insofar as one works upon oneself the "command" of Christ that we love one another.

30. One should keep in mind here Simone Weil's comments on detachment, self-effacement, and attention as expressed in *Gravity and Grace* (London: Routledge, 1963), and in her essay "Reflections on the Right Use of School Studies with a View to the Love of God," in *Waiting for God* (New York: Harper and Row, 1973).

13

Between Exclusivity
and Plurality

*Toward a Postmodern Christian
Philosophy of Other Religions*

ANDREW J. DELL'OLIO

This essay attempts to articulate a postmodern Christian philosophy of other religions primarily by employing two key interpretative strategies within postmodern philosophy—the hermeneutics of suspicion and the hermeneutics of finitude.[1] While most discussions of religious diversity revolve around the issue of salvation, this essay will focus on the issue of truth. That is, instead of asking the question, "Is there salvation in non-Christian religions?" the question this essay asks is, "What attitude or posture ought the Christian take with regard to the truth of other religions?" While I acknowledge that this question is especially important precisely because matters of salvation are implicated, an attempt at a postmodern Christian philosophy of other religions, as opposed to a theology of other religions, best brackets the issue of salvation and speaks instead of truth.[2]

Using the standard typology of positions on religious diversity—exclusivism, inclusivism, and pluralism—I will argue that the postmodern Christian philosopher ought to reject the position of religious exclusivism (Christianity is true and all other religions are false) on the grounds that it fails to take seriously the hermeneutics of suspicion—in particular, the strong link between exclusive claims of knowledge and exclusionary postures of power. As such, religious exclusivism is closed to the claims of the other and, in its worst forms, seeks the domination of the other by ignoring or silencing its voice. I will also argue that the philosophy of religious pluralism, while taking a more open stance to the other than does exclusivism, ought to be rejected on the grounds that it is insufficiently cognizant of the insights of the hermeneutics of finitude. In the form it has been given by its foremost spokesperson, John Hick, religious pluralism is forgetful of its own particularity.

Between exclusivism and pluralism stands religious inclusivism, a position one may not readily associate with the postmodern perspective, but nonetheless the position I suggest the postmodern Christian philosopher best take with regard to the truth of other religions. A postmodern version of Christian inclusivism maintains that divine truth is revealed definitively in Jesus Christ, but that Christianity—the religion—does not enjoy full possession of this truth. Postmodern Christian inclusivism thereby refrains from granting the teachings and practices of the Christian religion any absolute status vis-à-vis other religions. Indeed, it recognizes and is open to the revelation of divine truth in other religions. In this postmodern form, the particularity of Christian inclusivism gives witness not only to its uniquely Christian perspective but also to its finitude, while its openness to the other serves to hold in check exclusionary plays of power.

I should also note that I will not argue here for why a Christian philosopher ought to take the tenets of postmodernism seriously. Others have done this admirably already,[3] and it is my assumption that their assessments are correct. For example, I assume first that the hermeneutics of finitude in all its forms helps Christian philosophers to appreciate more fully their limitations as creaturely knowers and to curb their pretensions to have achieved absolute certainty and finality in matters of truth, that is, their desire to be the creator, to be God; and second that the hermeneutics of suspicion aids Christian philosophers in seeing to what extent their sinfulness, in the form of self-centered, self-interested exercises in power, is at work in their claims of knowledge. In other words, I assume that anything that helps the Christian steer clear of the sin of pride is a good thing and that postmodern philosophy can do this, in this case, in the arena of the encounter of religions.

I. Religious Exclusivism and the Politics of Exclusion

According to one postmodern Christian philosopher, John Caputo, "'Postmodern' thinking, if it means anything at all, means a philosophy of 'alterity,' a relentless attentiveness and sensitivity to the 'other.'

Postmodernism stands for a kind of hyper-sensitivity to many 'others':
the other person, other species, 'man's' other, the other of the West, of
Europe, of Being, of the 'classic,' of philosophy, of reason, etc. (The
list goes on.)"[4] One way in which this list goes on is by the addition
of other religions. Following Caputo, the Christian philosopher who
would appropriate the postmodern perspective would then adopt a certain posture toward other religions, namely, a posture of hyper-sensitivity.

What would it mean to be hyper-sensitive to another religion? At
the very least, it would be to stand in a posture of openness to the other
religion. It is to approach the other with an open mind and open heart,
a willingness to listen to the other's voice, whether it is a cry or a proclamation. It is to strive to understand the other's claims as best one can
and to take seriously the other's claims to truth, especially truths the
other regards with utmost seriousness, with ultimate concern.

The typical posture of the religious exclusivist with regard to the
truth of other religions is anything but open. Christian exclusivism, in
its strongest sense, maintains that Christianity is the one, true religion
and all other religions are false. As one Christian exclusivist, Ronald H.
Nash, puts it, "Christian exclusivists *begin* by believing that the tenets
of one religion—in this case, Christianity—are true and that any religious beliefs that are logically incompatible with these tenets are
false."[5] It is worth noting that exclusivists begin—that is, they take
their stance with regard to other religions—with an adversial posture.
In effect, the exclusivist initiates the encounter with the other with the
assertion, "I am in exclusive possession of truth. And the truth of my
central beliefs implies the falsity of yours."

The problem here is not so much that exclusivists deny the truth of
beliefs that seemingly contradict their own. One could argue that logic
requires as much. Rather, the problem is that the beliefs of the other
are condemned as false a priori, thereby closing off the possibility of
finding truth in the claims of the other. Exclusivists turn a deaf ear
to the non-Christian other, failing to recognize that, as another person made by God for God—that is, as a being open to the divine—the
other might also have had divine truth revealed to him. He might then
have something true to say about divine matters, and is therefore worthy of the Christian's respectful listening. But to refuse to listen to the
non-Christian other with openness, that is, as one would listen to a
person worthy of a voice, is, in effect, to silence him. From such a posture, there can be no open dialogue, only a confrontation and an attempt at proselytization—a talking to, not a talking with.

Of course, the exclusivist does not regard the substitution of proselytization for dialogue to be an insensitive act. Rather, it is considered

an act of charity. This is because the exclusivist maintains that salvation requires explicit belief that Jesus Christ is the savior, and other religions, since they deny this claim, are not only false but are to be condemned as leading their adherents toward damnation. For while exclusivists might recognize that other religions possess some true beliefs, some kind of general revelation, these truths are not regarded as salvific.[6] The Christian exclusivist thereby holds that other religions are excluded from the possession of the truth that really counts, the truth that packs the most punch, that wields the most power. In this sense, the other religions are false religions.

What is the basis of these exclusivistic claims? With Karl Barth, whose views have been widely regarded as representative of Christian exclusivism,[7] the exclusivist might locate the basis for his claims in the distinction between religion and revelation. For Barth, "Revelation is God's self-offering and self-manifestation. . . . In revelation God tells man that he is God, and that as such he is his Lord. In telling him this, revelation tells him something new, something which apart from revelation he does not know and cannot tell either himself or God."[8] In this sense, revelation, God's self-disclosure to human beings, stands in judgment of religion or "the religions" as "unbelief," that is, as the attempt of human beings to seize or capture God through their own means. The former contains the truth that saves, whereas the latter does not.

Now, to be sure, in Barth's view, Christianity, insofar as it is a religion, may also be regarded as unbelief and subject to human finitude or sinfulness.[9] Yet for Barth, Christianity is privy to the revelation of God in Christ as attested to by Holy Scripture. The possession of such a revelation, according to Barth, can "exalt" a religion and "justify" it.[10] "Revelation can adopt religion and mark it off as true religion," Barth claims, and goes on to add, "we need have no hesitation in saying that the Christian religion is the true religion."[11]

For all Barth's similarities to the postmodern perspective—his critique of religion as the human pretension to reach up to God is reminiscent of Heidegger's critique of ontotheology, and his insistence that God's disruptive revelation to us as "wholly other" echoes Levinas' statements about the interruptive demand of the human face[12]—his perspective nonetheless harbors a very non-postmodernist insensitivity to the other. For Barth is not open to the possibility that the religion of the other is also exalted by revelation, even though this is a claim the other religion makes. True to the logic of the exclusivist position, for Barth, this possibility is closed off from the start. When asked, for example, how he knew that Hinduism was unbelief when he had never met a Hindu, Barth simply replied, *"A priori."*[13]

The postmodern Christian philosopher, on the other hand, is chary of any a priori dismissal of the possibility that genuine revelation occurs in the other religion. For postmodern Christian philosophers take their cues from Levinas, who notes that the claim of the Other (*Autrui*, in French, the other that can only be a person) on me is "'older' than the *a priori*."[14] For Levinas, the Other's claim on me is a "reality that does not fit into any *a priori* idea, which overflows all of them."[15] As such, postmodern Christian philosophers recognize their obligation to the other as primordial, as prior to anything else, including their a priori stance on what is true or good, what is genuine revelation and what is not. This primordial obligation to the Other (*Autrui*) is nothing less than the respect one must have for another subject, another person.[16] One aspect of this respect for another person is the acknowledgment of the other's openness to divine revelation and his claims of a divine truth that claims him. For these claims are part and parcel of the identity of the other. They constitute who the Other is. As such, they are constitutive of his personhood.

From a postmodern perspective, part of the problem with the exclusivist position is its tendency to reduce religious truth to a matter of propositions which one may possess or own as so much currency or capital.[17] Postmodern Christian philosophers, following Levinas, are uncomfortable with the idea of knowledge as a matter of what one possesses for oneself. In the case of religious knowledge, my possession of divine truth can easily become an excuse for why I can dominate the other or force him to convert, or in some other way do violence to him.[18] Religious discourse which proceeds from this posture is what Levinas decries as totalization: it is *religious* philosophy as politics, as "the art of foreseeing war and of winning it by every means."[19]

It is not difficult to see this warring attitude at work in the history of the encounter of religions. For the history of religious exclusivism is the history of crusades, of jihad, of winning souls for the kingdom, of the Church Militant en route to the Church Triumphant. One need not be a seasoned practitioner of the hermeneutics of suspicion to see Christian exclusivists' claims to be in sole possession of the absolute divine truth as tantamount to the brute assertion of their very own wills to power, their wills to dominate the other. Instead, following Levinas, postmodern Christian philosophers recognize that the practitioners of other religions too have their place in the sun. By denying others their claim to be claimed by the divine other simply because we have been so claimed, Christian exclusivists do the equivalent of denying these others their place in the sun. And, with Levinas, may we not ask of such usurpations of sacred space, "are they not acts of repulsing, excluding, exiling, stripping, killing?"[20]

At this point, one may wonder whether this critique of exclusivists is just a bit overblown. Exclusivists have been accused of many things—arrogance, egoism, self-serving arbitrariness, imperialism, and oppression—and now are charged with being insensitive killers. Alvin Plantinga, for one, has recently sought to defend the exclusivist against such moral objections. For Plantinga, the exclusivist is simply stating a simple truth: my belief that *p* is true excludes your belief that *p* is false. I cannot hold both *p* and not-*p* at the same time. "That's no more than simple logic," writes Plantinga.[21] The exclusivist is no more immoral than anyone else who holds beliefs that contradict the incompatible beliefs of others.

There are two problems with this kind of response. First, in a manner characteristic of the exclusivist stance, Plantinga puts forward much too propositional a notion of religious truth for the postmodern Christian philosopher. Like Kierkegaard's Johannes Climacus, the postmodern Christian locates religious truth primarily in the "how," not the "what," that is, in the manner with which one appropriates divine revelation, not in the mere assent to certain propositions.[22]

Furthermore, the postmodern Christian philosopher is aware of Derrida's analysis of how signs, propositions, always refer elsewhere; they always differ from what they signify and defer their meaning to what is not present.[23] In this sense, the presence of the sign reveals the absence of the signified. It conceals more than it discloses and it excludes more than it includes. Indeed, for Derrida, the logocentric ideal which places the presence of the sign at some fixed center of the structure of language is deeply rooted in the history of the West.[24] It is at work not only in its languages but also in the concern of the West with its place in the world, with its desire to be at the geopolitical center at the exclusion of others. If Derrida is correct, our morally egregious history of ethnocentricism and cultural imperialism are traceable to this metaphysics of presence. And given the link between religion and culture, it would not be difficult to trace a similar connection in the history of Christian exclusivism.[25]

Thus, postmodern Christian philosophers take seriously the advice of both Climacus and Derrida against attributing any finality to claims to truth, advice that goes double for claims to religious truth. Since these propositions are our formulations, they bear the mark of our finitude. They are not themselves the transcendental signified. At best, the claims we make about the ultimate truth that claims us are approximations to that truth. There is no logical scaffolding supporting these claims; to hold fast to these approximations is always a risk, a leap over 70,000 fathoms.

Secondly, Plantinga's response is not cognizant enough of the context of philosophical and religious discourse. As Merold Westphal puts it, "A philosophy of religion that situates itself immediately in the heavenly world of propositions immunizes itself all but completely thereby from any concern for the uses to which those propositions are put in the earthly world of daily life. In other words, it isolates itself from the awkward questions raised by the hermeneutics of suspicion."[26] Such isolation from the difficult questions regarding the practical effects of one's exclusionary propositions betrays the kind of insensitivity to other religions we have claimed to be at work in Christian exclusivism. In hiding their heads in the sand of the logic of propositions, exclusivists choose not to see the connections between their claims of knowledge and their claims of power over those who fall outside of their own regime of truth. Exclusivists, however well-intentioned, fail to pay heed to Foucault's warning that "everything is dangerous"[27] and fail to see how the denial of the other's claims to be claimed by the divine—the denial of the "what" of the other's beliefs—too easily leads to the seizure of the other's space to live out the "how" of those claims. They do not see how their otherwise innocent use of the law of the excluded middle too readily becomes a destructive, violent act of politcal exclusion.[28]

For the postmodern Christian philosopher, Plantinga's defense is an act of self-justification which places the self prior to and over against the other. The fundamental posture of the postmodern Christian philosopher, on the other hand, is one of a de-centered self, that is, a self which has been interrupted and claimed by the other as it is interrupted and claimed by God. From this perspective, religious exclusivism, like ontotheology, is seen as yet another way to use God to do one's own philosophical (and political) bidding vis-à-vis the other.

What the exclusivist, following Barth, ought to acknowledge is that even if religious knowledge could be possessed, that is, represented in human concepts and categories, divine revelation cannot. As in our encounter with the human other—the human face—revelation breaks through our conceptual categories from the outside, on its own terms, not on ours. It claims us, but we have no claim on it. And we have no claim on where else it might occur.

II. The Pretensions of Religious Pluralism

It is as part of the effort at a more tolerant and open Christian posture toward other religions that John Hick has developed his philosophy of religious pluralism. Hick's pluralism denies that one religion is true while the others are false or that one religion is salvific while the others are not. For Hick, there is no privileged religion. He puts it this way: "In Christian theological terms, there is a plurality of divine revelations, making possible a plurality of forms of saving human response."[29] This is not to say that there are a plurality of truths in the universe of faith. Hick avoids the problem of many truths and hence conflicting truth-claims by denying truth in any real sense to the religions. Employing the Kantian distinction between reality as it is in-itself (the noumenal) and reality as it is perceived or conceived by us (the phenomenal), Hick maintains that the Divine Ultimate Reality is unknowable in itself. The plurality of divine revelations are the ways in which the Divine Ultimate Reality are perceived by us. The truth of any particular revelation is a constructed one; it is only the Real as it is conceptually or socially constructed by different religious communities within their very diverse cultural contexts. As Hick writes, "Stated philosophically such a pluralism is the view that the great world faiths embody different perceptions and conceptions of, and correspondingly different responses to, the Real or Ultimate from within the major variant cultural ways of being human."[30] So not only are religions culturally conditioned responses to divine revelation, but revelations themselves are culturally conditioned perceptual constructs. The truth of any particular revelation is a constructed one—it is not the Real as such but the Real as it is conceptually or socially constructed by different religious communities within diverse cultural contexts.

While Hick's pluralistic position takes a more open stance to the other than does religious exclusivism, for postmodern Christian philosophers, it is nonetheless insufficiently cognizant of the insights of the hermeneutics of finitude. The Kantian epistemological framework of Hick's pluralism proposes a universal perspective on the truth of all particular religions. As such, it fails to acknowledge its own particular cultural and historical embeddedness, its own epistemological finitude. Hick's religious pluralism retains the modernist, Western Enlightenment aim of a non-particular perspective on religious truth, a "view from nowhere," to borrow Thomas Nagel's phrase.[31] Postmodern Christian philosophers, however, realize that all perspectives are "views from somewhere" and that no one perspective possesses the privileged God's-eye view.

Furthermore, Hick's universal perspective on the truth of the world's religions, while successfully relativizing the truth of each religion, nonetheless totalizes the religions themselves. The differences in the religions are rendered irrelevant as they are all reduced to the same. Each religion's own understanding of itself and its truth is replaced by the pluralist's understanding of them, and, insofar as they all claim to be recipients of revealed truth in some ultimate sense, they are all mistaken. As such, a subtle form of philosophical (and, some would add, political) oppression is at work.[32] For in denying the religions' claims to be, through their revelations, grasped by a truth that claims ultimacy, Hick is denying the very religiosity of the religions' truth-claims and a fortiori the very religiosity of the religions themselves. While Hick's philosophy of religious pluralism purports to promote tolerance and respect among the religions, his position fails to tolerate what Mircea Eliade and others have found to be the most fundamental aspect of the religions themselves—the claim to participate directly in the Real or the Ultimate. And it fails to respect and listen to the religions' own understanding of how their revelations reflect this participation.[33]

The epistemic pride of Hick's religious pluralism may lead postmodern Christian philosophers to characterize it as another form of ontotheology, particularly for its attempt to fit God into a philosophical theory rooted in representational thinking. God becomes the Divine Ultimate Reality and fits neatly into the pluralist's conceptual scheme, even if as its limiting concept (it fits by not fitting and therefore serves the pluralists' theoretical purpose). As such, its construal of revelation as constructed representation is not only open to Heideggerian criticism against representational thinking about God—ontotheology—but fails to do justice to what Barth regarded to be the interruptive character of divine revelation, a character which, as was already noted, bears similarities to Levinas' account of the immediacy of the human face. In this Levinasian view, revelation is like the other "presenting" himself directly in person.[34] As such, it interrupts and ruptures representational schemes.

Postmodern Christian philosophers would abandon Hick's constructivist model of revelation for something like an iconic model following Jean-Luc Marion in *God without Being* (1991). Hick's treatment of revelation as human construction would fall under Marion's description of a conceptual idol. With the conceptual idol, our perception is satisfied and our gaze is frozen and brought to rest on this model of the divine. It does not open itself up to what transcends it, as does the icon. The conceptually constructed idol limits the revelation of the divine to the measure of the human gaze as it is "measured by what the scope of particular human eyes can support."[35] The iconic revelation, on the other hand, retains an openness to what transcends human measure as it "summons the gaze to surpass itself by never freezing on a visible."[36]

This iconic model of revelation allows for the kind of direct encounter with the divine that religions claim to enjoy. To be sure, it is still an encounter that occurs through the mediation of our concepts, yet it is one which is not fixed by our concepts or bounded by the horizons of our consciousness. For the immediacy is an openness to a divine, infinite abyss that cannot be traversed or mastered by us. Revelation is experienced as a direct lead to the sacred center, but one that shows us that we ourselves do not inhabit that center and cannot speak from its purview. We can point *to* it, but we cannot speak *for* it since we cannot speak its language. We can only speak our own language. As another postmodern philosopher, Ludwig Wittgenstein, might put it: it can be *shown*, but it cannot be *said*.

III. Between Exclusivity and Plurality

As a *via media* between exclusivism and pluralism, I put forward religious inclusivism as the position postmodern Christian philosophers ought to take with regard to the truth of other religions. Christian inclusivism is committed to the central belief of Christianity, that divine truth is revealed definitively in God's self-disclosure in Christ. Yet Christian inclusivism also recognizes divine truth, indeed the revelation of Christ—as the Word or Logos, the Wisdom or Truth of God—in other religions.[37] It is a position that remains open to the true and the good in other religions, recognizing that all truth is God's truth and all that is good is a reflection of the divine goodness. Inclusivism, by maintaining that divine truth is revealed definitively in Jesus Christ, retains the particularity of exclusivism, thereby avoiding pluralism's "view from nowhere." Yet in recognizing that the divine truth that the Christian knows to be revealed in Christ may also be revealed in other religions, the inclusivist avoids the exclusionary posture of the exclusivist.

Like Christian exclusivists, Christian inclusivists borrow Barth's distinction between religion and revelation but put it to different uses. Christian inclusivists understand Christianity, the religion, to be one particular way of speaking about the divine truth that is revealed in Christ. It is regarded as the most authoritative or definitive religion, to be sure, by virtue of its witness to the Logos or Word made flesh in Jesus of Nazareth. Yet inclusivists also regard other religions as legitimate ways of speaking about the divine truth that Christians know in Christian terms. In this sense, inclusivists consider the faithful of other religions who are moved and transformed by the grace and truth of God to be implicit disciples of what is for them the "unknown" Christ.[38] The faithful of other religions are thereby regarded as fellow hearers of the truth, or, in what is intended as a term of respect, as "anonymous Christians."[39]

The recognition of divine truth in the other religion allows inclusivists to begin their encounters with the other religion with an open rather than closed posture. Like Donald Davidson, who declares we must begin our encounter with people of other perspectives, other ways of thinking, and other languages, with the presumption that, like us, they, too, are rational,[40] Christian inclusivists insist that we begin the encounter with other religions with the presumption of these religions' truth, rather than their falsity—even if that truth is understood by the Christian in Christian terms, in a Christian translation.

While Christian inclusivists regard their own views as normative, as good postmodern, Rortyian ironists, they do so admittedly without universally accepted epistemic justification.[41] For postmodern Christian inclusivists recognize that the Christian perspective is a particular and contingent one, and so its acceptance as normative involves all the uncertainty, all the risk that comes with contingency. Yet inclusivists embrace the particularity of the Christian perspective, as does Gadamer, out of the sense that truth must be given a particular form and articulated in particular ways through particular traditions. Thus, contrary to pluralists, inclusivists admit their own finitude and accept the fact that Christians cannot give up their particular perspective when encountering other religions. Christian inclusivists acknowledge that we must state claims in our own way about the revealed truth that claims us. And we must be honest enough to state to the other, "from where I stand, this is how I see the truth that claims me—and this is how I see the truth that claims you." Christians would then enter the dialogue of religions without apologizing for their unique perspective—that is, they can engage in what William Placher calls an "unapologetic" theology of religions, but without exclusivist insensitivity.[42]

Pluralists such as Hick and others, however, find the inclusivist attitude toward other religions to be little better than the exclusivist posture. Hick believes inclusivism remains chauvinistic and paternalistic, thus hampering open dialogue among religions. The term "anonymous Christian" is particularly problematic, as it is deemed condescending and offensive to non-Christians. As Hick puts it, the term is "an honorary status granted unilaterally to people who have not expressed any desire for it."[43] Other critics claim that inclusivism does not take the other religions on their own terms and prejudes the issue of truth.[44] In postmodern terms, inclusivists may be said to be guilty of insensitivity to difference, of totalizing the other by understanding the truth of the other's religious tradition in Christian terms.

In response to these objections, Christian inclusivists can note that their position is a Christian position intended for other Christians. It is not meant for non-Christians, and it is not formulated for their acceptance. Rather, as Gavin D'Costa has pointed out, it "is addressed by a Christian to his or her, and the Church's, own self-understanding."[45] Within the context of Christian self-understanding, the regarding of the other as a Christian is to treat the other with the highest possible respect. It is like regarding the other as "another oneself," which Aristotle tells us is the salient characteristic of true friendship.[46]

Christian inclusivists can respond to the charge that they have pre-judged the truth of the other religion and have thereby failed to take the teaching of the other religion on its own terms by recalling Gadamer's account of understanding as a "fusion of horizons" and the unavoidability of pre-judice in all interpretation.[47] The understanding of another is always mediated through one's prior understanding, including one's language and the historical tradition in which one is situated. Such fore-understanding or pre-judging is the only context within which one can make sense of the other. In other words, the Christian can only understand the other and what the other understands to be divine truth in terms of the Christian understanding of divine truth. In order to recognize truth in the other religion, the Christian must understand it in terms of the truth as the Christian knows it, that is, in the way the divine is revealed in Christ. But this is simply to admit the finitude of one's understanding.

This partial fusion of horizons, this overlapping of one's own contextual, conceptual finitude with that of the other, need not constitute the totalization of the other. Through my initial openness to the other in the only way I know how, through the medium of my own self-understanding and fore-understanding, I am as vulnerable to the other as the other is to me. The fusion of horizons need not mean a limitation or destruction of the horizon of the other. It means, ultimately, an expansion of one's own horizon through the play of similarity and difference, the familiar and the strange.[48]

Nor is the regarding of the other as another self necessarily an instance of totalization, or of doing violence to the other as Other. As Derrida suggests in his discussion of Levinas in "Violence and Metaphysics," there is an inescapable symmetry in the openness to the other.[49] For to recognize the other as Other, that is, as a subject, I recognize that the Other is both like and not like me. It is my obligation to the Other to regard him, in some sense, as another self, as a person like me, as an alter ego. If I do not treat the Other as like me, in this sense—as a fellow person or subject—then I reduce him to the status of an object, to an it and not a Thou. And in this I do violence to him.

Finally, while Christian inclusivists remain true to the central beliefs of Christianity and hence retain a particular perspective on divine truth, they also recognize that this particular perspective is not exhaustive of divine truth. The Christian perspective on divine truth, even on the revelation of God in Christ, is a human perspective. It is not itself ultimate, but provisional. It is a relative way of speaking of the absolute.[50] This recognition, informed by a non-exclusivist understanding of the Barthian distinction between religion and revelation, sets limits to the absolute status of the Christian perspective and is consistent with the postmodern hermeneutics of finitude. For while God's self-disclosure in Christ may be regarded by Christians as the definitive revelation of divine truth, the teachings and practices of Christians may not. That is, while Christians may hold that Christ has been most fully revealed in their own scriptures and tradition, they must acknowledge that the Christian religion mediates this revelation and, as such, cannot itself be regarded as the unmediated revelation of divine truth. For while Christians may regard Christian thought and practice as normative vis-à-vis other religions, Christians should always be prepared for a reformation of their doctrines and practices in light of God's self-disclosure to other religions. That is, the Logos or Divine Truth which is revealed in Christ may be reflected in other religions in a way that allows Christians to deepen their own understanding of the Christian revelation and hence to modify teachings or practices that have fallen short of the fullness of divine truth. And in light of our finitude and fallenness, we may expect that they always will.

This attitude of epistemic humility, combined with a hermeneutics of suspicion turned toward the self, would serve to curb any inclusivist attempts at what Foucault, in "The Subject and Power," calls "pastoral power." Thus, to ensure that the regarding of the religious other as a friend, as an another self or fellow Christian of sorts (anonymously or otherwise), stems from my limitations as a knower and not my desire to dominate and define the other for my own self-serving aims, an openness to the other's interpretation and judgment of oneself and one's tradition is needed. Just as Christians must make judgments of other religious traditions from their own particular perspective, the Christian tradition must also be willing to stand and be judged from the perspective of truth of the other tradition.[51]

In other words, to use Marion's terminology, we cannot know—a priori, in any case—if the religion of the other is idolatrous or iconic. And while we must make our own claims on the truth that claims us, and, with irony, take them to be normative, we must also be ready to judge our own claims as idols in light of the icons of the other religion. For postmodern Christian inclusivists recognize that there is more truth than can be stated in Christian doctrine and practice. They recognize that our knowledge of the divine can never be complete and that we may not know every instance of God's self-disclosure and saving grace. For Christians believe that the spirit of God, like the wind, "blows where it wills, and you hear the sound of it, but you do not know whence it comes and whither it goes" (John 3:8). And this is consistent with what the postmodern philosopher has discovered, namely, that any particular expression of truth conceals more than it discloses.[52]

Notes

1. I am indebted to Merold Westphal for an understanding of the ways in which these two interpretive strategies characterize postmodern philosophy.

2. Focusing on truth rather than salvation also has the advantage of sidestepping recent criticisms of the three principal theologies of other religions—exclusivism, pluralism, and inclusivism—for failing to recognize that the world's religions have aims other than "salvation." To think otherwise commits what S. Mark Heim calls the error of "soteriocentrism." See Heim, *Salvations: Truth and Difference in Religion* (Maryknoll, N.Y.: Orbis Books, 1995). See also J. A. DiNoia, *The Diversity of Religions: A Christian Perspective* (Washington, D.C.: Catholic University of America Press, 1992). For a useful discussion of postmodern theologies of religion, but one which does not make the distinction I am drawing between truth and salvation, see Terrence W. Tilley, *Postmodern Theologies: The Challenge of Religious Diversity* (Maryknoll, N.Y.: Orbis Books, 1995), pp. 155–68.

3. See, for example, John D. Caputo, *Radical Hermeneutics* (Indianapolis: Indiana University Press, 1987), chap. 10; and Merold Westphal, "Postmodernism and Religious Reflection," *International Journal of the Philosophy of Religion*, 38, no. 1–3 (December 1995), among others.

4. John D. Caputo, "The Good News about Alterity: Derrida and Theology," *Faith and Philosophy* 10, no. 4 (October 1993): 453.

5. Ronald H. Nash, *Is Jesus the Only Savior?* (Grand Rapids, Mich.: Zondervan Publishing House, 1994), pp. 11–12 (my italics).

6. See Hendrick Kraemer, *Why Christianity of All Religions?* (Philadelphia: Westminster Press, 1962).

7. See Alan Race, *Christians and Religious Pluralism* (Maryknoll, N.Y.: Orbis Books, 1983), and Gavin D'Costa, *Theology and Religious Pluralism* (Oxford: Basil Blackwell, 1986).

8. Karl Barth, *Church Dogmatics*, vol. 1, part 2, trans. G. W. Bromiley (Edinburgh: T. and T. Clark, 1956), p. 301.

9. Indeed, as I will attempt to show, Barth's distinction between religion and revelation can be usefully employed in the critique of any absolutistic claims put

forth on behalf of the Christian religion. In other words, the distinction between religion and revelation need not serve an exclusivist agenda; it may actually serve to undermine it.

10. Barth, *Church Dogmatics*, p. 326.

11. Ibid.

12. See Graham Ward, "The Revelation of the Holy Other as the Wholly Other: Between Barth's Theology of the Word and Levinas's Philosophy of Saying," *Modern Theology* 9, no. 2 (April 1993), pp. 159–80. For comparisons of Barth and Derrida, see Walter Lowe, *Theology and Difference* (Indianapolis: Indiana University Press, 1993), and Graham Ward, *Barth, Derrida and the Language of Theology* (Cambridge: Cambridge University Press, 1995). Cf. chapter 5 above.

13. Quoted in Race, *Christians and Religious Pluralism*, p. 16.

14. Emmanuel Levinas, *The Levinas Reader*, ed. Sean Hand (Oxford: Basil Blackwell, 1989), p. 90.

15. Emmanuel Levinas, *Collected Philosophical Papers*, trans. Alphonso Lingis (Dordrecht: Martinus Nijhoff, 1987), p. 59. I have been aided in my understanding of this aspect of Levinas' thought by Merold Westphal, "Levinas and the Immediacy of the Face," *Faith and Philosophy* 10, no. 4 (October 1993), pp. 486–502.

16. See Emmanuel Levinas, *Totality and Infinity*, trans. Alphonso Lingis (Pittsburgh: Duquesne University Press, 1969), p. 39. See also the useful discussions in Westphal, "Levinas and the Immediacy of the Face," p. 492, and John D. Caputo, *Against Ethics* (Indianapolis: Indiana University Press, 1991), p. 119.

17. See Levinas, *Totality and Infinity*, p. 33, for a critique of the tendency in Western philosophy to regard knowledge, particularly with respect to the Other, as a form of possession.

18. This kind of power play can occur within a religion as well as between religions. See, for example, Michel Foucault's discussion of "pastoral power" in "The Subject and Power," in Hubert L. Dreyfus and Paul Rabinow, *Michel Foucault: Beyond Structuralism and Hermeneutics* (Chicago: University of Chicago Press, 1983), p. 214.

19. Levinas, *Totality and Infinity*, p. 21.

20. Levinas, *Levinas Reader*, p. 82.

21. See Alvin Plantinga, "A Defense of Religious Exclusivism," in *The Rationality of Belief and the Plurality of Faith: Essays in Honor of William P. Alston*, ed. Tomas D. Senor (Ithaca, N.Y.: Cornell University Press, 1995), p. 197; see also pp. 191–215. Plantinga also defends exclusivism against certain epistemic objections. Since my critique of exclusivism is primarily a moral one, I will not discuss Plantiga's response to the epistemic objections.

22. Gary Percesepe has suggested to me that a fuller account of a postmodern philosophy of other religions ought to provide a thorough, nuanced treatment of the "how" of religious truth in such a way as to move beyond the debate between exclusivists, inclusivists, etc. Percesepe's suggestion is helpful and worth pursuing, but I am unable to do so in this essay. For helpful accounts of the notion of truth as subjectivity in Kierkegaard, see C. Stephen Evans, *Kierkegaard's "Fragments" and "Postscript": The Religious Philosophy of Johannes Climacus* (Atlantic Highlands, N.J.: Humanities, 1983), esp. chap. 7; and Merold Wesphal, *Becoming a Self: A Reading of Kierkegaard's Concluding Unscientific Postscript* (West Lafayette, Ind.: Purdue Uni-

versity Press, 1996), chap. 8. For accounts of the connection between Kierkegaard and postmodern philosophy, see Merold Westphal, "Kierkegaard's Climacus: A Kind of Postmodernist," in *International Kierkegaard Commentary: Concluding Unscientific Postscript,* ed. Robert L. Perkins (Macon. Ga.: Mercer University press, 1997), pp. 53 71, and "The Transparent Shadow: Kierkegaard and Levinas in Dialogue," in *Kierkegaard in Post/Modernity,* ed. Merold Westphal and Martin J. Matsusik (Indianapolis: Indiana University Press. 1995), pp. 265–81.

Jean-Luc Marion's distinction between the idol and the icon may be seen as a way of expressing the proper "how" within the sphere of religious thought. See *God without Being,* translated by Thomas A. Carlson (Chicago: University of Chicago Press, 1991), pp. 7–13.

23. See Jacques Derrida, "Structure, Sign, and Play in the Discourse of the Human Sciences," in *Writing and Difference,* trans. Alan Bass (Chicago: University of Chicago Press, 1978), pp. 278–93.

24. See also Derrida, *The Gift of Death,* trans. David Wills (Chicago: University of Chicago Press, 1995).

25. See Andrew J. Dell'Olio, "Multiculturalism and Religious Diversity: A Christian Perspective," *Christian Scholar's Review* 25, no. 4 (June 1996), pp. 459–77.

26. Westphal, "Postmodernism and Religious Reflection," p. 132.

27. Michel Foucault, "On the Genealogy of Ethics," afterword to Hubert L. Dreyfus and Paul Rabinow, *Michel Foucault,* p. 231.

28. For a moving fictionalized account of the violence that can inadvertently befall upon a community confronted by exclusivistic Christian missionaries, see Chinua Achebe's *Things Fall Apart* (New York: Random House, 1959).

29. John Hick, "Religious Pluralism," in *The World's Religious Traditions: Essays in Honour of Wilfred Cantwell Smith,* ed. Frank Whaling (New York: Crossroad, 1985), p. 153. The most complete account of Hick's position may be found in his *An Interpretation of Religion* (New Haven, Conn.: Yale University Press, 1989); see also John Hick, *A Christian Theology of Religions* (Louisville, Ky.: Westminster/John Knox Press, 1995).

30. Hick, "Religious Pluralism," p. 156.

31. Thomas Nagel, *The View from Nowhere* (New York: Oxford University Press, 1986). Hick's position may also be described as a form of modern romanticism, what George Lindbeck calls "experiential-expressivism"; Lindbeck, *The Nature of Doctrine* (Philadelphia: Westminster, 1984), p. 16.

32. See Kenneth Surin, "A 'Politics of Speech': Religious Pluralism in the Age of the McDonald's Hamburger," in Gavin D'Costa, ed., *Christian Uniqueness Reconsidered: The Myth of a Pluralistic Theology of Religions* (Maryknoll, N.Y.: Orbis Press, 1990), pp. 192–212.

33. See Mircea Eliade, *The Sacred and the Profane* (New York: Harcourt, Brace, Jovanovich, 1959), pp. 20–65. David Tracy makes a similar point, with explicit reference to the issue of religious diversity, in *Dialogue with the Other* (Louvain, Belgium: Peeters Press, 1990). Along the lines of my critique of Hick's pluralism, John V. Apczynski has made the point that despite Hick's claims, Hick's position is implicitly exclusivistic. See Apczynski, "John Hick's Theocentrism: Revolutionary or Implicitly Exclusivist?", *Modern Theology* 8, no. 1 (January 1992), pp. 39–52.

34. Levinas, *Totality and Infinity*, p. 262.

35. Jean-Luc Marion, *God without Being*, p. 14.

36. Ibid., p. 18.

37. At first glance, one might think the inclusivist's reliance on logos theology to be at odds with postmodern philosophy's antipathy to logocentrism. But a theology of the Logos need not be logocentric in the Derridean sense that it privileges the spoken word over the written word. For the Logos is always encountered in a sign: it is the Word made flesh. As such, theologically, it functions like Marion's icon: it shows itself, but its signification (significance?) cannot be fully encaptured or possessed by us. The revelation of the Logos in whatever form signifies as much by its absence as by its presence. Its fullness is always deferred to the future, the promised time for which we presently await. But the postmodern Christian inclusivist who wishes to avoid logos-talk might also understand the divine truth within other religions in trinitarian terms. See, for example, Raimundo Panikkar, *The Trinity and the Religious Experience of Man: Icon–Person–Mystery* (Maryknoll, N.Y.: Orbis, 1973); Gavin D'Costa, "Christ, the Trinity, and Religious Pluralism" in *Christian Uniqueness Reconsidered* (1990); and the essays in *The Trinity in a Pluralistic Age*, ed. Kevin J. Vanhoozer (Grand Rapids, Mich.: Eerdmans, 1997).

38. See, for example, Raimundo Panikkar, *The Unknown Christ of Hinduism*, rev. ed. (Maryknoll, N.Y.: Orbis Press, 1981).

39. According to Rahner, "Christianity does not simply confront the member of an extra-Christian religion as a mere non-Christian but as someone who can and must already be regarded in this or that respect as an anonymous Christian"; see Rahner, *Theological Investigations* (New York: Seabury Press, 1961–84), vol. 5, pp. 122–23.

40. See Donald Davidson, "On the Very Idea of a Conceptual Scheme," in *Inquiries into Truth and Interpretation* (Oxford: Clarendon Press, 1984).

41. See Richard Rorty, *Contingency, Irony, and Solidarity* (Cambridge: Cambridge University Press, 1989).

42. William Placher, *Unapologetic Theology: A Christian Voice in a Pluralistic Conversation* (Louisville, Ky.: Westminster/John Knox Press, 1989.)

43. John Hick, "Whatever Path Men Choose is Mine," in *Christianity and Other Religions*, ed. John Hick and Brian Hebblethwaite (Philadelphia: Fortress, 1980), p. 179.

44. See Alan Race, *Christians and Religious Pluralism*, p. 56.

45. D'Costa, *Theology and Religious Pluralism*, p. 89.

46. Aristotle, *Nicomachean Ethics*, 1166a30.

47. See Hans-Georg Gadamer, *Truth and Method* (New York: Crossroad, 1986), pp. 235–74.

48. This process of understanding with regard to other religions would employ what David Tracy calls the "analogical imagination." See *The Analogical Imagination* (New York: Crossroad, 1981), pp. 446–56.

49. Jacques Derrida, "Violence and Metaphysics," in *Writing and Difference*, pp. 125–31. See also Caputo's helpful discussion of Derrida's critique of Levinas in *Against Ethics*, p. 264.

50. What I have in mind here is similar to Langdon Gilkey's category of "relative absolutes." Gilkey writes of the "interplay of absolute and relative—of being

a Christian, Jew or Buddhist, and *affirming* that stance, and yet at the same time relativizing that mode of existence"; Gilkey, "Plurality and Its Theological Implications," in *The Myth of Christian Uniqueness,* ed. John Hick and Paul F. Knitter (Maryknoll, N.Y.: Orbis Books, 1987), p. 47. This is one way the postmodern version of inclusivism differs from Rahnerian inclusivism wherein the claims of Christianity are given absolute status. While all human beings are searching for the immediate, concrete presence of the absolute, for Rahner, "among all religions only Christianity has the courage seriously to make an absolute claim"; Rahner, "Christianity," *Sacramentum Mundi* (New York: Seabury Press, 1968–70), vol. 1, p. 302.

51. Allen Verhey makes a similar point with regard to the relationship between Christian ethics and secular or philosophical theories of morality. See *The Great Reversal: Ethics and the New Testament* (Grand Rapids, Mich.: Eerdmans, 1984), p. 193.

52. I would like to thank Merold Westphal and all the members of the Calvin College Summer Seminar, particularly John Apczynski, Steve Bouma-Prediger, and Gary Percesepe, for their helpful comments on earlier drafts of this paper.

CONTRIBUTORS

Steven Bouma-Prediger is associate professor of religion at Hope College in Holland, Michigan.

John D. Caputo is the David R. Cook Professor of Philosophy at Villanova University.

George Connell is professor of philosophy and chair of the philosophy department at Concordia College in Moorhead, Minnesota.

Andrew J. Dell'Olio is assistant professor of philosophy at Hope College in Holland, Michigan.

Garrett Green is professor of religious studies at Connecticut College.

Lee Hardy is chair of the philosophy department at Calvin College.

Brian D. Ingraffia is associate professor of American literature and critical theory at Biola University in La Mirada, California.

Walter Lowe is professor of systematic theology at the Candler School of Theology, Emory University.

Jean-Luc Marion is professor of philosophy at the University of Paris–Sorbonne and at the University of Chicago.

Gary Percesepe teaches philosophy at the University of Dayton and in the Common Learning Program at Wittenberg University.

Merold Westphal is distinguished professor of philosophy at Fordham University.

Norman Wirzba is assistant professor of philosophy at Georgetown College in Georgetown, Kentucky.

W. Jay Wood is chair of the department of philosophy at Wheaton College.

Edith Wyschogrod is the J. Newton Rayzor Professor of Philosophy and Religious Thought at Rice University.

INDEX